Fodor's 1st Edition

Chile

The complete guide, thoroughly up-to-date

Packed with details that will make your trip

The must-see sights, off and on the beaten path

What to see, what to skip

Mix-and-match vacation itineraries

City strolls, countryside adventures

Smart lodging and dining options

Essential local do's and taboos

Transportation tips, distances and directions

Key contacts, savvy travel tips

When to go, what to pack

Clear, accurate, easy-to-use maps

Fodor's Travel Publications • New York, Toronto, London, Sydney, Auckland
www.fodors.com

Fodor's Chile

EDITOR: Mark Sullivan

Editorial Contributors: Gregory Benchwick, Pete Nelson, Jeffrey Van Fleet.
Editorial Production: Tom Holton
Maps: David Lindroth, Inc., *cartographer;* Rebecca Baer and Bob Blake, *map editors*
Design: Fabrizio La Rocca, *creative director;* Guido Caroti, *art director;* Jolie Novak, *senior picture editor;* Melanie Marin, *photo editor*
Cover Design: Pentagram
Production/Manufacturing: Robert B. Shields
Cover Photograph: Jorg Brockmann

Copyright

First Edition

ISBN 0–676–90114–X

ISSN 1535–5055

Special Sales

Fodor's Travel Publications are available at special discounts for bulk purchases for sales promotions or premiums. Special editions, including personalized covers, excerpts of existing guides, and corporate imprints, can be created in large quantities for special needs. For more information, contact your local bookseller or write to Special Markets, Fodor's Travel Publications, 280 Park Ave., New York, NY 10017. Inquiries from Canada should be directed to your local Canadian bookseller or sent to Random House of Canada, Ltd., Marketing Department, 2775 Matheson Boulevard East, Mississauga, Ontario L4W 4P7. Inquiries from the United Kingdom should be sent to Fodor's Travel Publications, 20 Vauxhall Bridge Road, London SW1V 2SA, England.

PRINTED IN THE UNITED STATES OF AMERICA

10 9 8 7 6 5 4 3 2 1

Important Tip

Although all prices, opening times, and other details in this book are based on information supplied to us at press time, changes occur all the time in the travel world, and Fodor's cannot accept responsibility for facts that become outdated or for inadvertent errors or omissions. So **always confirm information when it matters,** especially if you're making a detour to visit a specific place.

CONTENTS

Maps

ON THE ROAD WITH FODOR'S

THE MORE YOU KNOW before you go, the better your trip will be. Chile's most fascinating small museum (or its most chaotic outdoor market or trendiest seafood restaurant) could be just around the corner from your hotel, but if you don't know it's there, it might as well be on the other side of the globe. That's where this book comes in. It's a great step toward making sure your next trip lives up to your expectations. As you plan, check out the Web as well. Guidebooks have been helping smart travelers find the special places for years; the Web is one more tool. Whatever reference you consult, be savvy about what you read, and always consider the source. Images and language can be massaged to make places appear better than they are. And one traveler's quaint is another's grimy. Here at Fodor's, and at our on-line arm, fodors.com, our focus is on providing you with information that's not only useful but accurate and on target. Every day Fodor's editors put enormous effort into getting things right, beginning with the search for the right contributors—people who have objective judgment, broad travel experience, and the writing ability to put their insights into words. There's no substitute for advice from a like-minded friend who has just come back from where you're going, but our writers, having seen all corners of Chile, are the next best thing. They're the kind of people you'd poll for tips yourself if you knew them.

San Francisco-based freelance writer **Gregory Benchwick** first fell in love with Latin America when he traveled via chicken bus from Costa Rica to Belize in 1995. Returning to Latin America in 1999, this time to Chile, Gregory first glimpsed the rugged, enchanting, and often inhospitable landscape of El Norte Chico and El Norte Grande, which he wrote about for this book. A former editor for *The Bolivian Times*, Gregory has written extensively about travel in South America.

After earning a master's degree in poetry from Sarah Lawrence College, **Michael de Zayas** spent a year backpacking around Spain researching a book on Spanish fiestas. He returned to Spain to write several chapters for *upCLOSE Spain*, then headed south to check out Santiago, the Central Coast, and the Central Valley for this book, as well as the Pampas for *Fodor's Argentina* and Uruguay for *Fodor's South America*. The New York City resident writes about travel for the *New York Post* and the *Miami Herald*. He enjoys heli-skiing and pastries.

The son of an international airline executive, **Pete Nelson** spent most of his youth living abroad. He subsequently worked for over 20 years in hospitality marketing, including a stint of several years in Chile. Fluent in French and Spanish, he writes regularly for local and regional lifestyle magazines.

Editor **Mark Sullivan** has traveled in South America from the vast grasslands of Venezuela to the towering glaciers of Tierra del Fuego, but no place was quite so far off the beaten path as mysterious Easter Island. He is also editor of *Fodor's South America* and *upCLOSE Central America*.

Costa Rica-based freelance writer and pharmacist **Jeffrey Van Fleet** divides his time between Central America and Wisconsin, but always looks for opportunities to enjoy the more cosmopolitan ambience of South America's southern cone. He is a regular contributor to Costa Rica's English-language *Tico Times*. Jeff updated the Lake District and Chiloé chapters for this book.

We'd also like to thank Martin Mosley and the staff of LanChile Airlines, Marisol Cabello of the Embassy of Chile, and Misty Pinson of MSP Communications.

Don't Forget to Write

Your experiences—positive and negative—matter to us. If we have missed or misstated something, we want to hear about it. We follow up on all suggestions. Contact the Chile editor at editors@fodors.com or c/o Fodor's, 280 Park Avenue, New York, New York 10017. And have a fabulous trip!

Karen Cure
Editorial Director

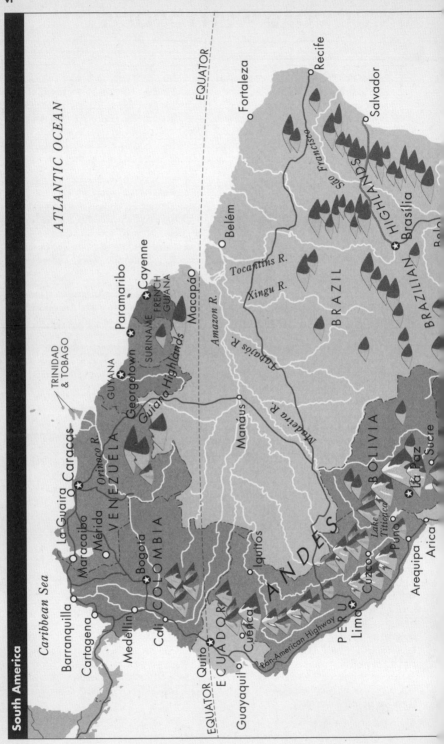

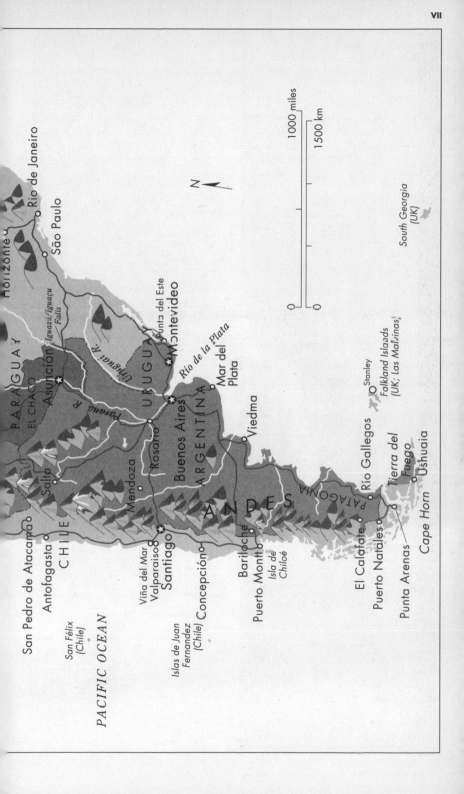

VII

PACIFIC OCEAN

San Pedro de Atacama

Antofagasta

San Félix
(Chile)

CHILE

Viña del Mar
Valparaíso
Santiago

Islas de Juan
Fernandez
(Chile)

Concepción

Puerto Montt

Bariloche

Isla de
Chiloé

El Calafate

Puerto Natales

Punta Arenas

Cape Horn

Salta

Mendoza

Rosario

Buenos Aires

ARGENTINA

ANDES

PATAGONIA

Río Gallegos

Tierra del
Fuego

Ushuaia

PARAGUAY

EL CHACO

Asunción

Paraná R.

URUGUAY

Iguazú/Iguaçu
Falls

Uruguay R.

Punta del Este

Montevideo

Río de la Plata

Mar del
Plata

Viedma

Stanley

Falkland Islands
(UK; Las Malvinas)

Horizonte

Río de Janeiro

São Paulo

N

South Georgia
(UK)

0 ____ 1000 miles

0 ____ 1500 km

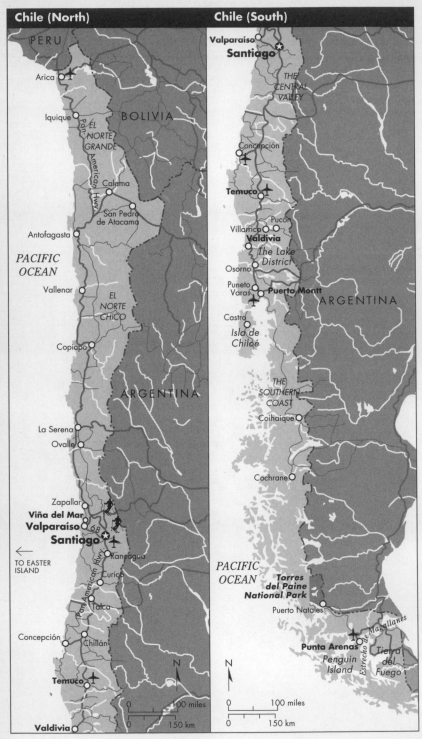

Chile (North)

PERU

Arica

Iquique

EL NORTE GRANDE

BOLIVIA

Calama

San Pedro de Atacama

Antofagasta

PACIFIC OCEAN

Vallenar

EL NORTE CHICO

Copiapó

ARGENTINA

La Serena

Ovalle

Zapallar

Viña del Mar

Valparaíso

68

Santiago

TO EASTER ISLAND

Rancagua

Curicó

Talca

Concepción

Chillán

Temuco

Valdivia

Pan American Hwy

Pan American Hwy

N

0   100 miles

0   150 km

Chile (South)

Valparaíso

Santiago

THE CENTRAL VALLEY

Concepción

Temuco

Pucón

Villarrica

Valdivia

The Lake District

Osorno

Puneto Varas

Puerto Montt

ARGENTINA

Castro

Isla de Chiloé

THE SOUTHERN COAST

Coihaique

Cochrane

PACIFIC OCEAN

Torres del Paine National Park

Puerto Natales

Punta Arenas

Penguin Island

Estrecho de Magallanes

Tierra del Fuego

N

0   100 miles

0   150 km

SMART TRAVEL TIPS A TO Z

Basic Information on Traveling in Chile, Savvy Tips to Make Your Trip a Breeze, and Companies and Organizations to Contact

ADDRESSES

The most common street terms in Spanish are *avenida* (avenue) and *calle* (street). Numbering individual buildings isn't as popular in South America as it is elsewhere. In some of this guide's listings, establishments have necessarily been identified by the street they're on and their nearest cross street—Calle Bolívar and Avenida Valdivia, for example. In extreme cases, where neither address nor cross street is available, you may find the notation "s/n," meaning "no street number." In these cases the towns are usually so small that finding a particular building won't be a problem.

AIR TRAVEL

Most international flights head to Santiago's Comodoro Arturo Merino Benítez International Airport (SCL), about 30 minutes west of the city. The beautifully designed metal-and-glass structure is alongside the rather dilapidated old terminal that now services only domestic flights. Miami and New York are the primary departure points for flights to Chile from the United States, though there are also daily flights from Dallas and Atlanta. Other international flights often connect through other major South American cites like Buenos Aires and Lima.

Arriving from abroad, American, Canadian, and Australian citizens must pay a "reciprocity" fee (to balance out fees Chileans pay upon entering foreign countries) of $45, $55, and $30, respectively. Only cash is accepted. A departure tax of $18 is included in the cost of your ticket.

BOOKING

When you book **look for nonstop flights** and **remember that "direct" flights stop at least once.** Try to avoid connecting flights, which require a change of plane. For more booking tips and to check prices and make online flight reservations, log on to www.fodors.com.

CARRIERS

The largest North American carrier is American Airlines, which has direct service from Dallas and Miami. United flies from Miami and New York, while Delta flies from Atlanta. No Canadian airlines fly directly to South American destinations, though Canadian Airlines has a partnership with American and Air Canada has one with United.

The major Chilean airline is Lan-Chile, which flies directly to Santiago from New York and Miami. Many South American airlines have connecting flights to Santiago: Aerocontinente connects through Lima, Peru; Aerolíneas Argentinas has connections in Buenos Aires; Avianca flies through Bogota, Colombia; LAB flies through La Paz and other Bolivian cities; Saeta connects through the Ecuadoran cities of Guayaquil and Quito; Tam flies through Asunción, Paraguay; and Varig stops in the Brazilian cities of Fortaleza, Manaus, Rio de Janeiro, and São Paulo.

From the United Kingdom, British Airways has service from London Gatwick to Santiago. LanChile offers service from London to Santiago via Frankfurt or Madrid. You can take American or United from London Heathrow and fly to South America via Miami or New York.

From Australia, LanChile flies directly from Sydney to Santiago and Easter Island.

➤ NORTH AMERICAN AIRLINES: **American Airlines** (☎ 2/690–1090 in Santiago, ☎ 800/433–7300 in North America). **Delta Airlines** (☎ 2/690–1551 in Santiago, ☎ 800/221–1212 in North America). **United Airlines**

SMART TRAVEL TIPS A TO Z

(☎ 2/690–1179 in Santiago, ☎ 800/538–2929 in North America).

➤ CENTRAL AND SOUTH AMERICAN AIRLINES: **Aerocontinente** (☎ 2/690–1192 in Chile, ☎ 888/586–9400 in North America). **Aerolíneas Argentinas** (☎ 2/690–1090 in Chile, ☎ 800/474–7424 in North America). **Aeromexico** (☎ 2/690–1141 in Chile, ☎ 800/237–6639 in North America). **Avianca** (☎ 2/690–1050 in Chile, ☎ 800/284–2622 in North America). **LAB** (☎ 2/690–1130 in Chile). **Lacsa** (☎ 2/690–1276 in Chile, ☎ 800/225–2272 in North America). **Lan-Chile** (☎ 2/601–9081 in Chile, ☎ 800/735–5526 in North America). **Tam** (☎ 2/690–1155 in Chile, ☎ 888/235–9826 in North America). **TAME** (☎ 2/690–1112 in Chile). **Varig** (☎ 2/690–1342 in Chile, ☎ 800/468–2744 in North America).

➤ FROM THE U.K.: **Aerolíneas Argentinas** (☎ 020/7494–1075). **American Airlines** (☎ 0345/789–789). **British Airways** (☎ 0345/222–111). **LanChile** (☎ 129/359–6606). **United Airlines** (☎ 0845/844–4777). **Varig** (☎ 020/7287–3131).

➤ FROM AUSTRALIA AND NEW ZEALAND: **Air New Zealand** (☎ 0396/703–700 in Australia, 0800/737–000 in New Zealand). **Qantas** (☎ 13–13–13 in Australia, 0800/808–767 in New Zealand).

CHECK-IN & BOARDING

Assuming that not everyone with a ticket will show up, airlines routinely overbook planes. When everyone does, airlines ask for volunteers to give up their seats. In return, these volunteers usually get a certificate for a free flight and are rebooked on the next flight out. If there are not enough volunteers, the airline must choose who will be denied boarding. The first to get bumped are passengers who checked in late and those flying on discounted tickets, so **get to the gate and check in as early as possible,** especially during peak periods.

Always **bring a government-issued photo I.D. to the airport;** a passport is best. You may be asked to show it before you are allowed to check in.

CUTTING COSTS

The least expensive airfares to Chile must usually be purchased in advance and are nonrefundable. It's smart to **call a number of airlines, and when you are quoted a good price, book it on the spot**—the same fare may not be available the next day. Always **check different routings** and look into using different airports.

Consolidators are another good source. They buy tickets for scheduled international flights at reduced rates from the airlines, then sell them at prices that beat the best fare available directly from the airlines, usually without restrictions. Sometimes you can even get your money back if you need to return the ticket. Carefully read the fine print detailing penalties for changes and cancellations, and **confirm your consolidator reservation with the airline.**

➤ CONSOLIDATORS: **Cheap Tickets** (☎ 800/377–1000). **Discount Airline Ticket Service** (☎ 800/576–1600). **Pino Welcome Travel** (☎ 800/247–6578). **Unitravel** (☎ 800/325–2222). **Up & Away Travel** (☎ 212/889–2345). **World Travel Network** (☎ 800/409–6753).

ENJOYING THE FLIGHT

Traveling between the Americas is usually less tiring than traveling to Europe or Asia because you cross fewer time zones. New York is in the same time zone as Santiago, and Los Angeles is three hours behind Santiago. London is four hours ahead of Santiago.

If you have a choice when to fly, **take a night flight.** You'll arrive the next morning with plenty of time to start exploring. Flying into Chile from the north you'll be treated to lovely sunrises over the mountains (assuming you're seated on the plane's left side).

For more legroom, **request an emergency-aisle seat.** Don't sit in the row in front of the emergency aisle or in front of a bulkhead, where seats may not recline. If you have dietary concerns, **ask for special meals when booking.** These can be vegetarian, low-cholesterol, or kosher, for example. On long flights, try to maintain a normal routine to help fight jet lag. At night, **get some sleep.** By day, **eat light meals, drink water** (not alcohol), and **move around the cabin** to stretch your legs. For additional jet-lag tips consult *Fodor's FYI: Travel Fit & Healthy* (available at bookstores everywhere).

Some carriers have prohibited smoking throughout their systems; others allow smoking on certain routes. Make sure to **contact your carrier regarding its smoking policy.**

FLYING TIMES

The major North American departure points for Santiago are New York (11½ hours) and Miami (9 hours). If you're traveling from Canada and connecting in the United States the Toronto–New York flight is just over an hour, while the flight to Miami is about 3 hours. Note that flight times may vary according to the size of the plane.

HOW TO COMPLAIN

If your baggage goes astray or your flight goes awry, complain right away. Most carriers require that you **file a claim immediately.**

➤ AIRLINE COMPLAINTS: U.S. Department of Transportation **Aviation Consumer Protection Division** (✉ C-75, Room 4107, Washington, DC 20590, ☎ 202/366–2220, 𝗪𝗘𝗕 www.dot.gov/airconsumer). **Federal Aviation Administration Consumer Hotline** (☎ 800/322–7873).

RECONFIRMING

Always **reconfirm your flight,** even if you have a ticket and a reservation. This is particularly true for travel within South America, where flights tend to operate at full capacity— usually with passengers who have a great deal of baggage to process before departure.

BIKE TRAVEL

Riding a bike will put you face to face with the people and landscapes of Chile. However, the rugged terrain and varying road conditions pose considerable challenges. **Consider a mountain bike,** since basic touring bikes are too fragile for the potholes of even the best roads. Many tour operators in Santiago and other places offer bike trips—sometimes including equipment rental—that range in length from a half day to several days. Always remember to **lock your bike when you make stops,** and **avoid riding in congested urban areas,** where it's difficult (and dangerous) enough getting around by car, let alone by bike.

BOAT & FERRY TRAVEL

Boats and ferries are the only way to reach many places in Chile, such as Chiloé and the Southern Coast. They are also a great alternative to flying when your destination is a southern port like Puerto Natales or Punta Arenas. Details on boat travel are discussed in the various chapter A to Z sections throughout this guide.

BUS TRAVEL

Bus travel in Chile is relatively cheap and safe, provided you use one of the better lines. Intercity bus service is a comfortable, safe, and reasonably priced alternative for getting around. Luxury bus travel between cities costs about one-third that of plane travel and is more comfortable, with wide reclining seats, movies, drinks, and snacks. The most luxurious and expensive service offered by most bus companies is called *salon cama* or *semi-cama.* The business-class-style sleeper buses offer all of the usual amenities, as well as pillows and blankets and a bow-tied attendant who serves surprisingly palatable meals.

Without doubt, the low cost of bus travel is its greatest advantage; its greatest drawback is the time you need to cover the distances involved and, in some outlying areas, having to allow for delays due to faulty equipment or poor road conditions. When traveling by bus, **pack light and dress comfortably** and be sure to **keep a close watch on your belongings.**

FARES

Bus fares are substantially cheaper than in North America or Europe. In Chile you'll usually pay no more than $2 per hour of travel (some ritzy sleeper buses are more). Competing bus companies serve all major and many minor routes, so it can really pay to shop around. Always speak to the counter clerk, as cut-throat competition may mean you can ride for less than the official fare.

Tickets are sold at bus-company offices and at city bus terminals. Note that in larger cities there may be different terminals for buses to different destinations, and some small towns may not have a terminal at all. You'll be picked up and dropped off at the bus line's office, invariably in a central location. **Expect to pay with cash** as Tur-Bus is one of the few companies that accepts credit cards.

RESERVATIONS

Note that reservations for advance-ticket purchases aren't necessary except for trips to resort areas in high season or during major holidays. You should **arrive at bus stations extra early for travel during peak seasons.** Companies are notoriously difficult to reach by phone, so it's often better to stop by the terminal to check on prices and schedules.

BUSINESS HOURS

Most retail businesses are open weekdays 10–7 and Saturday until 2; most are closed Sunday. Many businesses close for lunch between about 1 and 3 or 4, though this is becoming less common, especially in larger cities.

BANKS & OFFICES

Most banks are open weekdays 9–2. Casas de cambio are open weekdays 9–2 and 3–6.

GAS STATIONS

Gas stations in major cities tend to be open 24 hours. Others follow regular business hours.

MUSEUMS & SIGHTS

Most tourist attractions are open during normal business hours during the week and for at least the morning on Saturday and Sunday. Most museums are closed on Monday.

SHOPS

Shops generally are open weekdays 10–7 and Saturdays 10–2. In small towns, shops often close for lunch between 1 and 3 or 4.

CAMERAS & PHOTOGRAPHY

Chile, with its majestic landscapes and varied cityscapes, is a photographer's dream. Chileans seem amenable to having picture-taking tourists in their midst, but you should always **ask permission before taking pictures of individuals.** Be aware that photos shouldn't be taken in or around government or military areas. Photography is not permitted of Chilean war ships docked in Valparaíso. The *Kodak Guide to Shooting Great Travel Pictures* (available at bookstores everywhere) is loaded with tips.

To avoid the blurriness caused by hand shake, **buy a mini tripod**—they're available in sizes as small as 6 inches. **Get a small beanbag to support your camera on uneven surfaces.** If you'll be visiting the Andes, **get a skylight (81B or 81C) or polarizing filter to minimize haze and light problems.** The higher the altitude, the greater the proportion of ultraviolet rays. Light meters don't read these rays and consequently, except for close-ups or full-frame portraits where the reading is taken directly off the subject, photos may be overexposed. These filters may also help with the glare caused by white adobe buildings, sandy beaches, and so on. **Invest in a telephoto lens to photograph wildlife:** even standard zoom lenses of the 35–88 range won't capture a satisfying amount of detail. **Bring high-speed film to compensate for low light in the rain forest.** The thick tree canopy blocks out more light than you realize.

Casual photographers should **consider using inexpensive disposable cameras** to reduce the risks inherent in traveling with sophisticated equipment. One-use cameras with panoramic or underwater functions can be nice supplements to a standard camera.

EQUIPMENT PRECAUTIONS

Always **keep your film and tape out of the sun** and on rain forest trips **keep your equipment in resealable plastic bags** to protect it from the dampness. As petty crime is a problem throughout South America, **keep a close eye on your gear.** At airports you should **be prepared to turn on** your camera or camcorder to prove to security personnel that the device is real. Always **ask for hand inspection of film,** which becomes clouded after successive exposures to X-ray machines, and **keep videotapes away from metal detectors.**

FILM & DEVELOPING

Remember to **bring plenty of film** if you are traveling to remote areas where your favorite brand may not be available. Plan on shooting a minimum of one 36-exposure roll per week of travel. If you don't want the hassle of keeping a shot log, **make a quick note whenever you start a new roll**—it will make identifying your photos much easier when you get home.

CAR RENTAL

Many seasoned travelers like to drive in Chile. Certain areas are most enjoyable when explored on your own in a car, such as the wineries of the Central Valley and the ski areas east of Santiago. And some regions, such as the Atacama Desert, are nearly impossible to reach without your own wheels.

It is by far easier to rent a car in Santiago, where all the international agencies have branches at the airport and in town. You'll find mostly local rental agencies in the rest of the country. Local companies are often a cheaper option.

Always **give the rental car a once-over** to make sure that the headlights, jack, and tires (including the spare) are in working condition. Make sure to **alert the agency about any scratches and dents** before you set off on your trip or you may be held liable for damages you didn't cause.

➤ MAJOR AGENCIES: **Alamo** (☎ 800/ 522–9696; 020/8759–6200 in the U.K.). **Avis** (☎ 800/331–1084; 800/ 879–2847 in Canada; 02/9353–9000 in Australia; 09/525–1982 in New Zealand; 0870/606–0100 in the U.K.). **Budget** (☎ 800/527–0700; 0870/607–5000 in the U.K., through affiliate Europcar). **Dollar** (☎ 800/ 800–6000; 0124/622–0111 in the U.K., through affiliate Sixt Kenning; 02/9223–1444 in Australia). **Hertz** (☎ 800/654–3001; 800/263–0600 in Canada; 020/8897–2072 in the U.K.;

02/9669–2444 in Australia; 09/256– 8690 in New Zealand). **National Car Rental** (☎ 800/227–7368; 020/8680– 4800 in the U.K., where it is known as National Europe).

CUTTING COSTS

To get the best deal, **book through a travel agent who will shop around.** Also **price local rental companies.** Remember to ask about required deposits, cancellation penalties, and drop-off charges if you're planning to pick up the car in one city and leave it in another. If you're traveling during a holiday period, also make sure that a confirmed reservation guarantees you a car.

If you don't want to drive yourself, **consider hiring a car and driver** through your hotel concierge, or **make a deal with a taxi driver** for some extended sightseeing at a longer-term rate. Drivers charge an hourly rate regardless of the distance traveled. You'll often spend less than you would for a rental car.

INSURANCE

The price of a rental in Chile comes with collision and theft insurance, usually with a deductible of around $400. When driving a rented car you're generally responsible for any damage to or loss of the vehicle as well as for any property damage or personal injury that you may cause. Before you rent **see what coverage your personal auto-insurance policy and credit cards already provide.**

REQUIREMENTS & RESTRICTIONS

Your own driver's license and an International Driving Permit make it legal for you to drive. The minimum age for driving in Chile is 18; you can drive with an adult with a restricted license at 17. To rent a car you usually have to be 25, but a few companies let you rent at 22.

SURCHARGES

Before you pick up a car in one city and leave it in another, **ask about drop-off charges or one-way service fees,** which can be substantial. Note, too, that some rental agencies charge extra if you return the car before the time specified in your contract.

CAR TRAVEL

Between May and August, roads, underpasses, and parks can flood when it rains. It's very dangerous, especially for drivers who don't know their way around. Avoid driving if it has been raining for several hours. Keep in mind that the speed limit is 50 kmh (31 mph) in cities and 100 kmh (62 mph) on highways unless otherwise posted.

Some common-sense rules of the road: before you set out **establish an itinerary.** Be sure to **plan your daily driving distance conservatively.** Always **obey speed limits and traffic regulations.** And above all, **if you get a traffic ticket, don't argue**—and plan to spend longer than you want settling it.

AUTO CLUBS

The Automóvil Club de Chile offers low-cost road service and towing in and around the main cities to members of the Automobile Association of America (AAA).

➤ IN CHILE: **The Automóvil Club de Chile** (⊠ Av. Vitacura 8620, Santiago, ☎ 2/212–5702, FAX 2/211–9208).

➤ IN AUSTRALIA: **Australian Automobile Association** (☎ 02/6247–7311).

➤ IN CANADA: **Canadian Automobile Association** (CAA, ☎ 613/247–0117).

➤ IN NEW ZEALAND: **New Zealand Automobile Association** (☎ 09/377–4660).

➤ IN THE U.K.: **Automobile Association** (AA, ☎ 0990/500–600), **Royal Automobile Club** (RAC, ☎ 0990/722–722 for membership; 0345/121–345 for insurance).

➤ IN THE U.S.: **American Automobile Association** (☎ 800/564–6222).

GASOLINE

In Chile, gasoline is cheap—half of what it costs in neighboring Argentina. At press time a liter of gas cost about 50¢. To make sure you don't run out of gas, always **ask about gas stations** en route.

CHILDREN IN CHILE

Chileans love children, and having yours along may prove to be your special ticket to meeting the locals. Children are welcomed in most hotels and restaurants, especially on weekends, when families go out for lunch in droves. The *balnearios* (beach towns) along Chile's Central Coast expect you to bring the kids—the most common form of lodging are family-size bungalows. Children are also a common sight in the pine-covered mountains of the Lake District and the ski resorts of the Central Valley.

For general advice about traveling with children, consult *Fodor's FYI: Travel with Your Baby* (available in bookstores everywhere).

FLYING

If your children are two or older, **ask about children's airfares.** As a general rule, infants under two not occupying a seat fly at greatly reduced fares or even for free. When booking, **confirm carry-on allowances** if you're traveling with infants. In general, for babies charged 10% of the adult fare you are allowed one carry-on bag and a collapsible stroller; if the flight is full, the stroller may have to be checked or you may be limited to less.

Experts agree that it's a good idea to use safety seats aloft for children weighing less than 40 pounds. Airlines set their own policies: U.S. carriers usually require that the child be ticketed, even if he or she is young enough to ride free, since the seats must be strapped into regular seats. Do **check your airline's policy about using safety seats during takeoff and landing.** And since safety seats are not allowed everywhere in the plane, get your seat assignments early.

When reserving, **request children's meals or a freestanding bassinet** if you need them. But note that bulkhead seats, where you must sit to use the bassinet, may lack an overhead bin or storage space on the floor.

LODGING

Most hotels in Chile allow children under a certain age to stay in their parents' room at no extra charge, but others charge for them as extra adults; be sure to **find out the cutoff age for children's discounts.**

SIGHTS & ATTRACTIONS

There's plenty for kids to do in Chile. Santiago is filled with interesting museums that will appeal to the entire family. Every town has public parks where parents can relax while their children romp. Kids are fascinated by the *ascensores* (funiculars) of Valparaíso. The ferries around Puerto Montt are a great way to see the coastline. And even the youngest members of your family will delight at the penguin colonies near Punta Arenas.

Places that are especially appealing to children are indicated by a rubber-duckie icon (🦆) in the margin.

COMPUTERS ON THE ROAD

If you're planning to bring a laptop computer into the country, **check the manual** first to see if it requires a converter. Newer laptops will only require an adapter plug. Chile uses the same phone plugs as the United States, so plan accordingly if you'll be using a modem. Remember to **ask about electrical surges** before plugging in your computer. Carrying a laptop computer could make you a target for thieves; **conceal your laptop in a generic bag** and **keep it close to you at all times.** Note that South America's luxury hotels typically offer business centers with computers.

CONCIERGES

Concierges, found in many urban hotels, can help you find your way around. A good one with connections—which are always key in Chile—may be able to get you seats for a hot show or prime-time dinner reservations at the restaurant of the moment. You can also turn to your hotel's concierge for help with travel arrangements, sightseeing plans, services ranging from aromatherapy to zipper repair, and emergencies. **Always tip a concierge** who has been of assistance.

CONSUMER PROTECTION

Whenever shopping or buying travel services in South America, **pay with a major credit card,** if possible, so you can cancel payment or get reimbursed if there's a problem. If you're doing business with a particular company for the first time, **contact your local Better Business Bureau and the attorney general's offices** in your state and (for U.S. businesses) the company's home state as well. Have any complaints been filed? Finally, if you're buying a package or tour, always **consider travel insurance** that includes default coverage (☞ Insurance, *below*).

➤ BBBs: **Council of Better Business Bureaus** (✉ 4200 Wilson Blvd., Suite 800, Arlington, VA 22203, ☎ 703/276–0100, FAX 703/525–8277, WEB www.bbb.org).

CUSTOMS & DUTIES

When shopping, **keep receipts** for all purchases. Upon reentering the country, **be ready to show customs officials what you've bought.** If you feel a duty is incorrect or object to the way your clearance was handled, note the inspector's badge number and ask to see a supervisor. If the problem isn't resolved, write to the appropriate authorities, beginning with the port director at your point of entry.

IN AUSTRALIA

Australian residents who are 18 or older may bring home $A400 worth of souvenirs and gifts (including jewelry), 250 cigarettes or 250 grams of tobacco, and 1,125 ml of alcohol (including wine, beer, and spirits). Residents under 18 may bring back $A200 worth of goods. Prohibited items include meat products. Seeds, plants, and fruits need to be declared upon arrival.

➤ INFORMATION: **Australian Customs Service** (Regional Director, ✉ Box 8, Sydney, NSW 2001, Australia, ☎ 02/9213–2000, FAX 02/9213–4000, WEB www.customs.gov.au).

IN CANADA

Canadian residents who have been out of Canada for at least seven days may bring home C$500 worth of goods duty-free. If you've been away fewer than seven days but more than 48 hours, the duty-free allowance drops to C$200; if your trip lasts 24–48 hours, the allowance is C$50. You may not pool allowances with family members. Goods claimed under the C$500 exemption may follow you by mail; those claimed under the lesser exemptions must accompany you.

SMART TRAVEL TIPS A TO Z

Alcohol and tobacco products may be included in the seven-day and 48-hour exemptions but not in the 24-hour exemption. If you meet the age requirements of the province or territory through which you reenter Canada, you may bring in, duty-free, 1.14 liters (40 imperial ounces) of wine or liquor *or* 24 12-ounce cans or bottles of beer or ale. If you are 16 or older you may bring in, duty-free, 200 cigarettes and 50 cigars. Check ahead of time with Revenue Canada or the Department of Agriculture for policies regarding meat products, seeds, plants, and fruits.

You may send an unlimited number of gifts worth up to C$60 each duty-free to Canada. Label the package UNSOLICITED GIFT—VALUE UNDER $60. Alcohol and tobacco are excluded.

➤ INFORMATION: **Revenue Canada** (✉ 2265 St. Laurent Blvd. S, Ottawa, Ontario K1G 4K3, Canada, ☎ 613/993–0534; 800/461–9999 in Canada, FAX 613/991–4126, WEB www.ccra-adrc.gc.ca).

IN CHILE

You may bring into Chile up to 400 cigarettes, 400 grams of tobacco, 50 cigars, two open bottles of perfume, 2 liters of alcoholic beverages, and gifts. Visitors, although seldom questioned, are prohibited from leaving with handicrafts and souvenirs worth more than $500.

IN NEW ZEALAND

Homeward-bound residents 17 or older may bring back $700 worth of souvenirs and gifts. Your duty-free allowance also includes 4.5 liters of wine or beer; one 1,125-ml bottle of spirits; and either 200 cigarettes, 250 grams of tobacco, 50 cigars, or a combination of the three up to 250 grams. Prohibited items include meat products, seeds, plants, and fruits.

➤ INFORMATION: **New Zealand Customs** (Custom House, ✉ 50 Anzac Ave., Box 29, Auckland, New Zealand, ☎ 09/300–5399, FAX 09/359–6730), WEB www.customs.govt.nz).

IN THE U.K.

From countries outside the EU, including Chile, you may bring home, duty-free, 200 cigarettes or 50 cigars; 1 liter of spirits or 2 liters of fortified or sparkling wine or liqueurs; 2 liters of still table wine; 60 ml of perfume; 250 ml of toilet water; plus £136 worth of other goods, including gifts and souvenirs. If returning from outside the EU, prohibited items include meat products, seeds, plants, and fruits.

➤ INFORMATION: **HM Customs and Excise** (✉ Dorset House, Stamford St., Bromley, Kent BR1 1XX, U.K., ☎ 020/7202–4227, WEB www.hmce.gov.uk).

IN THE U.S.

U.S. residents who have been out of the country for at least 48 hours (and who have not used the $400 allowance or any part of it in the past 30 days) may bring home $400 worth of foreign goods duty-free.U.S. residents 21 and older may bring back 1 liter of alcohol duty-free. In addition, regardless of your age, you are allowed 200 cigarettes and 100 non-Cuban cigars. Antiques, which the U.S. Customs Service defines as objects more than 100 years old, enter duty-free, as do original works of art done entirely by hand, including paintings, drawings, and sculptures.

You may also mail or ship packages home duty-free: up to $200 worth of goods for personal use, with a limit of one parcel per addressee per day (except alcohol or tobacco products or perfume worth more than $5); label the package PERSONAL USE and attach a list of its contents and their retail value. Do not label the package UNSOLICITED GIFT or your duty-free exemption will drop to $100. Mailed items do not affect your duty-free allowance on your return.

➤ INFORMATION: **U.S. Customs Service** (✉ 1300 Pennsylvania Ave. NW, Washington, DC 20229, WEB www.customs.gov; inquiries ☎ 202/354–1000; complaints c/o ✉ 1300 Pennsylvania Ave. NW, Room 5.4D, Washington, DC 20229; registration of equipment c/o ✉ Resource Management, ☎ 202/927–0540).

DINING

The restaurants (all of which are indicated by a ✕ symbol) that we list are the cream of the crop in each price category. Properties indicated by a ✕⚏ are lodging establishments whose restaurant warrants a special trip. For details on food and drink, mealtimes, and paying, *see* Dining *in* Pleasures and Pastimes at the start of each chapter. It is customary to tip 10% in Chile; tipping above this amount is uncommon among locals. Price categories are as follows:

CATEGORY	COST*
$$$$	over 9,000 pesos
$$$	6,000–9,000 pesos
$$	3,000–6,000 pesos
$	under 3,000 pesos

per person, for a main course at dinner.

MEALS & SPECIALTIES

Chile serves an incredible variety of foods. With such a long coastline, it's no surprise that you can get wonderful seafood. Salmon is caught off the southern coast and raised in farms in the Lake District, and sea bass, conger eel, and reineta are found along the Central Coast. Ceviche is fish marinated in lemon juice and seasonings like cilantro. In Santiago you might find it served with roasted corn.

But fish isn't the only dish available. Valparaíso is known for its *chorillada*—a mountain of beef, onions, and eggs, atop french fries. In many parts of the country you'll find *cazuela de vacuno* (beef stew) and *chuleta con arroz* (steak served with rice). Everywhere you'll find the *empanada*, a fried or baked pastry filled with chopped beef, eggs, olives, onions, and seasonings.

The national drink is pisco, a type of brandy. A pisco sour is pisco with lemon, egg whites, and sugar. A good number of Chilean wines, especially cabernet sauvignons, are on par with top European and American counterparts. They are also a terrific value.

MEALTIMES

Lunch, which usually begins 1 or 2 PM, is the biggest and most important meal of day. It can take two hours or more. Some Chileans forgo dinner, making do with an *once*, a light evening meal similar in style to a high tea. Many restaurants have once meals, which include a sandwich (often ham and cheese), fresh juice, tea, and a dessert. Once is served from 5 to 8; dinner is eaten later than in North America, usually starting anywhere from 8 to 10. Unless otherwise noted, the restaurants listed in this guide are open daily for lunch and dinner.

RESERVATIONS & DRESS

Reservations are always a good idea: we mention them only when they're essential or not accepted. Book as far ahead as you can, and reconfirm as soon as you arrive. We mention dress only when men are required to wear a jacket or a jacket and tie.

DISABILITIES & ACCESSIBILITY

Although international chain hotels in Santiago and a few other cities have some wheelchair-accessible rooms, Chile isn't very well equipped to handle travelers with disabilities. There are few ramps and curb cuts, and it takes effort and planning to negotiate cobbled city streets, get around museums and other buildings, and explore the countryside. Some regions, such as the Atacama Desert, are a challenge for those with mobility problems. Valparaíso, with its hillside topography and unending staircases, could be unmanageable.

RESERVATIONS

When discussing accessibility with an operator or reservations agent, **ask hard questions.** Are there any stairs, inside *or* out? Are there grab bars next to the toilet *and* in the shower/tub? How wide is the doorway to the room? To the bathroom? For the most extensive facilities meeting the latest legal specifications, **opt for newer accommodations.**

SIGHTS & ATTRACTIONS

Few sights in Chile were designed with travelers in wheelchairs in mind, and fewer still have been renovated to meet their needs. Newer destinations may have the necessary facilities, but don't count on it. Call ahead or ask someone who has visited before.

➤ COMPLAINTS: **Aviation Consumer Protection Division** (☞ Air Travel, *above*) for airline-related problems. **Civil Rights Office** (✉ U.S. Department of Transportation, Departmental Office of Civil Rights, S-30, 400 7th St. SW, Room 10215, Washington,

DC 20590, ☎ 202/366–4648, FAX 202/366–9371, WEB www.dot.gov/ost/docr/index.htm) for problems with surface transportation. **Disability Rights Section** (✉ U.S. Department of Justice, Civil Rights Division, Box 66738, Washington, DC 20035-6738, ☎ 202/514–0301 or 800/514–0301; 202/514–0383 TTY; 800/514–0383 TTY, FAX 202/307–1198, WEB www.usdoj.gov/crt/ada/adahom1.htm) for general complaints.

TRAVEL AGENCIES

In the United States, the Americans with Disabilities Act requires that travel firms serve the needs of all travelers. Some agencies specialize in working with people with disabilities.

➤ TRAVELERS WITH MOBILITY PROBLEMS: **Access Adventures** (✉ 206 Chestnut Ridge Rd., Scottsville, NY 14624, ☎ 716/889–9096, dltravel@prodigy.net), run by a former physical-rehabilitation counselor. **CareVacations** (✉ 5-5110 50th Ave., Leduc, Alberta T9E 6V4, Canada, ☎ 780/986–6404 or 877/478–7827, FAX 780/986–8332, WEB www.carevacations.com), for group tours and cruise vacations. **Flying Wheels Travel** (✉ 143 W. Bridge St., Box 382, Owatonna, MN 55060, ☎ 507/451–5005 or 800/535–6790, FAX 507/451–1685, WEB www.flyingwheelstravel.com).

DISCOUNTS & DEALS

Be a smart shopper and **compare all your options** before making decisions. A plane ticket bought with a promotional coupon from travel clubs, coupon books, and direct-mail offers or on the Internet may not be cheaper than the least expensive fare from a discount ticket agency. And always keep in mind that what you get is just as important as what you save.

DISCOUNT RESERVATIONS

To save money, **look into discount reservations services** with toll-free numbers, which use their buying power to get a better price on hotels, airline tickets, even car rentals. When booking a room, always **call the hotel's local toll-free number** (if one is available) rather than the central reservations number—you'll often get a better price. Always ask about special packages or corporate rates.

When shopping for the best deal on hotels and car rentals, **look for guaranteed exchange rates,** which protect you against a falling dollar. With your rate locked in, you won't pay more, even if the price goes up in the local currency.

➤ HOTEL ROOMS: **Steigenberger Reservation Service** (☎ 800/223–5652, WEB www.srs-worldhotels.com). **Travel Interlink** (☎ 800/888–5898, WEB www.travelinterlink.com). **Turbotrip.com** (☎ 800/473–7829, WEB www.turbotrip.com).

PACKAGE DEALS

Don't confuse packages and guided tours. When you buy a package, you travel on your own, just as though you had planned the trip yourself. Fly/drive packages, which combine airfare and car rental, are often a good deal.

ELECTRICITY

Unlike the United States and Canada—which have a 110- to 120-volt standard—the current in Chile is 220 volts, 50 cycles alternating current (AC). To use an appliance from home, **bring a converter.**

If your appliances are dual-voltage—as many laptops are these days—you'll need only an adapter. Don't use 110-volt outlets, marked FOR SHAVERS ONLY, for high-wattage appliances such as hair dryers.

EMBASSIES

➤ CHILE: **Canada** (✉ Nueva Tajamar 481, p. 12 Torre Norte, Las Condes, Santiago, ☎ 2/362–9600). **United Kingdom** (✉ Av. El Bosque N 0125, p. 3, Providencia, Santiago, ☎ 2/231–3737). **United States** (✉ Av. Andrés Bello 2800, Providencia, ☎ 2/232–2600).

➤ AUSTRALIA: **Chile** (✉ Box 69, Monaco Crescent, ACT 2603, Australia, ☎ 616/286–2430).

➤ CANADA: **Chile** (✉ 151 Slater St., Suite 605, Ottawa, Ontario, K1P 5A9, Canada, ☎ 613/235–4402).

➤ NEW ZEALAND: **Chile** (✉ 1-3 Willeston St., 7th floor, Wellington, New Zealand, ☎ 644/472–5180).

➤ UNITED KINGDOM: **Chile** (✉ 12 Devonshire St., London, W1N 2DS, England, ☎ 020/7580–6392).

➤ UNITED STATES: **Chile** (✉ 1140 Connecticut Ave. NW, Suite 703, Washington, DC 20036, ☎ 202/785–1746).

EMERGENCIES

The numbers to call in case of emergency are the same all over Chile.

➤ NUMBERS: **Ambulance** (☎ 131); **Fire** (☎ 132); **Police** (☎ 133).

GAY & LESBIAN TRAVEL

Although the government repealed its law banning sex between people of the same gender, it's still difficult for many Chilean gay men and lesbians to be out of the closet. This may be why the gay scene remains very subdued. There are gay bars and clubs in Santiago and a few other cities, but they often can be difficult to find. For details about the gay and lesbian scene, consult *Fodor's Gay Guide to the USA* (available in bookstores everywhere).

GAY AND LESBIAN WEB SITES

For specific information about Chile's gay scene, try the online Gay Chile. It lists all the local gay bars and clubs and gay-friendly hotels. Spanish speakers can try the online Lambda News. The best site online for general information about gay travel is Out and About. Here you can scour though the back issues for information on gay-friendly destinations. You also can try PlanetOut and Gay.Com, two general-interest gay sites.

➤ GAY AND LESBIAN WEB SITES: www.gaychile.com, www.lambdanews.cl, www.planetout.com/travel, www.outandabout.com, www.gay.com

➤ GAY- & LESBIAN-FRIENDLY TRAVEL AGENCIES: **Different Roads Travel** (✉ 8383 Wilshire Blvd., Suite 902, Beverly Hills, CA 90211, ☎ 323/651–5557 or 800/429–8747, FAX 323/651–3678, lgernert@tzell.com). **Kennedy Travel** (✉ 314 Jericho Turnpike, Floral Park, NY 11001, ☎ 516/352–4888 or 800/237–7433, FAX 516/354–8849, WEB www.kennedytravel.com).

Now Voyager (✉ 4406 18th St., San Francisco, CA 94114, ☎ 415/626–1169 or 800/255–6951, FAX 415/626–8626, WEB www.nowvoyager.com). **Skylink Travel and Tour** (✉ 1006 Mendocino Ave., Santa Rosa, CA 95401, ☎ 707/546–9888 or 800/225–5759, FAX 707/546–9891, WEB www.skylinktravel.com), serving lesbian travelers.

HEALTH

From a health standpoint, Chile is one of the safer countries in which to travel. To be on the safe side, **take the normal precautions** you would traveling anywhere in South America.

ALTITUDE SICKNESS

Altitude sickness—which causes shortness of breath, nausea, and splitting headaches—may be a problem when you visit Andean countries. The best way to prevent *soroche* is to **ascend slowly.** Spend a few nights at 6,000–9,000 ft before you head higher. If you must fly straight in, plan on doing next to nothing for your first few days. If you begin to feel ill, the traditional remedy is herbal tea made from coca leaves. Over-the-counter analgesics and napping also help. If symptoms persist, return to lower elevations. Note that if you have high blood pressure and/or a history of heart trouble, check with your doctor before traveling to the mountains.

DIVERS' ALERT

Scuba divers take note: **Do not fly within 24 hours of scuba diving.** Neophyte divers should have a complete physical exam before undertaking a dive. If you have travel insurance, **make sure your policy applies to scuba-related injuries,** as not all companies provide this coverage.

FOOD & DRINK

Visitors seldom encounter problems with drinking the water in Chile. Almost all drinking water receives proper treatment and is unlikely to produce health problems. If you have any doubts, stick to bottled water. Mineral water is good and comes in carbonated (*con gas*) and noncarbonated (*sin gas*) incarnations.

Food preparation is strictly regulated by the government, so outbreaks of food-borne diseases are very rare. But it's still a good idea to use the same common-sense rules you would in any other part of South America. Don't risk restaurants where the hygiene is suspect or street vendors where the food is allowed to sit around unrefrigerated. Always **avoid raw shellfish,** such as ceviche. Remember to **steer clear of raw fruits and vegetables** unless you know they've been thoroughly washed and disinfected.

MEDICAL PLANS

No one plans to get sick while traveling, but it happens, so **consider signing up with a medical-assistance company.** Members get doctor referrals, emergency evacuation or repatriation, hot lines for medical consultation, cash for emergencies, and other assistance.

➤ MEDICAL-ASSISTANCE COMPANIES: International SOS Assistance (WEB www.internationalsos.com; ✉ 8 Neshaminy Interplex, Suite 207, Trevose, PA 19053, ☎ 215/245–4707 or 800/523–6586, FAX 215/244–9617; ✉ 12 Chemin Riantbosson, 1217 Meyrin 1, Geneva, Switzerland, ☎ 4122/785–6464, FAX 4122/785–6424; ✉ 331 N. Bridge Rd., 17-00, Odeon Towers, Singapore 188720, ☎ 65/338–7800, FAX 65/338–7611).

OVER-THE-COUNTER REMEDIES

Mild cases of diarrhea may respond to Imodium (known generically as loperamide), Pepto-Bismol (not as strong), and Lomotil. Paregoric, another antidiarrheal agent that requires a doctor's prescription in the United States, can be purchased over the counter in South America. Drink plenty of purified water or tea—chamomile (*manzanilla* in Spanish) is a good folk remedy.

SHOTS & MEDICATIONS

All travelers to Chile should get up-to-date tetanus, diphtheria, and measles boosters, and a hepatitis A inoculation is recommended. Children traveling to Chile should have current inoculations against mumps, rubella, and polio. Always **check with your doctor** about which shots to get.

According to the Centers for Disease Control and Prevention, there's no risk of contracting malaria, but a limited risk of cholera, typhoid, hepatitis B, dengue, and Chagas. While a few of these you could catch anywhere, most are restricted to jungle areas. The best way to avoid these diseases is to **prevent insect bites** by wearing long pants and long-sleeve shirts and by using insect repellents with DEET. If you plan to visit remote regions or stay for more than six weeks, **check with the CDC's International Travelers Hot Line.**

➤ HEALTH WARNINGS: **National Centers for Disease Control and Prevention** (CDC; National Center for Infectious Diseases, Division of Quarantine, Traveler's Health Section, ✉ 1600 Clifton Rd. NE, M/S E-03, Atlanta, GA 30333, ☎ 888/232–3228 or 800/311–3435, FAX 888/232–3299, WEB www.cdc.gov).

HOLIDAYS

New Year's Day (Jan. 1); Labor Day (May 1); Day of Naval Glories (May 21); Corpus Christi (in June); Feast of St. Peter and St. Paul (June 29); Anniversary of Coup (Sept. 11); Independence Celebrations (Sept. 18–19); Discovery of the Americas (Oct. 12); Day of the Dead (Nov. 1); Immaculate Conception (Dec. 8); Christmas (Dec. 25).

Many shops and services are open on these days, but transportation is always heavily booked up on and around the holidays.

INSURANCE

The most useful travel-insurance plan is a comprehensive policy that includes coverage for trip cancellation and interruption, default, trip delay, and medical expenses (with a waiver for preexisting conditions).

Without insurance you will lose all or most of your money if you cancel your trip, regardless of the reason. Default insurance covers you if your tour operator, airline, or cruise line goes out of business. Trip-delay covers expenses that arise because of bad weather or mechanical delays. Study the fine print when comparing policies.

If you're traveling internationally, a key component of travel insurance is coverage for medical bills incurred if you get sick on the road. Such expenses are not generally covered by Medicare or private policies. U.K. residents can buy a travel-insurance policy valid for most vacations taken during the year in which it's purchased (but check preexisting-condition coverage). British and Australian citizens need extra medical coverage when traveling overseas.

Always **buy travel policies directly from the insurance company**; if you buy them from a cruise line, airline, or tour operator that goes out of business you probably will not be covered for the agency or operator's default, a major risk. Before making any purchase, **review your existing health and home-owner's policies** to find what they cover away from home.

➤ TRAVEL INSURERS: In the United States: **Access America** (✉ 6600 W. Broad St., Richmond, VA 23230, ☎ 804/285–3300 or 800/284–8300, FAX 804/673–1586, WEB www.previewtravel.com), **Travel Guard International** (✉ 1145 Clark St., Stevens Point, WI 54481, ☎ 715/345–0505 or 800/826–1300, FAX 800/955–8785, WEB www.noelgroup.com).

➤ INSURANCE INFORMATION: In the United Kingdom: **Association of British Insurers** (✉ 51–55 Gresham St., London EC2V 7HQ, U.K., ☎ 020/7600–3333, FAX 020/7696–8999, WEB www.abi.org.uk). In Canada: **Voyager Insurance** (✉ 44 Peel Center Dr., Brampton, Ontario L6T 4M8, Canada, ☎ 905/791–8700, 800/668–4342 in Canada). In Australia: **Insurance Council of Australia** (✉ Level 3, 56 Pitt St., Sydney NSW 2000, ☎ 03/9614–1077, FAX 03/9614–7924). In New Zealand: **Insurance Council of New Zealand** (✉ Box 474, Wellington, New Zealand, ☎ 04/472–5230, FAX 04/473–3011, WEB www.icnz.org.nz).

INTERNET ACCESS

Chileans are generally savvy about the Internet. It is not as widely used as in the United States, which may be partly due to the sluggish connection speeds. Only the most expensive hotels have business centers with Internet-linked computer terminals. If your hotel doesn't have one, ask at the front desk or at any Sernatur office for directions to one of the increasing number of Internet cafés. Connection fees are generally no more than $1 for a half hour. There is at least one Internet café in every city. Smaller towns may not have one, so make sure you check your e-mail before you leave urban areas.

LANGUAGE

Chile's official language is Spanish, so it's best to learn at least a few words and carry a good phrase book. Chilean Spanish is fast, clipped, and chock-full of colloquialisms. For example, the word for police officer isn't *policía*, but *carabinero*. Even foreigners with a good deal of experience in Spanish-speaking countries may feel like they are encountering a completely new language. However, receptionists at most upscale hotels speak English, as do many taxi drivers and salespeople.

A phrase book and language-tape set can help get you started. *Fodor's Spanish for Travelers* (available at bookstores everywhere) is excellent.

LANGUAGE SCHOOLS

The Wall Street Institute, an international chain of language schools, has a branch in Santiago. Berlitz, another internationally recognized language school, has a number of schools in Santiago, Concepción, and Viña del Mar. The Instututo Chileno-Norteamericano, based in Valparaíso, has a good reputation for having more student-teacher contact. There are branches in most Chilean cities.

➤ LANGUAGE SCHOOLS: **Berlitz** (✉ Padre Mariano 305, Santiago, ☎ 2/236–1557, FAX 2/236–1563, WEB www.berlitz.com). **Instututo Chileno-Norteamericano** (✉ Esmerelda 1069, Valparaíso, ☎ 32/254–844). **Wall Street Institute/Agustinas** (✉ Agustinas 1138, Santiago, ☎ 2/672–2827, FAX 2/698–0654, WEB www.wallstreetinstitute.com).

LODGING

The lodgings (all indicated with ⊞) that we list are the cream of the crop in each price category. We always list the facilities that are available—but we don't specify whether they cost extra: When pricing accommodations, always ask what's included and what costs extra. All hotels listed have private bath unless otherwise noted. Properties indicated by ✕⊞ are lodging establishments whose restaurant warrants a special trip. Price categories are as follows:

CATEGORY	COST*
$$$$	over 90,000 pesos
$$$	60,000–90,000 pesos
$$	30,000–60,000 pesos
$	under 30,000 pesos

*for a double room in high season, excluding taxes

It's always good to **look at any room before accepting it.** Expense is no guarantee of charm or cleanliness, and accommodations can vary dramatically within one hotel. If you ask for a double room, you'll get a room for two people, but you're not guaranteed a double mattress. If you'd like to avoid twin beds, you'll have to **ask for a cama de matrimonio** (no wedding ring seems to be required). Many older hotels in Chile have rooms with wrought-iron balconies or spacious terraces; ask if there's a room *con balcón* or *con terraza* when checking in.

Hotels in Chile do not charge taxes to foreign tourists. Knowing this in advance can save you some cash. When checking the price, make sure to **ask for the precio extranjero, sin impuestos** (foreign rate, without taxes).

HOSTELS

No matter what your age, you can **save on lodging costs by staying at hostels.** Youth hostels in Chile are not very popular, perhaps due to the prevalence of *residenciales* and other low-cost lodging. But if staying in a hostel is your thing, Hostelling International (HI), the umbrella group for a number of national youth-hostel associations, offers single-sex, dorm-style beds and, at many hostels, couples rooms and family accommo-

dations. Membership in any HI national hostel association, open to travelers of all ages, allows you to stay in HI-affiliated hostels at member rates (one-year membership is about $25 for adults; hostels run about $10–$25 per night). Members also have priority if the hostel is full; they're eligible for discounts around the world, even on rail and bus travel in some countries.

➤ ORGANIZATIONS: **Australian Youth Hostel Association** (✉ 10 Mallett St., Camperdown, NSW 2050, Australia, ☎ 02/9565–1699, FAX 02/9565–1325, WEB www.yha.com.au). **Hostelling International—American Youth Hostels** (✉ 733 15th St. NW, Suite 840, Washington, DC 20005, ☎ 202/783–6161, FAX 202/783–6171, WEB www.hiayh.org). **Hostelling International—Canada** (✉ 400–205 Catherine St., Ottawa, Ontario K2P 1C3, Canada, ☎ 613/237–7884, FAX 613/237–7868, WEB www.hostellingintl.ca). **Youth Hostel Association of England and Wales** (✉ Trevelyan House, 8 St. Stephen's Hill, St. Albans, Hertfordshire AL1 2DY, U.K., ☎ 0870/8708808, FAX 01727/844126, WEB www.yha.org.uk). **Youth Hostels Association of New Zealand** (✉ Box 436, Christchurch, New Zealand, ☎ 03/379–9970, FAX 03/365–4476, WEB www.yha.org.nz).

HOTELS

Only Chile's larger cities and resort areas have hotels that offer all of the amenities that are taken for granted in North America and Europe, such as room service, a restaurant, or a swimming pool. Elsewhere you may not have television or a phone in your room, although you will find them somewhere in the hotel. Rooms that have a private bath may only have a shower, and in some cases, there will be a shared bath in the hall. In all but the most upscale hotels, you may be asked to leave your key at the reception desk whenever you leave.

➤ TOLL-FREE NUMBERS: **Best Western** (☎ 800/528–1234, WEB www.bestwestern.com). **Choice** (☎ 800/221–2222, WEB www.hotelchoice.com). **Clarion** (☎ 800/252–7466, WEB www.hotelchoice.com). **Embassy Suites** (☎ 800/362–2779, WEB www.

embassysuites.com). **Holiday Inn** (☎ 800/465–4329, WEB www.basshotels. com). **Hyatt Hotels & Resorts** (☎ 800/233–1234, WEB www.hyatt.com). **Panamericana Hoteles** (WEB www. panamericanahoteles.cl).

RESIDENCIALES

Private homes that rent rooms, *residenciales,* are a unique way to get to know Chile, especially if you're on a budget. Many are under $10. Some will be shabby, but others can be substantially better than hotel rooms. They also offer the added benefit of allowing you to interact with locals, who likely speak English.

MAIL & SHIPPING

Postage on regular letters and post-cards to Canada and the United States costs 200 pesos. The postage to Britain and Australia is 250 pesos. The postal system is efficient and, on average, letters take five–seven days to reach the United States or Europe. Vendors often sell stamps at the entrances to larger post offices. If you want to save a potentially long wait in line, the stamps are valid, and selling them this way is legal.

MONEY MATTERS

Always **check exchange rates** in your local newspaper for the most current information; at press time there were approximately 372 Chilean pesos to the Canadian dollar, 562 pesos to the U.S. dollar, and 821 pesos to the British pound. Chilean coins come in units of 1, 5, 10, 50, and 100 pesos; bills are issued in 500, 1,000, 5,000, 10,000, and 20,000 pesos. Note that acquiring change for larger bills, especially from small shopkeepers, can be difficult. Make sure to **get smaller bills** when you exchange money.

Credit cards and traveler's checks are accepted in most resorts and in many shops and restaurants in major cities, though you should **always carry some local currency** for minor expenses like taxis and tipping. Once you stray from the beaten path, you can often only pay with pesos.

Prices throughout this guide are given for adults. Substantially reduced fees are almost always available for children, students, and senior citizens.

For information on taxes, *see* Taxes, *below.*

ATMS

ATMs are widely available, and you can get cash with a Cirrus- or Plus-linked debit card or with a major credit card. Most ATMs in Chile have a special screen—accessed after entering your PIN code—for foreign account withdrawals. In this case, merely selecting a "cash withdrawal" won't work—you need to access your account first via the "foreign client" option. Although ATM fees may be higher than back home, Cirrus and Plus offer excellent exchange rates because they are based on wholesale rates offered only by major banks.

Before leaving home, **make sure that your credit cards have been programmed for ATM use in Chile.** Make sure to **ask your bank about a getting debit card,** which works like a bank card but can be used at any ATM displaying a MasterCard or Visa logo.

➤ ATM LOCATIONS: **MasterCard Cirrus** (☎ 800/424–7787, WEB www. mastercard.com/atm). **Visa Plus** (☎ 800/843–7587, WEB www.visa. com/atm).

CREDIT CARDS

It may be easier to **use your credit card whenever possible.** The exchange rate only varies by a fraction of a cent, so you won't need to worry whether your purchase is charged on the day of purchase or at some point in the future. Note, however that you may get a slightly better deal if you pay with cash.

Throughout this guide, the following abbreviations are used: **AE,** American Express; **DC,** Diners Club; **MC,** MasterCard; and **V,** Visa.

➤ REPORTING LOST CARDS: **American Express** (☎ 1801–964–6665); **MasterCard** (☎ 1230-020-2012); **Visa** (☎ 1230–020–2136).

CURRENCY EXCHANGE

For the most favorable rates, **change money through banks.** You won't do as well at exchange booths in airports or rail and bus stations, in hotels, in restaurants, or in stores.

➤ EXCHANGE SERVICES: **International Currency Express** (☎ 888/278–6628 for orders, WEB www.foreignmoney. com). **Thomas Cook Currency Services** (☎ 800/287–7362 for telephone orders and retail locations, WEB www. us.thomascook.com).

TRAVELER'S CHECKS

Do you need traveler's checks in Chile? It depends on where you're headed. If you're going to rural areas and small towns, go with cash; traveler's checks are best used in cities. Lost or stolen checks can usually be replaced within 24 hours. To ensure a speedy refund, buy your own traveler's checks—don't let someone else pay for them: irregularities like this can cause delays. The person who bought the checks should make the call to request a refund.

PACKING

In Chile you'll need to **pack for all seasons**—no matter what time of year you're traveling. For sightseeing and leisure, casual clothing and good walking shoes are both desirable and appropriate. For the beach, you'll need lightweight sportswear, a bathing suit, a sun hat, and sunscreen. Travel in the forests requires long-sleeve shirts, long pants, socks, sneakers, a hat, a light waterproof jacket, a bathing suit, and insect repellent. Light colors are best, since mosquitoes avoid them. If you're visiting Patagonia or the Andes, bring a jacket and sweater, or plan to acquire one of the hand-knit sweaters or ponchos crowding the marketplaces.

Other useful items include a screw-top water bottle that you can fill with bottled water, a money pouch, a travel flashlight and extra batteries, a Swiss Army knife with a bottle opener, a medical kit, binoculars, and a pocket calculator to help with currency conversions. A sarong or light cotton blanket can have many uses: beach towel, picnic blanket, and cushion for hard seats, among other things. You can never have too many large resealable plastic bags (bring a whole box), which are ideal for storing film, protecting things from rain and damp, quarantining stinky socks, and more.

In your carry-on luggage, **pack an extra pair of eyeglasses or contact lenses** and **enough of any medication you take** to last the entire trip. You may also ask your doctor to write a spare prescription using the drug's generic name, since brand names may vary from country to country. In luggage to be checked, **never pack prescription drugs or valuables.** To avoid customs delays, carry medications in their original packaging. And don't forget to carry with you the addresses of offices that handle refunds of lost traveler's checks.

Check *Fodor's How to Pack* (available in bookstores everywhere) for more tips.

CHECKING LUGGAGE

How many carry-on bags you can bring with you is up to the airline. Most allow two, but not always, so make sure that everything you carry aboard will fit under your seat or in the overhead bin, and get to the gate early. Note that if you have a seat at the back of the plane, you'll probably board first, while the overhead bins are still empty.

If you are flying internationally, note that baggage allowances may be determined not by piece but by weight—generally 88 pounds (40 kilograms) in first class, 66 pounds (30 kilograms) in business class, and 44 pounds (20 kilograms) in economy.

Airline liability for baggage is limited to $1,250 per person on flights within the United States. On international flights it amounts to $9.07 per pound or $20 per kilogram for checked baggage (roughly $640 per 70-pound bag) and $400 per passenger for unchecked baggage. You can buy additional coverage at check-in for about $10 per $1,000 of coverage, but it excludes a rather extensive list of items, shown on your airline ticket.

Before departure, **itemize your bags' contents** and their worth, and label the bags with your name, address, and phone number. (If you use your home address, cover it so potential thieves can't see it readily.) Inside each bag, **pack a copy of your itinerary.** At check-in, **make sure that each bag is correctly tagged** with the destination airport's three-letter code. If your bags arrive damaged or fail to arrive at all, file a written report with the airline before leaving the airport.

PASSPORTS & VISAS

Citizens of the United States, Canada, Australia, New Zealand, and the United Kingdom need only a passport to enter Chile. Before traveling, **make two photocopies of your passport's data page** (one for someone at home and another for you, carried separately from your passport). While sightseeing in Chile it's best to carry the copy of your passport and leave the original in your hotel's safe. If you lose your passport promptly call the nearest embassy or consulate and the local police.

Upon arrival in Chile, you will be given a flimsy, minute piece of paper that is your three-month tourist visa. This has to be handed in when you leave; because getting a new one involves waiting in many lines and a lot of bureaucracy, put it somewhere safe.

PASSPORT OFFICES

The best time to apply for a passport or to renew is in fall and winter. Before any trip, check your passport's expiration date, and, if necessary, renew it as soon as possible.

➤ AUSTRALIAN CITIZENS: **Australian Passport Office** (☎ 131–232, WEB www.dfat.gov.au/passports).

➤ CANADIAN CITIZENS: **Passport Office** (☎ 819/994–3500; 800/567–6868 in Canada, WEB www.dfait-maeci.gc.ca/passport).

➤ NEW ZEALAND CITIZENS: **New Zealand Passport Office** (☎ 04/494–0700, WEB www.passports.govt.nz).

➤ U.K. CITIZENS: **London Passport Office** (☎ 0870/521–0410, WEB www.ukpa.gov.uk) for fees and documentation requirements and to request an emergency passport.

➤ U.S. CITIZENS: **National Passport Information Center** (☎ 900/225–5674; calls are 35¢ per minute for automated service, $1.05 per minute for operator service; WEB www.travel.state.gov/npicinfo.html).

SAFETY

Areas frequented by tourists are generally safe, provided you use common sense. Wherever you go, **don't wear expensive clothing, don't wear flashy jewelry,** and **don't handle money in public.** It's a good idea to **keep your money in a pocket rather than a wallet,** which is easier to steal. On buses and in crowded areas, hold purses or handbags close to the body; thieves use knives to slice the bottom of a bag and catch the contents as they fall out. **Keep cameras in a secure camera bag,** preferably one with a chain or wire embedded in the strap. Always **remain alert for pickpockets,** and **don't walk alone at night,** especially in the larger cities.

TRAVEL ADVISORIES

Before heading to Chile or any other country in South America, **get the latest travel warnings and advisories.** The U.S. State Department has a 24-hour hot line, a "fax on demand" (just dial the number and follow the instructions) number, and a Web site.

➤ U.S. GOVERNMENT ADVISORIES: **U.S. Department of State** (✉ Overseas Citizens Services Office, Room 4811 N.S., 2201 C St. NW, Washington, DC 20520; ☎ 202/647–5225 for interactive hot line; 301/946–4400 for computer bulletin board; FAX 202/647–3000 for interactive hot line; WEB www.travel.state.gov.); enclose a self-addressed, stamped, business-size envelope.

WOMEN IN CHILE

Many women travel alone or in groups in Chile with no problems. Chilean men are more subtle in their machismo than men in other South American countries, but it's still an aspect of the culture, and foreign women are considered fair game. Men are apt to misinterpret a casual, informal attitude or friendly behavior.

SENIOR-CITIZEN TRAVEL

There's no reason that active, well-traveled senior citizens shouldn't visit Chile, whether on an independent vacation, an escorted tour, or an adventure vacation. Before you leave home, however, determine what medical services your health insurance will cover outside the United States; note that Medicare doesn't provide for payment of hospital and medical services outside the United States. If you need additional travel insurance, buy it (☞ Insurance, *above*).

Chile is full of good hotels and competent ground operators who will meet your flights and organize your sightseeing. To qualify for age-related discounts **mention your senior-citizen status up front** when booking hotel reservations (not when checking out) and before you're seated in restaurants (not when paying the bill). When renting a car **ask about promotional car-rental discounts,** which can be cheaper than senior-citizen rates.

➤ EDUCATIONAL PROGRAMS: **Elderhostel** (✉ 11 Ave. de Lafayette, Boston, MA 02111-1746, ☎ 877/426–8056, ℻ 877/426–2166, WEB www.elderhostel.org).

STUDENTS IN CHILE

Although airfares to and within South America are high, you can take buses in Chile for mere dollars, and you can usually find safe, comfortable, affordable accommodations for a fraction of what it might cost back home. Many cities, especially Santiago and Valparaíso, have vibrant student populations.

➤ I.D.s & SERVICES: **Council Travel** (CIEE; ✉ 205 E. 42nd St., 15th floor, New York, NY 10017, ☎ 212/822–2700 or 888/268–6245, ℻ 212/822–2699, WEB www.councilexchanges.org) for mail orders only, in the United States. **Travel Cuts** (✉ 187 College St., Toronto, Ontario M5T 1P7, Canada, ☎ 416/979–2406 or 800/667–2887 in Canada, ℻ 416/979–8167, WEB www.travelcuts.com).

TAXES

An 18% value-added tax (VAT, called IVA here) is added to the cost of most goods and services in Chile; often you won't notice because it's included in the price quoted. When it's not, the seller gives you the price plus IVA. At many hotels you may receive an exemption from the IVA if you pay in American dollars or traveler's checks; some also offer this discount if you use an American Express card.

TELEPHONES

Having numerous telephone companies mean that Chilean public phones all look different. All require a 100 peso deposits. Telefónica and other companies sell telephone cards, but many locals continue to use coins. If you will only be making a few local calls, it's not necessary to purchase a phone card.

AREA & COUNTRY CODES

The country code for Chile is 56. When dialing a Chilean number from abroad, drop the initial 0 from the local area code.

DIRECTORY ASSISTANCE

You can reach directory assistance in Chile by calling 103.

INTERNATIONAL CALLS

An international call at a public phone requires a 500-peso deposit, which will give you 68 seconds of talk.

LOCAL CALLS

A 100-peso piece is required to make a local call in a public phone booth, allowing 143 seconds of conversation between the hours of 9 AM and 8 PM, and 239 seconds of talk from 8 PM to 9 AM. Prefix codes are not needed for local dialing. Most public phones allow you to make several calls in succession, provided you don't hang up in between: There's a special button to push—marked with an "R"—that cuts off one call and starts another. Some phones also include English-language instructions, accessed by pressing a button marked with a flag icon. Most city areas have standing phone booths, but phones are also found at restaurants, calling centers, and even newsstands. You may have to wait several seconds after picking up the receiver before a steady humming sound signals that you may dial. After dialing, you'll hear a characteristic beep-beep as your call goes through; then there's a pause, followed by a long tone signaling that the other phone is ringing. A busy signal is similar but repeats itself with no pause in between.

LONG-DISTANCE SERVICES

AT&T, MCI, and Sprint access codes make calling long distance relatively convenient, but you may find the local access number blocked in many hotel rooms. First ask the hotel operator to connect you. If the hotel operator balks, ask for an international operator, or dial the international operator yourself. One way to improve your odds of getting connected to your long-distance carrier is to travel with more than one company's calling card (a hotel may block Sprint, for example, but not MCI). If all else fails, call from a pay phone.

➤ ACCESS CODES: **AT&T Direct** (☎ 800/225–288). **MCI Worldcom** (☎ 800/444–4444). **Sprint Express** (☎ 800/793–1153).

PHONE CARDS

If you plan to call abroad while in Chile, it's in your best interest to buy a local phone card (sold in varying amounts at kiosks and calling centers) or use a calling center. To dial an international number directly from a private phone, you first dial the three-digit number of the carrier you want to use. Then dial 0, followed by the country code, the area or city code, and the phone number. Price differences among carriers can be large; to verify rates, dial the carrier's number, followed by 123. Telefónica del Sur has the best rates, offering 114 seconds of international time per 500 pesos.

➤ PHONE COMPANIES: **Transam**, dial 113; **Entel**, dial 123; **Mundo Telefónica**, dial 188; **Chilesat**, dial 171; **Bellsouth**, dial 181; **Telefónica del Sur**, dial 121; **Carrier 120**, dial 120.

TIME

Chile is aligned with Eastern Standard Time and three hours ahead of Pacific Standard Time. Daylight savings time in Chile begins in October and ends in March.

TIPPING

The usual tip, or *propina*, in restaurants is 10%. Leave more if you really enjoyed the service. City taxi drivers don't usually expect a tip because most own their cabs. If you hire a taxi to take you around a city, you should consider giving a good tip. Hotel porters should be tipped at least $1. Also give doormen and ushers about $1. Beauty- and barber-shop personnel generally get around 5%.

TOURS & PACKAGES

Because everything is prearranged on a prepackaged tour or independent vacation, you'll spend less time planning—and often get it all at a good price.

BOOKING WITH AN AGENT

Travel agents are excellent resources. But it's a good idea to collect brochures from several agencies as some agents' suggestions may be influenced by relationships with tour and package firms that reward them for volume sales. If you have a special interest, **find an agent with expertise in that area**; ASTA (☞ Travel Agencies, *below*) has a database of specialists worldwide.

Make sure your travel agent knows the accommodations and other services of the place they're recommending. Ask about the hotel's location, room size, beds, and whether it has a pool, room service, or programs for children, if you care about these. Has your agent been there in person or sent others whom you can contact?

Do some homework on your own, too: local tourism boards can provide information about lesser-known and small-niche operators, some of which may sell only direct.

BUYER BEWARE

Each year consumers are stranded or lose their money when tour operators—even large ones with excellent reputations—go out of business. So **check out the operator.** Ask several travel agents about its reputation, and try to **book with a company that has a consumer-protection program.** (Look for information in the company's brochure.) In the United States, members of the National Tour Association and the United States Tour Operators Association are required to set aside funds to cover your payments and travel arrangements in the event that the company defaults. It's also a good idea to choose a company that participates in the American Society of Travel Agents' Tour Operator Program (TOP); ASTA will act as mediator in any disputes between you and your tour operator.

Remember that the more your package or tour includes the better you can predict the ultimate cost of your vacation. Make sure you know exactly what is covered, and **beware of hidden costs.** Are taxes, tips, and transfers included? Entertainment and excursions? These can add up.

➤ TOUR-OPERATOR RECOMMENDATIONS: **American Society of Travel Agents** (☞ Travel Agencies, *below*). **National Tour Association** (NTA; ✉ 546 E. Main St., Lexington, KY 40508, ☎ 859/226–4444 or 800/ 682–8886, WEB www.ntaonline.com). **United States Tour Operators Association** (USTOA; ✉ 342 Madison Ave., Suite 1522, New York, NY 10173, ☎ 212/599–6599 or 800/468–7862, FAX 212/599–6744, WEB www.ustoa.com).

TRAIN TRAVEL

Good train service is a thing of the past in Chile. There is no longer northbound service from Santiago. There are daily departures between Santiago and Temuco, but be prepared for frequent delays and a painfully slow journey (Traveling from Santiago to Temuco takes about 12 hours). Reservations, which can be made in Santiago at the Estación Central, are recommended.

TRAVEL AGENCIES

A good travel agent puts your needs first. Look for an agency that has been in business at least five years, emphasizes customer service, and has someone on staff who specializes in your destination. In addition, **make sure the agency belongs to a professional trade organization.** The American Society of Travel Agents (ASTA), with more than 26,000 members in some 170 countries, is the largest and most influential in the field. Operating under the motto "Without a travel agent, you're on your own," it maintains and enforces a strict code of ethics and will step in to help mediate any agent-client disputes if necessary. ASTA also maintains a Web site that includes a directory of agents. (If a travel agency is also acting as your tour operator, *see*

Buyer Beware *in* Tours & Packages, *above*.)

➤ LOCAL AGENT REFERRALS: **American Society of Travel Agents** (ASTA; ☎ 800/965–2782 24-hr hot line, FAX 703/739–7642, WEB www.astanet. com). **Association of British Travel Agents** (✉ 68–71 Newman St., London W1T 3AH, U.K., ☎ 020/7637–2444, FAX 020/7637–0713, WEB www. abtanet.com). **Association of Canadian Travel Agents** (✉ 130 Albert St., Suite 1705, Ottawa, Ontario K1P 5G4, Canada, ☎ 613/237–3657, FAX 613/237–7502, WEB www.acta.net). **Australian Federation of Travel Agents** (✉ Level 3, 309 Pitt St., Sydney NSW 2000, Australia, ☎ 02/9264–3299, FAX 02/9264–1085, WEB www.afta.com.au). **Travel Agents' Association of New Zealand** (✉ Box 1888, Wellington 10033, New Zealand, ☎ 04/499–0104, FAX 04/499–0827, WEB www .taanz.org.nz).

VISITOR INFORMATION

The national tourist office Sernatur (Servicio Nacional de Turismo) has branches in Santiago and in major tourist destinations around the country. Sernatur offices, often the best source for general information about a region, are generally open daily from 9 to 6, with lunch generally from 2 to 3.

Municipal tourist offices, often located near a central square, usually offer better information about their town's sights, restaurants, and lodging. Many have shorter hours or close altogether during low season, however.

➤ U.S. GOVERNMENT ADVISORIES: **U.S. Department of State** (✉ Overseas Citizens Services Office, Room 4811 N.S., 2201 C St. NW, Washington, DC 20520, ☎ 202/647–5225 for interactive hot line, WEB www.travel. state.gov/travel_warnings.html); enclose a self-addressed, stamped, business-size envelope.

WEB SITES

Do check out the World Wide Web when planning your trip. You'll find everything from weather forecasts to virtual tours of famous cities. Be sure

SMART TRAVEL TIPS A TO Z

to **visit Fodors.com,** a complete travel-planning site. You can research prices and book plane tickets, hotel rooms, rental cars, vacation packages, and more. In addition, you can post your pressing questions in the Travel Talk section and, in the site's Rants & Raves section, read comments about some of the restaurants and hotels in this book—and chime in yourself. Other planning tools include a currency converter and weather reports, and there are loads of links to other travel resources.

On Spanish-language sites, watch for the name of the country, region, state, or city in which you have an interest. The search terms for "look," "find," and "get" are *mirar* and *buscar* in Spanish. "Next" and "last" (as in "next/last 10") are *próximo* and *último/anterior* in Spanish. Keep an eye out for such words as *turismo* (tourism), *turístico* (tourist-related), *hoteles* (hotels), *residenciales* (guest houses), *restaurantes* (restaurants), *gobierno* (government), *estado* (state), *región* (administrative region), *ciudad* (city), *carabinero* (police officer), and *municipalidad* (town hall).

The following sites are good places to start a search (unless otherwise noted, these sites have information in English): www.gochile.cl has travel info and online booking; www.chilnet.cl has business listings; and www.winesofchile.com is a site for true oenophiles. For Spanish speakers, www.granvalparaiso.cl serves as a guide to Valparaíso with articles on current national issues. Also in Spanish, www.emol.com is the online edition of the national newspaper *El Mercurio.*

WHEN TO GO

CLIMATE

Chile's seasons are the reverse of North America's—that is, June–August is Chile's winter. Tourism peaks during the hot summer months of January and February, except in Santiago, which tends to empty as most Santiaguinos head for the coast. Though prices are at their highest, it's worth braving the summer heat if you're interested in lying on the beach or enjoying the many concerts, folklore festivals, and outdoor theater performances offered during this period.

If you're heading for the Lake District or Patagonia and want good weather without the crowds, the shoulder seasons of December and March are the months to visit. The best time to see the Atacama Desert is late spring, preferably in November, when temperatures are bearable and air clarity is at its peak. In spring Santiago blooms, and the fragrance of the flowers will distract even the most avid workaholic. A second tourist season occurs in the Chilean winter, as skiers flock to Chile's mountaintops for some of the world's best skiing, available at the height of northern summers. Winter smog is a good reason to stay away from Santiago during July and August, unless you're coming for a ski holiday and won't be spending much time in the city.

➤ FORECASTS: **Weather Channel Connection** (☎ 900/932–8437), 95¢ per minute from a Touch-Tone phone.

The following are the average daily maximum and minimum temperatures for Santiago and Punta Arenas.

SANTIAGO

Jan.	85F	29C	May	65F	18C	Sept.	66F	19C
	53	12		41	5		42	6
Feb.	84F	29C	June	58F	14C	Oct.	72F	22C
	52	11		37	3		45	7
Mar.	80F	27C	July	59F	15C	Nov.	78F	26C
	49	9		37	3		48	9
Apr.	74F	23C	Aug.	62F	17C	Dec.	83F	28C
	54	7		39	4		51	11

SMART TRAVEL TIPS A TO Z

PUNTA ARENAS

Jan.	58F	14C	May	45F	7C	Sept.	46F	8C
	45	7		35	2		35	2
Feb.	58F	14C	June	41F	5C	Oct.	51F	11C
	44	7		33	1		38	3
Mar.	54F	12C	July	40F	4C	Nov.	54F	12C
	41	5		31	0		40	4
Apr.	50F	10C	Aug.	42F	6C	Dec.	57F	14C
	39	4		33	1		43	6

1 DESTINATION: CHILE

TRAVELING IN A THIN COUNTRY

LIVE NOW IN A COUNTRY AS SOFT as the autumnal flesh of grapes," begins "Country," a poem by Pablo Neruda. With his odes to the place of his birth, the Nobel Prize winner sang Chile into being and taught us to inhale the bouquet of its salty breezes and its soaring Andean peaks before we hold them to our lips and drink them down.

Chile is as luminous and pungent, as rustic and romantic, as any of Neruda's poems describing it. It encompasses a bone-dry desert that blooms in a riot of color once or twice a decade, sprawling glaciers that bellow like thunder, and snow-covered volcanos that perpetually smoulder—all in one sliver of land squeezed between the Andes and the Pacific Ocean. In some places the 320-km (200-mi) territorial limit is actually wider than the country itself, making Chile as much water as earth.

As might be expected in a country with a coastline stretching 6,435 km (3,999 mi), many parts of Chile are inaccessible by land. Because of the unusual topography, highways simply end when they reach fjords or ice fields. You'll need to take a ship to see the mammoth glacier in the heart of Parque Nacional Laguna San Rafael. A ferry ride is necessary to visit Chiloé, an archipelago where you'll find charming wooden churches built by missionaries. Distant Easter Island, in the middle of the Pacific Ocean, is reachable only by a five-hour flight from the mainland.

The region known today as Chile has been inhabited for millennia. One of the oldest known people were the Chinchorros, who lived along the coast of El Norte Grande beginning at about 6,000 BC. This nomadic people learned the process of mummifying their dead 5,000 years ago—thousands of years before the Egyptians. Nearby in the antiplano lived the Aymara, who herded llamas and alpacas and cultivated barley and potatoes. In El Norte Chico were the Diaguitas, whose finely detailed bowls and pitchers are among the most beautiful of pre-Columbian ceramics, and the Molles, who carved the intricate petroglyphs in the Valle de Encanto.

The first invaders did not come from Europe, but from elsewhere in South America. The Mapuches crossed the Andes from what is today Argentina and established a stronghold in the Lake District. In the process they gradually absorbed the peoples already living in the region. The Incas, who arrived in the 15th century, were much more brutal. Pushing southward from their empire in Peru, the Incas dismantled existing cultures, forcing indigenous peoples to give up their language and their rituals. Only the fierce resistance of the Mapuches halted the expansion of the Inca empire.

The first European to reach Chile barely gave it a glance: Spanish conquistador Hernando de Magallanes left his name and little else behind when he journeyed up the southern coast in 1520. Diego de Almagro was the first Spaniard actually to explore the region. Setting out from Peru in 1535, Almagro and a ragged crew of 500 adventurers marched south in search of fame and fortune. When the band reached the Aconcagua Valley, they fled after an extended battle with the Mapuches. Pedro de Valdivia, who led another gang of adventurers south along the roads constructed by the Incas, broke ground for Santiago in 1541. He founded several other towns, including Concepción and Villarrica, before he died during a skirmish with the Mapuches.

Spain had its hands full with the rest of its empire in South America, so Chile was pretty much ignored. The residents, even those who had profited under colonial rule, eventually grew tired of having others govern their land. After Chile won its independence from Spain in a war that lasted from 1810 to 1818, the new nation sought to establish firm control of its entire territory. In 1843, it sent a frigate carrying a ragtag contingent of 19 men to the Strait of Magellan. There the men built a wooden fort called Fuerte Bulnes, thus establishing the country's first permanent settlement in the southernmost reaches of Patagonia. Chile also began to dream about expansion northward. The 1879 War of the Pacific pitted Chile against its two neighbors to the north, Bolivia and Peru. Chile gained much of the nitrate-rich land of the Atacama Desert, and Bolivia lost its only outlet to the sea.

For more than 300 years, the Mapuches successfully defended much of the Lake District against the encroachment of the Spanish. But the proud people could not hold out against the Chileans. The last great rebellion of the Mapuche people failed in 1881, and soon afterward the Chilean government started shipping in German, Swiss, and other European colonists to fill the "empty" lands.

Chile's government was hampered for almost a century by an 1830 constitution that granted enormous powers to the president, thus encouraging autocratic rule. After a civil war in 1891, Congress seized control, diminishing the president to a mere figurehead. This unstable system, which caused constant clashes between the presidential and legislative branches, was replaced in 1925 when a new constitution that sought to find a delicate balance.

By the 1950s, left-wing political parties representing working-class people began to gain considerable strength. In 1970, the push for governmental reform led to the election of Salvador Allende, Chile's first socialist president. Although widely popular at first, Allende lost favor when he failed to find a way to shore up the country's sagging economy. Strikes by labor unions and protests by farm workers made it clear his administration was ailing.

From 1973 to 1990, Chile was virtually synonymous with the name of General Augusto Pinochet. With support from the United States, the military leader led a bloody coup in September 1973. He dissolved the legislature, banned political organizations, and exiled opponents. Tens of thousands are said to have been murdered during his years in power. In 2000 Pinochet returned to Chile to stand trial for alleged human rights abuses, but the trial has been repeatedly delayed.

Pinochet's regime discouraged many visitors, but in the decade since his fall from power tourism has steadily increased.

Chile's beaches draw sun-worshipers from all over South America, and its towering volcanos and roaring rivers draw adventure travelers from around the world. Fishing aficionados head south to the Lake District, while armchair archaeologists are attracted to the 5,000-year-old mummies of the Atacama. Today Chile is one of the most popular destinations in South America. It doesn't hurt that the country also has one of the continent's most stable economies.

NEW AND NOTEWORTHY

UNESCO designated 14 of the distinctive wooden churches on Chiloé as World Heritage Sites in December 2000. Among them are Castro's Iglesia de San Francisco and Achao's Iglesia Santa María de Loreto, two of the most interesting of the archipelago's 150 houses of worship.

The Chilean government continues to study the feasibility of construction of a suspension bridge between Chiloé and the mainland. The project would span the Strait of Chacao at its narrowest point on the northern end of the island, a distance of almost 3 km (2 mi).

The first segment of the new Sendero de Chile (Chilean Trail) opened within the boundaries of the Parque Nacional Conguillío in the Lake District in 2001. Modeled on the Appalachian Trail in the United States and geared toward both hikers and cyclists, the 6,000-km (3,600-mi) path will eventually run the length of Chile. The $20 million project, targeted for completion by 2010, will offer campsites and lodging about every 32 km (20 mi).

The Mapuches, the country's largest indigenous group, staged demonstrations to call attention to the deplorable conditions on their reservations. One group briefly occupied the Dutch embassy in Santiago. News reports occasionally report violence in remote areas of the Lake District, but these have occurred in areas way off the tourist path.

WHAT'S WHERE

Santiago

There are 15 million people in Chile, and more than a third of them call the sprawling metropolis of Santiago their home. Ancient and modern stand side-by-side in the heart of the city—one of the most common photographs on postcards is the neoclassical cathedral reflected in the windows of the glass office tower across the street. You may be amazed at the amount of green in a city so large. Downtown you're never far from the leafy Plaza de Armas or the paths that meander along the Río Mapocho. To take in the entire city, climb the maze of trails up Cerro Santa Lucía, or take the funicular to the top of Cerro San Cristóbal. Not that the views from the ground are so shabby—on a clear day you can see the majestic peaks of the Andes in the distance. Head in that direction for the hot springs of the Cajón de Maipo or skiing in the Valle Nevado.

The Central Coast

The Central Coast is the summer playground for Santiago's vacationing masses. Valparaíso and Viña del Mar, the country's second- and third-largest cities, overlook the Pacific Ocean from adjacent bays. Gritty Valparaíso, the country's largest port, provides many stunning views from the promenades atop its more than 40 hills. Glittery Viña del Mar boasts nonstop nightlife, streets lined with trendy boutiques and eateries, and the country's most popular stretch of shoreline. On the rugged beaches to the north you can get close to populations of penguins and sea lions. In the south, pay homage to the Nobel Prize–winning poet Pablo Neruda, whose hillside house faces the ocean at Isla Negra.

El Norte Chico

North of Santiago lies El Norte Chico, a land of dusty brown hills that stretches for some 700 km (435 mi) from Río Aconcagua to Río Copiapó. Once or twice a decade the barren land bursts into bloom in a phenomenon called *el desierto florido.* Some of Chile's most beautiful valleys cut through this region. In the lush Elqui Valley, just about everyone you meet is involved in growing the grapes used to make pisco, the heady brew that has become Chile's national drink. Inland lies Parque Nacional Nevado Tres Cruces, where four species of flamingos fly across dazzling white salt flats. On the coast is Parque Nacional Pan de Azúcar, home to sea lions and sea otters as well as some of El Norte Chico's most stunning beaches.

El Norte Grande

El Norte Grande, Chile's northernmost region, borders Peru to the north and Bolivia to the east. Extending for some 1,930 km (1,200 mi), it's one of the driest places on earth. Here you'll find the Atacama Desert, where some weather stations have never recorded even a drop of rain. The climate helped to preserve tantalizing clues of the indigenous peoples of the past, including the Chinchorro mummies near Arica. As you ascend into the Andes, the air becomes dramatically cooler. In Parque Nacional Lauca the landscape is dotted with a brilliant emerald-green moss called *llareta.* You come across not just llamas, but also groups of galloping vicuñas and alpacas.

The Central Valley

A paradise for oenophiles, this region south of Santiago is where most of the grapes that produce Chile's finest wines are grown. An easy drive from the capital is the Valle de Colchagua, where you can sample vintages at many wineries along a route called the *Ruta del Vino.* Also in the area are the beautiful manor houses of the *estancias,* or sprawling farms, once run by Chile's most powerful families. The region's many rivers, such as the Río Bío Bío in the southern part of the region, offer white-water rafting and other sporting opportunities.

The Lake District

Many visitors to the Lake District are surprised to find that the 400-km (240-mi) stretch of land between Temuco and Puerto Montt is bordered by a string of volcanos. More than 50 snow-covered peaks, many of them still smoldering, offer splendid hiking opportunities. The region's forested foothills, long the home of the Mapuche people, is where you'll find popular summer resorts such as Pucón and Villarrica. The last town is Puerto Montt—literally the end of the road, as you need to get on a boat or ferry to travel any farther south.

Chiloé

The rainy archipelago of Chiloé is made up of more than 40 islands sprinkled across the Golfo de Ancud. The largest by far, the appropriately named Isla Grande, measures 180 km (112 mi) long. The main draw here are the dozens of simple wooden churches, a remnant of the colonial era, dotting the landscape. Dense forests cover the western half of Isla Grande, while gently rolling farmland dominates the eastern part where most of its 130,000 residents live.

The Southern Coast

Although a highway called the Carretera Austral runs through much of this 4,300-km (2,672-mi) stretch of coastline between the Lake District and Patagonia, it's still one of the most remote regions on earth. So much of the Southern Coast is a labyrinth of icy fjords that you're likely to take a boat or plane to wherever you want to go. The only town of any size, Coihaique, is in the middle of everything and therefore makes a good base for exploring the area. To the north is the privately owned Parque Pumalín, home to one of the last-remaining temperate rain forests in the world. The most popular attraction, and the hardest to reach, in the spectacular glacier extending 4 km (2½ mi) from end to end that forms the centerpiece of Parque Nacional Laguna San Rafael.

Patagonia and Tierra del Fuego

Its impenetrable forests and impassable mountains meant that Chilean Patagonia went largely unexplored until the beginning of the 20th century. It's still sparsely inhabited. Here you'll find the colorful provincial city of Punta Arenas, which looks like it's about to be swept into the Strait of Magellan (and on a windy day feels that way, too). Drive north and you'll reach Parque Nacional Torres del Paine, the country's most magnificent natural wonder. Its snow-covered peaks seem to rise vertically from the plains below. To the east is mythical Tierra del Fuego, the windswept island at the continent's southernmost tip. Off the coast you'll find rocky Cape Horn, the bane of many a captain intent on sailing around the continent. For the most intrepid travelers, this is literally the end of the world.

Easter Island

Known to locals as "the loneliest place on earth," Easter Island lies 3,700 km (2,294 mi) off the Chilean coast. The tiny island in the middle of the South Pacific was unknown to the outside world until a Dutch explorer happened across it in 1722. Jacob Roggeveen's crew at first thought the island was inhabited by giants, but soon realized they were looking at hundreds of stone idols standing along the coast. A century later, nearly all had been toppled. Who carved them? How were they raised? Why were they destroyed? Most of the mysteries surrounding these carvings have yet to be solved, but many people travel to this windswept island hoping to come up with their own solutions.

PLEASURES AND PASTIMES

Dining

Kissing her shores from tip to toe, the Pacific Ocean is the breadbasket of Chile's cuisine, proffering delicacies like the conger eel, sea bass, king crab, and *locos* (abalone the size of fat clams). Raw shellfish is best avoided, but cooked with cheese or white wine, lemon, and fresh coriander, it's an excellent introduction to Chilean cuisine. Awaken your palate with a seafood appetizer, such as *choritos al vapor* (mussels steamed in white wine), *machas a la parmesana* (similar to razor clams but unique to Chile, grilled with tomatoes and Parmesan cheese), or *chupo de centolla* (king crab). Simply seasoned grilled fish is a Chilean favorite, usually garnished with steamed potatoes or an *ensalada a la chilena* (peeled tomatoes with onions marinated in brine to reduce their acidic flavor). Also worth tasting is the humble *merluza* (hake), which makes a delicious, cheap lunch.

But the Pacific isn't Chile's only answer to fine dining—European immigrants brought with them a love for robust country cooking; indeed, many simple country dishes are among the best offerings of Chilean cuisine. *Cazuela,* a superb soup that includes a piece of meat (beef, pork, chicken, or turkey, usually on the bone), potatoes, and corn on the cob in a thick broth, is a meal in itself. If your stomach's upset, a rich chicken cazuela may be just the remedy. In summer, *porotos granados,* a thick bean, corn, and squash soup, is all the rage with Chileans, as are *humitas,* ground corn seasoned and steamed in its own husk. At markets all over the country you'll be wooed by women selling the ubiquitous *pastel de choclo,* a cornmeal pastry pie that usually contains ground beef, a piece of chicken, and seasonings. *Empanadas* are the Chilean answer to hamburgers, but as with hamburgers, it's hard to find an outstanding one.

Pork is another Chilean specialty, especially in *arrollados* (a stuffed pork roll encased in pork rind), *costillares* (ribs, often covered in chili, known here as *ají*), *lomo* (roast pork loin), and *pernil* (the whole leg, so make sure you're hungry).

Some Spanish-inspired dishes like *guatitas* (intestines) send Chileans into states of culinary bliss, as do blood sausage, *chunchules* (a spicy stew of beef or pork intestines), and other odds and ends of edible beasts. If you order a *parillada* (a barbecue at your table), ask about the cuts being served so as to avoid those that are too peculiar for your taste.

In southern Chile, the limitations of dining in a small provincial city are compensated for in Punta Arenas by the delights of fresh seafood, especially salmon, king crab, and scallops, along with the local staple—lamb—whose flavor is slightly stronger than in other regions of Chile. Watch out for warnings of red tide, which makes shellfish toxic, but health authorities are strict about monitoring toxin levels, so you're unlikely to have problems.

Chileans know their sweets, with foamy meringues topping the list of indulgences, followed closely by *alfajor de manjar* (creamy, caramelized sugar smashed between wafers and bathed in chocolate). Spring and summer sunshine brings to life an unparalleled Chilean ice cream culture; parlors line almost any pedestrian walkway, and vats filled with exotic fruit flavors will tempt even the most dedicated of dieters. The German immigrants who came to the Lake District a century ago brought their tasty *küchen,* rich fruit-filled pastries.

Lodging

Power and wealth have historically orbited around Chile's capital—Santiago—so it has a wide range of luxury lodging options. In sluggish response to increased tourism, however, novel and new hotels have sprung up in the provinces. In the more heavily touristed areas you'll find cozy wooden cabins, hot-springs retreats, and elaborate hotels richly adorned in Patagonian hardwoods. The always homey and hospitable *residenciales* (bed-and-breakfasts) are found everywhere.

Traditionally, *hotel* referred to upscale accommodations; *hostería* and *hostal* denoted something more basic. Those distinctions have blurred, and there are some pretty snazzy hosterías and hostales to be found. A lodging that calls itself a *hospedaje* means your room will be in a private home. A *cabaña* is any type of lodging with detached cabin units, while a *refugio,* often found in national parks, has bunks and little else.

Outdoor Activities

Chile's Lake District is legendary for its fly-fishing. You can stay in a rustic lodge and enjoy the icy lakes and streams jumping with trout and salmon. Opportunities also abound for hiking and mountain biking in Chile's national parks, over its mountain trails, and through its forests. If you're a serious mountaineer, you know the challenges of Volcán Ojos del Salado in El Norte Chico. The world's highest active volcano, it soars to 6,893 meters (22,600 ft). There are dozens of other challenging climbs all along the eastern border of the country.

Since Chile's seasons are the opposite of those of North America, you can ski or snowboard from June to September. Most of Chile's ski resorts are in the Andes close to Santiago. With the top elevations at the majority of ski areas extending to 3,300 meters (11,000 ft), you can expect long runs and deep, dry snow.

Shopping

Chile is one of only three countries in the world that mine lapis lazuli, so it's worth checking out the workshops and stores in Santiago. The city's artisans are increasingly sophisticated, and you can find earrings, rings, and necklaces to please virtually every taste. Handicrafts you'll find all over Chile include warm sweaters that are hand-dyed, -spun, and -knitted in the southern parts of the country (it's cheaper to purchase them there) and ponchos whose designs vary according to the region; the best are by the Mapuche artisans in and around Temuco and by the Chilote women on Chiloé. Thick wool blankets are woven in Chiloé but are heavy to carry, as are the figures of reddish clay from Pomaire and the famous black clay ceramics of Quinchamalí. Purchase them at the end of your trip. Several towns specialize in wicker, particularly Chimbarongo (about an hour's drive from Santiago) and Chiloé, where baskets and woven effigies of that island's mythical figures abound.

Wine

Chilean wines have come a long way in the last decade. Many vineyards in the valleys around Santiago have been producing wine for more than 100 years, some with French vinestocks that date back to the middle of the 19th century. Chilean wines were introduced to the world in the 1980s, when formerly inexpensive California wines started to jump in price. Since that time, the Chilean wineries have been working furiously to keep pace with the broadening international demand while steadily trying to improve their product.

An oft-repeated fact about Chilean wine is that the best is reserved for the export market. Although you can find some good quality wines at upscale Chilean restaurants, the big vintners are still concentrating their energy on the international market. To that end, the best wineries are modernizing the growing and fermenting methods (with help from French and Californian oenological experts) to produce wines that are better suited for the European and North American markets. These changes have paid off in recent years with improved overall quality of Chilean wines. In fact, a small number of Chilean vintners are already turning out a few truly first-rate wines, including Concha y Toro's Don Melchor Reserve, Santa Rita's Casa Real, and Veramonte's Primus.

As a general rule, Chilean merlots and cabernet sauvignons are more likely to be the full-bodied wines that Americans and Europeans enjoy. Chardonnays and sauvignon blancs are usually not as pleasing to the palate. When you're considering these different varietals, keep in mind the name of Chile's largest winery, Concha y Toro. It has a number of different labels (some made exclusively for the Chilean market) that usually offer good value. At one end is the affordable and popular Casillero del Diablo label, at the other is the export-oriented Trio wines. Other reliable wineries that are strong in the domestic market include Errázuriz, Santa Carolina, and Santa Rita. Also, be on the lookout for the smaller Casa Lapostolle winery, whose reds are highly regarded but not as widely available.

FODOR'S CHOICE

Dining

Aquí Está Coco, Santiago. Flotsam and jetsam found on nearby beaches adds a whimsical touch to this restaurant cooking up the best fish and shellfish in the capital. *$$$$*

Casino Español, Iquique. Superb Moorish architecture that calls to mind the Alhambra Palace in Granada makes this former men's club a sight in its own right. *$$$–$$$$*

Azul Profundo, Santiago. Chileans favor heavy sauces on their fish dishes, but this Bellavista eatery serves unadorned seafood grilled to perfection. *$$$*

Bristol, Santiago. Innovative takes on traditional Chilean dishes make this downtown eatery a must for Santiago's movers and shakers. *$$–$$$*

Café Turri, Valparaíso. Dine in an elegant 19th-century mansion high above the city, then stroll along the hilltop promenades nearby. *$$–$$$*

Los Ganaderos, Punta Arenas. Spit-roasted lamb is the specialty at this restaurant resembling a rural *estancia*. To put you in the mood, the waiters dress as gauchos. *$$–$$$*

El Barco Rojo, Papudo. Fashioned from sundry parts of a sunken ship, this eclectic beachfront eatery was a favorite of poet Pablo Neruda. $$

Historic Sights

Iglesia Santa María de Loreto, Achao. Of the dozens of wonderful wooden churches on the archipelago of Chiloé, this one on the island of Achao is the most fascinating.

Isla Negra, The Central Coast. A mecca for his ardent admirers, Pablo Neruda's seaside hideaway is filled with mementos and memorabilia from the poet's fascinating life.

Ranu Raraku, Easter Island. When it comes to the famous stone heads, this is the mother lode. Researchers have counted 397 moais—nearly half of those found on the island—at the quarry in this long-extinct volcano.

Lodging

Hotel Antumalal, Pucón. Perched on the side of a cliff, this Bauhaus beauty has cozy rooms with roaring fireplaces and huge windows overlooking shimmering Lago Villarrica. $$$$

Hotel Explora, Parque Nacional Torres del Paine. Tucked away on the southeast corner of Lago Pehoé, this lodge is a luxurious alternative to roughing it. The interior is Scandinavian in design, with local woods used for ceilings, floors, and furniture. $$$$

Hotel José Nogueira, Punta Arenas. Once the home of a wealthy wool baron's widow, this opulent 19th-century mansion retains the original crystal chandeliers, marble floors, and polished bronze accents that were imported from France. $$$$

Hotel Plaza San Francisco, Santiago. Across from the Iglesia de San Francisco, this historic hotel pampers you with unparalleled luxury. $$$$

Termas de Puyuhuapi, The Southern Coast. Accessible only by boat, this world-class resort gives new meaning to the word "secluded." Its redwood structures have lots of windows to take full advantage of the gorgeous scenery. $$$–$$$$

Hotel Pedro de Valdivia, Valdivia. Lavish furnishings and peerless service are the hallmarks of this magnificent pink palace on the Río Calle Calle. $$$

Hotel Terrantai, San Pedro de Atacama. Wood-beam ceilings and river-stone walls are your first clue that this hotel is something special. The rustic rooms, bathed in light from the wide windows, have handmade furniture and beds piled high with down comforters. $$$

Isla Seca, Zapallar. A trail of black-and-white tiles at this ultra-chic hotel leads you to a tented terrace where you can gaze out to the blue of the Pacific. $$–$$$

Hotel Rocas de Bahia, Bahía Inglesa. This sprawling modern hotel right on one of El Norte Grande's prettiest beaches has fantastic views from the rooftop pool. $$

Hotel Unicornio Azul, Castro. The rambling Blue Unicorn makes many twists and turns as it climbs up a hillside, but there are big windows at every landing to catch the stunning views of the sea. $$

Hostería Ancud, Ancud. Stately and dignified, Chiloé's best-known hotel stands watch on the bluff overlooking the Canal de Chacao, defending the island much as the nearby forts did centuries ago. $$

Brighton B&B, Valparaíso. This bed-and-breakfast, housed in a lemon-yellow Victorian-style house, is one of the pretty port town's most recognizable landmarks. $–$$

Museums

Museo Arqueológico Gustavo Le Paige, San Pedro de Atacama. This awe-inspiring collection of artifacts from the region traces the history of the Atacama Desert from pre-Columbian times through the Spanish colonization.

Museo Arqueológico de San Miguel de Azapa, Arica. In an 18th-century olive-oil refinery, this museum houses an impressive collection of artifacts, including the Chinchorro mummies that date back to 5000 BC.

Museo de Arte Precolombino, Santiago. Artifacts of Central and South America's indigenous peoples are on display here in the city's beautifully restored Royal Customs House.

Museo Regional de Castro, Castro. This museum of life on Chiloé holds everything from the farming and fishing implements of indigenous peoples to the looms, spinning wheels, and plows of European settlers.

Museo Regional de Magallanes, Punta Arenas. This restored mansion provides an intriguing glimpse of the wealthy family's life at the beginning of the 20th century. Lavish Carrara marble hearths, English bath fixtures, and cordovan leather walls are among the original accoutrements.

Natural Wonders

Atacama Desert, El Norte Grande. The world's driest desert hold many natural wonders, such as La Cordillera de Sal, a mountain range composed almost entirely of salt.

Cerros Pintados, El Norte Grande. Part of the Reserva Nacional Pampa del Tamarugal, the Painted Hills hold the largest group of geoglyphs in the world.

Parque Nacional Fray Jorge, El Norte Chico. Incongruously set in the middle of the region's dusty hills, northern Chile's only cloud forest is a great retreat from the relentless sun.

Parque Nacional Laguna San Rafael, The Southern Coast. The Ventisquero San Rafael, a spectacular glacier extending 4 km (2½ mi), is one of the country's greatest natural wonders.

Parque Nacional Torres del Paine. Glaciers that swept through the region millions of years ago created the ash-gray spires that dominate this unforgettable national park.

Parque Pumalín, The Southern Coast. American conservationist Doug Tompkins has spent more than $15 million to purchase the 800,000 acres that make up this private park in one of the world's last remaining temperate rain forests.

Volcán Villarrica, The Lake District. You don't need climbing experience to reach the 3,116-meter (9,350-ft) summit of this perpetually smouldering volcano.

GREAT ITINERARIES

When Chileans joke that the Creator made their nation of the universe's leftovers, they are only partly jesting. Chile's thin ribbon of territory comprises some of nature's most spectacular anomalies: the looming Andes impose the country's eastern boundaries, stretching from the desolate Atacama Desert to the archipelagos and fjords of forbidding Patagonia, where the concept of the final frontier is still fresh in the hearts of its inhabitants. Just above Puerto Montt lies a land of alpine lakes, with its distinctively German and Swiss cultural enclaves. The central Maipo Valley, fertile home of Chile's famous vineyards and fruit fields, also houses the frenzy of cosmopolitan Santiago.

West of the capital is the rustic port city of Valparaíso and the glittery resort town of Viña del Mar. For those with more time on their hands, Easter Island and its mysterious stone heads lie some 3,700 km (2,300 mi) west of mainland, in the middle of the Pacific Ocean.

Great Itineraries

If You Have 6 Days

Take at least three days to explore and enjoy Santiago, Chile's capital and largest city. Skiers may opt for spending a day in one of the nearby ski resorts. On your fourth day, hop a bus to Valparaíso in the morning, meandering among this port city's picturesque hills and many funiculars. Spend the next day in neighboring Viña del Mar, exploring its chic cafés and restaurants and relaxing on its miles of beaches. On your last day head back to Santiago to catch your flight home.

If You Have 10 Days

After spending four days exploring Santiago and the nearby beach resorts, fly north of your fifth day to San Pedro de Atacama, in the middle of the driest desert in the world. Spend two days exploring the bizarre moonscape of the Valle de la Luna and the desolate salt flats of the Salar de Atacama. On your eighth day drive up the coast to Iquique, where you can visit the Gigante de Atacama, the world's largest geoglyph. The next day head to Arica, the northernmost city in Chile. Visit the Museo Arqueológico de San Miguel de Azapa to see the Chinchorro mummies. On your last day fly back to Santiago.

If You Have 14 Days

Spend your first four days exploring Santiago and the beach towns along the Central Coast. Fly south to Puerto Montt and explore the lovely resort towns of the Lake District on your fifth and sixth days. Make sure to take time to relax in one of the region's many hot springs. From Puerto Montt, take a three-night cruise down the coast to the unforgettable glacier in Parque Nacional Laguna San Rafael. When you return to Puerto Montt, take a spectacular morning flight over the Andes to the Patagonian city of Punta Arenas. On your 12th day drive to Puerto Natales, gateway to the Parque National Torres del Paine. You'll need at least two days to wander through the wonders of the park's granite spires. On your final day head back to Punta Arenas, stopping en route at one of the penguin sanctuaries, and catch your flight back to Santiago.

FESTIVALS AND SEASONAL EVENTS

SUMMER

DECEMBER:➤ The **Fiesta Grande** (Big Festival), honoring the patron saint of miners, culminates with frenzied festivities on December 26 in Andacolla, a small town in El Norte Chico. More than 100,000 pilgrims come to watch the masked dancers.

JANUARY:➤ In January, **Semanas Musicales** (Music Weeks) in the Lake District town of de Frutillar offers virtuoso performances of classical music. The Lake District town of Villarrica hosts the **Muestra Cultural Mapuche** (Mapuche Cultural Show) from January 3 to February 28. Here you'll find examples of the indigenous people's art and music. Look for the reproduction of a ruka, the Mapuche traditional dwelling. **Fiestas Costumbristas,** a celebration of Chilote customs and folklore, take place over several weekends during January and February in the Chiloé towns of Ancud and Castro.

The annual **Tapati Rapa Nui** festival, a two-week celebration of Easter Island's heritage, takes place every year in January and February. The normally laid-back village of Hanga Roa bursts to life in a colorful festival that includes much singing and dancing. The pastoral quiet of Isla Huapi is broken in late January or early February with the annual harvest festival called **Lepún.** It's one of the Lake District's most interesting celebrations. The **Festival Folclórico** (Folklore Festival) is held in Santiago during the fourth week of January.

FEBRUARY➤ The **Fiesta de la Virgen de la Candelaria,** a three-day romp that begins on February 2, is held in the tiny antiplano village of Parinacota. It includes music and traditional dancing. The annual **Festival Internacional de la Canción** (International Song Festival) takes place over a week in mid-February in Viña del Mar. The concerts are broadcast live on television. February 9 is the beginning of the two-month-long **Verano en Valdivia,** a favorite celebration for those living in the Lake District. It culminates with a spectacular fireworks display.

AUTUMN

MARCH➤ The four-day **Fiesta de la Vendimia,** the annual grape harvest festival, takes place in the Central Valley town of Curico the first weekend in March. It includes grape stomping contests and the selection of a queen, whose weight is measured out in grapes on a massive scale. A similar celebration is held in nearby Santa Cruz.

APRIL➤ **Semana Santa,** or Holy Week, is popular all over Chile. Different events are held each day between Palm Sunday and Easter Sunday. The Sunday after Easter is **Fiesta de Cuasimodo,** a celebration in which priests in decorated carriages ride through villages as parishioners cheer. The village of Colina, north of Santiago, has one of the largest gatherings.

MAY➤ The **Fiesta de las Cruces** (Festival of the Crosses), takes place in El Norte Grande on May 3.

WINTER

JUNE➤ In Valparaíso, colorful processions mark the **Día de San Pedro** (St. Peter's Day) on June 29. A statue of the patron saint of fishermen is paraded through town.

JULY➤ The town of La Tirana in El Norte Grande hosts one of the country's most famous celebrations from July 12 to July 18. During this time some 80,000 pilgrims converge on the central square to honor the **Virgen de la Tirana** with riotous dancing.

SPRING

SEPTEMBER➤ On September 18 **Fiestas Patrias** (patriotic festivals) take place all over the country to mark National Independence Day. The most fun is around Rancagua, where you'll find hard-fought rodeo competitions.

OCTOBER➤ **Fiesta Chica** (Little Festival), honoring the Virgen del Rosario, is held in Andacolla the first Sunday of October.

In the religious festival called the **Fiesta de San Francisco,** held October 4 in the Central Valley town of Huerta de Maule, over 200 cowboys gather from all over the country for a day of riding and roping.

NOVEMBER➤ November 1 is **Todos los Santos** (All Saints Day), when

Chileans traditionally tend to the graves of relatives. It's followed November 2 by **Día de los Muertos** (All Souls Day). In November, the Chilean wine industry shows off the fruits of its hard labor at the annual **Feria International de Vino del Hemisferio Sur** in Santiago.

pitys pikacio Cousiño

Few cities can boast a backdrop as dramatic as the one belonging to Chile's capital city. On the occasional day when the smog lifts, the snow-covered peaks of the Andes slice across the eastern horizon. In this city of 6 million people you'll find the best that Chile has to offer—trendy boutiques, enticing restaurants, and nonstop nightlife. And the surrounding countryside is just as exciting, with the finest vineyards and the most challenging skiing in South America less than an hour away.

By Michael
de Zayas

W HEN IT WAS FOUNDED by Spanish conquistador Pedro de
Valdivia in 1541, Santiago was little more than the triangular patch of land embraced by two arms of the Río
Mapocho. Today that area, known as Santiago Centro, is just one of
32 *comunas* that make up the city, each with its own distinct personality. You'd never mistake Patronato, a neighborhood north of downtown filled with Moorish-style mansions built by families who made
their fortunes in textiles, with Providencia, where the modern skyscrapers built by international corporations crowd the avenues. The chic shopping centers of Las Condes have very little in common with the dusty
outdoor markets in Bellavista.

Perhaps the neighborhoods have retained their individuality because
many have histories as old as Santiago itself. Nuñoa, for example, was
a hardworking farm town to the east. Farther away was El Arrayán,
a sleepy village in the foothills of the Andes. As the capital grew, these
and many other communities were drawn inside the city limits. If you
ask Santiaguinos you meet today where they reside, they are just as
likely to mention their neighborhood as their city.

Like many of the early Spanish settlements, Santiago suffered some se-
vere setbacks. Six months after the town was founded, a group of the
indigenous Picunche people attacked, burning every building to the
ground. Undeterred, the Spanish rebuilt in the same spot. The narrow
streets radiating out from the Plaza de Armas are the same ones that
can be still be seen today.

The Spanish lost interest in Santiago after about a decade, moving south
in search of gold. But fierce resistance from the Mapuche people in 1599
forced many settlers to retreat to Santiago. The population swelled,
solidifying the city's claim as the region's colonial capital. Soon many
of the city's landmarks, including the colorful Casa Colorada, were
erected.

It wasn't until after Chile won its independence from Spain in 1818
that Santiago took the shape it has today. Broad avenues extended in
every direction. Buildings befitting a national capital, such as the Congreso Nacional and the Teatro Municipal, won wide acclaim. Parque
Quinta Normal and Parque O'Higgins preserved huge swaths of green
for the people, and the poplar-lined Parque Forestal gave the increasingly proud populace a place to promenade.

Santiago today is home to almost 6 million people—nearly a third of
the country's total population. It continues to spread outward to the
so-called *barrios altos* (upper neighborhoods) east of the center. It's also
growing upward, as new office towers transform the skyline. Yet it many
ways, Santiago still feels like a small town. Residents are always likely
to bump into an acquaintance along the city center's crowded streets
and bustling plazas.

Pleasures and Pastimes

Dining
Dining is one of Santiago's great pleasures, and one of its most affordable
delectations. Everything from fine restaurants to informal *picadas* are
spread across the city. Menus run the gamut of international cuisines,
but don't miss the local bounty—seafood delivered directly from the
Pacific Ocean. You couldn't do better than enjoy a plate of fresh fish
at Mercado Central, the city's bustling market.

Lunch and dinner are served later than in many places—2 PM for lunch, 8 or 9 PM for dinner. People do dress smartly for dinner, but a coat and tie are rarely necessary. For details on price categories, *see* Dining *in* Smart Travel Tips A to Z.

Lodging

Santiago has more than a dozen five-star hotels, many of them in the burgeoning Providencia and Las Condes neighborhoods. With the increased popularity of Chile as a travel destination, most major international chains are represented here. You won't find better service than at newer hotels such as the lavish Sheraton Santiago. But don't write off the old standbys. The Carrera, which has been around for decades, is still one of Santiago's finest luxury hotels. Inexpensive small hotels, especially near the city center, are harder to find, but they do exist.

All the construction in the past few years means competition between hotels is heated. You can often find a room for considerably less than the high-season rates listed here. For details on price categories, *see* Lodging *in* Smart Travel Tips A to Z.

Shopping

In Santiago's markets you can easily find fresh produce, fine woolen items, and handicrafts from across the country. Trendy boutiques line the streets of Bellavista and Providencia, and luxury department stores in modern shopping malls lure dedicated shoppers to Las Condes. Keep an eye out for lapis lazuli—Chile is one of only three countries that produce this lovely stone, and the jewelers of Santiago show it off in every type of setting imaginable.

Wineries

Santiago is nestled in the Maipo Valley, the country's oldest wine-growing district. Some of Chile's largest and best wineries—Concha y Toro, Cousiño-Macul, and Santa Rita—are within an hour's drive of the city. November to March is the best time to visit if you want to see the winemaking process. The *vendimia*, or annual harvest, takes place in late February and early March.

EXPLORING SANTIAGO

Pedro de Valdivia wasn't very creative when he mapped out the streets of Santiago. He stuck to the same simple grid pattern you'll find in almost all of the colonial towns along the coast. The city didn't grow much larger before the meandering Río Mapocho impeded these plans. You may be surprised, however, at how orderly the city remains. It's difficult to get lost wandering around downtown Santiago.

Running through many neighborhoods is the city's major thoroughfare, the Alameda. No matter where you go in the city, you're likely to find this wide avenue is no more than a few blocks away. West of Plaza Baquedano it is called Avenida Libertador Bernardo O'Higgins, while to the east it is known as Avenida Providencia, where you'll find an upscale shopping district. Farther along it turns into Las Condes, the address of some of the city's fanciest houses.

Much of the city, especially communities such as Bellavista and Providencia, is best explored on foot. The subway is probably the quickest, cleanest, and most economical way to shuttle among neighborhoods. To travel to more distant neighborhoods, or to get anywhere in the evening after the subway closes, you'll probably want to hail a taxi.

16

Santiago

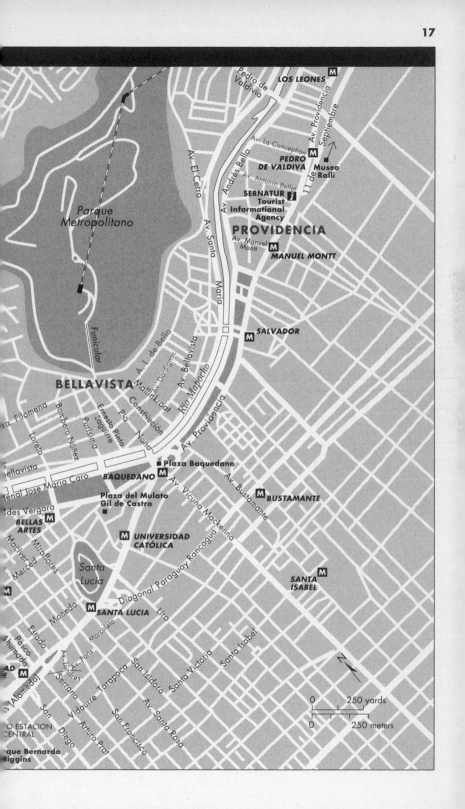

LOS LEONES

Pedro de Valdivia

Av. La Concepción

Av. Andrés Bello

Av. El Cerro

Parque Metropolitano

PEDRO DE VALDIVA

Museo Ralli

Av. Antonia Bellet

SERNATUR Tourist Informational Agency

PROVIDENCIA

Av. Manuel Montt

MANUEL MONTT

Av. Providencia

11 de Septiembre

Funicular

Av. Santa María

SALVADOR

A. L. de Bello

Av. Dardignac

Av. Bellavista

Mallinkroat

Río Mapocho

BELLAVISTA

Constitución

Po Nono

a. Filomena

Loreto

Bombero Núñez

Purísima

Ernesto Pinto Laqurre

Bellavista

Av. Providencia

Plaza Baquedano

renal José María Caro

BAQUEDANO

des Vergara

Plaza del Mulato Gil de Castro

Av. Bustamante

BUSTAMANTE

BELLAS ARTES

Av. Vicuña Mackenna

UNIVERSIDAD CATÓLICA

Maclver

Miraflores

Merced

Santa Lucía

Diagonal Paraguay Rancagua

SANTA ISABEL

Lira

SANTA LUCIA

Marcoleta

Moneda

Estado

Paseo Ahumada

Av. Londres

Av. París

Serrano

Vidaurre

Tarapacá

San Isidoro

Santa Victoria

Santa Isabel

AD

(Alameda)

San Diego

Arturo Prat

Av. Santa Rosa

San Francisco

 O ESTACIÓN CENTRAL

que Bernardo Higgins

N

0   250 yards

0   250 meters

Great Itineraries

IF YOU HAVE 3 DAYS

Santiago is a compact city, small enough that you can visit all the must-see sights in a few days. Consider the weather when planning your itinerary—on the first clear day your destination should be Parque Metropolitano, where you'll be treated to exquisite views from Cerro San Cristóbal. After a morning gazing at the Andes, head back down the hill and spend the afternoon wandering the bohemian streets of Bellavista, with a visit to Nobel laureate Pablo Neruda's Santiago residence, La Chascona. Check out one of the neighborhood's colorful eateries.

The next day, head to Parque Forestal, where you can stroll through the leafy park that runs along the Río Mapocho. Make sure to visit the lovely old train station, the Estación de Mapocho. After lunch at the Mercado Central, uncover the city's colonial past with a visit to Santiago Centro. Requisite sights include the Plaza de Armas, around which you'll find the Casa Colorada and the Museo de Arte Precolombino. Stop for tea in the afternoon at one of the quaint cafés in Plaza del Mulato Gil de Castro. On day three explore the sights along the Alameda, especially the presidential palace of La Moneda and the landmark church called the Iglesia San Francisco. For a last look at the city, make sure to climb Cerro Santa Lucía. That night put on your chicest outfit for dinner in the trendy neighborhoods of Providencia or Las Condes.

IF YOU HAVE 5 DAYS

In addition to the above itinerary, you can spend the good part of a day exploring the area around Parque Quinta Normal, where you can relax with a picnic while the youngsters scurry about flying kites. Ask your concierge to make reservations for a show that evening at the stunning Teatro Municipal. On the fifth day make a reservation for lunch at one of Chile's best wineries, Viña Santa Rita. If you're a fan of Chile's most famous export, spend the rest of the day touring the vineyards just south of Santiago. You'll undoubtedly find a few bottles to take back home. Treat yourself to dinner in Vitacura, where the dining district known as Borde Río offers just about every type of food imaginable.

IF YOU HAVE 7 DAYS

With a few extra days, you have plenty of time to head to the hills. Skiers should hit the slopes of nearby Valle Nevado, or travel a little farther north to the more exclusive resort of Portillo. If you're here in the few months when there isn't any snow, take a drive through the Cajón del Maipo. The Baños de Colina aren't easy to reach, but these relaxing hot springs are worth the journey.

When to Tour

No wonder Santiaguinos abandon their city every summer—it's hot and muggy from December to February. For walking around the city, spring and fall are better choices. If you're planning on driving through the Cajón del Maipo, this is when the scenery is at its peak. Winters in the city aren't especially cold—temperatures rarely dip below freezing—but days are gray and gloomy. Ski season, depending on the resort, runs mid-June through mid-September. Good weather conditions, however, mean six-month-long seasons beginning in May and ending in October.

Santiago Centro

Shiny new skyscrapers may be sprouting up in neighborhoods to the east, but Santiago Centro is the place to start if you really want to take the pulse of the city. After all, this is the historic heart of Santiago. All the major traffic arteries cross here (creating the usual traffic headaches) and all the subway lines converge here before whisking riders out to the suburbs. In Santiago Centro you'll find interesting museums, imposing governmental buildings, and bustling commercial streets. But don't think you'll be lost in a sprawling area—it takes only about 10 minutes to walk from one edge to the other.

Numbers in white bullets in the text correspond to numbers in black bullets in the margins and on the Santiago Centro and La Alameda map.

A Good Walk

To really know Santiago, get acquainted with the **Plaza de Armas** ①. Across Calle Catedral is a block-long threesome of historic buildings, centered by the the Palacio de la Real Audiencia, at one time the country's highest court and currently home to the **Museo Histórico Nacional** ②. To the west of the museum is the pastel pink **Correo Central** ③; to the east is the **Municipalidad de Santiago** ④. The **Catedral** ⑤, twice destroyed by earthquakes and once by fire before the current neoclassical structure was completed in the 18th century, looms over the western end of the plaza. A motley assortment of commercial arcades completes the fringes of the square, adding a touch of modernity to one of the city's most traditional neighborhoods.

Southwest of the Plaza de Armas on Calle Merced you'll find a beautifully restored colonial mansion called the **Casa Colorada** ⑥. The **Museo de Arte Precolombino** ⑦ is two blocks west on the corner of Calle Compañía and Calle Bandera. Across the street stands Chile's lordly **Tribunales de Justicia** ⑧. Encompassing an entire city block to the north is the **Ex Congreso Nacional** ⑨ and its gated gardens, offering refuge from the hustle and bustle of Santiago Centro.

TIMING AND PRECAUTIONS

The walk itself should take less than an hour. If you visit a few museums, wander around the squares, and rest here and there, this itinerary could take a full morning. Each of the small museums on this route should take about 45 minutes to see thoroughly.

Sights to See

⑥ **Casa Colorada.** Appropriately named the Red House, this structure was once the home of Mateo de Toro y Zambrano, Santiago's most prosperous businessman of the 18th century. Today it's one of the best-preserved colonial structures in all of Santiago. It houses the Museo de Santiago, a modest but informative museum that is an excellent place to dive into the history of the city. For an explanation of the exhibits, ask for an English guidebook. ⊠ *Merced 860,* ☎ *2/633–0723.* 🖃 *Admission Tues.–Sat., free Sun.* ☉ *Tues.–Fri. 10–6, Sat. 10–5, Sun. 11–2. Metro: Plaza de Armas.*

⑤ **Catedral.** Conquistador Pedro de Valdivia declared in 1541 that a house of worship would be constructed at this site bordering the Plaza de Armas. The first adobe building burned to the ground, and the structures that replaced it were destroyed by the earthquakes of 1647 and 1730. The finishing touches of the neoclassical cathedral standing today were added in 1789 by Italian architect Joaquín Toesca. Be sure to see the stunning interior—a line of gilt arches topped by stained-glass windows parades down the long nave. ⊠ *Plaza de Armas,* ☎ *2/696–2777.* ☉ *Mon.–Sat. 11, 12:30, and 7:30; Sun. 10, 11, and noon. Metro: Plaza de Armas.*

③ **Correo Central.** Housed in what was once the ornate Palacio de los Gobernadores, this building dating from 1715 is one of the most beautiful post offices you are likely to see. A recent face-lift has made waiting in long lines to mail a letter more tolerable. ⊠ *Plaza de Armas,* ☎ *2/699–4531.* ☉ *Weekdays 8–7, Sat. 8–2. Metro: Plaza de Armas.*

20

Santiago Centro and La Alameda

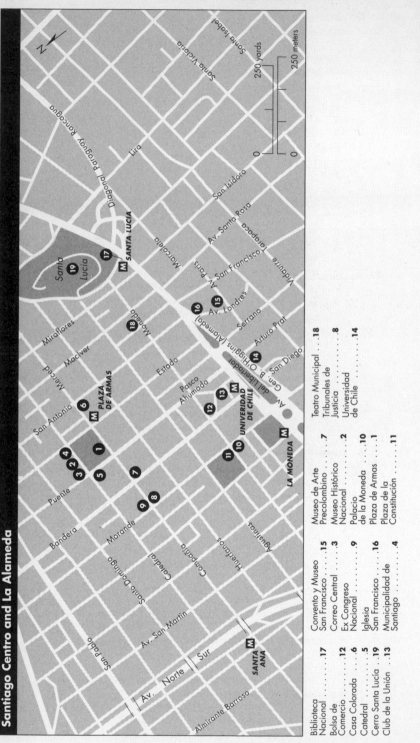

Biblioteca
Nacional **17**
Bolsa de
Comercio **12**
Casa Colorada **6**
Catedral **5**
Cerro Santa Lucía . .**19**
Club de la Unión . .**13**

Convento y Museo
San Francisco **15**
Correo Central **3**
Ex Congreso
Nacional **9**
Iglesia
San Francisco **16**
Municipalidad de
Santiago **4**

Museo de Arte
Precolombino **7**
Museo Histórico
Nacional **2**
Palacio
de la Moneda **10**
Plaza de Armas **1**
Plaza de la
Constitución **11**

Teatro Municipal . . .**18**
Tribunales de
Justicia **8**
Universidad
de Chile **14**

⑨ Ex Congreso Nacional. Once the meeting place for the National Congress (the legislature moved to Valparaíso in 1990), this palatial neoclassical building now houses the offices of the Ministry of Foreign Affairs. The original structure on the site, a church called the Iglesia de la Compañía de Jesús, was destroyed by a fire in 1863 in which 2,000 people perished. Inside the peaceful gated gardens is a monument commemorating the victims. ⊠ *Bandera 345, at Morandé. Metro: Plaza de Armas.*

④ Municipalidad de Santiago. Today's governmental center for Santiago can be found on the site of the colonial city hall and jail. The original structure, built in 1552, survived until a devastating earthquake in 1730. Joaquín Toesca, the architect who also designed the presidential palace and completed the cathedral, reconstructed the building in 1785, but it met its end in a fire a century later. In 1891, Eugenio Joannon, who favored an Italian Renaissance style, erected the structure standing today. On the facade hangs an elaborate coat of arms presented by Spain. The interior is not open to the public. ⊠ *Plaza de Armas. Metro: Plaza de Armas.*

★ **⑦ Museo de Arte Precolombino.** If you plan to visit only one museum in Santiago, it should be the Museum of Pre-Columbian Art, a block from the Plaza de Armas. The well-endowed collection of artifacts of Central and South America's indigenous peoples is housed in a beautifully restored Royal Customs House dating from 1807. The permanent collection showcasing textiles and ceramics from Mexico to Patagonia is on the upper floor. Unlike many of the city's museums, the displays here are well labeled in Spanish and English. ⊠ *Bandera 361, at Av. Compañía,* ☎ *2/695–3851 or 2/695–3627.* ⊡ *Admission Tues.–Sat., free Sun.* ☉ *Tues.–Sat. 10–6, Sun. 10–2. Metro: Plaza de Armas.*

② Museo Histórico Nacional. The colonial-era Palacio de la Real Audiencia served as the meeting place of Chile's first Congress. It functioned as a telegraph office before the museum moved here in 1911. It's worth the small admission charge to see the interior of the 200-year-old structure. Inside are large collections of coins, stamps, and traditional handicrafts, including more than 3,000 examples of native textiles. A model of the colonial city shows its regimented grid pattern, centered by the Plaza de Armas and bordered by La Alameda, which at that time, as its name denotes, was a grove of poplar trees. ⊠ *Plaza de Armas,* ☎ *2/638–1411.* ⊡ *Admission Tues.–Sat., free Sun.* ☉ *Tues.–Sat. 10–5:30, Sun. and holidays 10–5:30. Metro: Plaza de Armas.*

OFF THE
BEATEN PATH

PARQUE BERNARDO O'HIGGINS – Named for Chile's national hero whose troops were victorious against the Spanish, this park has plenty of open space for everything from ball games to military parades. Street vendors sell *volantines* (kites) outside the park year-round; high winds make September and early October the prime kite-flying season. ⊠ *Av. Jorge Alessandri Rodríguez between Av. Blanca Encalada and Av. General Rondizzoni,* ☎ *2/556–1927.* ⊡ *Free.* ☉ *Daily 9–7. Metro: Parque O'Higgins.*

★ **① Plaza de Armas.** The square has been the symbolic heart of Chile—as well as its political, social, religious, and commercial center—since Pedro de Valdivia established the city on this spot in 1541. Its northern edge is fronted by three recently renovated landmarks—the 1715 Palacio de los Gobernadores, the 1808 Palacio de la Real Audiencia, and the 1785 Municiplidad de Santiago. The dignified Catedral graces the western side of the square. In the middle of it all, distinctive fountains and gardens reveal the Chileans' pride about their history. Also here is a bronze well that once served as the city's main source of water. On any given day, the plaza teems with life—vendors selling religious icons, street performers juggling fire, and tourists clutching guidebooks mix in a swirl of activity. Watch older men play a game of chess in the southern corner of the plaza. ⊠ *Calle Compañia and Calle Estado. Metro: Plaza de Armas.*

❽ **Tribunales de Justicia.** During Pinochet's reign of terror, countless human-rights demonstrations were held outside the Courts of Justice, home to the country's Supreme Court. Protests are still held near this stately neoclassical building a block from the Plaza de Armas, including some in support of the former dictator. In front of the building, perhaps ironically, is a monument celebrating justice and the promulgation of Chile's civil code. ⊠ *Bandera 344.* ☉ *Mar.–Nov., weekdays 1–6:30; Dec.–Feb., Mon. 1–6:30 and Tues.–Fri. 8–1. Metro: Plaza de Armas.*

La Alameda

Avenida Libertador Bernardo O'Higgins, more frequently called La Alameda, is the city's principal thoroughfare. Along with the Avenida Norte Sur and the Río Mapocho, it forms the wedge that defines the city's historic district. Many of Santiago's most important buildings, including landmarks such as the Iglesia San Francisco, are found along the avenue. Others, like Teatro Municipal, are just steps away.

A Good Walk

Unthinkable only a few years ago, today you can walk unescorted into the courtyard of the **Palacio de la Moneda** ⑩, the nerve center of the Chilean government. Across Calle Modena you'll find **Plaza de la Constitución** ⑪, a formal square where you can watch the changing of the guard. Walk a block east along Calle Moneda to the cobblestone Calle La Bolsa. On this narrow diagonal street is the ornate **Bolsa de Comercio** ⑫, the country's stock exchange. A block down, at a dainty fountain, the street becomes Calle Nueva York, where you'll find the **Club de la Unión** ⑬. Across the street is the main building, or casa central, of the **Universidad de Chile** ⑭. Reach it by crossing under the Universidad de Chile Metro stop, which contains monumental murals depicting Chilean history painted by Mario Toral, part of the fine MetroArte series in all subway stops. Two blocks east are the **Convento y Museo San Francisco** ⑮ and the **Iglesia San Francisco** ⑯. To avoid the crazy drivers speeding down La Alameda, cross back to the other side via the Santa Lucía Metro station. Directly ahead of you is the **Biblioteca Nacional** ⑰, and a block beyond is the **Teatro Municipal** ⑱. Head east through Plaza Vicuña Mackenna to survey the entire city from **Cerro Santa Lucía** ⑲.

TIMING AND PRECAUTIONS

This walk itself is fairly short, but it's full of beautiful old buildings where you'll want to spend some time. You could spend an hour at La Moneda—try to time your visit with the changing of the guard. Across the Alameda, give yourself another hour to explore the Iglesia San Francisco and the adjacent museum. You could easily spend a bookish half-hour perusing the stacks at the Biblioteca Nacional. Plan for an hour or more at Cerro Santa Lucía—don't get here too late, as the hilltop park isn't safe after dark.

Sights to See

⑰ **Biblioteca Nacional.** Near the foot of Cerro Santa Lucía is the block-long classical facade of the National Library. With more than 3 million titles, this is one of the largest libraries in South America. The vast interior includes arcane collections; one of the most attractive spaces, the Sala Medina, holds the most important collection of prints by native peoples in

Latin America. ⌂ *Av. O'Higgins 651,* ☏ *2/360–5259.* ⌖ *Free.* ☉ *Weekdays 10–2 and 3:30–6:30, Sat. 10–2. Metro: Santa Lucía.*

⑫ **Bolsa de Comercio.** Chile's stock exchange is housed in an 1917 French neoclassical structure with an elegant clock tower surmounted by an arched slate cupola. During the week you can watch the shouting of traders in the three buying and selling circles called *redondeles.* ⌂ *Calle La Bolsa 64,* ☏ *2/698–2001,* WEB *www.bolsantiago.cl.* ⌖ *Free.* ☉ *Weekdays noon–1:20 and 4–4:30. Metro: Universidad de Chile.*

⑲ **Cerro Santa Lucía.** The mazelike park of St. Lucía is a hangout for souvenir vendors, park-bench smoochers, and photo-snapping tourists. Walking uphill along the labyrinth of interconnected paths and plazas takes about 30 minutes. An elevator two blocks north of the park's main entrance is a little faster, but its schedule is erratic. The crow's nest, reached via a series of steep and slippery stone steps, affords an excellent 360-degree view of the entire city. Be careful near dusk, as the park also attracts the occasional mugger. ⌂ *Santa Lucía and Av. O'Higgins,* ☏ *no phone.* ☉ *Winter, daily 9–7; summer, daily 9–8. Metro: Santa Lucía.*

⑬ **Club de la Unión.** This private club, whose roster has included numerous Chilean presidents, admits only members. The facade of this neoclassical building dating from 1925 is one of the city's finest. Inside is one of the largest private art galleries in the country. ⌂ *Av. O'Higgins at Calle Bandera. Metro: Universidad de Chile.*

⑮ **Convento y Museo San Francisco.** Beside San Francisco Church is this former convent which functions as a religious and colonial art museum. It's home to the best collection of 17th-century colonial paintings on the continent, with 54 large-scale canvases portraying the life of St. Francis and a plethora of religious iconography. Most pieces are labeled in both Spanish and English. Fans of literature shouldn't miss a small exhibit devoted to Gabriela Mistral, who won the Nobel Prize in 1945 for her poetry about Chile. ⌂ *Londres 4,* ☏ *2/638–3238.* ⌖ *Admission.* ☉ *Tues.–Sat. 10–1:30 and 3–6, Sun. 10–2. Metro: Santa Lucía, Universidad de Chile.*

⑯ **Iglesia San Francisco.** Santiago's oldest structure, greatest symbol, and principal landmark, the Church of St. Francis is the last trace of Santiago's 16th-century colonial architecture. Construction began on the massive structure in 1586. Though it survived all of the city's successive earthquakes, the tremors took their toll early on; portions had to be reconstructed in 1698. Today's neoclassical towers, which form the city's most recognizable silhouette, were added in 1857 by architect Fermín Vivaceta. Inside, rough stone-and-brick walls, marble columns, and ornate wood ceilings testify to the centuries of construction. Visible on the main altar is the image of the Virgen del Socorro (Virgin of Assistance) that Pedro de Valdivia carried to protect and guide him during his conquest of the region. ⌂ *Londres 4, at Av. O'Higgins,* ☏ *2/638–3238.* ☉ *Masses Tues.–Sat. 8, 10, noon, and 7:30; Sun. 9, 10, 11, noon, 1, and 7:30. Metro: Santa Lucía, Universidad de Chile.*

⑩ **Palacio de la Moneda.** Still called the "Palace of the Coin" because of its original purpose as the royal mint, this sober neoclassical edifice was built by Joaquín Toesca in 1805. It became the presidential palace in 1846 and served that purpose for more than a century. It was bombarded by the military in the 1973 coup, when Salvador Allende heroically defended his presidency against the assault of General Augusto Pinochet. The real cause of Allende's death is still a mystery—some say he went down fighting, others claim he took his own life before the future dictator entered the palace in triumph.

The building, once sadly neglected, was restored to its original splendor by a renovation in 2001 that cleaned up the smog-color facade. The two central courtyards are once again open to the public. Within Patio de los Cañones sit two bronze cannons; Patio de Naranjos gets its name from the orange trees growing there. In the center is a fountain, made in Lima in 1671, that once stood in the Plaza de Armas. Tours of the interior can be arranged at the reception desk. ⊠ *Plaza de la Constitución, Moneda between Teatinos and Morandé.* ⊙ *Daily 10–6. Metro: La Moneda.*

⓫ **Plaza de la Constitución.** The country's most formal square, Constitution Square is ringed by the Palacio de la Moneda and other governmental buildings. The changing of the guard takes place every other day at 10 AM within the triangle defined by 12 Chilean flags. Adorning the plaza are three monuments, each dedicated to a notable national figure: Diego Portales, founder of the Chilean republic; Jorge Alessandri, the country's leader from 1958 to 1964; and Don Eduardo Frei, president from 1964 to 1970. The plaza also serves as the roof of the underground bunker Pinochet had installed when he "redecorated" La Moneda. Four pillars in the corners of the square serve as ventilation ducts for the bunker, now a parking lot. Locals joke that these monoliths represent the four founding members of the military junta—they're made of stone, full of hot air, and no one knows their real function. In 2000, one of them was converted into a memorial honoring President Salvador Allende. One of his most famous quotes graces the monument: TENGO FE EN CHILE Y SU DESTINO (I have faith in Chile and its destiny). ⊠ *Moneda and Morande. Metro: La Moneda.*

⓭ **Teatro Municipal.** The opulent Municipal Theater is the city's cultural center, with performances of opera, ballet, and classical music from April to November. Originally built in 1857, with major renovations in 1870 and 1906 following a fire and an earthquake, the Renaissance-style building is one of the city's most refined monuments. The lavish interior deserves a visit. Tours can be arranged with a week's notice. ⊠ *Av. Agustinas at Av. San Antonio,* ☎ *2/369–0282. Metro: Universidad de Chile, Santa Lucía.*

⓮ **Universidad de Chile.** The main branch of the University of Chile, the country's largest educational institution, is one of the city's most attractive 19th-century buildings. The symmetrical ocher edifice was completed in 1872, when it was called the University Palace. It's not officially open to the public, but you are free to stroll through the grounds. ⊠ *Av. O'Higgins.* ⊙ *Metro: Universidad de Chile.*

Parque Forestal

After building a canal in 1891 to tame the unpredictable Río Mapocho, Santiago found itself with a thin strip of land that it didn't quite know what to do with. The area quickly filled with the city's refuse. A decade later, under the watchful eye of Enrique Cousiño, it was transformed into the leafy Forest Park. It proved to be enormously popular among Santiaguinos, and continues to be to this day. The eastern tip, near Plaza Baquedano, is distinguished by the Wagnerian-scale Fuente Alemana (German Fountain). Donated by the Germanic community of Santiago, the bronze and stone monolith commemorates the centennial of Chilean Independence.

A Good Walk

Santiago's tranquil Parque Forestal, which runs parallel to the Río Mapocho for several blocks, is the perfect antidote for the spirited Plaza de Armas. Near its eastern edge you'll find the wrought-iron **Mercado**

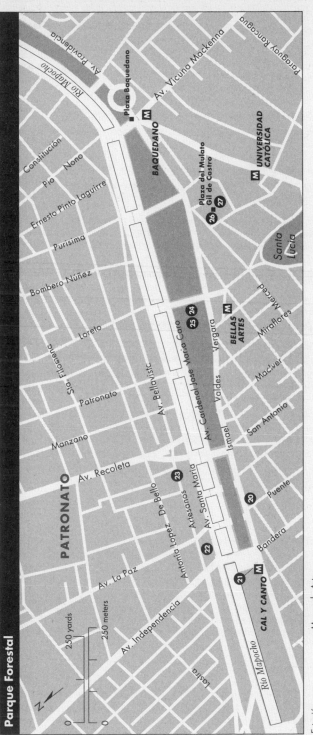

Parque Forestal

Central ⑳, the city's fish market. Stroll in the park along the Río Mapocho a block west to reach the former train terminal, the **Estación de Mapocho** ㉑. Cross the river and you'll be able to follow your nose to the flower market called the **Pérgola de las Flores** ㉒. If the Central Market feels like a tourist trap, turn east on Artesanos and walk until you see the lime-green entrance to the gritty **Vega Chica** ㉓. A full block to the north is the peach-color **Vega Central.**

Strolling east through the Parque Forestal will bring you to the jewel-like **Museo de Bellas Artes** ㉔ and the adjacent **Museo de Arte Contemporáneo** ㉕. Just south of the park, near where Calle Merced and Calle José Victorino Lastarria meet, you'll find the Plaza del Mulato Gil de Castro, a pleasant little nook with a handful of art galleries, bookshops, and cafés, as well as the **Museo Arqueológico** ㉖ and the **Museo de Artes Visuales** ㉗.

TIMING AND PRECAUTIONS

You can make a pleasant, relaxing day out of strolling through the city's most popular park, losing yourself in the art museums, and exploring Mercado Central. In Plaza Mulato Gil de Castro, allot at least 30 minutes for the Museo Arqueológico and the Museo de Artes Visuales. You can easily spend a few hours in the Museo de Bellas Artes and the Museo de Arte Contemporáneo. Vega Chica and Vega Central are usually very crowded, so keep an eye on your personal belongings. When the markets are closing around sunset, it's best to return to neighborhoods south of the river.

Sights to See

★ ㉑ **Estación Mapocho.** This mighty edifice, with its trio of two-story arches framed by intricate terra-cotta detailing, is as elegant as any train station in the world. While steam engines no longer pull into this old terminal, it's still one of the city's most attractive destinations. Inaugurated in 1913 as a terminus for trains arriving from Valparaíso and points north, the station was closed in 1987 after the dismantling of most of the country's rail service. Reopened in 1994 as the Centro Cultural Estación Mapocho, the cultural center houses two good restaurants, a fine bookstore and café, a large exhibition and arts space, and a shop selling traditional handicrafts. The cavernous space that once sheltered steam engines is now used for musical performances and other events. ✉ *Calle Balmaceda 1215,* ☎ *2/361–1761,* WEB *www.estacionmapocho.cl.* ⏱ *Daily 10–8. Metro: Puente Cal y Canto.*

㉒ **Mercado Central.** The lofty wrought-iron ceiling of the Central Market, reminiscent of a Victorian train station, was prefabricated in England and erected in Santiago between 1868 and 1872. Here you'll find a matchless selection of creatures from the sea. Depending on the season, you might see the delicate beaks of *picorocos,* the world's only edible barnacles; the orange stars of *erizos,* the prickly shelled sea urchins; or shadowy pails full of succulent bullfrogs. Diners are regaled by musicians in the middle of the market, where two restaurants compete for customers. If both are full, you can find a cheap, filling meal at the stands along the market's southern edge. ✉ *Ismael Valdés Vergara and Puente.* ⏱ *Sun.–Thurs. 7–4, Fri. and Sat. 7–8. Metro: Puente Cal y Canto.*

㉖ **Museo Arqueológico.** Some 3,000 artifacts bring the country's Mapuche, Aymara, Fueguino, Huilliche, and Pehuenche cultures vividly to life. The little Archaeological Museum—reopened in 2001 after a long renovation—is devoted specifically to the indigenous peoples of Chile. After taking in the museum, browse one of the bookstores or relax in one of the quiet cafés of Plaza del Mulato Gil de Castro. ✉ *José Victorino Lastarria 307, 2nd floor,* ☎ *2/664–9337.* ▱ *Free.* ⏱ *Tues.–Sun. 10:30–6:30. Metro: Baquedano, Universidad Católica.*

MK #1 - EL ARTE DE ENSEÑAR ARTE

NEED A BREAK? The pleasant Plaza del Mulato Gil de Castro, a cobblestone square off the colorful Calle José Victorino Lastarria, is an unexpected treat. In the midst of it is **R.** (✉ Plaza Mulato Gil de Castro, ☎ 2/664–9844), a cozy café serving English teas and light fare. Weary travelers relax beneath the kettles and cups hanging from the ceiling.

㉕ **Museo de Arte Contemporáneo.** On the opposite side of the building housing the Museo de Bellas Artes, the Museum of Contemporary Art has a collection of modern Latin American paintings, photography, and sculpture. The museum is run by the art school of the Universidad de Chile, so it isn't afraid to take risks; the rather dilapidated state of the interior is a perfect setting for the edgier art. Look for Fernando Botero's pudgy *Caballo* sculpture gracing the square out front. ✉ *Parque Forestal,* ☎ *2/639–6488.* 🎟 *Admission.* 🕐 *Tues.–Sat. 11–7, Sun. 11–2. Metro: Baquedano, Puente Cal y Canto.*

★ ㉗ **Museo de Artes Visuales.** You'll never confuse this dazzling new museum of contemporary art with the crumbling Museo de Arte Contemporáneo. Opened to the public in 2001, this gallery featuring the combined private holdings of Chilean construction moguls Manuel Santa Cruz and Hugo Yaconi holds what may be the world's finest collection of contemporary Chilean art. The building itself is a masterpiece—six gallery levels designed by local architect Christian Undurraga float into each other in surprising ways. The wood floors and Plexiglas-sided stairways create an open and airy space for paintings and sculptures by Roberto Matta, Arturo Duclos, Roser Bru, José Balmes, Eugenio Dittborn, and numerous others. ✉ *José Victorino Lastarria 307, Plaza del Mulato Gil de Castro,* ☎ *2/638–3502.* 🎟 *Admission* 🕐 *Tues.–Sun. 10:30–6:30. Metro: Baquedano, Universidad Católica.*

㉔ **Museo de Bellas Artes.** The Museum of Fine Arts is packed with paintings, drawings, and sculpture by 16th- to 20th-century Chilean and European artists. Originally intended to house the city's school of fine arts, the elegant building has an impressive glass-domed ceiling that illuminates the main hall. A theater on the second floor screens short films about the featured artists. ✉ *Parque Forestal,* ☎ *2/633–0655.* 🎟 *Admission, free Sun.* 🕐 *Tues.–Sun. 10–7. Metro: Baquedano, Puente Cal y Canto.*

OFF THE BEATEN PATH **PARQUE DE LAS ESCULTURAS –** Providencia is mainly a business district, but it has one of the city's most captivating—and least publicized—public parks. From the Pedro de Valdivia Metro stop, walk a block north to the Río Mapocho and cross the bridge. Here you'll find Parque de las Esculturas, where the gardens are filled with a score of sculptures by Chile's top artists. Because of its pastoral atmosphere, the park is quite popular with joggers. In the center is a wood pavilion that hosts very good changing sculpture exhibitions.

㉒ **Pérgola de las Flores.** The Trellis of Flowers is where Santiaguinos come to buy wreaths and flower arrangements to bring to the city's two cemeteries. *La Pérgola de las Flores,* a famous Chilean musical, is based on the conflict that arose in the 1930s when the mayor of Santiago wanted to shut down the market. Practice your Spanish with one of the chatty florists and learn all about it. ✉ *Corner of Av. La Paz and Artesanos,* ☎ *no phone.* 🕐 *Daily sunrise–sunset. Metro: Puente Cal y Canto.*

㉓ **Vega Central and Vega Chica.** From fruit to furniture, meat to machinery, these lively markets stock just about anything you can name. Alongside the more ordinary items you can often find rare delicacies like *piñones,* the giant pine nuts found on monkey puzzle trees. If you're undaunted by the crowds, try a truly typical Chilean meal in one of the closet-size eateries called *picadas*. Chow down with the locals on *pastel de choclo,* a cornmeal-covered pie filled with ground beef, chicken, and spices. ⊠ *Antonia López de Bello between Av. Salas and Av. Gandarilla. Metro: Puente Cal y Canto.*

Bellavista and Parque Metropolitano

If you happen to be in Santiago on one of the rare days when the smog dissipates, head straight for Parque Metropolitano. In the center is Cerro San Cristóbal, a hill reached via cable car or funicular. At the top you're rewarded with spectacular views in all directions. In the shadow of Cerro San Cristóbal is Bellavista. The neighborhood has but one sight—Pablo Neruda's hillside home of La Chascona—but it's perhaps the city's best place to wander. You're sure to discover interesting antiques shops, bustling outdoor markets, and the city's most adventurous and colorful eateries.

A Good Walk

Starting from Plaza Baquedano, cross the bridge over the Río Mapocho and you'll find yourself in Bellavista. The streets lined with acacia trees are filled with quaint cafés, trendy restaurants, and one-story homes painted in pinks, aquamarines, and blues. Walk three blocks north on Calle Pío Nono and turn right onto Calle Antonia López de Bello. Heading north along Constitución, you'll enter Santiago's most lively restaurant district. On Fernando Márquez de la Plata sits the house Pablo Neruda designed, **La Chascona** ㉘.

At the northern end of Calle Pío Nono you'll find Plaza Caupolicán, the entrance to Parque Metropolitano. The funicular, housed in an old castlelike terminus, climbs up Santiago's highest hill, **Cerro San Cristóbal** ㉙. Halfway up the hill, it stops at the **Jardín Zoológico de Santiago** ㉚. After reaching the summit, take in the expansive views of the city skyline. Follow the signs to the *telesférico* (cable car) and get out halfway at **Plaza Tupahue** ㉛. A short walk away is **Jardín Botánico Mapulemu** ㉜, an expansive botanical garden. After a 15-minute walk east and slightly downhill you'll reach the authentic and well-kept **Jardín Japonés** ㉝.

TIMING AND PRECAUTIONS

Figure on an entire day to see Parque Metropolitano's major attractions. During the week the park is almost empty, and you can enjoy the views in relative solitude. Avoid walking down if you decide to watch the sunset from the lofty perch—the area is not well patrolled. Give yourself at least an hour to wander through Bellavista, and another hour for a tour of La Chascona.

Sights to See

㉙ **Cerro San Cristóbal.** St. Christopher's Hill is one of the most popular tourist attractions in Santiago. From the western entrance at Plaza Caupolicán you can walk—it's a steep but enjoyable one-hour climb—or take the funicular. Either route leads you to the summit, which is crowned by a gleaming white statue of the Virgen de la Inmaculada. If you are coming from the eastern entrance, you can ascend in the cable car that leaves seven blocks north of the Pedro de Valdivia Metro stop. The ride, which seats two in a colored-glass bubble, can be terrifying for acrophobics. Tree branches whack at your lift as you glide over the park. ⊠ *Cerro San Cristóbal,* ☎ *2/777–6666 for park administration; 2/737–6669 for lift information,* WEB *www.parquemet.cl.* ☑ *Free; admission for round-trip lift.* ☉ *Park: Sun.–Thurs. 8 AM–10 PM, Fri.–Sat. 8 AM–midnight. Funicular: Mon. 1–8, Tues.–Sun. 10–8. Cable car:*

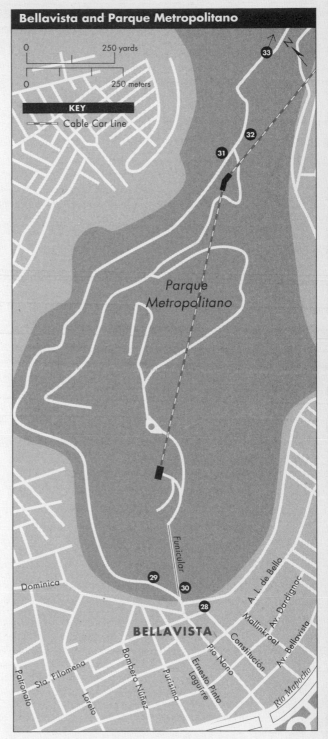

Bellavista and Parque Metropolitano

0   250 yards

0   250 meters

KEY
— — — Cable Car Line

Parque
Metropolitano

Funicular

Dominica

BELLAVISTA

Patronato

Sta. Filomena

Lorelo

Bombero Núñez

Purísima

Laguirre

Ernesto Pinto

Pío Nono

Constitución

Mallinkroat

A. L. de Bello

Av. Dardignac

Av. Bellavista

Río Mapocho

Mon. 2:30–7, Tues.–Fri. 12:30–7, weekends and holidays 10:30–7:30. Metro: Plaza Baquedano, Pedro de Valdivia.

NEED A
BREAK?
A short walk from La Chascona is Calle Antonia López de Bello, a Bellavista street overflowing with bars and restaurants. One of the best is **Off the Record** (⊠ Antonia López de Bello 155, ☎ 2/777–7710), a café with a decidedly bohemian air. The wooden booths, for instance, seem to have been designed with witty conversation and artistic bonhomie in mind. Black-and-white photographs recall visitors from Pablo Neruda to Uma Thurman.

㉜ Jardín Botánico Mapulemu. Gravel paths lead you to restful nooks in these acres of well-labeled local flora. The botanical star is the squat *jubea chilena*, the ubiquitous Chilean palm. Every path and stairway seems to bring you to better and better views of Santiago and the Andes—probably the best vistas from anywhere in the city. ⊠ *Cerro San Cristóbal,* ☎ *no phone.* ☺ *Free.* ☉ *Daily 8:30 AM–10 PM. Metro: Pedro de Valdivia.*

㉝ Jardín Japonés. This tranquil garden offers a sumptuous view over the skyscrapers of Las Condes and Bellavista. Walk past lily ponds on paths edged with bamboo and lit by Japanese lanterns. You'll find few more tranquil spots for a picnic than the gazebo beside a trickling fountain. ⊠ *Cerro San Cristóbal,* ☎ *no phone.* ☺ *Free.* ☉ *Daily 8:30 AM–10 PM. Metro: Pedro de Valdivia.*

㉚ Jardín Zoológico de Santiago. The Santiago Zoological Garden is a good place to see examples of many Chilean animals, some nearly extinct, that you might not otherwise encounter. As is often the case with many older zoos, the creatures aren't given a lot of room. Be careful with children, as some of the cages aren't properly protected, and the animals can bite. A larger, modern zoo is being built outside the city near the Universidad de Chile. ⊠ *Cerro San Cristóbal,* ☎ *no phone.* ☺ *Admission.* ☉ *Oct.–Mar., Tues.–Sun. 9–7; Apr.–Sept., Tues.–Sun. 10–6. Metro: Baquedano*

★ **㉘ La Chascona.** This house designed by the Nobel-winning poet Pablo Neruda was dubbed the "Woman with the Tousled Hair" after Mathilde Urrutia, the poet's third wife. The two met while strolling in nearby Parque Forestal, and for many years the house served as a romantic hideaway before the two were married. The pair's passionate relationship was recounted in the popular 1995 Italian film *Il Postino.* Tours allow you to step into the extraordinary mind of the poet whose eclectic designs led him to be called an "organic architect." Winding this way and that around Cerro San Cristóbal are garden paths, stairs, and bridges leading to the house where you'll find a library stuffed with books, a bedroom in a tower, and a secret passageway. Scattered about the rooms are the collections of butterflies, seashells, wineglasses, and other odd objects that inspired Neruda's tumultuous life and romantic poetry. Neruda, who died in 1973, had two other houses on the coast—one in Valparaíso and one in Isla Negra. All three are open as museums. Though it's not as magical as the other two, La Chascona can still set your imagination dancing. ⊠ *Fernando Márquez de la Plata 0192,* ☎ *2/777–8741.* ☺ *Admission.* ☉ *Tues.–Sun. 10–1 and 3–6. Metro: Baquedano.*

☾ **㉛ Plaza Tupahue.** The middle stop on the telesférico deposits you in the center of Parque Metropolitano. The main attraction here in summer is the delightful **Piscina Tupahue,** a 46-meter (150-ft) pool with a rocky crag running along one side. If this one is too crowded, try the nearby **Piscina Antilén.** Beside the pool is the 1925 **Torreón Victoria,** a stone tower surrounded by a trellis of bougainvillea. From Plaza Tupahue you can follow a path to **Plaza de Juegos Infantiles Gabriela Mistral**, a popular playground. ⊠ *Cerro San Cristóbal,* ☎ *no phone.* 🎟 *Admission.* ⊙ *Piscina Tupahue: Nov.–Mar., Tues.–Sun. 10–7. Piscina Antilén pool: Nov.–Mar., Wed.–Mon. 10–7. Metro: Pedro de Valdivia.*

Parque Quinta Normal Area

Just west of downtown is shady Parque Quinta Normal, a 1-acre park with three museums within its borders and another just across the street. This is an especially good place to take the kids, as all the museums were designed to stimulate eager young minds. Originally three times its current size, the park was created in 1841 as a place to experiment with new agricultural techniques. On weekdays this is a great place for quiet strolls; on weekends you'll have to maneuver around all the noisy families. Pack a picnic or a soccer ball and you'll fit right in.

A Good Walk

Take a cab or the subway to the Estación Central stop. Outside the Metro is the **Estación Central de Ferrocarriles,** a graceful colossus that is the city's only functioning train station. Across the street is the **Planetario,** found on the southeast corner of the Universidad de Santiago, one of the city's two large universities. Walk five blocks north on Avenida Matucana to Avenida Portales. Half a block west is the colorful **Museo Artequín.** Across the street is the main entrance to **Parque Quinta Normal,** where you'll find the **Museo Ferroviario.** Avenida Las Palmas, a wide pedestrian path, leads through the park to the **Museo Nacional de Historia Natural** and the **Museo de Ciencia y Tecnología.**

TIMING AND PRECAUTIONS

You can visit the museums in and around the park, stroll through along a wooded path, and even row a boat on a lake, all within a few hours. The hour-long presentation at the planetarium is shown only on weekends.

Sights to See

Estación Central de Ferrocarriles. Inaugurated in 1897, Central Station is the city's last remaining train station, servicing Concepción and points south. The greenish iron canopy that once shielded the engines from the weather is flanked by two lovely beaux-arts edifices. A lively market keeps this terminal buzzing with activity. ⊠ *Av. O'Higgins at Av. Matacuna,* ☎ *2/376–8460.* 🎟 *Free.* ⊙ *Daily 6 AM–midnight. Metro: Estación Central.*

★ ℭ **Museo Artequín.** The resplendent Pabellón París is home to this interactive museum that teaches the fundamentals of art to children, but the pavilion itself is the real jewel. Constructed in 1889 by French architect Henri Picq to house Chile's exhibition in the famous 1889 Paris International Exposition (the same fair that unveiled Gustave Eiffel's skyline-defining tower), the prefabricated structure was packed up and shipped back to Santiago when the show was over. Its glass domes, Pompeiian-red walls, and blue-steel columns and supports make this national monument a diaphanous box of exquisite beauty. Weekdays, school groups explore the two floors of reproductions of famous artworks (there are no originals here), touch-screen computers, and didactic areas with titles like "Light and Shade" and "Composition." On weekends there are more guides available to lead you through the space and give the pavilion's history. Call ahead to request an English-speaking tour. ⊠ *Av. Portales 3530,* ☎ *2/681–8656,* 🌐 *www.netup.cl/artequin.* 🎟 *Admission.* ⊙ *Tues.–Fri. 9–5, weekends and holidays 11–6. Metro: Estación Central.*

 🕭 **Museo de Ciencia y Tecnologia.** This science and technology museum for children is rather unfocused but has a good collection of old phonographs and a dark and moody astronomy wing with exhibits that resemble overgrown science projects. It's worth a visit for its Internet room, which offers connections for 50¢ an hour. ⊠ *Parque Quinta Normal,* ☎ *2/681–6022 or 2/689–8026,* WEB *www.corpdicyt.cl.* 🞅 *Admission.* 🕓 *Tues.–Fri. 10–5:30, weekends and holidays 11–8. Metro: Estación Central.*

OFF THE
BEATEN PATH

CEMENTERIO GENERAL – It may be an unusual tourist attraction, but this cemetery in the northern part of the city tells a lot about traditional Chilean society. After passing through the lofty stone arches of the main entrance you find yourself on well-tended paths lined with marble mausolea, the squat mansions belonging to Chile's wealthy families. The 8- or 10-story "niches" farther along—literally concrete shelves housing thousands of coffins—resemble middle-class apartment buildings. Their inhabitants lie here until the rent runs out and they're evicted. As you're walking through Santiago's burial grounds, look for former President Salvador Allende's final resting spot. This is an emotionally charged place around September 11, the anniversary of the coup that resulted in Allende's untimely death and Pinochet's rise to power.

 🕭 **Museo Ferroviario.** Chile's once-mighty railroads have been relegated to history, but this acre of Quinta Normal Park keeps alive a bit of the romance. More than a dozen steam locomotives and three passenger coaches are set within quiet gardens with placards in Spanish and English describing their history and origin. You can board two of the trains and view the underside of another. Among the collection is the cross-Andes express, which crossed the mountain range between 1911 and 1971. In a re-creation of a typical station are photos and exhibits. ⊠ *Parque Quinta Normal, at Av. Las Palmas,* ☎ *2/681–4627,* WEB *www.corpdicvt.cl.* 🞅 *Admission.* 🕓 *Tues.–Fri. 10–5:30, weekends and holidays 11–6. Metro: Estación Central.*

 🕭 **Museo Nacional de Historia Natural.** The National Museum of Natural History serves as the centerpiece of Parque Quinta Normal. Paul Lathoud, who designed many of the city's best-known monuments, created the building to serve as the site of Chile's first International Exposition in 1875. The neoclassical monument, rebuilt and enlarged after being damaged by various earthquakes, is one of the country's most important museums. Though the exhibits are slightly outdated and there are no English texts to guide you, the large dioramas of stuffed animals against painted backdrops are still intriguing, as are the numerous stone heads from Easter Island. In the large central hall hangs a skeleton of an enormous blue whale that is sure to delight kids. ⊠ *Parque Quinta Normal,* ☎ *2/680–4600,* WEB *www.mnhn.cl.* 🞅 *Admission.* 🕓 *Tues.–Fri. 10–5:30, weekends 11–6. Metro: Estación Central.*

Planetario. The Universidad de Chile's planetarium dome mimics a universe of stars with a weekend show. ⊠ *Av. O'Higgins,* ☎ *2/776–2624.* 🞅 *Admission.* 🕓 *Weekend shows: 10, 12, 3, and 5. Metro: Estación Central.*

DINING

Santiago is overwhelming when it comes to dining, as hundreds of restaurants are strewn about the city. No matter your mood, there are likely to be half a dozen eateries within easy walking distance. Tempted to taste hearty Chilean fare? Pull up a stool at one of the counters at Vega Central and enjoy a traditional *pastel de choclo*. Craving seafood? Head to the Mercado Central, where you can choose from the fresh fish brought in that morning. Want a memorable meal? Trendy new restaurants are opening every day in neighborhoods like Bellavista, the most colorful of the city's dining districts. Hip Santiaguinos head here to hit the latest hot spots.

Also drawing crowds is Vitacura, where a complex of 10 restaurants called Borde Río opened in 2001. A 15-minute taxi ride from the center of the city, the neighborhood attracts a slightly more upscale crowd. El Bosque is the name for the string of two dozen restaurants along Avenida El Bosque Norte and Avenida Isidora Goyenechea in Las Condes. The emphasis is on creative cuisine, so you'll often be treated to familiar favorites with a Chilean twist. Finally, *Suecia* is what locals call the bars and restaurants that line the pedestrian streets of Avenida Suecia and Calle General Holley in Providencia. The focus is less on food and more on fun: the priority here is people-watching.

One of the most pleasing aspects of the city's dining scene is the relatively low price of a meal. While rates for luxury hotel rooms are commensurate with those in many other world capitals, the price of a gourmet meal is disproportionately low. It is difficult to find an entrée in Santiago that tops $15, though a dish of similar quality in other cities would cost much more. The size of the wine lists may also come as a pleasant surprise, as most people assume the best vintages have been exported. Consuming fine Chilean wines has becomes as trendy here over the past decade or so as it has in the United States and Europe.

Bellavista

Chilean

$$$-$$$$ ★ ✕ **El Camino Real.** On a clear day, treat yourself to the stunning views of the city through the floor-to-ceiling windows at this excellent restaurant atop Cerro San Cristóbal. The menu is remarkably varied, featuring choices such as pork tenderloin in mustard sauce with caramelized onions and warm scallop salad with quail eggs and asparagus. Oenophiles will appreciate the 168-bottle wine list featuring many Chilean vintages. Neophytes can head across a central courtyard to Bar Dalí, where they can organize an impromptu *degustación* of a half dozen varietals. Ask for the English-speaking sommelier, who will gladly discuss the selections with you. Downstairs is a small wine museum (called the *enoteca*) in a cellarlike space scattered with maps and vitrines filled with local bottles. ✉ *Parque Metropolitano,* ☎ 2/232–3381 or 2/233–1238. *Reservations essential. AE, DC, MC, V. Metro: Pedro de Valdivia or Baquedano.*

$$$ ★ ✕ **Como Agua Para Chocolate.** Inspired by Laura Esquivel's romantic 1989 novel *Like Water for Chocolate,* this Bellavista standout is one part restaurant, one part theme park. The idea is to focus on the aphrodisiacal qualities of food, so it shouldn't be surprising that one long table is actually an iron bed, with place settings arranged on a crisp white sheet. The food compares to the decor like the film version compares to the book: it's good, but not nearly as imaginative. *Ave de la pasión,* for instance, means Bird of Passion. It may be just chicken with mushrooms, but it's served on a copper plate. ✉ *Constitución 88,* ☎ 2/777–8740. *AE, DC, MC, V. Metro: Baquedano.*

$-$$ ★ ✕ **El Venezia.** Long before Bellavista became fashionable, this bare-bones picada was where movie stars and TV personalities rubbed elbows with the common people. While gourmands now head a block or two in either direction to the latest hot spots, tacky El Venezia still fills to capacity each day at lunch. And what's not to like? The beer is icy, the waiters are efficient, and the food is abundant. The *congrío frito* (fried conger eel) is delicious, as are the *costillar de chancho* (pork ribs). What

Santiago Dining and Lodging

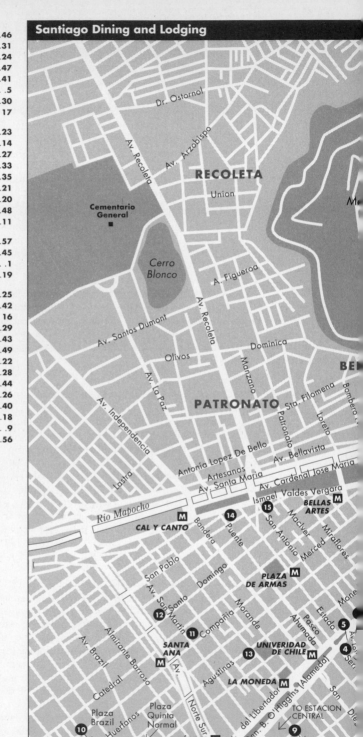

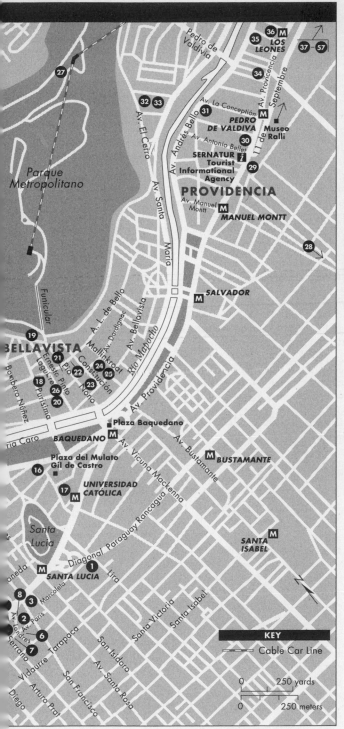

Lodging

they accomplish here is nothing short of a miracle—while you can't pinpoint exactly why, you leave tremendously satisfied. ⊠ *Pío Nono 200,* ☏ *2/737–0900. AE, DC, MC, V. Metro: Baquedano.*

$–$$ ✕ **Plaza Blue.** Awash in saffron and sky blue, the main dining room of this restaurant resembles a miniature town square. When students and young hipsters flock to this area on the weekends, live music accompanies the standard but solid Chilean fare. Try the *omelette al langostino* (crawfish omelet) or the *reineta a la plancha* (grilled sole). ⊠ *Pío Nono 185,* ☏ *2/732–3870. No credit cards. Closed Sun. Metro: Baquedano.*

Peruvian

$$ ✕ **Sarita Colonia.** Easily the most outrageous restaurant in Santiago, Sarita Colonia is a collection of colorful dining rooms, one more vibrant than the last. The food is authentic Peruvian—try the *cau cau* (scallops stewed with vegetables) or the *pollo al maní* (chicken with a spicy peanut sauce)—but the presentation is fun and fanciful. You can also stop by for a late-night cocktail in the second-floor lounge, relaxing on one of the plush white couches. ⊠ *Av. Dardignac 50,* ☏ *2/737–0242. No credit cards. Closed Sun. Metro: Baquedano.*

Seafood

$$ ✕ **Azul Profundo.** Not so many years ago, Deep Blue was the only restaurant you'd find on this street near Parque Metropolitano. Today it's but one of the dozens of restaurants in trendy Bellavista, but its two-level dining room, walls painted bright shades of blue and yellow and racks of wine stretching to the ceiling, ensure that it stands out in the crowd. Choose your fish from the extensive menu—swordfish, sea bass, shark, flounder, salmon, trout, and haddock are among the choices—and enjoy it or *a la plancha* (grilled) or *a la lata* (served on a sizzling plate with tomatoes and onions). Another popular dish called Isla Negra is reineta filled with cheese and chorizo. ⊠ *Constitución 111,* ☏ *2/738–0288. Reservations essential. AE, DC, MC, V. Metro: Baquedano.*

$$ ✕ **Todo Fresco.** As the name suggests, the seafood served here is the freshest possible—and to prove that fact, much of what's on the menu is displayed by the door. Peruvian chef Emilio Peschiera has designed a multitiered dining room flooded with natural light and filled with hanging plants. Try the *fettuccini a la sepia con salmón* (salmon with squid's ink pasta). ⊠ *Antonio Lopez de Bello 61,* ☏ *2/735–0988,* FAX *2/735–8215. AE, DC, MC, V. Metro: Baquedano.*

Spanish

$$ ✕ **La Esquina al Jerez.** After a thorough makeover, Bellavista's longtime favorite looks as good as any of the trendy newcomers. The iron lanterns and suits of medieval armor call to mind traditional Spanish restaurants, but the overall feeling here is contemporary, with billowing curtains and splashes of bright reds and yellows. The best dishes include a *paella de mariscos* (seafood with rice) and tapas like *calamares fritos al alioli* (fried squid with garlic mayonnaise). There are zarzuela dance performances and live jazz weekends. ⊠ *Dardignac 0192,* ☏ *2/777–4407. Reservations essential. AE, DC, MC, V. Closed Sun. Metro: Baquedano.*

$–$$ ✕ **La Bodeguilla.** This authentic Spanish restaurant is a great place to stop for a glass of sangria after a tour of Cerro San Cristóbal. After all, it's right at the foot of the funicular. The dozen or so tables are set among wine barrels and between hanging strings of garlic bulbs. *Chorizo riojano* (a piquent sausage), *pulpo a la gallega* (octopus with peppers and potatoes), and *queso manchego* (a mild white cheese) are tasty tapas you can share while perusing the long wine list. ⊠ *Av. Dominica 5,* ☏ *2/732–5215. AE, DC, MC, V. Metro: Baquedano.*

Vegetarian

$$ ✕ **El Viejo Verde.** A creative spirit fills this restaurant on a colorful street a block from Pablo Neruda's home of La Chascona. Rubén González, the amiable owner, has made everything from the menus to the flattened-leaf lamp shades. A patio in the back doubles as a performance space for lighthearted theatrical performances and live music on weekends. For an appetizer, try the cheese fondue or the *fondos de alcachofa* (artichokes stuffed with mushrooms and cheese). Sandwiches come on thick slices of bread (whole wheat is the specialty) that's baked on the premises twice a day. Homemade pastas come with a choice of four sauces: mushroom, herb, cheese, and fresh tomato. Desserts are also homemade, and the juices are freshly squeezed. ✉ *Antonio López de Bello 0110,* ☎ *2/735–0755. AE, DC, MC, V. Metro: Baquedano.*

Centro

Chilean

$$–$$$ ✕ **Bristol.** The indefatigable Guillermo Rodríguez, who has commandeered the kitchen here for more than a decade, has won just about all of the country's culinary competitions. No wonder he also serves as a private chef to Chilean President Ricardo Lagos. The restaurant's prime location in the Hotel Plaza San Francisco has made the lunch buffet a meeting point for Santiago's movers and shakers in politics and business. Besides the innovative takes on traditional Chilean dishes, the buffet includes unlimited access to a wine cart stocked with a dozen quality vintages. Friendly Alejandro Farias, the city's most prized sommelier, is happy to discuss the choices with you. His affable expertise is reason alone to visit. ✉ *Av. O'Higgins 816,* ☎ *2/360–4000,* ✆ *2/639–8975. AE, DC, MC, V. Metro: Universidad de Chile.*
★

$$ ✕ **Torres.** Facing Avenida O'Higgins, this longtime favorite claims to be the oldest eatery in Santiago Centro. The shiny wooden bar, lazily turning fans, and antique fixtures transport you back to an earlier era. Specialties range from classic Chilean dishes to lighter fare such as sandwiches, making it a perfect spot for lunch. On Thursday through Saturday nights, tango and bolero dancers take to the floor. ✉ *Av. O'Higgins 1570,* ☎ *2/698–6220. AE. Closed Sun. Metro: Los Héroes.*

French

$$ ✕ **Les Assassins.** Although it appears to be a rather somber bistro, nothing could be further from the truth. The service is friendly and the Provence-influenced food is first-rate. The steak au poivre and crêpes suzette would make a Frenchman's eyes water. If you want to practice your Spanish, there's always a line of talkative locals in the cozy ground-floor bar. ✉ *Merced 297,* ☎ *2/638–4280. AE, DC, MC, V. Closed Sun. Metro: Universidad Católica.*

Japanese

$$ ✕ **Japón.** Take off your shoes, settle onto a cushion, and prepare for authentic flavors from the floating kingdom. Frequented by Santiago's small but growing Japanese community, this restaurant off Plaza Baquedano offers a first-rate sushi bar and three comfortable dining rooms. The most patient waiters in town help you make a selection. The *unagi* (eel) is fantastic, and the noodle soup is a meal in itself. ✉ *Marcoleta 39,* ☎ *2/222–4517. AE, DC, MC, V. Metro: Santa Lucía.*

Peruvian

$$ ✕ **Cocoa.** Although Cocoa's two branches are probably the two smallest restaurants in Santiago, these longtime favorites make up for their lack of size with delicious Peruvian cuisine. The pisco sours are potent, and the ceviche is the best in town. There's no menu, as the daily specials are simply recited by the owner. The cheesecake is homemade, and

the *suspiro limeño* (a meringue-topped lemon dish) is so popular it is sold at other area establishments. ⊠ *José Victorino Lastarria 297,* ☎ *2/632–1272, Metro: Universidad Católica;* ⊠ *Antonia Lope de Bello 60,* ☎ *2/735–0634, Metro: Baquedano. AE, DC, MC, V. Closed Sun.*

Seafood

$–$$ ✕ **Donde Augusto.** Inside bustling Mercado Central, Donde Augusto
★ offers the best values on seafood in town. If you don't mind the un-hurried service and the odd tear in the tablecloth, you'll have the time of you life dining on everything from sea urchins to ceviche. Placido Domingo eats here on every visit to Chile, attended to by the white-bearded Segovian Augusto Vasquez, who has run this eatery for more than four decades. If you can't get a table, try one of the many stalls in the nearby fish market, which may not look especially clean but do serve the freshest seafood in Santiago. ⊠ *Mercado Central,* ☎ *2/672–2829. Reservations not accepted. AE, DC, MC, V. No dinner. Metro: Puente Cal y Canto.*

Vegetarian

$ ✕ **Govinda's.** Cheap but hearty vegetarian lunches are prepared here by Hari Krishnas. Card tables and lawn chairs are the extent of the decor, but the fresh juices and homemade bread are delicious. Try the yogurt with mixed fruit and honey for dessert. ⊠ *Av. Compañía 1489,* ☎ *2/673–0892. No credit cards. Closed weekends. Metro: Santa Ana.*

Las Condes

Chilean

$$–$$$ ✕ **Balthasar.** Contemporary cuisine with a Chilean twist is served in this carefully restored adobe stable on the eastern end of Las Condes. A rough-hewn wooden trestle table in the center of the small dining room groans under the weight of a buffet of exquisite salads and inventive hors d'oeuvres that borrow from Indonesian, Japanese, Chinese, Middle Eastern, and other flavorings. The scallops and stuffed trout with olive sauce are superb. ⊠ *Av. Las Condes 10690,* ☎ FAX *2/215–1090. AE, DC, MC, V. Closed Sun. No lunch. Metro: Escuela Militar.*

$$–$$$ ✕ **Gernika.** The Basque owners of this wood-and-stone restaurant have created a little slice of their homeland with black-and-white photos of traditional scenes, tapestries bearing an ancient coat of arms, and even jai alai equipment. Head upstairs to the more intimate upper level, which has three well-decorated private dining salons. Chilean seafood is cooked with Spanish flair, as in the *congrio donostiarra* (conger eel coated in chili sauce and fried in olive oil). The wine list includes several selections from Spain's Rioja region. ⊠ *Av. El Bosque Norte 227,* ☎ *2/232–9752. Reservations essential. AE, DC, MC, V. Metro: Tobalaba.*

German

$$–$$$ ✕ **München.** You can't help but question the authenticity of a restaurant that names itself after a German city but doesn't stock Löwenbräu—or any other brau, for that matter. Only three German dishes—bratwurst, sauerbraten, and strudel—can be found on the large menu of Chilean fare. Most people come not for the food, but to sit outside and watch shoppers stroll along fashionable Avenida El Bosque Norte. Unlike most restaurants in the area, which open at 1 for lunch and 8 for dinner, München is open from 11 AM until midnight. ⊠ *Av. El Bosque Norte 204,* ☎ *2/246–1222. AE, DC, MC, V. Metro: Tobalaba.*

Indian

$–$$ ✕ **Taj Mahal.** In a dining room adorned with silks of nearly every shade, this restaurant offers a spicy change from Chile's often bland cuisine. The curries aren't as fiery as you'd expect, but the flavors of the traditional tandoori dishes are as authentic as you'll find this far from India. ⌂ *Av. Isadora Goyenechea 3215,* ☎ *2/232–3606. AE, DC, MC, V. Metro: El Golf.*

Italian

$$$–$$$$ ✕ **Bice.** When it opened in mid-2001, Bice revolutionized Santiago's
★ notion of elegant dining. The small, two-tiered dining room has soaring ceilings that lend a dramatic flair without sacrificing intimacy. Gleaming floors of alternating stripes of dark and light wood and black leather banquettes in the bar add a touch of contemporary glamour. The service is a breed apart—a team of white-jacketed waiters are constantly zipping around to perform the actions your smallest gestures seem to imply. The *linguine alla Ciro* may be one of the more expensive dishes you'll find in Chile ($25 for one, $40 for two), but it's worth every peso: lobster comes in a split shell atop a generous plate of linguine mixed with scallops, razor clams, shrimp, and mussels. For dessert there's *cioccolatíssimo,* a hot chocolate soufflé with more melted chocolate on the inside, served with an exquisite *dulce de leche* ice cream over almonds and fruit slices. The wine list is an opinionated and refined account of Chile's finest bottles. ⌂ *Hotel Inter-Continental, Av. Luz 2920,* ☎ *2/381–5500. Reservations essential. AE, DC, MC, V. Metro: El Golf.*

$$–$$$ ✕ **Le Due Torri.** For excellent homemade pastas, head to this longtime favorite in Las Condes. The name, by the way, refers to the two towers erected by the dueling Garisenda and Asinelli families in the owner's native Bologna. If you think the agnolotti stuffed with ricotta cheese and spinach resembles a feathered hat, you're right. The owner, who lived in Italy during World War II, intentionally shaped it like a Red Cross nurse's cap. Another excellent dish is the agnolotti *panna e funghi,* which comes with mushrooms in a béchamel sauce. The rear of the dining room, with its small cypress trees and a corner pergola, is more traditional; seating in the front is stylish in a more contemporary mode. ⌂ *Av. Isadora Goyenechea 2908,* ☎ *2/231–4327. Reservations essential. AE, DC, MC, V. Metro: El Golf.*

Japanese

$–$$ ✕ **Matsuri.** With a sleek design that calls to mind Los Angeles as much as Tokyo, this restaurant in the Hyatt Regency is one of Santiago's most stylish eateries. The decor's eclectic and bold mix of materials includes porous stone from China and wood from Madagascar. Downstairs are a sushi bar and two tatami rooms (no shoes allowed, but slippers are provided) with sliding privacy screens, while upstairs are two grill tables. Try the eight-piece dragon roll—cucumber and eel covered with avocado and smelt roe. ⌂ *Av. Presidente Kennedy 4601,* ☎ *2/363–3051,* 🖷 *2/218–2513. AE, DC, MC, V. Metro: Tobalaba.*

Mexican

$–$$ ✕ **Santa Fe.** Decorated in bright shades of blue, pink, and ocher, this Tex-Mex restaurant is always packed with Santiago's twentysomething crowd. If you're over 6 ft tall you'll have to stoop over in the main dining room, but it's worth it for the authentic guacamole, sizzling fajitas (with seafood or meat fillings), and frozen margaritas. Don't head here if you want a quiet meal, as it's always noisy. ⌂ *Av. Las Condes 10690,* ☎ *2/215–1091. AE, DC, MC, V. Metro: Escuela Militar.*

Seafood

$$–$$$ ✕ **Isla Negra.** The sails flying from the roof signal to diners that if it's seafood they're seeking, Isla Negra means business. It's named for a coastal town south of Santiago that was Nobel laureate Pablo Neruda's last home. The poet's favorite dish was conger eel soup, and you'll find it served here as a starter. Don't miss the empanadas stuffed with everything from cheese to razor clams. The *chupe de marisco*, a delicious seafood chowder, is served in a quaint earthenware bowl. ✉ *Av. El Bosque Norte 325,* ☎ *2/231–3118. Reservations essential. AE, DC, MC, V. Metro: Tobalaba.*

Thai

$–$$ ✕ **Anakena.** This spacious Thai eatery in the Hyatt Regency serves some
★ of the finest spicy food in Santiago. It also offers a unique way of ordering: you select a piece of fish or meat and then tell the chefs whether you want it cooked in the wok or on the grill. There's also a buffet with a terrific choice of dishes, including pork with walnuts and celery in a tangy sauce, and tiger prawns with lemongrass and cashews. The large terrace overlooks a lovely pool and gardens. ✉ *Av. Presidente Kennedy 4601,* ☎ *2/363–3177. AE, DC, MC, V. Metro: Tobalaba.*

Nuñoa

Chilean

$–$$ ✕ **Restorán Don Peyo.** For first-rate Chilean food, join the families that
★ pack into Don Peyo. With low ceilings and patched stucco walls, what this place lacks in aesthetics it makes up for in flavor. The hot sauce and the garlic spread are tasty, but meat dishes—especially a Chilean roast beef called *plateada*—are what put this restaurant on the map. ✉ *Av. Grecia 448 and Lo Encalada 465,* ☎ *2/274–0764. AE, DC, MC, V. Closed Sun. Metro: Irrazaval.*

Providencia

Chilean

$$–$$$ ✕ **El Cid.** Considered by critics to be among the city's top restaurants, El Cid is the culinary centerpiece of the classic Sheraton Santiago. The dining room is relatively small and simple, with views of the pool. All the excitement here is provided by the food, which is served with a flourish unmatched anywhere in town. Don't miss the famous *parrillada* of grilled seafood—king crab, prawns, squid, and scallops are served with a sweet, spicy sauce. If you're new to Chilean cuisine, you can't go wrong with the excellent lunch buffet, which includes a wide range of appetizers, entrées, and desserts, as well as unlimited wine. Afterwards, zip up to the hotel's 21st floor for an exhilarating view of Santiago. ✉ *Av. Santa María 1742,* ☎ *2/233–5000,* ☎ *2/234–1729. AE, DC, MC, V. Metro: Pedro de Valdivia.*

$–$$ ✕ **Liguria.** This extremely popular picada has three branches in the city where you can get reliable, typical Chilean food cheaply. A large selection of Chilean wine accompanies such favorites as *jardín de mariscos* (a shellfish stew) and the filling *casuela* (a stew of beef and potatoes). ✉ *Av. Providencia 1373,* ☎ *2/235–7914, Metro: Manuel Montt;* ✉ *Av. Providencia 2682,* ☎ *2/232–4918, Metro: Los Leones;* ✉ *Av. Las Condes 12265,* ☎ *2/243–6121, Metro: Escuela Militar. No credit cards.*

Seafood

$$–$$$$ ✕ **Aquí Está Coco.** The best seafood in Santiago is served up in a din-
★ ing room whose walls are covered with flotsam and jetsam found on Chilean beaches. Ask your waiter—or friendly owner "Coco" Pacheco—which fish was caught that day. This is a good place to try Chile's famous *machas* (clams) served with tomatoes and Parmesan cheese or

corvina (sea bass) grilled with plenty of butter. Don't miss the cellar, where you can sample wines from the extensive collection of Chilean vintages. ⊠ *La Concepción 236,* ☎ *2/235–8649,* FAX *2/236–2636. Reservations essential. AE, DC, MC, V. Closed Sun. Metro: Pedro de Valdiva*

Vegetarian

$$ ✕ **Café del Patio.** Hidden in the back of quaint Galería del Patio, this eatery is transformed into a bar at night. The chef uses all organic produce, half of which is grown in the owners' own garden. The chef's salad—with lettuce, tomato, hearts of palm, and Gruyère cheese—is exquisite. The menu also includes a handful of dishes with an Asian flair. ⊠ *Providencia 1670,* ☎ *2/236–1251. AE, DC, MC, V. Closed Sun. Metro: Pedro de Valdiva.*

$$ ✕ **El Huerto.** In the heart of Providencia, this vegetarian eatery has become a hangout for hip young Santiaguinos. Even the decor, with its wood paneling and high windows, feels healthy. Simple dishes like stir-fried veggies (made with organic produce) and pancakes stuffed with asparagus and mushrooms are full of flavor, but it is the hearty soups and freshly squeezed juices that register the highest praise. Try the tasty *jugo de zanahoria* (carrot juice). Besides lunch and dinner, those in the know also drop by for afternoon tea. ⊠ *Orrego Luco 054,* ☎ *2/233– 2690. AE, DC, MC, V. No lunch Sun. Metro: Pedro de Valdiva.*

Vitacura

Moroccan

$$–$$$ ✕ **Zanzibar.** Although you can order a tabouleh salad or lamb tagine, ★ this ostensibly Moroccan restaurant is more about conjuring up an exotic atmosphere than re-creating the cuisine of the region. (The first clue would be that Zanzibar isn't anywhere near Morocco.) The food is tasty, but the real reason to come is to glide across the multicolored mosaic floors and settle into a chair placed beneath dozens of silver lanterns. Tables are just as fanciful, with designs made from pistachio nuts, red peppers, beans, and other items. It's over-the-top, but it's the most fun you can have at the Borde Río restaurant complex. ⊠ *Av. Monseñor Escrivá de Balaguer 6400,* ☎ *2/218–0119. Reservations essential. AE, DC, MC, V.*

Seafood

$$–$$$ ✕ **Ibis de Puerto Varas.** The decor at this Borde Río restaurant is nattily nautical: sails stretch taut across the ceiling, pierced here and there by mastlike wood columns. The walls are a splashy blue. Choose from appetizers such as baby eels with hot pepper and garlic or shrimp and squid with an orange sauce. *Panqueque Ibis* is a pancake stuffed with shrimp, calamari, and scallops; the whole is sautéed in butter, flambéed in cognac, and served with a spinach and cream sauce. ⊠ *Av. Monseñor Escrivá de Balaguer 6400,* ☎ *2/218–0111,* FAX *2/218–0112. Reservations essential. AE, DC, MC, V.*

LODGING

Santiago's accommodations range from luxurious *hoteles* to comfortable *residenciales,* the Chilean equivalent of bed-and-breakfasts. The number of five-star properties has jumped in the past few years; the city now has more than a dozen—even more than Buenos Aires. Most newer hotels are in Providencia and Las Condes, a short taxi ride from Santiago Centro.

All this new construction means that although the official room rates are pricey, you'll undoubtedly find discounts. Call several hotels and ask for the best possible rate. It's still a good idea to reserve well in advance during the peak seasons (January–February and July–August).

The 18% hotel tax is removed from your bill if you pay in U.S. dollars or with a credit card. All hotels listed here include breakfast in the rate; the more expensive choices usually pull out the stops with an elaborate breakfast buffet.

Bellavista

$ ⊞ **Hotel Castillo.** The neon HOTEL sign doesn't do justice to this three-story mansion dating from 1925. The hotel is big with budget-minded travelers intent on spending their nights in the bars of Bellavista, so they don't seem to mind the basic accommodation and small baths. But with a savvier management this could be a lovely boutique hotel. It's hard not to look at the blue or green stained glass, the Spanish roof tile, and the delightful wooden balcony without asking yourself "what if?" ⊠ *Av. Pío Nono 420,* ☏ *2/735–0243. 18 rooms. AE, DC, MC, V. Metro: Baquedano.*

Centro

$$$$ ⊞ **Carrera.** Santiago's oldest luxury hotel, the Carrera occupies a
★ prominent corner of Plaza de la Constitución. The rooftop restaurant provides a matchless view of the country's most important square. Because it has been around for more than 60 years, the Carrera has the prestige that newer hotels lack. Like New York City's famed Waldorf Astoria, constructed around the same time, it has an opulent two-story lobby that preserves its original art deco murals. The suites overlooking the plaza have an air of distinction lent by the chintz draperies, prints of hunting scenes, and comfortable armchairs. The Copper Room is a great place to relax come lunch or dinner, and features a full sushi bar. The dark-paneled bar, enlivened by live jazz performances, is popular among business executives and politicos. ⊠ *Teatinos 180,* ☏ *2/698–2011; 800/223–6800 in the U.S.,* ℻ *2/672–1083,* Ⅷℰℬ *www.carrera.cl. 325 rooms, 30 suites. 3 restaurants, sushi bar, piano bar, in-room VCRs, minibars, no-smoking rooms, room service, pool, hair salon, golf privileges, aerobics, gym, racquetball, shops, solarium, laundry service, baby-sitting, concierge, business services, meeting room, travel services, free parking. AE, DC, MC, V. Metro: La Moneda, Plaza de Armas.*

$$$$ ⊞ **Hotel Plaza San Francisco.** Facing the historic Iglesia San Francisco,
★ this centrally located hotel has everything corporate travelers need, from business services to a convention center. Between meetings there's plenty to do—take a dip in the lovely pool, stroll through the art gallery, or select a bottle from the well-stocked wineshop. Bristol, the restaurant, has perhaps Chile's most talented chef. The hotel's cozy rooms have large beds, lovely antique furniture, and marble-trim baths. And while all these amenities are tremendous draws, one of the best reasons to choose this hotel is for its helpful, professional staff. ⊠ *Av. O'Higgins 816,* ☏ *2/360–4000,* ℻ *2/639–8975,* Ⅷℰℬ *www.hotelsanfrancisco.cl. 160 rooms, 20 suites. Restaurant, piano bar, lobby lounge, in-room data ports, in-room safes, minibars, room service, indoor pool, hot tub, massage, sauna, gym, laundry service, business services, convention center, meeting rooms, free parking. AE, DC, MC, V. Metro: Universidad de Chile.*

$$ ⊞ **Hotel Majestic.** Towering white pillars, peaked archways, and glittery brass ornaments welcome you to this Indian-inspired hotel. A welcoming staff and a location several blocks from the Plaza de Armas make the Majestic a good choice. Even though the bright, airy rooms have "soundproof" windows, ask for one facing away from the street. ⊠ *Santo Domingo 1526,* ☏ *2/695–8366,* ℻ *2/697–4051,* Ⅷℰℬ

www.hotel-majestic.co.cl. 50 rooms. Restaurant, bar, café, in-room safes, minibars, pool, free parking. AE, DC, MC, V. Metro: Santa Ana.

$ ⚏ **El Marqués del Forestal.** A good budget alternative for families, these small apartments sleep up to four people. The simply furnished rooms also have kitchenettes. The hotel has a great location overlooking Parque Forestal not far from Mercado Central. ⊠ *Ismael Valdés Vergara 740, ☎ 2/633–3462, ℻ 2/639–4157. 14 apartments with shower. Bar, kitchenettes, free parking. AE, DC, MC, V. Metro: Puente Cal y Canto.*

$ ⚏ **Foresta.** This seven-story hotel across the street from Cerro Santa Lucía gives you the feeling that you're staying in an elegant old home. Guest rooms with bronze and marble accents have cheery floral wallpaper and lovely antique furnishings. The best ones are those on the upper floors overlooking the hill. A rooftop restaurant and bar are a great place to enjoy the view. The quaint cafés and shops of Plaza Mulato Gil de Castro are just around the corner. ⊠ *Victoria Subercaseaux 353, ☎ ℻ 2/639–6261. 35 rooms, 8 suites. Restaurant, bar, piano bar. AE, DC, MC, V. Metro: Universidad Católica.*

$ ⚏ **Hotel Los Arcos.** Off Plaza Brasíl, this simple hotel has become a haven for young foreigners on a budget. Rooms are simple but clean, and some have windows overlooking an interior courtyard and café. ⊠ *Agustinas 2173, ☎ 2/699–0998 or 2/696–5602, ℻ 2/699–7998. 21 rooms. Café, room service, laundry service. DC, MC, V. Metro: República.*

$ ⚏ **Hotel Vegas.** This colonial-style building, adorned with a bullet-shape turret on the corner, is in the heart of the charming Londres/París neighborhood. To the north is the stunning Iglesia San Francisco. Rooms here have plenty of windows—ask for one with a view of gently curving Avenida Londres. ⊠ *Londres 49, ☎ 2/632–2498 or 2/632–2514, ℻ 2/632–5084. 20 rooms. Bar, café, room service, laundry service. AE, DC, MC, V. Metro: Universidad de Chile.*

$ ⚏ **Residencial Londres.** Built in the 1920s, this inexpensive hotel in the
★ picturesque Londres/París neighborhood is a stone's throw from most of the city's major sights. Rooms are spacious, with high ceilings ringed by detailed moldings and expansive wood floors. The best rooms have stone balconies overlooking this charmingly atypical neighborhood. The hosts are friendly and helpful. ⊠ *Londres 54, ☎ ℻ 2/638–2215. 27 rooms. No credit cards. Metro: Universidad de Chile.*

Las Condes

$$$$ ⚏ **Hotel Inter-Continental.** In late 2000 the Inter-Continental inaugurated a new wing, more than doubling the hotel's size. The new two-story marble lobby announces that you have entered one of the city's top hotels; once past the welcome desk, there are comfortable lounges, including one next to an indoor waterfall. In the back is Bice, one of the city's most memorable restaurants. Among the new design touches added during the renovation are doors made from handsome panels of the native blond wood called *mañio*. Inside the sumptuous rooms, a menu card offers a choice of five types of pillows, from "very soft" to "stiff." Five executive floors feature express check-in, a sleek private dining area with open bar, and an elegant meeting room. ⊠ *Av. Vitacura 2885, ☎ 2/394–2000, ℻ 2/251–7814, ⅦⒺⒷ www.interconti.com. 285 rooms, 10 suites. 2 restaurants, 2 bars, lobby lounge, piano bar, in-room data ports, in-room safes, in-room VCRs, kitchenettes, minibars, no-smoking floors, room service, indoor pool, massage, sauna, aerobics, gym, shops, laundry service, concierge, business services, convention center, meeting rooms, travel services, free parking. AE, DC, MC, V. Metro: El Golf.*

$$$$ ⚏ **Hyatt Regency.** The soaring spire of the Hyatt Regency leaves a lasting impression, especially if you're shooting up a glass elevator through

a 24-story atrium. An architectural eye-catcher, the hotel has rooms that wrap around the cylindrical lobby, providing you with a truly panoramic view of the Andes. Executive suites in the upper-floor Regency Club offer express check-in, a billiards room, and a private dining area. Duke's, the spitting image of an English pub, fills to standing capacity each day after work hours. The hotel's three restaurants—Tuscan, Thai, and Japanese—are all worth the trip. A glass-walled health club, in a separate three-story wing, has trainers on hand to help you with your workout. If tennis is your game, instructors are on call. Children enjoy the delightful lagoon-style pool, complete with a wide 10-ft waterfall. ⊠ *Av. Presidente Kennedy 4601,* ☎ *2/218–1234,* FAX *2/218–2513,* WEB *www.santiago.hyatt.com. 287 rooms, 22 suites. 3 restaurants, bar, lobby lounge, sushi bar, in-room data ports, in-room fax, in-room VCRs, minibars, no-smoking floor, room service, pool, barbershop, hair salon, massage, sauna, 2 tennis courts, aerobics, health club, baby-sitting, laundry service, concierge, business services, convention center, meeting rooms. AE, DC, MC, V.*

$$$$ 🏨 **Radisson Royal.** Santiago's most dynamic office building, the World
★ Trade Center, is also home to the Radisson Royal, a combination that will make sense to many corporate travelers. The hotel offers amenities—personal mobile phones, fine linen bedding, a boutique line of beauty products in the baths—that let you know service is a priority. Most high-rise hotels in Las Condes and Providencia have great views; the windows here are huge, with three wide glass panels for triptych perspectives of the city and the Andes beyond. The upholstered leather chairs and wood paneling in meeting rooms make it clear the hotel is serious in its attitude toward luxury. That includes, of course, rooftop parking for your helicopter. ⊠ *Av. Vitacuria 2610,* ☎ *2/203–6000 or toll free 123/00–206657 in Chile,* FAX *2/203–6003,* WEB *www.radisson.com/santiagocl. 159 rooms, 25 suites. Restaurant, bar, in-room data ports, in-room safes, minibars, no-smoking rooms, room service, indoor pool, gym, library, baby-sitting, laundry service, concierge, business services, meeting rooms, helipad, free parking. AE, DC, MC, V. Metro: Tobalaba.*

$$$ 🏨 **Hotel Tarapacá.** This smaller hotel may have a smudge here and there, but its location in fashionable Las Condes makes up for it. Rooms facing the commercial hub of Avenida Apoquindo are susceptible to traffic noise, so ask for one in the back. Better yet, pay a few extra dollars for one of two spacious suites on the 11th floor. The dormer windows make you feel that you're in a garret. ⊠ *Vecinal 40, at Av. Apoquindo,* ☎ *2/245–1430,* FAX *2/245–1440. 52 rooms. Restaurant, bar, in-room safes, minibars, room service, sauna, laundry service, meeting rooms, free parking. AE, DC, MC, V. Metro: El Golf or Tobalaba.*

$$ 🏨 **Hotel Montebianco.** This four-floor hotel has a professional attitude that many larger places lack. The rooms, which wind around a central staircase, are on the small side; the king-size beds take up most of the space. A few dollars more secures a room with more elbow room. The hotel is in Las Condes, right on one of the city's main dining thoroughfares. ⊠ *Av. Isidora Goyenechea 2911,* ☎ *2/232–5034,* FAX *2/233–0420,* WEB *www.hotelmontebianco.co.cl. 33 rooms. Bar, cafeteria, in-room safes, minibars, laundry service, airport shuttle. AE, DC, MC, V. Metro: El Golf.*

Providencia

$$$$ 🏨 **Four Points Sheraton.** This small luxury hotel, which opened in 2000, is just steps from the Río Mapocho and the heart of Providencia's shopping district. The cool rooftop terrace is a real pleasure in summer, when you can relax with a pisco sour while enjoying the panoramic views of the city. For those more interested in nightlife, the hotel is adjacent to one of the city's main party thoroughfares: A sidewalk links the hotel to the pedestrian streets of Calles General Holley and Avenida Suecia, lined with pubs, restaurants, and discos. Rooms that face these streets can be noisy, even through double-paned windows. ⊠ *Av. Santa Magdalena 111,* ☎ *2/750–0300,* FAX *2/750–0350,* WEB *www.fourpoints.com. 112 rooms, 16 suites. Restaurant, bar, in-room data ports, in-room safes, no-smoking rooms, room service, pool, sauna, gym, solarium, laundry service, business services, convention center, meeting rooms, travel services, free parking. AE, DC, MC, V. Metro: Los Leones.*

$$$$ 🏨 **Park Plaza.** It bills itself as a "classic European-style" hotel, and the receptionists that greet you from behind individual mahogany desks certainly call to mind the Continent. The refined decor, with rich burgundy and cream accents, extends to the adjoining Park Lane restaurant, whose chef masterfully combines international and Chilean cuisine. The glass-covered pool on the top floor offer great views of the city. ⊠ *Av. Ricardo Lyon 207,* ☎ *2/233–6363,* FAX *2/233–6668,* WEB *www.parkplaza.cl. 104 rooms, 6 suites. Restaurant, bar, indoor pool, sauna, health club, business services. AE, DC, MC, V. Metro: Los Leones.*

$$$$ 🏨 **Sheraton Santiago and San Cristóbal Tower.** Two distinct hotels stand
★ side-by-side at this unrivaled resort. The Sheraton Santiago is a luxury hotel with all the amenities that you would expect. The adjoining San Cristóbal Tower, on the other hand, is in a class all its own. Constructed in 1998, it has become the favorite of business executives and foreign dignitaries who value its efficiency, elegance, and impeccable service. A labyrinthine marble lobby—which links the two hotels, three fine restaurants, and the city's largest hotel convention center—is lavish in a way unthinkable here a decade ago. Rooms are tastefully decorated in soft cream tones and come equipped with stereos, VCRs, and CD players. But pampering is not all that goes on at the San Cristóbal Tower—the attentive staff at the business center provide guests with everything from secretarial services to Internet access. The complex is at the foot of Parque Metropolitano, providing some of the best views to be found in Santiago. ⊠ *Av. Santa María 1742,* ☎ *2/ 233–5000,* FAX *2/234–1732,* WEB *www.sheraton.cl. Sheraton Santiago: 379 rooms, 14 suites; San Cristóbal Tower: 139 rooms, 12 suites. 3 restaurants, 2 bars, lobby lounge, picnic area, in-room data ports, in-room safes, minibars, 2 pools, sauna, gym, laundry service, concierge, business services, convention center, meeting rooms, travel services. AE, DC, MC, V. Metro: Pedro de Valdiva.*

$$ 🏨 **Hotel Bonaparte.** Resembling a small château, this charming hotel on tree-lined Avenida Ricardo Lyon is often overshadowed by its showier neighbors. The rooms with the most light are on the top floor, but all are tastefully decorated and have large baths. On the ground floor is a small restaurant and a cozy lounge. There's also free Internet access. ⊠ *Av. Ricardo Lyon 1229,* ☎ *2/274–0621,* FAX *2/204–8907,* WEB *www.hotelbonaparte.com. 25 rooms, 2 suites. Restaurant, lobby lounge, room service, pool, sauna, laundry service, free parking. AE, DC, MC, V. Metro: Los Leones.*

$$ 🏨 **Hotel Orly.** This is a rare find—a moderately priced hotel with all
★ the comforts of those costing twice as much. That you can find a treasure like this in the middle of Providencia is nothing short of a miracle. The shiny wood floors, country-manor furnishings, and glass-domed breakfast room make this hotel as sweet as it is economical. Most of the credit can go to the owner, who decorated it herself. Rooms come in all shapes and sizes, so ask to see a few before you decide. Cafetto, the downstairs café, has some of the finest coffee drinks in town. ⊠ *Av. Pedro de Valdivia 27,* ☎ *2/231–8947,* FAX *2/252–0051,* WEB *www.orlyhotel.com. 25 rooms, 3 suites. Restaurant, café, in-room data ports,*

in-room safes, minibars, room service. AE, DC, MC, V. Metro: Pedro de Valdivia.

Vitacura

$$$ 🏨 **Hotel Kennedy.** This glass tower may seem impersonal, but the small details—such as beautiful vases of flowers atop the wardrobes—show the staff cares about each guest. Bilingual secretarial services and an elegant boardroom are among the pluses for visiting executives. The Aquarium restaurant has a first-rate French chef, delicious international cuisine, and a cellar full of excellent Chilean wines. ⊠ *Av. Presidente Kennedy 4570,* ☎ *2/219–4000,* ℻ *2/218–2188,* 🌐 *www.hotelkennedy.cl. 133 rooms, 10 suites. Restaurant, bar, room service, pool, beauty salon, gym, laundry service, business services, meeting rooms, travel services, free parking. AE, DC, MC, V.*

$$ 🏨 **Acacias de Vitacura.** This hotel's extraordinary location, in the midst of towering eucalyptus and acacia trees thought to be more than a century old, is unforgettable. You'll want to have your morning coffee in the lush garden under one of the oversize umbrellas. The rooms here are simple but have lots of light. The owner's collection of old carriages gives the hotel a quirky personality. ⊠ *El Manantial 1781,* ☎ *2/211–8601,* ℻ *2/212–7858,* 🌐 *www.hotelacacias.cl. 36 rooms, 2 suites. Dining room, minibars, pool, meeting room. AE, DC, MC, V.*

NIGHTLIFE AND THE ARTS

After years of curfews and crackdowns under Pinochet's regime, Santiago has become a more interesting place after dark. Although it still can't rival Buenos Aires or Rio de Janeiro, Santiago buzzes with increasingly sophisticated bars and clubs. Santiaguinos often meet for drinks during the week, usually right after work when most bars have happy hour. Then they call it a night, as most people don't really cut loose until Friday and Saturday. Weekends commence with dinner beginning at 9 or 10, and then a drink at a pub. (This doesn't refer to an English beer hall—it means bars with loud music and a lot of seating.) No one thinks of heading to the dance clubs until 1, and they stay until 5 or 6.

With dozens of museums scattered around the city, it's clear Santiaguinos also have a strong love of culture. Music, theater, and other artistic endeavors supplement weekends spent dancing the night away.

Nightlife

Bars and clubs are scattered all over Santiago, but a handful of streets have such a concentration of establishments that they resemble block parties on Friday and Saturday nights. Try pub-crawling with all the well-heeled young locals on Avenida Suecia in the chic neighborhood of Providencia. Calle General Holley, which runs parallel to it, is also worth a try. Most establishments here try to lure you in with drink specials; it takes a while to get used to people bartering with you as you walk past. The crowd here is very young, as the drinking age is 16. To the east in Las Condes, Paseo San Damián is an outdoor complex of bars and clubs. It's the newest and most fashionable of nighttime destinations. If you're looking for something a little more bohemian, head for Avenida Pío Nono, the main drag through the colorful neighborhood of Bellavista. Although slightly seedy, the web of streets is filled with cutting-edge clubs.

What you should wear depends on your destination. Bellavista has a mix of styles ranging from blue jeans to basic black. Avenida Suecia has a stricter dress code (sneakers might bar you from admission), as does Paseo San Damián. Note that establishments referred to as "night clubs" are female strip shows.

Bars and Clubs

BELLAVISTA

As hip as ever, **Oz** (⊠ Chucre Mansur 6, ☎ 2/737–7066) is still among the best dance clubs in Bellavista. The DJs play a good mix of techno, hip-hop, and jazz-funk. A huge stairway winds down from the upper bar to the wide dance floor, so if you want to make a spectacle of yourself, this is the place to do it. **Tantra** (⊠ Ernesto Pinto Lagarrigue 154, ☎ 2/732–3268) is a sleek, stylish newcomer. Stop by for a drink earlier in the evening and watch the restaurant transform itself into a disco at midnight. The beat goes on until 6 AM, unless one of the frequent after-hours parties keep it open even later. Upstairs are king-size beds used as tables—reserve one for a memorable evening.

The **Libro Café** (⊠ Purísima 165, Bellavista, ☎ 2/735–0928) is a late-night haunt for starving artists and those who wish they were. If you're hungry, head here for a *tortilla malageña* and a carafe of the house red.

CENTRO

From the doorway, **Casa de Cena** (⊠ Almirante Simpson 20, Santiago Centro, ☎ 2/635–4418) looks like your average hole in the wall. It's actually a gem. Most nights a band wanders through the maze of wood-paneled rooms singing folk songs while the bartender listens to endless stories from inebriated regulars.

PROVIDENCIA

The **Phone Box** (⊠ Av. Providencia 1670, ☎ 2/235–9972) is a fairly convincing recreation of a British pub that serves steak-and-kidney pie to homesick Brits. You'll easily spot the entrance—it's through a red phone booth. If you feel like playing some eight ball, **Boomerang** (⊠ General Holley 2285, ☎ 2/334–5081) is a raucous pub with a few pool tables.

Most of the neighborhood's nightspots are found along the pedestrian street of Avenida Suecia. One of the most popular is **Mister Ed** (⊠ Av. Suecia 152, ☎ 2/231–2624), the best place to hear up-and-coming local bands. Next door to Mr. Ed is the **Green Bull** (⊠ Av. Suecia 150, ☎ 2/334–5619), which competes for pretty much the same crowd with live performances nightly.

Entre Negros (⊠ Suecia 188, ☎ 2/334–2094) might be the most popular of Avenida Suecia's discos. This longtime favorite also features live music on weekends. **Cayo Hueso** (⊠ Av. Suecia 170, ☎ 2/334–7724) books bands playing all types of music, from pop to rock.

Gay and Lesbian Clubs

Once mostly underground, Santiago's gay scene is starting to assert itself. Although some bars are so discreet they don't have a sign, others are known by just about everyone. Clubs like Bunker, for example, are so popular that they attract a fair number of nongays. There's no real gay district, but a cluster of gay restaurants and bars are found on the streets parallel to Avenida Pío Nono in Bellavista.

While there are few open displays of same-sex affection in public, Chile is at least as tolerant of gays as most other South American countries. The government eliminated the prohibition on gay sex in 1999.

Bunker (⊠ Bombero Nuñez 159, Bellavista, ☎ 2/737–1716), a mainstay of the gay scene, is in a cavernous space with numerous platforms overlooking the dance floor. Don't get here too early—people don't arrive until well after midnight. On Bellavista's main drag, **Bokhara**

(✉ Pío Nono 430, Bellavista, ☎ 2/732–1050) is one of the city's most popular gay discos. It has two dance floors playing house and techno.

In business for more than 20 years, the venerable **Fausto** (✉ Av. Santa María, Providencia, ☎ 2/777–1041) has polished wood paneling that calls to mind a gentlemen's club. The disco is pumping until the wee hours. **Blondie** (✉ Av. O'Higgins 2879, Centro, ☎ no phone) attracts a young crowd with its loud music and outlandish drag shows.

Look, it's Cher! New on the scene in Bellavista is **Drag Queen** (✉ Bombero Nuñez 169, Bellavista, ☎ 2/738–2301), a two-story bar where performers dressed as Madonna and other celebrities entertain a mixed crowd. If you're looking for a place to kick back with a beer, **Vox Populi** (✉ Ernesto Pinto Lagarrigue 342, Bellavista, ☎ no phone) is a tiny bar with a patio where you can sit on sunny days.

There's not much for lesbians in Santiago, although some women can be found at most establishments catering to men. **Sui Generis** (✉ Bombero Nuñez 363, ☎ no phone) is the only honest-to-goodness lesbian bar in town.

Salsa Clubs

Cimarrón (✉ Av. Irarrázabal 1730, Nuñoa, ☎ 2/225–1627), with salsa and tango classes on Wednesday and Thursday nights, is the perfect spot to learn how to shake to a tropical beat. On Fridays and Saturdays this *salsoteca* comes alive with sensuous salsa, merengue, and milonga.

For salsa and merengue, try **Ilé Habana** (✉ Bucarest 95, Providencia, ☎ 2/231–5711), where you can boogie to the beat of a live band. There are free salsa lessons Tuesday to Saturday at 9:30 PM. **Arriba de la Bola** (✉ General Holley 171, Providencia, ☎ 2/232–7965) gets things going with a live Cuban band. It gets packed, so reservations are necessary.

The Arts

Dance
The venerable **Ballet Nacional Chileno** (✉ Av. Providencia 43, Santiago Centro, ☎ 2/634–4746), founded in 1945, performs from its repertoire of more than 150 pieces at at the Teatro Universidad de Chile near Plaza Baquendano.

Film
Santiago's dozens of cinemas screen movies in English with Spanish subtitles. Movie listings are posted in *El Mercurio,* the country's largest newspaper, as well as the other dailies. Admission is $2.50 to $5, with half-price shows on Wednesdays. The newest multiplexes—with mammoth screens, plush seating, and fresh popcorn—are in the city's malls. Among the best theaters in town is the **Cinemark 12** (✉ Av. Presidente Kennedy 9001, Las Condes, ☎ 2/213–1323), in the Alto Las Condes mall. Its dozen screens show the latest releases. In the Parque Arauco mall, **Showcase Cinemas** (✉ Av. Presidente Kennedy 5413, Las Condes, ☎ 2/224–7707) has the city's most modern facility. Two smaller theater complexes have opened in Santiago Centro. **Hoyts Huérfanos** (✉ Huérfanos 735, Santiago Centro, ☎ 600/500–0400) boasts six screens. **Hoyts San Agustín** (✉ San Antonio 144, Santiago Centro, ☎ 600/500–0400) has nine screens. Most of the city's art cinemas tend to show international favorites. The old standby is **El Biógrafo** (✉ José Victorino Lastarria 181, Santiago Centro, ☎ 2/633–4435), which shows foreign films on its single screen. It's on a colorful street lined with cafés. **Cine Arte Normandie** (✉ Av. Tarapacá 1181, Santiago Centro, ☎ 2/697–2979) is a popular theater south of Iglesia San Fran-

cisco. Affiliated with one of the city's universities, the **Centro de Extensión Universidad Católica** (⊠ Av. O'Higgins 390, Santiago Centro, ☎ 2/635–1994) only screens the classics.

Galleries

The city's galleries are scattered around the city. Admission is usually free. Near Plaza Baquendano, **Sala de Arte Fundación Telefónica** (⊠ Av. Providencia 111, Santiago Centro, ☎ 2/634–4746) has very good exhibits of painting and sculpture in the lobby of the foundation's 32-story headquarters. It's open Tuesday to Sunday 10–8. At the foot of Cerro San Cristóbal, **Galería del Cerro** (⊠ Antonía López de Bello 135, Bellavista, ☎ 2/737–3500, WEB www.delcerro.cl) features works by prominent local artists. The bright and airy gallery is a short walk from Pablo Neruda's home of La Chascona. It's open weekdays 10:30–6:30 and Saturday 10:30–2. **Galería Isabel Aninat** (⊠ Alonso de Córdova 3053, Providencia, ☎ 2/263–2729) hosts exhibitions of international artists. It's open weekdays 10–8, Saturday 11–2 and 4–7, and Sunday 11–2.

Music

The city has two outstanding venues for classical music. The **Teatro Municipal** (⊠ San Antonio at Agustinas, Santiago Centro, ☎ 2/633–2549), Santiago's 19th-century theater, presents excellent classical concerts, opera, and ballet by internationally recognized artists throughout the March–December season. The Coro Sinfónico and the Orquestra Sinfónica, the city's highly regarded chorus and orchestra, perform near Plaza Baquendano at the **Teatro Universidad de Chile** (⊠ Providencia 43, Santiago Centro, ☎ 2/634–4746).

Theater

Provided that you understand at least a little Spanish, you should take in a bit of Chilean theater. Its widely regarded to be among the best in Latin America. Performances take place all year, mainly from Thursday to Sunday at around 8 PM. In February the year's best plays are performed across the city in a program called *Teatro A Mil,* referring to the admission price of 1,000 pesos (less than $2). Contact the tourist office for details.

The well respected ICTUS theater company performs in the **Teatro la Comedia** (⊠ Merced 349, Santiago Centro, ☎ 2/639–1523). **Teatro la Feria** (⊠ Crucero Exeter 0250, Bellavista, ☎ 2/737–7371) mounts Chilean versions of English comedies. **El Conventillo** (⊠ Bellavista 173, Bellavista, ☎ 2/777–4164) produces a mixed offering of Latin American comedies and dramas.

OUTDOOR ACTIVITIES AND SPORTS

Participant Sports

Athletic Clubs and Spas

All of Santiago's larger hotels have health clubs on the premises, usually with personal trainers on hand to assist you with your workout. Even if you aren't staying at a particular hotel, you can usually pay to use the facilities for the day. **Balthus** (⊠ Av. Monseñor Escivá De Balaguer 5970, Vitacura, ☎ 2/218–1831), is the city's top health club. This high-tech marvel, which opened in 2001, features all the latest equipment. You feel healthier just by walking into the complex, a sleek series of riverside structures in concrete and glass designed by Santiago's ArchiPlan. There are eight tennis courts, spas, pools, and numerous fitness programs.

The modern **Günter Mund** (⊠ Cardenal Belarmino 1075, Vitacura, ☎ 2/211–6104) is a sprawling aquatic spa where you can relax in saunas and hot tubs. Better yet, pamper yourself with one of the range of facials that are available. **Agua y Bién** (⊠ Americo Vespucio Norte 1440, Vitacura, ☎ 2/371–6554), a smaller club, also offers massage, hydrotherapy, and other spa treatments.

Bicycling

Santiago has no shortage of public parks, and they offer good opportunities to see the city. If you're ambitious you can even pedal up Cerro San Cristóbal, the city's largest hill. Rent mountain bikes at **Bys** (⊠ Av. Miraflores and Av. Santo Domingo, Santiago Centro, ☎ 2/633–7600).

Spectator Sports

Horse Racing

Betting on the horses is popular in Santiago, which is the reason the city has two large racetracks. The **Club Hípico** (⊠ Blanco Encalada 2540, ☎ 2/683–6535) is south of downtown next to Parque O'Higgins. Races are Mondays and alternating Wednesdays. El Ensayo, an annual race that's a century-old tradition, is held here in early November. **Hipódromo Chile** (⊠ Hipódromo Chile 1715, Independencia, ☎ 2/736–9276) is the home of the prestigious Gran Premio Internacional, which draws competitors from around South America. Regular races are held Saturdays and alternating Wednesdays.

Soccer

Chile's most popular spectator sport is soccer, but a close second is watching the endless bickering among owners, trainers, and players whenever a match isn't going well. First division soccer matches, featuring the city's handful of local teams, are held in the **Estadio Nacional** (⊠ Av. Grecia 2001, ☎ 2/238–8102), south of the center of the city. The season is March through December, and most matches are held on weekends. Even if you're not a soccer fan, the Estadio National is worth a visit, as it was here that Pinochet's henchmen killed thousands of political opponents in 1973, including Chilean folk singer Victor Jara. To assure he would never again provoke Chileans to action with his music, Jara's hands were mutilated before he was put to death.

SHOPPING

Providencia, the city's most popular shopping district, has a wide range of exclusive boutiques catering to wealthy Santiaguinos. Avenida Providencia slices through the neighborhood, branching off for several blocks into the parallel Avenida 11 de Septiembre. The shops continue east to Avenida El Bosque Norte, after which Avenida Providencia changes its name to Avenida Apoquindo and the neighborhood becomes Las Condes. In this chic district you'll find an ever-increasing number of thoroughly modern shopping malls filled with hundreds of specialty shops.

Bohemian Bellavista attracts those in search of the perfect woolen sweater or the right piece of lapis lazuli jewelry. Santiago Centro is much more down to earth. The Mercado Central may feel as if it's intended for tourists, but nearby markets like Vega Chica and Vega Central are the real thing. Stores downtown usually face the street, which makes window-shopping much more entertaining. The city's pedestrian streets around the Plaza de Armas are crowded with children licking ice cream cones, older women strolling arm in arm, and business executives sitting under wide umbrellas having their shoes shined.

Markets

Los Graneros de Alba is a "village" of more than 200 shops where you can find everything from fine leather to semiprecious stones, as well as a wonderful display of cockatoos and other live birds. It's a nice place to visit, especially on weekends when traveling musicians entertain the crowds. The market is on the outskirts of the city, nestled in the foothills of the Andes. ⊠ *Av. Apoquindo 9085, Las Condes,* ☎ *2/ 245–4152.* ☉ *Tues.–Sun. 10:30–9.*

Bellavista's colorful **Feria Artesanal Pío Nono,** held in the park along Avenida Pío Nono, comes alive every night of the week. It's even busier on weekends, when more vendors gather in Parque Domingo Gómez to display their handicrafts.

Centro Artesanal Santa Lucía, an art fair at the base of Cerro Santa Lucía, is an excellent place to find Aymara and Mapuche crafts.

Shopping Malls

In Santiago, the shopping malls are so enormous that they have become attractions in their own right. Some even offer free transportation from the major hotels. **Alto Las Condes** (⊠ Av. Presidente Kennedy 9001, Las Condes, ☎ 2/299–6999) contains a supermarket that has appropriately been named Jumbo, where the staff wear roller skates while restocking the shelves. It has a wide range of excellent Chilean wines. The mall has 245 shops, three department stores, a multiplex, and a seemingly endless food court. It's open daily 10 to 10.

Parque Arauço (⊠ Av. Presidente Kennedy 5413, Las Condes, ☎ 2/ 242–0600) is a North American–style shopping center with an eclectic mix of designer boutiques, including clothing outlets like Benetton. Chile's three largest department stores—Falabella, Ripley, and Almacenes París—offer everything from perfume to plates. There's even a McDonald's for those suffering from homesickness.

The **Mall del Centro** (⊠ Puente 689, Santiago Centro, ☎ 2/361–0011) is a smaller version of Parque Arauco, with a more central location.

Specialty Shops

Handicrafts

For handicrafts, head to **Artesanías de Chile** (⊠ J.V. Lastarria 307, Santiago Centro, ☎ 2/633–0081). This shop in Plaza Mulato Gil de Castro has a good selection of creative jewelry and handwoven clothing. In the middle of Parque Metropolitano is **Cooperativa Almacén Campesino** (⊠ Torreón Victoria, Bellavista, ☎ 2/335–4443), a cooperative of artisans from various indigenous cultures. This shop sells the best handicrafts from all over Chile.

Jewelry

Chile is one of the few places in the world where lapis lazuli, a brilliant blue mineral, is found in abundance. **Lapis Lazuli House** (⊠ Bellavista 14, Bellavista, ☎ 2/732–7081) sells jewelry made from lapis lauli and other precious and semiprecious stones. **Rocco** (⊠ J.V. Lastarria 53, Santiago Centro, ☎ 2/633–4036) sells fine jewelry and other items.

Wine and Liquor

Chileans have discovered just how good their vintages are, and wineshops are popping up everywhere. In Las Condes, **El Mundo del Vino** (⊠ Isidora Goyenechea 2931, Las Condes, ☎ 2/244–8888) is a world-class store with an international selection, in-store tastings, wine classes, and books for oenophiles. It also offers sturdy boxes to protect your purchases on the flight home. **La Vinoteca** (⊠ Av. Isidora Goynechea 2966, Las Condes, ☎ 2/334–1987) proudly proclaims that it was Santiago's first fine wineshop. It offer personalized service and an excellent selection. **Vinopolis** (⊠ Av. El Bosque Norte 380, Las Condes, ☎ 2/333–0080; ⊠ Av. Pedro de Valdivia 36, Providencia, ☎ 2/333–0816) has two locations in the city, as well as a shop at the airport for last-minute purchases. The selection is top-notch. **The Wine House** (⊠ Av. El Bosque Norte 500, Providencia, ☎ 2/207–3520) offers an enviable selection of Chilean wines.

SIDE TRIPS FROM SANTIAGO

For more than a few travelers, Santiago's main attraction is its proximity to the continent's best skiing. Three world-class ski resorts are just outside the city, and another is a little farther away. Others are curious to see the region where their favorite wines are produced. The wineries around Santiago provide the majority of the country's excellent exports. The Cajón del Maipo, deep in the Andes, is irresistible for those want to soak in a natural hot spring, stroll through picturesque mountain villages where low adobe houses line the roads, or just take in the stark but majestic landscape.

Cajón del Maipo

The Cajón del Maipo, a stunning river valley southeast of Santiago, is so expansive that you can easily spend several days exploring the area. A narrow road runs parallel to the Río Maipo, the river that supplies Santiago with most of its drinking water, as it snakes up into the Andes. As you ascend, you'll be treated to views of the massive mountains of sedimentary rock, heaved up and thrown sideways millions of years ago when the Andes were formed. On a sunny day, the colors here are subtle but glowing, ranging from oranges and reds to ochers, buffs, beiges, browns, and even elusive greens. Along the way, small mountain villages cling precipitously to the hillsides. Locals in roadside stands sell homemade *chicha* (cider) and *miel* (honey). At the far end of the valley, if you drive this far, you'll find an austere landscape where hot springs spill from the earth and the mountains display vibrant shades of blue and violet.

Whatever you do, don't hurry through the Cajón del Maipo. Any of the villages you pass is worth a visit. As the valley is a popular weekend getaway for Santiaguinos, most villages have small cafés offering basic meals and simple lodgings. There are also plenty of mercados where you can pick up supplies for a picnic. The canyon's main town, San José de Maipo, is a great place to get acquainted with small-town life in the Andes.

San Alfonso

About 65 km (40 mi) from Santiago is San Alfonso, a small but charming village where you'll find fantastic houses that look as if they've been stolen from a fairy tale. Just past San Alfonso is the abandoned mining town of **El Volcán,** where you can visit the old abandoned copper-mine shafts and peer into the decaying, cramped miners' quarters. The going gets tougher after this point, as the road is no longer paved. Make sure you have a four-wheel-drive vehicle if you want to venture farther, especially if there's rain in the forecast.

LODGING

$ 🏨 **Cascada de las Animas.** Set on its own 10,000-acre nature reserve in the foothills of the Andes, Cascada de las Animas offers breathtaking views in all directions. You won't want to sit still for long, as the family-run establishment offers excellent guides that bring you white-water rafting down the Río Maipo and horseback riding high up into the mountains. Back at the complex of whimsical cabins you'll find a healing center where you can learn yoga, get a massage, or relax in a soothing hot tub. The restaurant has a huge terrace where you can dine with a view of the river below. Book well ahead in the busy season. ⊠ *Casilla 57, San Alfonso,* ☎ *2/861–1303,* FAX *2/861–1833,* WEB *www.cascadadelasanimas.cl. 15 cabins. Restaurant, bar, pool, hot tub, sauna, hiking, horseback riding, meeting room. MC, V.*

$ 🍴 **Hostería los Ciervos.** At this pleasant hostelry you can enjoy a filling lunch of traditional Chilean dishes like pastel de choclo or *porotos granados* (a thick vegetable stew). The nine simple guest rooms are set beside a lovely garden with a small pool. ⊠ *Av. Argentina 711, San Alfonso,* ☎ FAX *2/861–1581. 9 rooms. Restaurant, outdoor pool. AE, MC, V.*

Lo Valdés

Past El Volcán, the gravel road leads higher into the jagged mountains. Green slopes give way to sheer mountain cliffs of gray and purple. Here you'll be able to spot layer upon layer of sedimentary rock, packed with fossils from the time when this whole area was under the ocean. About 12 km (8 mi) beyond El Volcán you'll pass by the tiny town of Baños Morales, where Santiaguinos go to soak their tired muscles in the hot springs. In Baños Morales you'll find the **Monumento Natural El Morado,** named for an impressive peak called "The Purple One" because of its unusual color. An 8-km (5-mi) hike that passes a glacier takes about three hours.

Take the right fork to reach Lo Valdés, a charming village that makes an excellent place to stop for the night. About 11 km (7 mi) past Lo Valdés, along a poorly maintained road through an impressive moonscape of mauves, grays, and steely blues, are the isolated and picturesque **Baños de Colina.** These huge natural bowls, scooped out of the mountain edge and overflowing with water from the hot springs, are well worth the trip. Here you can slip into a bathing suit (in your car, as there are no changing rooms) and choose the pool that has the temperature most to your liking. Let your body float gently in the mineral-rich waters and enjoy the view down the valley as your fellow soakers trade medical advice, offer salt and lemons to suck on, and speculate about the medicinal properties of the waters.

LODGING

$$ 🍴 **Refugio Alemán.** Santiago's German Alpine Club built the Refugio Alemán in 1931 as a base camp for members scaling the heights of the Andes. The charming stone building looks as if it could be situated in the Alps. The accommodations are spartan, but the location couldn't be better. To top it off, all meals are included. ⊠ *Lo Valdés,* ☎ *2/232–0476,* FAX *2/231–2096,* WEB *www.terraincognita.cl. 11 rooms. Restaurant, mineral baths, hiking.*

Ski Resorts

No wonder skiing aficionados from around the world head to Chile—the snowcapped mountains to the east of Santiago have the largest number of runs not just in Chile or South America, but the entire southern hemisphere. The other attraction is that the season here lasts from June to September, so savvy skiers can take to the slopes when everyone else is hitting the beach.

There are three distinct ski areas within easy reach of Santiago—Valle Nevado, Farellones, and La Parva. These resort regions have a total of 43 lifts that can carry you to the top of 1,260 acres of groomed runs. Follow La Alameda eastward until you leave the city. At the base of the mountain you begin a long and arduous journey up the Andes, making 40 consecutive hairpin turns. The road forks when you reach the top, with one road taking the relatively easy 16-km (10-mi) route east to Valle Nevado, the other following a more difficult road north to Farellones and La Parva.

About 160 km (100 mi) north of Santiago is Portillo, the oldest ski area in South America. It's farther from Santiago than the other resorts—a three-hour drive—so making a day trip out of it would be exhausting. The only accommodation around is Hotel Portillo, which accepts guests with a minimum one-week stay. From Santiago, head north on the Pan-American Highway, following signs to the town of Los Andes. From there take the International Highway (Ruta 60) east until you reach the resort at the edge of the Argentine border.

Farellones

The closest ski area to Santiago is Farellones, at the foot of Cerro Colorado. This area, consisting of a couple of ski runs for beginners, is used mainly by locals out for a day trip. Facilities are scanty—just a couple of unremarkable restaurants and a few drink stands. Farther up the road is El Colorado, which has 568 acres of groomed runs—the most in Chile. There are 18 runs here: seven beginner, four intermediate, three advanced, and four expert. There are a few restaurants and pubs in the village. Ski season here runs mid-June to mid-October.

DINING AND LODGING

$$ ✕☷ **La Cornisa.** On the road to Farellones, this family-run hotel is open
★   all year. It's great for those wanting to get to the slopes early, as there's free shuttle service to and from the nearby ski areas. The quaint old inn, run by the same family for years, has 10 rooms with wood floors and heaters to keep out the chill. The best are the two corner rooms, which are a bit larger and have wide windows with excellent views. The rate includes breakfast and dinner in the small restaurant, warmed by a fireplace and looking directly down the mountain to Santiago. ✉ *Los Cóndores 636, Farellones,* ☎ FAX *2/220–7581. 10 rooms. Restaurant. AE, DC, MC, V.*

La Parva

About 3 km (2 mi) up the road is La Parva, a colorful conglomeration of private homes set along a handful of mountain roads. At the resort itself there are 14 ski runs, most for intermediate level skiers. La Parva is positioned perfectly to give you a stunning view of Santiago, especially at night. The season at La Parva tends to be a little longer than at the neighboring resorts. The slopes usually open in May, meaning the season can sometimes last six months.

LODGING

$$$$ ☷ **Condominio Nuevo Parva.** The only place to stay in La Parva is this complex of apartments that sleep six or eight. You can rent only by the week, so plan for a lot of skiing. Valle Nevado and the other ski areas are a short drive away. ✉ *Nueva La Parva 77,* ☎ *2/211–4400,* FAX *2/220–8510. Kitchenettes. AE, MC, V. Closed Oct.–May.*

Valle Nevado

Just 13 km (8 mi) beyond La Parva is Chile's largest ski area, Valle Nevado. This luxury resort area has 11 ski lifts that take you up to 27 runs on more than 300 acres of groomed trails. More lifts are being built to provide skiing fanatics with even more options. There are a few slopes for beginners, but Valle Nevado is intended for skiers up for a challenge. Three of the extremely difficult runs from the top of

Cerro Tres Puntas are labeled "Shake," "Rattle," and "Roll." That does-n't intimidate you? Then you might be ready for some heliskiing. A Bell 407 helicopter whisks you to otherwise inaccessible peaks where you can ride a vertical drop of up to 2,500 meters (8,200 ft).

Valle Nevado has a ski school giving pointers to everyone from beginners to experts. As most of the visitors here are European, the majority of the 50 instructors are from Europe. Equipment rental runs about $30 a day. The ski season here runs June 15–October.

Three hotels dominate Valle Nevado; staying at one gives you access to the facilities at the other two. The larger two—Puerta del Sol and Valle Nevado—are a part of the same complex. The three hotels share eight restaurants with a variety of cuisines: Italian, Japanese, American, Chilean, Swiss, and French. Rates include lift tickets, ski equipment, and all meals. Rooms are most expensive during the high season in July and August; you can often get the same room for half the price if you stay during the shoulder season of June or September.

LODGING

$$$$ 🏨 **Puerta del Sol.** The largest of the Valle Nevado hotels, Puerta del Sol can be identified by its signature sloped roof. Rooms here are larger than Tres Puntas, but still rather small. One good option are the "altillo rooms," which feature a loft bed that gives you more space. North-facing rooms (which cost more) have unobstructed views of the slopes. Since all three hotels share facilities, Puerta del Sol is your best value. ✉ *Valle Nevado*, ☎ *2/206–0027; 800/669–0554 in the U.S.; 888/301–3248 in Canada,* FAX *2/208–0697,* WEB *www.vallenevado.com. 124 rooms. 2 restaurants, minibars, room service, massage, sauna, gym, dance club. AE, DC, MC, V. Closed Oct.–June 14.*

$$$$ 🏨 **Tres Puntas.** It bills itself as a hotel for young people, and Tres Puntas may indeed remind you of a college dormitory. The closet-size rooms come with either bunk beds or two single beds. That's it for decor, except for maybe a night table. In short, the rooms are for those who intend to be on the slopes all day. It may be consoling to know that the tiny wooden balconies (just big enough for two people) are as small as those at the pricier Puerta del Sol. Inside is a pub and an American-style restaurant complete with a jukebox. ✉ *Valle Nevado*, ☎ *2/206–0027; 800/669–0554 in the U.S.; 888/301–3248 in Canada,* FAX *2/208–0697,* WEB *www.vallenevado.com. 89 rooms. Restaurant, pub, billiards. AE, DC, MC, V. Closed Oct.–June 14.*

$$$$ 🏨 **Valle Nevado.** Valle Nevado's most expensive lodge offers ski-in/ski-out convenience. Rooms here, while slightly larger than at the other two hotels, are tiny compared with those in comparably priced lodgings in Santiago. Only the handful of suites can be accurately called spacious, with separate living areas, kitchenettes, big baths, and balconies. ✉ *Valle Nevado*, ☎ *2/206–0027; 800/669–0554 in the U.S.; 888/301–3248 in Canada,* FAX *2/208–0697,* WEB *www.vallenevado.com. 40 rooms, 6 suites. 4 restaurants, bar, lobby lounge, minibars, room service, massage, sauna, gym, dance club. AE, DC, MC, V. Closed Oct.–June 14.*

Portillo

A completely separate ski area north of Santiago, Portillo is renowned for its slopes, where numerous world speed records have been recorded. It also has the best views of any of the area's ski resorts. The slopes here were discovered by engineers building the now-defunct railroad that linked Chile to Argentina. After the railroad was inaugurated in 1910, skiing aficionados headed here despite the fact that there were no facilities available. The hotel opened its doors in 1949, making Portillo the country's first ski resort.

The Hotel Portillo is still the only hotel in the area. The facilities are reserved for hotel guests, but you can dine in the *auto-servicio* (cafeteria-style) restaurant if you're here just for the day. Ski season is mid-June to mid-October.

LODGING

$$$$ 🏨 **Hotel Portillo.** Staying at this hotel feels a bit like going off to camp: every Saturday a new group settles in for a week's worth of outdoor activities. Besides skiing there's skating on the Laguna del Inca and even swimming in the heated outdoor pool. The hotel has almost as many employees as guests, which means service is excellent and the mood relaxed. The rooms have big windows showcasing the view of the mountains, or the more prized view of the lake. Family-style apartments come with bunk beds for children. Rates include all meals. ✉ *Portillo*, ☎ *2/ 361–7000; 800/829–5325 in the U.S.*, FAX *2/361–7080*, WEB *www.skiportillo.com. 150 rooms, 5 suites, 15 apartments. 2 restaurants, pool, massage, sauna, gym, recreation room, billiards, dance club, ski shop, theater, baby-sitting. AE, DC, MC, V. Closed Oct.–June 14.*

Wineries

The wineries in the valley below Santiago are some of the oldest in Chile. Here you'll find most of the biggest and best-known vineyards in the country. For years tourists were virtually ignored by these wineries, but they are finally getting attention. Now you'll find many wineries are throwing their doors open to visitors for the first time, often letting them see behind-the-scenes activities like harvesting and pressing.

Valle de Maipo

One of the most recognizable of Chile's wine appellations is the Valle de Maipo, an area that stretches south from Santiago. Viña Santa Rita is the only vineyard in the area with a restaurant, and it's a good one. Others worth a visit are Viña Concha y Toro, the country's largest wine maker; Viña Undurraga, known for its lovely grounds; and Viña Cousiño-Macul, which has been making wine in the region since 1856.

Chile's largest wine maker, **Viña Concha y Toro** produces 11 million cases annually. Some of its table wines—identifiable by the short, stout bottles—are sold domestically for about $2. The best bottles, though, fetch sky-high prices abroad. This is one of the oldest wineries in the region. Melchor de Concha y Toro, who once served as Chile's minister of finance, built the *casona,* or main house, in 1875. He imported vines from Europe, significantly improving the quality of the wines he was able to produce. Hour-long tours begin with an introductory video, a stroll through the vineyards and the century-old gardens, a look at the modern facilities, and a tasting. Reserve a week ahead for Saturday tours. ✉ *Virginia Subercaseaux 210, Pirque*, ☎ *2/821–7000*, WEB *www.conchaytoro.cl.* 🎫 *Admission.* ☉ *Weekdays 10:30–6, Sat. 10– 12. English tours weekdays 11:30–3, Sat. 11 AM.*

Residential development keeps creeping closer to **Viña Cousiño-Macul,** a 625-acre estate where grapes have been grown since the mid-16th century. For the moment the venerable vineyard has managed to hang on. The Cousiño family home, set next to a beautiful 110-acre park, isn't open to the public, but you can visit the rest of the facilities. Especially interesting is the vaulted brick cellar, built in 1872, which can store more than 1 million bottles. ✉ *Av. Quilín 7100, Peñalolén, Santiago*, ☎ *2/284–1011*, WEB *www.cousinomacul.cl.* 🎫 *Free.* ☉ *Tours Mon.–Sat. 11 AM.*

Chile's third-largest winery, **Viña Santa Rita** played an important historical role in Chile's battle for independence. In 1814, 120 soldiers led by revolutionary hero Bernardo O'Higgins hid here in the cellars. Paula Jaraquemada, who ran the estate, refused to let the Spanish enter, saving the soldiers. (Santa Rita's domestic line of wines, called 120, commemorates the event.) At the center of Santa Rita's Maipo Valley estate half an hour south of Santiago, the lovely colonial hacienda now serves as the winery's headquarters. A restaurant on the premises, La Casa de Doña Paula, is a delightful place to have a bite after a tour of the vineyard.

Tours take you down into the winery's musty cellars, which are worthy of Edgar Allen Poe. Built by French engineers in 1875 using a lime-and-stone technique called *cal y canto,* the fan-vault cellars have been named a national monument. You then see the 125-year-old barrels made of *raulí* wood where the wine once was aged before eventually reaching the stainless-steel towers that serve the same purpose today. Unfortunately, the wonderful gardens and the original proprietor's house, with its chapel steeple peeking out from behind a thick canopy of trees, are not part of the tour. At the wineshop you can pick up Santa Rita's quality Medalla Real label of cabernet sauvignon, chardonnay, and sauvignon blanc. ⊠ *Camino Padre Hurtado 695, Alto Jahuel–Buín,* ☎ 2/ 362–2594 or 2/362–2000, WEB *www.santarita.com.* ⊠ *Admission.* ☉ *Tours Tues.–Fri. 11:30, 12:25, 3, 4; weekends 12:30 and 3.*

Don Francisco Undurraga Vicuña founded **Viña Undurraga** in 1885 in the town of Talagante, 34 km (21 mi) southwest of Santiago. The opulent mansion he built here has hosted various visiting dignitaries, from queen of Denmark to king of Norway. Today you can tour the house and the gardens—designed by Pierre Dubois, who planned Santiago's Parque Forestal—take a look at the facilities, and enjoy a tasting. Reservations are recommended. ⊠ *Camino a Melipilla Km 34, Talagante,* ☎ 2/817–2346, WEB *www.undurraga.cl.* ⊠ *Admission.* ☉ *Tours weekdays 9:30–4, Sat. 10–3.*

DINING

$$ ✕ **La Casa de Doña Paula.** Viña Santa Rita's restaurant is housed in
★   a two-century-old colonial hacienda with thick adobe walls. Under a peaked wood ceiling, the restaurant is decorated with old religious sculptures and portraits, including one of Paula Jaraquemada, who once ran the estate. If you plan to lunch here, it's a good idea to arrange to take the winery's 12:15 tour. *Camarones al pi-pil* (shrimp in an olive oil and chili sauce) makes a tasty starter. Locally grown meats are the draw here; try the delicious *costillar de cerdo* (pork ribs). For dessert, the house specialty is *ponderación,* a crisp swirl of fried dough atop vanilla ice cream and caramel syrup. The wine list, not surprisingly, features all of Santa Rita's offerings, as well as those from the sister winery of Viña Carmen. ⊠ *Viña Santa Rita, Camino Padre Hurtado 695, Alto Jahuel–Buín,* ☎ 2/821–4211. *Reservations essential. Closed Mon. No dinner. AE, DC, MC, V.*

SANTIAGO A TO Z

To *research prices, get advice from other travelers, and book travel arrangements, visit www.fodors.com.*

AIR TRAVEL TO AND FROM SANTIAGO
Santiago's Comodoro Arturo Merino Benítez International Airport is about a 30-minute drive west of the city. The new facility is an efficiently and beautifully designed metal-and-glass structure that contains far better facilities than its predecessor.

Among the U.S. carriers, American serves Santiago from Dallas and Miami, while Delta connects from Atlanta and United has daily service from

Miami. LanChile flies nonstop to Santiago from both Miami and Los Angeles. From London, the British Airways' flight that stops in Buenos Aires is the best bet. Most of the major Central and South American airlines also fly to Santiago, including Aerocontinente, Aerolíneas Argentinas, Aeromexico, Avianca, Lacsa, Lloyd Aéreo Boliviano, and Varig.

LanChile and Ladeco, its domestic subsidiary, have daily flights from Santiago to most destinations in Chile.

➤ NORTH AMERICAN AIRLINES: **American Airlines** (☎ 2/690–1090 in Santiago; 800/433–7300 in North America). **Delta Airlines** (☎ 2/690–1551 in Santiago; 800/221–1212 in North America) flies daily from Atlanta. **United Airlines** (☎ 2/690–1179 in Santiago; 800/538–2929 in North America).

➤ CENTRAL AND SOUTH AMERICAN AIRLINES: **Aerocontinente** (☎ 2/690–1192 in Chile; 888/586–9400 in North America). **Aerolíneas Argentinas** (☎ 2/690–1090 in Chile; 800/474–7424 in North America). **Aeromexico** (☎ 2/690–1141 in Chile; 800/237–6639 in North America). **Avianca** (☎ 2/690–1050 in Chile; 800/284–2622 in North America). **Lacsa** (☎ 2/690–1276 in Chile; 800/225–2272 in North America). **LanChile** (☎ 2/601–9081 in Chile; 800/735–5526 in North America). **Lloyd Aéreo Boliviano** (☎ 2/690–1130 in Chile). **Varig** (☎ 2/690–1342 in Chile; 800/468–2744 in North America).

➤ AIRPORTS: **Comodoro Arturo Merino Benítez International Airport** (☎ 2/220–7610).

AIRPORTS AND TRANSFERS

You have several options for getting to and from the airport. The most expensive is a taxi, which should cost you less than $15 for a trip downtown. Less expensive, especially if you are traveling alone, are the comfortable minibuses operated by Transfer. They whisk you from the airport to any location downtown for about $5.

Centropuerto, which runs buses every 10 minutes between the airport and Terminal Los Héroes, charges about $2. Tur-Bus offers similar service between the airport and its own terminal near the Los Héroes Metro station. There is no Metro connection at the airport.

➤ TAXIS & SHUTTLES: **Centropuerto** (☎ 2/601–9883). **Transfer** (☎ 2/677–3000). **Tur-Bus** (☎ 2/270–7500).

BUS TRAVEL TO AND FROM SANTIAGO

All the country's major highways pass through Santiago, which means you won't have a problem catching a bus to almost any destination. Finding that bus, however, can be a problem. The city has several terminals, each with buses heading in different directions. Terminal Los Héroes is located on the edge of Santiago Centro near the Los Héroes Metro station. Several companies have buses to points north and south. The other three stations are clustered around the Universidad de Santiago Metro station. The modern Terminal San Borja has buses headed north. Terminal Santiago is the busiest, with dozens of small companies with service to the coast and the south. Terminal Alameda, which handles only Tur-Bus and Pullman Bus, is for coastal and southern traffic. Terminal Los Héroes and Terminal Santiago also handle a few international routes, heading to far-flung destinations such as Buenos Aires, Rio de Janeiro, and Lima.

If you're headed to the Andes, several companies run regularly scheduled service in the winter. Skitotal heads to all of the ski resorts except Portillo. Buses depart at 8:45 AM; a round-trip ticket is $13. Also available for hire here are taxis—($90 including driver) and 12-person minibuses ($125). Manzur Expediciones runs buses to Portillo on Wednesday, Saturday, and Sunday for about the same price. Buses leaves at 8:30 AM.

Bus service to the Cajón del Maipo is frequent and inexpensive—Manzur offers a round-trip ticket to Refugio Alemán for less than $10. Only the 7:30 AM bus makes the two-hour trek to Baños Colina, however. Sit on the right side of the bus for a good view of the river.

➤ BUS COMPANIES: **Manzur** (✉ Sótero del Río 475, Santiago, ☎ 2/777–4284, FAX 2/643–5651). **Pullman Bus** (✉ Terminal Alameda, ☎ 2/779–2026). **Skitotal** (✉ Av. Apoquindo 4900, ☎ 2/246–0156). **Tur-Bus** (✉ Terminal Alameda, ☎ 2/270–7500).

➤ BUS TERMINALS: **Terminal Alameda** (✉ Av. O'Higgins 3714, ☎ 2/776–1038). **Terminal Los Héroes** (✉ Tucapel Jiménez 21, ☎ 2/696–9076, 2/696–9080, or 2/696–9082). **Terminal San Borja** (✉ San Borja 184, ☎ 776–0645). **Terminal Santiago** (✉ Av. O'Higgins 3848, ☎ 2/779–1385).

BUS TRAVEL WITHIN SANTIAGO

Bus service has improved, but it is still too confusing for most newcomers. (It's confusing for most residents, too.) For one thing, there are dozens of private companies operating on hundreds of routes around the city. For another, drivers almost invariably say they go where you want to go, whether they do or not. Bus fare is usually less than 50¢, paid upon boarding. Drivers are good about providing change for small bills.

CAR RENTALS

Renting a car is convenient in Santiago, as most companies have offices at the airport and downtown. The international agencies such as Avis, Budget, and Hertz offer compact cars with unlimited mileage for about $50 a day. They can provide ski-equipped vehicles for climbs to the Andes. Two reputable local agencies are Atal and Diamond, whose rates are as low as $30 a day.

➤ RENTAL AGENCIES: **Atal** (✉ Av. Costanera 1051, ☎ 2/235–9222). **Avis** (✉ airport, ☎ 2/690–1382; ✉ Av. Santa María 1742, Providencia, ☎ 2/274–7621; ✉ Av. San Pablo 9900, Providencia, ☎ 2/601–9747). **Budget** (✉ airport, ☎ 2/601–9421; ✉ Av. Francisco Bilbao 1439, Providencia, ☎ 2/601–9421). **Diamond** (✉ Av. Manqueque Sur 851, Las Condes, ☎ 2/212–1523). **Hertz** (✉ airport, ☎ 2/601–0477; ✉ Av. Costanera 1469, Las Condes, ☎ 2/420–5200)

CAR TRAVEL

You don't need a car if you're not going to venture outside the city limits, as most of the downtown sights are within walking distance of each other. To get to other neighborhoods, taxis are inexpensive and the subway system is safe and efficient. After you dodge a line of cars speeding through a red light or see the traffic snarls during rush hour you'll be glad you didn't have to drive in the city.

A car is still the best way to see the surrounding countryside, however. Although the highways around Santiago are generally well maintained, weather conditions can make them dangerous. Between May and August, rain can cause roads in low-lying areas to flood. Avoid driving if it has been raining for several hours. If you're headed north or south, you'll probably use the Pan-American Highway, also called Ruta 5. To reach Valparaíso, Viña del Mar, or the northernmost beach resorts on the Central Coast, take Highway 68; for the southern beaches, take Ruta 78.

It can take up to two hours to reach the region's three major ski resorts, which lie 48–56 km (30–35 mi) from Santiago. The road is narrow, winding, and full of Chileans racing to get to the top. If you decide to drive, make sure you have either a four-wheel-drive vehicle or snow chains, which are rented along the way. The chains are installed for about $10. Don't think you need them? There's a police checkpoint just before the road starts to climb into the Andes, and if the weather is rough they'll make you turn back. To reach Valle Nevado, Farellones, and La Parva, take Avenida Presidente Kennedy or Avenida las Condes east. Signs direct you once you get into the mountains. Portillo, three hours north of Santiago, is quite a distance from the other resorts. Call ahead to find out about road conditions.

To reach the Cajón del Maipo, head south on Avenida José Alessandri until you reach the Rotonda Departamental, a large traffic circle. There you take Camino Las Vizcachas, following it south into the canyon.

EMERGENCIES
➤ EMERGENCY NUMBERS: **Ambulance** (☎ 131). **Fire** (☎ 132). **Police** (☎ 133).
➤ HOSPITALS: **Clinica Alemana** (✉ Av. Vitacura 5951, ☎ 2/212–9700). **Clinica Vitacura** (✉ Av. Presidente Kennedy 3210, ☎ 2/228–9043).

ENGLISH-LANGUAGE MEDIA
The Instituto Chileno-Norteamericano de Cultura has a selection of books in English, as well as English-language periodicals. Larraín Hudson Ltda. sells secondhand English books. Librería Inglesa sells new books, but the prices are high. For popular newspapers and magazines in English (often from weeks before), check the kiosks on the pedestrian mall of Paseo Ahumada in Santiago Centro.
➤ BOOKSTORES: **Instituto Chileno-Norteamericano de Cultura** (✉ Moneda 1467, Santiago Centro, ☎ 2/696–3215). **Larraín Hudson Ltda.** (✉ Av. Providencia 1652, Providencia, ☎ 2/235–1205). **Librería Inglesa** (✉ Av. Pedro de Valdivia 47, Providencia, ☎ 2/231–6270).

HEALTH
In terms of the food, Santiago is one of the safest cities in South America. Because of strict health codes, you shouldn't worry too much about the food in most restaurants. If you decide to sample something from a street vendor, make sure it has been thoroughly cooked. The tap water in Santiago and elsewhere in Chile is quite safe, but if you want to be extra careful take advantage of the bottled water available everywhere.

Altitude sickness—which is marked by difficulty breathing, dizziness, headaches, and nausea—is a danger when heading to the Andes. It's caused when your body gets less oxygen than usual. The best way to ward off altitude sickness is to take it slow. Try to spend a day or two acclimatizing before any physical exertion. When skiing, rest more often and drink as much water as possible. If symptoms continue, return to a lower altitude.

INTERNET
In Santiago there are plenty of Internet cafés; you're likely to find several around your hotel. Most larger hotels offer business services, but these can be costly. Cyber Café, in Providencia, is open Monday–Saturday 10–10. Easy@Net, also in Providencia, lets you punch in a special access code so you only pay for the amount of time you are online. It's open daily 10–10.
➤ INTERNET CAFÉS: **Cyber Café** (✉ Pedro de Valdivia 27, Providencia, ☎ 2/236–1416). **Easy@Net** (✉ Paseo Las Palmas 2213, Providencia, ☎ 2/333–7112).

MAIL AND SHIPPING
The Correo Central, housed in the ornate Palacio de los Gobernadores, is located in Santiago Centro on the north side of the Plaza de Armas. There is a second downtown branch near the Palacio de la Moneda, as well as one in Providencia near the Manuel Montt Metro stop.

For overnight delivery, DHL and Federal Express both have offices in Santiago Centro.

➤ OVERNIGHT SERVICES: **DHL** (✉ San Francisco 301, Santiago Centro, ☎ 2/280–2000). **Federal Express** (✉ San Camilo 190, Santiago Centro, ☎ 2/361–6000).

➤ POST OFFICES: **Centro** (✉ Moneda 1155; ✉ Plaza de Armas). **Providencia** (✉ Av. Providencia 1466).

MONEY MATTERS

Unlike other South American countries, U.S. dollars are rarely accepted as currency in Chile. (The exception is larger hotels, where prices are often quoted only in dollars.) Credit cards and travelers checks are accepted everywhere in Santiago's most heavily touristed areas. When you stray off the beaten path, it's a good idea to have a few pesos on you.

There are many places to exchange money in Santiago Centro, including American Express and Citibank. Banks in Santiago are usually open weekdays 9–2, while casas de cambio are open weekdays 9–2 and 3–6.

Automatic teller machines only dispense Chilean pesos. To use an ATM issued by a foreign bank, select the "foreign client" option from the menu. Citibank, with the most ATMs in town, has instructions in English and is linked to both the Plus and Cirrus systems. ATMs belonging to Chilean banks are often only linked to Cirrus. There are two ATMs on the second floor of the airport.

➤ BANKS: **American Express** (✉ Av. Andres Bello 2711, Las Condes, ☎ 2/350–6955). **Citibank** (✉ Teatinos 180, Santiago Centro, ☎ 2/338–5000; ✉ Av. Andrés Bello 2681, Providencia, ☎ 2/338–5000; ✉ Av. Apoquindo 5470, Las Condes, ☎ 2/338–5000).

SAFETY

Santiago Centro, Providencia, Las Condes, and other areas frequented by tourists are generally very safe. Use the same precautions you would anywhere—don't wear wear flashy jewelry and watches, keep your camera in a secure bag, and don't handle money in public. Remain alert for pickpockets, especially in crowded markets and parks.

SUBWAY TRAVEL

Santiago's excellent subway system is the best way to get around town. The Metro is comfortable, inexpensive, and safe. The system operates Monday–Saturday 6:30 AM to 10:30 PM and Sunday 8 AM to 10:30 PM. Línea 1 runs east–west along the axis of the Río Mapocho. This is the most popular line, and is especially useful for visitors because it runs past most of the heavily touristed areas. Línea 2 runs north–south; it's rarely used by nonresidents because it heads to residential areas. Línea 3 also runs north–south except at its northern tip, when it bends to the west to connect with the Bellas Artes and Plaza de Armas stations. Every station has an easy-to-read map of all the stations and the adjoining streets. Buy tickets in any station at the glass booths or at the nearby machines. Individual tickets cost 300 to 350 pesos (50¢–55¢), depending on the time of day. A *boleto inteligente* (smart ticket) or *boleto valor* (value ticket) costs about $5 and is good for up to 10 trips; they save you time, if not money. After depositing your ticket in the turnstile, pass through and retrieve it to use again later. Single-ride tickets are not returned.

TAXIS

With some 50,000 taxis in Santiago, you easily can flag one down on most streets. The average ride costs around $5. Radio-dispatched cabs from such companies as Andes Pacífico are slightly more expensive, but will pick you up at your door.

Most taxi drivers are willing to be hired for the day. To increase your bargaining power, head for the taxi stand at Calle Huérfanos and Calle MacIver in the heart of downtown, where you can negotiate with more than one driver.

➤ TAXI COMPANIES: **Andes Pacífico** (☎ 2/225–3064 or 2/204–0104).

TELEPHONES
When calling Santiago from other parts of the country, use the area code of 02. Within the city, skip the area code and dial the seven-digit local number. For calls to Santiago from outside the country, use the international access code 011, then the country code 56, the area code 2, and finally the seven-digit phone number.

PUBLIC PHONES
Public phones use either coins or phone cards. For calls to the United States, EntelTicket phone cards, available in denominations of 1,000, 3,000, and 5,000 pesos, are the best deal. Regular phone cards cost about a dollar a minute; the EntelTicket costs about 25¢ a minute.

TIPPING
Most Santiaguinos tip about 10% in restaurants, leaving a bit more for excellent service. Taxi drivers own their cabs and therefore don't expect tips.

TOUR OPERATORS
Sernatur, the national tourism agency, maintains a listing of experienced individual tour guides who will take you on a half-day tour of Santiago and the surrounding area for about $35. These tours are a great way to get your bearings when you have just arrived in the city. They can also greatly enrich your visit. In museums, for example, they often provide interesting information not generally available to the public. They are especially helpful in the museums with little or no signage in English.

With more than a dozen locations, Turismo Cocha is one of the city's biggest private tour operators. Founded in 1951, it offers tours of the wineries of the Cajón del Maipo and the beach resorts of Valparaíso and Viña del Mar, besides the usual city tours. It also has offices in the domestic and international terminals of the airport as well as in some of the larger hotels. Across Chile, Chilean Travel Services, and Sportstour handles tours of both Santiago and other parts of Chile.

For more adventurous travelers, Altué Expediciones and Cascada Expediciones offer adventure trips such as white-water rafting on nearby rivers and hiking to the mouths of volcanoes.

➤ TOUR COMPANIES: **Across Chile** (⌗ Av. Santa María 172, Providencia, ☎ 2/737–5131, FAX 2/735–8406, WEB www.acrosschile.com). **Altué Expediciones** (⌗ Encomenderos 83, Las Condes, ☎ 2/232–1103, FAX 2/233–6799). **Cascada Expediciones** (⌗ Orrego Luco 019, Providencia, ☎ 2/234–2274, FAX 2/233–9768). **Chilean Travel Services** (⌗ Antonio Bellet 77, Office 101, Providencia, ☎ 2/251–0400, FAX 2/251–0426). **Sportstour** (⌗ Moneda 970, Santiago Centro, ☎ 2/549–5200, FAX 2/698–2981). **Turismo Cocha** (⌗ Av. El Bosque Norte 0430, Las Condes, ☎ 2/464–1267, FAX 2/203–5110; ⌗ Santa María 1642, Providencia, ☎ 2/335–6616; ⌗ Pedro de Valdivia 0169, Providencia, ☎ 2/464–1600; ⌗ Teatinos 180, Santiago Centro, ☎ 2/464–1990, FAX 2/699–3290, WEB www.cocha.com).

TRAIN TRAVEL
Chileans once boasted about the country's excellent rail service, but there's little left besides the limited service from Santiago to points south.

Santiago's Estación Central, in Santiago Centro at the Metro station of the same name, is where you catch trains headed to the Central Valley. Trains run from Santiago through the larger cities of Rancagua, Curicó, Talca, Chillán, Concepción, and Temuco. In between they stop at the smaller towns of San Bernardo, San Javier, Linares, Parral, San Carlos, Bulnes, Cabrero, Monte Aguila, Yumbel, San Rosendo, Talcamavida, Hualqui, Laja, Santa Fe, Renaico, Mininco, Collipulli, Victoria, and Lautaro.

➤ TRAIN INFORMATION: **Estación Central** (✉ Av. O'Higgins 853, Santiago Centro, ☎ 2/376–8313 and 2/376–8460, WEB www.efe.cl).

VISITOR INFORMATION

Sernatur, the national tourist service, has an office in Providencia. The office, located between the Manuel Montt and Pedro de Valdivia Metro stops, is open daily 9 AM–10 PM. There is a complete stock of maps and brochures, and a large and friendly staff that speaks English.

➤ TOURIST INFORMATION: **Sernatur** (✉ Av. Providencia 1550, Providencia, ☎ 2/236–1416, FAX 2/251–8469).

3 THE CENTRAL COAST

The rugged Central Coast is Chile's summer playground. Its sleepy fishing villages are awakened each January by the thousands of Santiaguinos who come to sample the world-famous sea bass and conger eel, relax on the wide beaches, and visit the colonies of penguins and sea lions. In the middle of it all are the odd couple of Chile's second- and third-largest cities: gritty Valparaíso, where century-old funiculars cable you up a collection of 45 hills overlooking the sea, and chic Viña del Mar, which glistens with luxury apartments and trendy shops.

by Michael
de Zayas

M OST PEOPLE HEAD TO THE CENTRAL COAST for a single reason: the beaches. Yes, some come to see the populations of
sea lions and penguins, and others want to experience the
rough grandeur of the windswept coastline, but those in search of nature generally head south to Chiloé and Patagonia or to the north to
the Atacama Desert. Yet this stretch of coastline west of Santiago offers much more than sun and surf.

The biggest surprise is the charm of Valparaíso, Chile's second- largest
city. Valparaíso shares a bay with Viña del Mar, but the similarities end
there. Valparaíso is a bustling port town with a jumble of colorful cot-
tages nestled in the folds of its many hills. Viña del Mar has polished
parks and modern high-rises. Together they form an interesting contrast of past and future. The smaller coastal towns (locals call them
balnearios) have their own character, often defined by their coastal topography.

Santiago's proximity to the resorts south of Valparaíso may explain
why they are more developed—some might say overdeveloped—than
the beaches north of Viña del Mar. Except for Quintay, which has remained relatively isolated, the towns to the south form an uninterrupted
stretch of small restaurants and hotels. The northern resorts have a rus-
ticity about them, a character that matches the expanse of rough terrain found here.

At the beginning of the 20th century, Santiago's elite started building
summer homes along the coastal towns. Soon after, when trains connected the capital to beaches to the north and south, middle-class families could spend their summers at the shore. Improved highway access
in the past few decades has brought Chileans of all economic levels.
December and January, when schools let out for summer vacation, finds
the beaches packed with pleasure seekers. But the rest of the year the
coast is comparatively deserted, and the quiet shores are yours to explore.

Pleasures and Pastimes

Beaches
The Humboldt Current, which flows northward along the coast of Chile,
carries cold water to almost all the beaches of the Central Coast. If
you plan to surf or windsurf, you'll need a wet suit; if you plan to swim,
you'll need thick skin. The current also means that pollution is often
a problem. Because of dangerous undertow and the roughness of the
waves, pay attention to beach warnings. A red flag means swimming
is prohibited. A green flag, usually accompanied by a sign reading PLAYA
APTA PARA NADAR (beach suitable for swimming), is a go-ahead signal.

Dining
"In the turbulent sea of Chile lives the golden conger eel," wrote
Chilean poet Pablo Neruda in simple verse that leaves the real poetry
for the dinner table. To many, dining is the principal pleasure of a trip
to the Central Coast. Along with the succulent eel, Chile's most ex-
ported catch, menus here typically feature *corvina,* or sea bass, and
reineta, a mild whitefish. For a filling, quick, always inexpensive lunch,
try *merluza frita,* or fried hake.

Fish dishes are usually served with an *agregado* (side dish) of french
fries, salad, or mashed potatoes. Always brought to the table as an ac-
companiment are bread, a bowl of lemons, and a sauce called *pebre,*
which is a mix of tomato, onion, coriander, parsley, and often chili.

The Central Coast

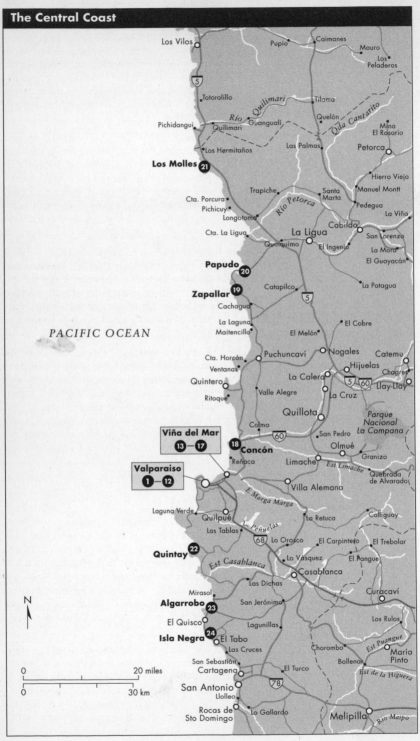

PACIFIC OCEAN

Los Vilos
Pupio
Caimanes
Mauro
Los Peladeros
5
Totoralillo
Tilama
Quelón
Mina El Rosario
Pichidangui
Quilimari
Guanguali
Las Palmas
Petorca
Los Hermitaños
Los Molles 21
Hierro Viejo
Trapiche
Santa Marta
Manuel Montt
Cta. Porcura
Pichicuy
Pedegua
La Viña
Longotoma
Río Petorca
Cabildo
San Lorenzo
Cta. La Ligua
La Ligua
La Mora
Quinquimo
El Ingenio
El Guayacán
Papudo 20
Catapilco
La Patagua
Zapallar 19
Cachagua
El Cobre
La Laguna
Maitencillo
El Melón
Cta. Horcón
Puchuncaví
Nogales
Catemu
Ventanas
Hijuelas
Chagres
Quintero
La Calera
5 60
Llay-Llay
Ritoque
Valle Alegre
La Cruz
Colmo
Quillota
Parque Nacional La Campana
60
San Pedro
Viña del Mar 13 — 17
18 **Concón**
Olmué
Granizo
Reñaca
Limache
Est Limache
Quebrada de Alvarado
Valparaíso 1 — 12
E. Marga Marga
Villa Alemana
Laguna Verde
Quilpué
Las Tablas
L. Peñuelas
La Retuca
Colliguay
68
Lo Orosco
El Carpintero
El Trebolar
Quintay 22
Lo Vásquez
El Rangue
Est Casablanca
Casablanca
Mirasol
Las Dichas
Curacaví
Algarrobo 23
San Jerónimo
El Quisco
Lagunillas
Los Rulos
Isla Negra 24 El Tabo
Las Cruces
Chorombo
Est Puangue
María Pinto
San Sebastián
Bollenar
Est de la Higuera
Cartagena
El Turco
San Antonio
78
Llolleo
Rocas de Sto Domingo
Lo Gallardo
Melipilla
Río Maipo

Río Quilimari
Oda Cantarito
N
0   20 miles
0   30 km

Valparaíso is known for a hearty, cheap meal called *chorillana*—a mountain of steak, onions, and eggs on a bed of french fries.

With the exception of major holidays, reservations are almost never required for restaurants in the Central Coast. For details on price categories, *see* Dining *in* Smart Travel Tips A to Z.

Lodging

Designed for Santiago families vacationing in January and February, *cabañas* are the most common accommodations in towns along the coast. Most have at least one bedroom, and many have additional beds in the living room or in a second bedroom intended for children. Almost all cabañas come equipped with kitchenettes; the fancier ones also have microwaves and ovens. As for hotels, Viña del Mar is the only place along the Central Coast with a wide selection. In fact, there are only a handful scattered throughout the entire region.

A more affordable option are guest houses known as *residenciales*. As these are usually rooms in private homes, the quality varies considerably. You'll receive more personalized attention than in a hotel, and get a better feel for the town. For details on price categories, *see* Lodging *in* Smart Travel Tips A to Z.

Shopping

Viña del Mar has, by far, the best shopping on the Central Coast. Here you'll find everything from large department stores and outlet malls to trendy boutiques and antiques shops. You'll also find some of the largest markets selling Chilean *artesanías,* or crafts. All summer long, souvenirs are sold in stands on the beaches up and down the coast.

Exploring the Central Coast

Valparaíso is the only city in the Central Coast capable of holding your attention for long; you could spend a week exploring its winding streets and not even scratch the surface. Viña del Mar, laid out in a neat grid pattern, is far less interesting. The small towns along the coast, found wherever the current has carved out a beach, can each be toured in a few hours. They have no museums, monuments, or even shops. Most offer little more than a chance to explore their coastline—which can often be exhilarating. As you head farther north along the coast, the towns become more distinctive. The resorts to the south, on the other hand, tend to differ very little from each other.

To reach the balnearios south of Valparaíso, take Highway 68 to Casablanca, where a road takes you to most of the coastal towns (Quintay is reached via another road a few miles west of Casablanca). Viña del Mar and towns to the north to Papudo are all accessible by the coastal road referred to as "La Costanera." Los Molles and other towns farther to the north can also be reached from the Pan-American Highway.

Great Itineraries

IF YOU HAVE 3 DAYS

Plan to spend your nights in the bustling beach town of Viña del Mar, which is centrally located and has the best lodging options. On the first day explore Viña de Mar, focusing on **Plaza José Francisco Vergara** ⑬, the botanical gardens and museum at **Quinta Vergara** ⑮, and the miles of splendid shoreline. On the second day head to Valparaíso, walking the **Cerro Concepción** ⑥, riding a few funiculars, and visiting Pablo Neruda's home of **La Sebastiana** ⑦. The stately mansions of **Zapallar** ⑲ should be your goal the next morning, followed by the astounding coastline of **Los Molles** ㉑.

Unless you find a specific lodging that suits you, stay in Viña del Mar and make day trips. Spend the first day in Viña del Mar and the next two in Valparaíso. Tour the hilltop promenades one day and delve into the various museums the next. On the fourth day, head south to Pablo Neruda's other home in **Isla Negra** ㉔. On the fifth day, explore the towns north of Viña, making sure to see **Zapallar** ⑲ and **Los Molles** ㉑.

When to Tour

It seems that all of Chile heads to the coast in the summer months of December, January, and February. If you're planning a visit during these peak times, make reservations a few months in advance or you may not be able to find a place to stay. The climate in the spring and fall is ideal—warm and breezy during the day, slightly cool at night. November and March are excellent months to visit—nobody's around, leaving the natural wonders for you to explore in solitude.

VALPARAÍSO AND VIÑA DE MAR

Valparaíso and Viña del Mar ("Paradise Valley" and "Vineyard of the Sea," respectively) each maintain an aura that warrants their dreamy appellations. Only minutes apart, these two urban centers are nevertheless as different as twin cities could be. Valparaíso won the heart of Pablo Neruda, who praised its "cluster of crazy houses." It is, at its heart, still a fishing town. Viña del Mar, Valparaíso's glamorous sibling, showcases miles of pristine beaches, a glitzy casino, and shopping galore.

Valparaíso's dramatic topography—45 precipitous hills overlooking the ocean—requires the use of winding pathways and charming wooden *ascensores,* or funiculars, to get up many of the grades. The city installed the first ascensor in 1883. The word means elevator, though only the Ascensor Polanco travels vertically; the rest are pulled up steep inclines by steel cables. The slopes are covered by colorful wooden houses; there are almost no apartments in the city. Valparaíso's lack of beaches keeps its mind on matters more urban, if not urbane. Viña del Mar, by contrast, is lined with tall, modern luxury apartments buildings. Viña, especially the neighborhood of Reñaca, is synonymous with the best of life for vacationing Chileans. Its beaches gleam, its casino rolls, and its discos sizzle.

Valparaíso

120 km (75 mi) west of Santiago.

Valparaíso has served as Santiago's port for hundreds of years. Before the Panama Canal opened, Valparaíso was the biggest port in South America. Harsh realities—changing trade routes, industrial decline, and political unrest—diminished its importance. But it is still the largest and most important port in Chile.

The handful of parallel streets off the bay are called the *plan* (probably from *plano,* which means flat). It's here most of the businesses—banks, cinemas, stores—set up shop. But *porteños* (the name for locals, referring to the port) live in the surrounding hills in an undulating array of colorful homes. Glance up any of the dozens of stairways and you're likely to see an unobstructed vista of blue sky. At the top you'll find *paseos,* or promenades, with spectacular views; many are named after prominent Yugoslavian, Basque, and German immigrants.

But some details—the unbelievable jumble of power, telephone, and cable lines that tangle above your head, or the hundreds of privately run buses that slow, but never completely stop, to pick up agile rid-

ers—constantly remind you that you're in a city. There's the crime you'd
find in every metropolis—keep a hold of valuables at all times. That
said, walking around Valparaíso reveals much you'll find nowhere else.

Numbers in white bullets in the text correspond to numbers in black
bullets in the margins and on the Valparaíso map.

A Good Walk

Almost any bus in town will drop you off in the northern part of town
at the Plaza Aduana, where you'll find the scarlet Dirección Nacional
de Aduana, the 19th-century customs house still in use today. Next to
this building is the Ascensor Artillería, a funicular that carries you up
to the **Paseo 21 de Mayo** ①. On this promenade with a sweeping view
of the bay you'll find the **Museo Naval y Marítimo de Valparaíso** ②.
There's an interesting stairway that winds around back near the base
of the customs house. Back down, walk southeast along Calle Cochrane.
The first block has some tawdry bars—note the WELCOME SAILOR
signs—so be on your guard here, especially at night. Continue southeast down Cochrane to **Plaza Sotomayor** ③ and its dignified Monumento a los Héroes de Iquique.

Past the square is the **Muelle Prat** ④, where you'll find the tourist office,
the Estación Puerto for trains bound for Viña del Mar, and boats leaving for short tours of the bay. Cross Plaza Sotomayor to Calle Prat. Beyond the massive gray Primera Zona Naval is a small square which houses
the classical facade of the courthouse called the Tribunales de Justicia.
Tucked away to the side here is the Ascensor El Peral, which leads to the
lovely neighborhood of Cerro Alegre. At the top you'll find the art nouveau **Museo de Bellas Artes** ⑤. Return to Calle Prat and head southeast
until you reach the clock tower of the Edificio Turri. Across the street is
the Ascensor Concepción (also called Ascensor Turri), which takes you
to Paseo Gervasoni and the beautiful neighborhood of **Cerro Concepción** ⑥.

If you continue along Calle Prat past where it becomes Calle Esmerelda
you'll pass the neoclassical structure that houses the world's oldest Spanish-language newspaper, *El Mercurio de Valparaíso.* Esmerelda then
curves south to Plaza Pinto. Head east on Calle Condell, then turn south
on Avenida Ecuador. Here you'll find taxis to take you to **La Sebastiana** ⑦. Back on Calle Condell head east and you'll reach the old Palacio Lyon, which houses the **Museo de Historia Natural de Valparaíso** ⑧
and the **Galería Municipal de Arte** ⑨. The first street heading south,
Calle Huito, leads to Ascensor Espíritu Santo, which takes you up to
explore the **Museo a Cielo Abierto** ⑩. A block farther east on Calle Condell is **Plaza Victoria** ⑪. Four blocks east on Avenida Montt is Parque
Italia; five more blocks east is Plaza O'Higgins, where you'll find the
stern **Congreso Nacional** ⑫.

TIMING

You'll need a good pair of shoes to fully appreciate Valparaíso. Walking past all the sights on the tour will take about six hours. If you want
to explore the museums, it will take two days. One good idea is to skip
La Sebastiana and visit it the following day. Should you get tired or
get lost while exploring the city's twisting streets, taxis and buses are
always easy to find. You're sure to soak up a lot of sun on an afternoon walking tour—sunblock is not a bad idea.

Sights to See

⑥ **Cerro Concepción.** Ride Ascensor Turri to the top of this hill and you'll
find Paseo Gervasoni, a wide promenade that runs by some of the city's
most stately mansions. Over the balustrade is an incredible view of the
city. For another perspective, head a block east to Paseo Atkinson. ⊠
Off Calle Papudo. ▣ *Free.*

Bahía de Valparaíso

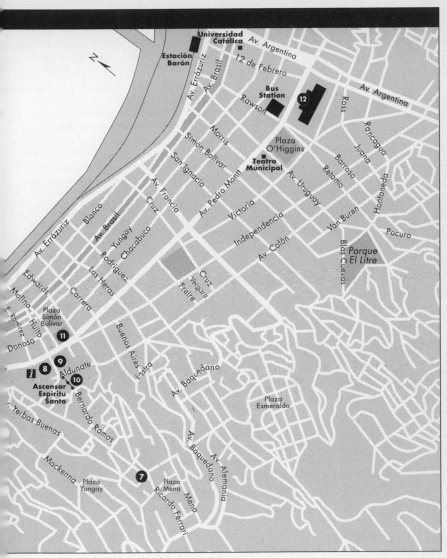

Universidad Católica

Estación Barón

Av. Argentina

12 de Febrero

Bus Station

Rawson

Av. Argentina

Ross

Rancagua

Juana

Barroso

Retamo

Hontaneda

Von Buren

Pocuro

Blas Cuevas

Parque El Litre

Morris

Simón Bolívar

San Ignacio

Av. Francia

Cruz

Plaza O'Higgins

Teatro Municipal

Av. Uruguay

Victoria

Independencia

Av. Colón

Av. Pedro Montt

Av. Errázuriz

Av. Brasil

Blanco

Av. Brasil

Yungay

Chacabuco

Rodríguez

Las Heras

Cruz

Vergara

Freire

Edwards

Molina

E. Ramírez

Huito

Donoso

Carrera

Plaza Simón Bolívar

11

8

9

7

Aldunate

10

Ascensor Espíritu Santo

Bernardo Ramos

Buenos Aires

Ushra

Av. Baquedano

Plaza Esmeralda

Av. Yerbas Buenas

Mackenna

Plaza Yungay

7

Plaza Mena

Ricardo Ferrari

Mena

Av. Baquedano

Av. Alemania

While exploring Cerro Concepción, **Café Color** (⊠ Calle Papudo 526,
☎ 32/746–136) is a delightful place to stop in for breakfast, a snack,
or to surf the Internet. You can sit at one of the colorful tables and
choose from dozens of teas, fruit juices blended on the spot, and sandwiches. While you wait you can browse through books and assorted
handicrafts made by Concepción Hill artists.

⑫ Congreso Nacional. Pinochet ordered the construction of this heavy-
handed structure on the site of one of his boyhood homes. The dictator relinquished power before its completion, however. It was here that,
after a 16-year hiatus, the National Congress resumed meeting in
1990. The first three weeks of each month you can watch the 120 *diputa-
dos,* or representatives, Tuesday to Thursday noon–2:30 and 4–6.
Meetings of the Senate, which consists of 40 elected members and two
senadores vitalicios (former presidents who were granted senator-for-
life status) are closed to the public. Free tours in English explain the
bicameral workings of Chile's government. ⊠ *Plaza O'Higgins.* 🎫 *Free.*
⊙ *Weekdays 10–6.*

⑨ Galería Municipal de Arte. This crypt in the basement of the Palacio
Lyon is the finest exhibition space in the city. Changing presentations
by top-caliber local artists are displayed on stone walls under a series
of brick arches. It's easy to miss the entrance, which is on Calle Condell beyond the Museo de Historia Natural de Valparaíso. ⊠ *Calle Condell 1550,* ☎ *32/251–071.* 🎫 *Free.* ⊙ *Mon.–Sat. 10–7.*

★ ⑦ La Sebastiana. Some say the views from the windows of Pablo Neruda's
hillside house are the best in all of Valparaíso. People come to La Sebastiana to marvel at the same ocean that inspired so much of his poetry. The house is named for Sebastián Collado, a Spanish architect
who began it as a home for himself but died before it was finished.
The incomplete building stood abandoned for 10 years before Neruda
finished it, revising the design (Neruda had no need for the third-floor
aviary or the helicopter landing pad) and adding curvaceous walls, narrow stairways, and a tower. With its many polymorphous levels, the
house looks like a ragged tugboat in the heart of the city.

A maze of twisting stairwells leads to an upper room where a video
shows Neruda enunciating the five syllables of the city's name over and
again as he rides the city's ascensores. His upper berth here contains
his desk, books, and some original manuscripts. What makes the visit
to La Sebastiana memorable, however, is Neruda's nearly obsessive delight in physical objects. The house is a shrine to his many cherished
objects, such as the beautiful orange-pink bird he brought back em-
balmed from Venezuela. His lighter spirit is here also, in the carousel
horse and the pink and yellow bar room stuffed with potent kitsch.

To get here, share the cheap cooperative cab at the taxi stand at
Plazuela Ecuador (180 pesos, or about 25¢), or walk all the way up
Calle Ferrari from Plaza Victoria. ⊠ *Ferrari 692, Cerro Florida,* ☎ *32/
256–606.* 🎫 *Admission.* ⊙ *Mar.–Dec., Tues.–Sun. 10:30–2:30, 3:30–
6; Jan.–Feb., Tues.–Sun. 10:30–6:50.*

④ Muelle Prat. The Prat Dock is a great place to watch the ships in the
harbor. To get a closer look, hop aboard one of the *lanchas* (boats) that
take tourists around the bay. The dock is flanked by the tourist information office and a row of souvenir shops.

⑩ Museo a Cielo Abierto. The Open Sky Museum is a winding walk of
20 official murals (and a handful of unofficial ones) by some of Chile's
best painters. There's even one by the country's most famous artist,
Roberto Matta. The path is not marked—in fact, there is no real fixed

route—as the point is to get lost in the city's history and culture. Ride the Ascensor Espíritu Santo up to Cerro Buenavista. When you get out, you'll be in the middle of the museum. ☒ *Cerro Buenavista.* ☜ *Free.*

★ **⑤ Museo de Bellas Artes.** The city's fine arts museum is closed while a complete renovation of its palatial home, the art nouveau Palacio Baburizza, is underway. In the meantime, it's worth a visit for a look at the exterior. Especially noteworthy are the fanciful decorative motifs reminiscent of Spain's Antoni Gaudí. The palace was the former residence of Pascual Baburizza, who donated his large collection of European paintings to the city. The museum is expected to reopen by the end of 2002, by which time it will have added state-of-the-art wings. The entire collection will also have been restored. The palace itself, besides undergoing a general renovation, will acquire a complete wardrobe of period furniture. ☒ *Paseo Yugoslavo,* ☎ *32/915–1028,* WEB *www.museobaburizza.cl.* ☜ *Free.*

⑧ Museo de Historia Natural de Valparaíso. Within the Palacio Lyon, one of the few buildings to survive the devastating 1906 earthquake, is this rather outdated natural history museum. Among the more unusual exhibits are a precolonial mummy, newborn Siamese twins in formaldehyde, and stuffed penguins. ☒ *Condell 1546,* ☎ *32/257–441.* ☜ *Admission.* ☉ *Tues.–Fri. 10–1, 2–6; Sat. 10–6; Sun. 10–2.*

② Museo Naval y Maritimo de Valparaíso. Atop Cerro Artillería is the large neoclassical mansion that is home to the maritime museum. Cannons positioned on the front lawn frame the excellent view of the ocean. Displays document the port and the ships that once defended it. ☒ *Paseo 21 de Mayo,* ☎ *32/915–1028.* ☜ *Free.* ☉ *Tues.–Sun. 10–5.*

NEED A BREAK?	If you can't get enough of the views from Paseo 21 de Mayo, grab a bite at **Poseidon** (☒ Subida Artillería 99, ☎ 32/346–713), a quick skip down the stairs that run parallel to the ascensor. With a terrace superbly perched on a high corner overlooking the city, Poseidon makes a great spot for a traditional *once* snack in the early evening. The inexpensive (about $4) *once completo* includes a sandwich, coffee or tea, fresh juice (try the *frutilla*, or strawberry), and great homemade pie.

❶ Paseo 21 de Mayo. Ascensor Artillería pulls you uphill to Paseo 21 de Mayo, a wide promenade surrounded by well-tended gardens and stately trees from which you can survey the port and a goodly portion of Valparaíso. It's in the middle of Cerro Playa Ancha, one of the city's nicest neighborhoods. ☒ *Paseo 21 de Mayo.* ☜ *Free.*

❸ Plaza Sotomayor. Valparaíso's most impressive square, Plaza Sotomayor serves as a gateway to the bustling port. In the middle of the open square (beware of traffic—it gives the impression of being for pedestrians, but cars and buses come suddenly from all directions) is the **Monumento de los Héroes de Iquique**, honoring Arturo Prat and other heroes of the War of the Pacific. Nearby you can look down through glass tiles into the **Museo del Sitio**. This curious underground museum contains artifacts from the city's mid-19th century port. On display are parts of the recently unearthed dock that once stood on this spot. At one end of the plaza, the **Primera Zona Naval**, headquarters of the *Armada de Chile,* rises to a turreted pinnacle above a mansard roof.

⓫ Plaza Victoria. The heart of the lower part of the city is this green plaza with a lovely fountain bordered by four female figures representing the seasons. Two black lions at the edge of the park look across the street to the neo-Gothic **cathedral** and its unusual freestanding bell tower. To the north is **Plaza Simon Bolívar**, which delights children with carnival rides, swings, slides, and a fun promenade ramp that winds across the square.

Dining and Lodging

$$-$$$$ ✕ **Coco Loco.** This impressive *giratorio* (revolving restaurant) offers unparalleled views from atop a bay-front luxury apartment building. It takes over an hour to turn the full 360 degrees, but you'll appreciate every minute savoring the fresh seafood. The *parrillada de mariscos* is served in two clay dishes that are opened to reveal salmon, sea bass, squid, crab, and fish marinated in a garlic sauce. It's accompanied by butter and pebre. For the quality of food and the fun of going around, the menu is quite inexpensive. ⊠ *Blanco 1781,* ☎ *32/227–614,* 𝔽𝔸𝕏 *32/ 227–617. Reservations essential. AE, DC, MC, V.*

$$-$$$ ✕ **Café Turri.** Near the top of Ascensor Turri, this 19th-century man-
★   sion commands one of the best views of Valparaíso. It also offers some of the finest seafood. The corvina in almond sauce alone is worth driving to the coast for, and the *tortilla de erizos* (Spanish-style omelet filled with local sea urchin) is an adventure. There is a terrace outside and two floors of dining within the house. The service here is the city's best. ⊠ *Templeman 147, Paseo Gervasoni,* ☎ *32/252–091,* 𝔽𝔸𝕏 *32/259–198. AE, DC, MC, V.*

$$-$$$ ✕ **La Colombina.** This fine restaurant is housed in an old home on Cerro Alegre, one of the city's most beautiful neighborhoods. The small dining room, notable for its stained-glass ceiling, has views of the sea. *Trilogia del Mar* comes with salmon, sea bass, and conger eel in a white-wine sauce with mushrooms and vegetables. There is also a large selection of national wines. ⊠ *Paseo Yugoslavo 15,* ☎ *32/236–254. No credit cards. Closed Mon.*

$$ ✕ **Bote Salvavidas.** This restaurant at the end of Muelle Prat offers great views of the harbor and, naturally, specializes in seafood. Fish dishes such as panfried conger eel with sea-urchin sauce and fish soup with mussels and clams in a paprika-flavored broth are among the popular specialties served in the plant-filled dining room. ⊠ *Muelle Prat,* ☎ *32/251–477. AE, DC, MC, V. No dinner Sun.*

$$ ✕ **J. Cruz.** Located at the end of a bleak corridor off Calle Condell, you enter this eccentric restaurant at the CASINO SOCIAL MUSEO sign. You pass through a sociable, if odd, museum. Vitrines choked with dusty trinkets—steins, necklaces, medallions—surround the tiny dining room where a wooden propeller, bells, and a bomb hang from the ceiling. This restaurant enjoys a legendary status among locals who give it credit for inventing a staple called *chorillana* (steak with onions and eggs atop a bed of french fries). There is no menu—choose either chorillana or *carne mechada* (stuffed beef and pork), with a side of french fries, rice, or tomato salad. The handful of tables are covered with plastic tablecloths, but nobody seems to mind, at least judging from the laudatory graffiti that covers the walls. "J. Cruz takes us on an infinite voyage," one visitor wrote, "but we are here, in this indelible, wonderful porteña reality." ⊠ *Condell 1466,* ☎ *32/211–225. No credit cards.*

$-$$ ✕ **Bar Inglés.** Boasting the longest bar in Valparaíso, Bar Inglés incorporates Dutch lamps and American oak furnishings to imitate an English country pub. The specialty is international cooking, particularly hot and cold soups, beef, and shellfish baked with cheese, sautéed with garlic, or dipped in mayonnaise. Also try such imaginative vegetable dishes as an artichoke, mushroom, and asparagus combination. ⊠ *Cochrane 851,* ☎ *32/214–625. No credit cards. Closed weekends and holidays.*

$-$$ ✕ **Brighton.** This café atop Cerro Concepción, with its black-and-
★   white-tiled balcony overlooking the city's glittering lights, is the most romantic spot in Valparaíso for late-night drinks. An old phonograph and vintage theater posters help create a relaxed mood in this charm-

ing Victorian-style house. The *tabla mixta*, an attractive assortment of meats, cheeses, and breads for two, makes an excellent compliment to the wine list. The bar's selection of piscos, tequilas, gins, rums, vodkas, and whiskeys may be the most extensive in town. There is live bolero music and dancing late Friday nights, and tangos late Saturday. ⊠ *Paseo Atkinson 151,* ☎ *32/223–513. AE, DC, MC, V.*

$–$$ ✕ **Los Porteños I & II.** The seafood is so good at these neighboring restaurants that you'll leave with a new respect for the ocean. Famous are the *empanadas de mariscos* (deep-fried turnovers stuffed with seafood), which make excellent appetizers. The *chupes* (chowders) and *mariscales* (seafood soups) are excellent and inexpensive. The *jardín de marisco* (seafood garden) comes with clams, mussels, shrimp, and fish and is flavored with coriander. Special touches—the house wine comes in small soda bottles—leave you feeling right at home. ⊠ *Valdivia 169,* ☎ *32/252–511;* ⊠ *Cochrane 102,* ☎ *32/251–915. No credit cards.*

$$ ▥ **Puerta de Alcalá.** A five-story atrium flooded with light is the centerpiece of this hotel. Rooms here are basic and modern. Clean tiled bathrooms have little extras like hair dryers. The rooms facing the street in front can be quite noisy on weekends on account of the bars facing Subida Ecuador; if you're looking for sleep, ask for a quiet room in the back. ⊠ *Pirámide 524,* ☎ *32/227–478,* ℻ *32/745–642,* WEB *www.chileinfo.cl/puertadealcalahotel. 40 rooms. Restaurant, bar, minibars, room service, meeting room. AE, D, MC, V.*

$–$$ ▥ **Brighton B&B.** There may be no structure in town more prominent
★ than this bright yellow Victorian house on Cerro Concepción. It has a great location in a charming neighborhood beside an ascensor for easy access. The house is furnished with antiques chosen by owner Nelson Morgado, who taught architecture for two decades at the University of Barcelona. Three of the six rooms have ocean views. One, though small, has a wonderful private balcony overlooking the bay. The staff speaks excellent English, and prices include a Continental breakfast in the great café. ⊠ *Paseo Atkinson 151,* ☎ *32/223–513,* ℻ *32/598–802. 6 rooms. Restaurant, bar. AE, D, MC, V.*

$ ▥ **Alojamiento Monique Markowicz.** If you're willing to make some concessions—like sharing a cramped bathroom and sleeping beside walls that could use some fresh paint—you can live as the locals do in this private home. You can use the kitchen to prepare your own meals, and the plant-filled balcony with its stunning views of the entire city is alone worth the price of the stay. ⊠ *Subida Artillería 105, near Paseo 21 de Mayo,* ☎ ℻ *32/283–790. 3 rooms. Dining room, library, laundry services. AE, D, MC, V.*

$ ▥ **Porto Principal.** For its small size and unassuming location, this hotel is surprisingly comfortable. You enter through a restaurant where complimentary breakfast is served. The rooms are modern, secure, and as clean as they come in Valparaíso. ⊠ *Calle Huito 361,* ☎ ℻ *32/745–629. 6 rooms. Restaurant, bar, room service. AE, D, MC, V.*

Nightlife and the Arts

Since Valparaíso is a university town, the nightlife is reliably rowdy. On Thursday, Friday, and Saturday nights young people are out on the streets until daybreak. Subida Ecuador near Plazuela Ecuador crawls with pubs, and Avenida Errázuriz, facing the port, has the best discos.

BARS

To bump elbows and bottoms with Valparaíso's young and spirited crowd, venture up Subida Ecuador, just a few blocks west of Plaza Victoria. Since all these establishments are side by side, they're easy to find. Live jazz on weekends can be found at **La Curva** (⊠ Calle Ecuador 95). **L'O Devi** (⊠ Calle Ecuador 48) has a downstairs bar with live music and an upstairs disco with a bumping techno beat. **Mr. Egg** (⊠ Calle

Ecuador 50), conveniently located next door, also has a dance floor. **Bar Azul** (✉ Calle Ecuador 75) plays alternative music.

Valparaíso Eterno (✉ 150 Almirante Señoret, ☎ 32/228–374) one block from Plaza Sotomayor, gets it name from a famous song that pays homage to the city. This bar, covered with paintings of Valparaíso and floor-to-ceiling graffiti lovingly supplied by patrons, is a paean in its own right. There is live music on weekends. If you're hungry, the chorillana is as good as chorillana gets. The huge antique mirrors of **Bar La Playa** (✉ Serrano 567), just west of Plaza Sotomayor, give it an eclectic flare. A crowd gathers for poetry readings on Wednesdays at 11 PM, and this is the best time to soak up this bar's irresistible atmosphere.

DANCE CLUBS

On weekends you can dance to live tango music at the warm, unassuming Valparaíso classic, **Cinzano** (✉ Plaza Anibal Pinto 1182, ☎ 32/213–043). The newest dance clubs are found on and around the street directly opposite the bay, Avenida Errázuriz. Among the top discos in Valparaíso is **La Cueva Del Chivato** (✉ 1156 Av. Errázuriz, ☎ no phone). Next door to La Cueva Del Chivato you'll find another popular dance club, **Bulevar** (✉ 1154 Av. Errázuriz, ☎ no phone).

FILM

Cine Hoyts (✉ Av. Pedro Montt 2111, ☎ 32/594–709), across from Parque Italia, is a state-of-the-art theater showing American releases on five screens. The restaurant **Valparaíso Mi Amor** (✉ Papudo 612, ☎ 32/219–891) has a room dedicated to showing the 16mm films about Valparaíso made by owner Nelson Cabrera.

THEATER

Off Plaza O'Higgins, the lovely old **Teatro Municipal de Valparaíso** (✉ Uruguay 410, ☎ 32/214–654) hosts symphonies, ballet, and opera between May and November. The restored **Teatro Mauri** (✉ Av. Alemania 6985) directly behind La Sebastiana, is once again home to live performances. The **Ex-Cárcel de Valparaíso** (✉ El Castro s/n, Cerro Cárcel, ☎ 32/250–891), in a crumbling former prison in the middle of the city, is a haunting space for contemporary theater productions. Photo exhibitions keep alive the memory of political prisoners who were held captive here during Pinochet's regime.

Outdoor Activities and Sports

BEACHES

If it's beaches you're after, head to Viña del Mar. Valparaíso has only one notable beach, **Playa Las Torpederas,** a small sheltered crescent of sand south of the port.

BOATING

Ship owners and operators at **Muelle Prat** take groups on a circuit of the bay for about $2 per person. The half-hour ride, which passes in front of anchored warships, doesn't go very far out into the bay, but offers a panoramic view of the city. If you have several people, consider hiring your own boat for about $20.

SOCCER

The **Valparaíso Wanderers** (✉ Independencia 2061, ☎ 32/217–210), is Valparaíso's first division soccer team. The team was formed when a British football squad introduced the sport to the country. Catch a match, which usually takes place Mondays at the Estadio Municipal in Playa Ancha.

Shopping

The **Cooperativa Artesanal de Valparaíso,** a market where you can buy locally produced crafts, is at the corner of Avenida Pedro Montt and

Calle Las Heras. On the weekends, the **Feria de Antigüedades,** a flea market on Avenida Argentina at Plaza O'Higgins, offers an excellent selection of antiques.

Chile's major department store, **Ripley** (⊠ Calle Condell 1646, ☎ 32/ 622–531), is across from Plaza Victoria. The fifth floor has a food court.

Viña del Mar

130 km (85 mi) northwest of Santiago, 10 km (6 mi) north of Valparaíso.

In contrast to Valparaíso's hodgepodge of hillside houses, Viña de Mar has stylish new high-rise apartment buildings that tower above its excellent shoreline. Here you'll find wide boulevards lined with palms, lush parks with sharply edged landscaping, and manicured beaches that stretch for miles. It's been known for years as Chile's tourist capital (a title challenged today by several other hot spots).

To some, all this means that Viña del Mar is modern and exciting; to others, it means the city is lacking in character. But there's no denying that Viña del Mar has a little of everything—trendy boutiques, luxury hotels, beautiful mansions, interesting museums, a glitzy casino, and, of course, some of the best beaches in the country.

Numbers in white bullets in the text correspond to numbers in black bullets in the margins and on the Viña del Mar map.

A Good Walk

Don't expect twisting streets and steep stairways in Viña del Mar. The downtown area is completely flat and organized on a grid. To make things even easier, almost all of the streets are numbered. The only confusing aspect is that to the left and right of Avenida Libertad are streets with the same number, but they are labeled *Poniente* (West) and *Oriente* (East).

Plaza José Francisco Vergara ⑬ is the heart of the city. Just to the south is a smaller square called Plaza Sucre. Grandly filling the east end of the square is the redoubtable **Club Viña del Mar** ⑭. Walking south past Plaza Sucre you'll reach the magnificently landscaped gardens of the **Quinta Vergara** ⑮, where you'll find the Museo de Bellas Artes.

Return to Plaza Vergara and head north across the Estero Marga Marga via the Puente Libertad bridge. Gondolas once floated through the estuary, but today it's nearly dry outside of the rainy months of July and August. Walk north along Avenida Libertad and head east on 4 Norte. You'll immediately see the **Museo de Arqueológico e Historia Francisco Fonck** ⑯, renowned for its Easter Island artifacts. Continue east two more blocks until the street ends at the lovely **Palacio Rioja.** ⑰.

TIMING

The terrain in Viña del Mar is flat, making walking easy. You can take in all the sights on this tour in a few hours. Give yourself plenty of time for the beach—it's the real scene here, especially in summer.

SIGHTS TO SEE

⑭ **Club Viña del Mar.** It would be a shame to pass up a chance to see this private club's magnificent interior. The neoclassical building, constructed in 1901 of materials imported from England, is where wealthy locals come to play snooker. It often hosts art shows that are open to the public, which allows you to circumambulate the second-floor interior balcony. ⊠ *Plaza Sucre s/n,* ☎ *32/680–016.* ⊠ *Free.* ⊙ *Hrs vary.*

⑯ **Museo de Arqueológico e Historia Francisco Fonck.** A 500-year-old stone head brought from Easter Island guards the entrance to this archaeo-

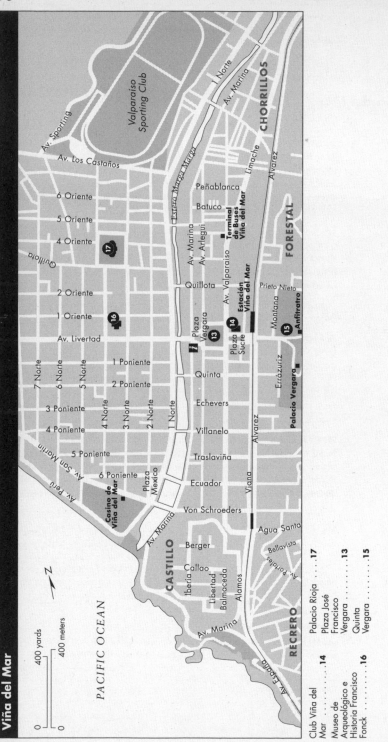

Viña del Mar

PACIFIC OCEAN

N

| 0 | 400 yards |
| 0 | 400 meters |

Valparaiso Sporting Club

Av. Sporting

Av. Los Castaños

Quillota

6 Oriente

5 Oriente

4 Oriente

2 Oriente

1 Oriente

Av. Livertad

Estero Marga Marga

Peñablanca

Batuco

Av. Marina

Av. Arlegui

Quillota

Av. Valparaiso

Terminal de Buses Viña del Mar

Estación Viña del Mar

Plaza Vergara

Plaza Sucre

Prieto Nieto

Montana

Limache

Alvarez

CHORRILLOS

FORESTAL

Anfitratro

Palacio Vergara

Erázuriz

7 Norte

6 Norte

5 Norte

4 Norte

3 Norte

2 Norte

1 Norte

1 Poniente

2 Poniente

3 Poniente

4 Poniente

5 Poniente

6 Poniente

Quinta

Echevers

Villanelo

Traslaviña

Ecuador

Von Schroeders

Alvarez

Viana

Agua Santa

Av. San Martin

Av. Perú

Plaza Mexico

Casino de Viña del Mar

Av. Marina

Berger

Callao

Iberia

Libertad

Balmaceda

Alamos

Av. Marina

Av. España

CASTILLO

RECRERO

Bellavista

Av. Portales

logical museum. The most interesting exhibits document the history of the isolated island that indigenous people call Rapa Nui. Besides the stone head, artifacts include wood tablets displaying ancient hieroglyphics. The museum, named for groundbreaking archaeologist Francisco Fonck, a native of Viña del Mar, has an extensive library of documents relating to the island. ⊠ *4 Norte 784,* ☏ *32/686–753.* 🖃 *Admission.* ⊙ *Tues.–Fri. 9:30–6, weekends and holidays 9:30–2.*

⑰ Palacio Rioja. This grand palace was built by Spanish banker Francisco Rioja immediately after the earthquake that leveled much of the city in 1906. Inside is a decorative arts museum showcasing a large portion of Rioja's belongings; it's worth the price to take in the century-old splendor. Also inside is a conservatory, so you'll often hear music in the air. If you're lucky you can catch a performance in the main ballroom. The beautifully landscaped grounds around the palace, open to the public, are great for shady lounging or a picnic. An art-house cinema is in the rear. ⊠ *Quillota 214,* ☏ *32/883–322.* 🖃 *Admission.* ⊙ *Tues.–Sun. 10–2, 3–6.*

⑬ Plaza José Francisco Vergara. Viña del Mar's central square, Plaza Vergara is lined with majestic palms. Here's where you can strap on your in-line skates or take a ride in a horse-drawn carriage past some of the city's stately mansions. Presiding over the east end of the plaza is the patriarch of coastal accommodations, the venerable Hotel O'Higgins. Opposite the hotel is the neoclassical Teatro Municipal, where you can see ballet, theater, and music performances. To the south is Avenida Valparaíso, the city's main shopping strip.

★ **⑮ Quinta Vergara.** Viña del Mar has one of Chile's best botanical gardens. You can easily feel lost on the paths that wind amid soaring eucalyptus trees. Here you'll find an amphitheater where an international music festival, the *Festival Internacional de la Canción de Viña del Mar,* is held in February. The neo-Gothic Palacio Vergara is home to the **Museo de Bellas Artes.** The fine-arts palace was erected after the 1906 earthquake as the residence of the wealthy Vergara family. Inside you'll find a collection of classical paintings dating from the 15th to the 19th centuries. Highlights include works by Rubens and Tintoretto. ⊠ *Av. Errázuriz 563,* ☏ *32/684–137.* 🖃 *Admission.* ⊙ *Museum Tues.–Sun. 10–1:45, 3–6; gardens daily 7:30–7.*

NEED A BREAK?	Even die-hard shoppers can feel overwhelmed by the myriad shops along Avenida Valparaíso. Take a load off at **286 Rue Valparaíso** (⊠ Av. Valparaíso 286, ☏ 32/710140), an Internet café—here you can make free international calls via the Internet (headphones are provided). The French owner makes delicious, sugary milk shakes—with ice cream and milk—something not easily found in Chile. It's open past midnight.

Dining and Lodging

$$–$$$ ✕ **La Fontana.** Inside the Casino de Viña del Mar, this elegant Italian restaurant is decorated with bougainvilleas and images of Venice. La Fontana offers a complete fish and shellfish menu, but it's the pasta and risotto dishes that shine. After a plate of fettuccine with fresh salmon and caviar, you'll feel ready to gamble the night away. ⊠ *San Martín 199,* ☏ *32/500–600. AE, DC, MC, V. No lunch.*

$$ ✕ **Cap Ducal.** This ship-shaped restaurant rises from the sea and affords excellent views of the shore. The creative kitchen specializes in European-style cooking as well as its own inventions, including a popular eel stew and grilled fish in a spicy herb sauce. ⊠ *Av. Marina 51,* ☏ *32/626–655. AE, DC, MC, V.*

$$ ✕ **Delicias del Mar.** Don't be fooled by the Marilyn Monroe photos—
★   this nationally renowned restaurant's Basque-style seafood is tasty, even
though the decor may not be. The *machas curadas* (steamed clams with
dill and Parmesan cheese) are fantastic, as is the grilled sea bass in a
cognac sauce with shrimp and mushrooms. Top your meal off with one
of the fine desserts and you'll know why chef Raúl Madinagoitía has
his own television program. Oenophiles should peruse the excellent wine
list. ✉ *San Martín 459,* ☏ *32/901–837. AE, DC, MC, V.*

$$ ✕ **Fogón Criollo.** In an unassuming area with many good little restaurants, this is the most authentically Chilean spot. The specialty is
brasero al estilo Fogón Criollo, a large clay pot full of chunks of pot
roast, chicken, sausages, and potatoes in a hearty broth. Note the old
black-and-white photos of Viña de Mar. ✉ *5 Norte 476,* ☏ FAX *32/
973–312. AE, DC, MC, V.*

$$ ✕ **Rendez Vous.** The twinkling lights of Valparaíso provide a roman-
tic backdrop for this restaurant in the Hotel Oceanic. The views are
just as good during the day, when you can watch the rough surf pound
the coast from an outdoor terrace. As the name suggests, you can order
French-inspired dishes such as *filete café de Paris* (bacon-wrapped
steak with herb butter) and *filete a la francesa* (sole sautéed in butter
with lemon, parsley, white wine, and a little garlic). Fresh flowers on
the tables are a simple touch missing nearly everywhere else on the coast.
✉ *5 Norte 476,* ☏ *32/973–312. AE, DC, MC, V.*

$$$ ▦ **Hotel Gala.** This 14-story luxury hotel not far from the Avenida Val-
paraíso shopping strip offers modern rooms with panoramic views of
the city. For corporate travelers there's a state-of-the-art business center. ✉ *Arlegui 273,* ☏ *32/686–688,* FAX *32/689–568. 64 rooms, 13 suites.
Restaurant, bar, in-room data ports, minibars, pool, massage, sauna,
health club, business services, convention center, meeting rooms. AE,
DC, MC, V.*

$$$ ▦ **Hotel Oceanic.** Large, luxurious rooms overlook the rocky coast at
★   this hotel on the road to Reñaca. Comfort abounds, from the fireplace
warming the lobby to the pool overlooking the entire bay. The nicest
rooms have terraces. While there's no beach access here, the sands of
Salinas and Reñaca are close by. ✉ *Av. Borgoño 12925, Reñaca,* ☏
32/830–006, FAX *32/830–390. 22 rooms, 6 suites. Restaurant, bar, in-
room data ports, in-room safes, minibars, room service, pool, hot tub,
massage, sauna, business services, meeting rooms. AE, DC, MC, V.*

$$$ ▦ **Hotel O'Higgins.** This elegant grand dame, built in 1935, presides
over one corner of Plaza Vergara. An oak-paneled bar off the lobby
shows off the classic style that made this hotel famous. Rooms are huge,
with soaring ceilings. Many parts of the block-long hotel are in need
of renovation, but if you don't mind the occasional faded curtain and
worn carpet, you can enjoy ample space, charm, and traditional service. ✉ *Plaza José Francisco Vergara,* ☏ *32/682–000,* FAX *32/883–537.
262 rooms, 2 suites. Restaurant, bar, minibars, room service, pool, dance
club, business services, meeting rooms. AE, DC, MC, V.*

$$ ▦ **Best Western Marina Del Rey.** A few blocks south of the estuary,
this modern seven-story hotel has everything a business traveler could
ask for, from a business center to plenty of space for meetings. In the
clean, generously proportioned rooms, the windows are double-paned
to keep out noise from the road. There's also a pleasing breakfast area
and restaurant. ✉ *Ecuador 299,* ☏ *32/710–071,* FAX *32/710–513,* WEB
*www.marinadelrey.co.cl. 103 rooms, 5 suites. Restaurant, bar, in-
room data ports, minibars, room service, laundry service, baby-sitting,
business services, convention center, meeting rooms. AE, DC, MC, V.*

$$ ▦ **Hotel Alcazar.** Have you always wanted to stay in your own little
house near the beach? You can get that feeling by renting one of the
charming cabañas at Hotel Alcazar. Accessible through a passageway

from the street, these cabins in a lush courtyard are cheaper than the standard-issue rooms in the hotel itself. ⊠ *Alvarez 646,* ☎ *32/685–112,* FAX *32/884–245. 52 rooms, 22 cabins. Restaurant, bar, minibars, meeting rooms. AE, DC, MC, V.*

$$ 🖫 **Magno Hotel.** This modern hotel is near most of Viña del Mar's major sights. The rooms are small, but they have double-paned windows to keep out the street noise. ⊠ *Arlegui 372,* ☎ *32/881–172,* FAX *32/993–316. 26 rooms. Bar, free parking. AE, DC, MC, V.*

$ 🖫 **Hotel Rokamar.** On the main road into town, Hotel Rokamar is an excellent alternative to some of Viña del Mar's overpriced properties. Three floors of large rooms surround a paneled lobby with a raulí-wood reception desk. The staff is very friendly and helpful. In the restaurant are large murals depicting scenes of life in old Viña. ⊠ *Viana 107,* ☎ FAX *32/690–019. 24 rooms, 2 suites. Free parking. AE, DC, MC, V.*

$ 🖫 **Residencia 555.** In business since 1978, Residencia 555 has twice been named the city's top guest house. A stay in this charming wood-frame building makes you feel like a local. A large winding staircase leads to the rooms on the second floor. Breakfast is included. ⊠ *5 Norte 555,* ☎ *32/972–240,* FAX *32/972–240,* WEB *www.gratisweb.com/residencial555. 12 rooms. Breakfast room, parking. MC, V.*

Nightlife and the Arts

Viña's nightlife varies considerably according to the season, with the most glittering events concentrated in the summer months of January and February.

CASINOS

With a retro style that wouldn't be out of place in a classic James Bond movie, **Casino de Viña del Mar** (⊠ Av. San Martín 199, ☎ 32/500–600) has a restaurant, disco, cabaret, and—of course—games of the roulette and blackjack sort. It's open nightly until the wee hours; formal dress is encouraged in the game rooms. There's a $5 cover charge.

DANCE CLUBS

Many of the most popular dance clubs are a few miles north of Viña de Mar in Reñaca. **News** (⊠ Av. Borgon 13101, Reñaca, ☎ 32/837–345), in a miniature castle perched on the cliff between Viña de Mar and Reñaca, is always packed on the weekends. The dance floor often keeps pumping until 8 AM. Bartenders here mix Chile's best *caipirinha* (Brazil's national drink, made with a potent sugar cane liquor called cachaça). Another top dance spot is **Kamikaze** (⊠ Av. Vicuña Mackenna 1106, Reñaca, ☎ 32/834–667).

New Topsy (⊠ Av. Borgon 13101, Reñaca, ☎ 32/837–345), has salsa dancing on Fridays. Flashy **Skuba** (⊠ Caleta Abarca, ☎ 32/837–345) is a dance club on the coast at the southern edge of Viña del Mar. In the center of town the most popular disco is **Santa Fe** (⊠ 8 Norte 303, ☎ 32/691–725).

FILM

Cine Palacio Rioja (⊠ Quillota 214, ☎ 32/883–322) is an art-house theater in the rear of the Palacio Rioja. Viña del Mar's two Cinemark movie theaters outsize everything else on the coast. Both show recent American movies. **Cinemark Marina Arauco** (⊠ Av. Libertad 1348, ☎ 32/688–188) has four screens. **Cinemark Viña Shopping** (⊠ Av. 15 Norte 961, ☎ 32/993–388), a little far from the center of town, has eight screens.

Outdoor Activities and Sports

BEACHES

Just north of the rock wall along Avenida Peru you'll find the stretch of shoreline that draws visitors from all over South America. Viña del

Mar really has just one long beach, but it's called by different names—heading north you find **Playa Los Marineros, Playa Las Salinas,** and after the dock, **Playa El Sol** and **Playa Blanca.** All of them are packed with sun-loving crowds all summer long. The most popular beach in all Chile, **Playa Reñaca,** is 2 km (1 mi) north. In summer, crowds here blanket the entire beach—literally.

GOLF

You can play 18 holes at **Granadilla Country Club** (⊠ Camino Granadilla s/n, ☎ 32/689–249), a historic course north of downtown Viña del Mar in the Santa Inés section of town.

HORSE RACING

Valparaíso Sporting Club (⊠ Av. Los Castaños 404, ☎ 32/689–393) hosts horse racing every Friday. The Clásico del Derby, Chile's version of the Kentucky Derby, takes place the first Sunday in February. Rugby, polo, cricket, and other sports are also played here.

SOCCER

Everton is Viña del Mar's soccer team. After poor play in the first division in 2000, the team was demoted to second division for 2001. Matches are held at the 19,000-seat **Estadio Sausalito** (⊠ Laguna Sausalito, ☎ 32/978–250), which hosted World Cup matches in 1962.

Shopping

Outside of Santiago, there are more opportunities for shopping in Viña del Mar than anywhere else in Chile. Hundreds of stores along **Avenida Valparaíso** sell shoes, electronics, clothing, and other goods. On Plaza Sucre you'll find the city's two largest department stores. **Ripley** (⊠ Sucre 290, ☎ 32/384–480) sells everything from perfume to electronics. **Falabella** (⊠ Sucre 250, ☎ 32/264–740) also has linens and designer clothing. For one-stop shopping, locals head to **Shopping Viña** (⊠ 15 Norte 961).

A market of locally produced crafts, **Cooperativa de Artesania de Viña del Mar** is on Quinta between Viana and Valparaíso. More crafts stands are set up a block to the east on Pasaje Cousiño. On the beach, just off Vergara dock, the **Feria Artesanal Muelle Vergara** is a crafts fair open daily in summer and on weekends the rest of the year.

THE NORTHERN BEACHES

Once north of Viña del Mar, the Pacific collides with the rocky offshore islands and stony shores of the coast. The greater distance between towns—each is set around a beach—lends them a sense of independence and character. Just north of Concón begins the wide sand dunes that eventually give way to expanses of frolicking coastline.

Concón

⑱ *16 km (10 mi) north of Viña del Mar.*

How to explain the lovely name Concón? In the language of the Changos, *co* meant water, and the duplication of the sound refers to the confluence of the Río Aconcagua and the Pacific. When the Spanish arrived in 1543, Pedro de Valdivia created an improvised shipyard here that was destroyed by natives, leading to one of the first clashes between indigenous and Spanish cultures in central Chile.

This suburb of Viña del Mar has a few good beaches, and some elegant summer houses were built in the 1930s. But the most interesting sights are outside of town. Visible from the highway as you drive toward Concón is **Isla de Lobos,** a small rocky island that is home to a permanent population of sea lions. A kilometer (½ mile) farther north, the **Roca Oceánico** overlooks the rocky coastline. The gneiss and quartz rocks here have occasional impressive veins of black volcanic rock, especially on the south side of the promontory.

Dining and Lodging

$$-$$$ ✕ **Edelweiss.** Pass by Edelweiss and you'll miss the finest food in town. Edelwiess has one of the best wine lists on the coast, including selections of French and Spanish labels—a rarity in this region. Some dishes are just as unexpected: *salmón a la Florentina* comes with a spinach cream sauce; *camarones Bombay* consists of prawns in a curry sauce with bananas, cherries, and pineapple braised in butter; fondues are another specialty. Set off the highway south of town, the restaurant has wide windows with views of the rough ocean swells. ✉ *Av. Borgoño 19200,* ☎ *32/811–683. AE, DC, MC, V.*

$$$ 🏨 **Hippocampus Resort.** This nine-story resort near the beach provides a level of comfort unmatched by any other accommodation on the Central Coast. The terrace, landscaped with palms and flowers, has an indoor heated pool that offers a sunning alternative to the beaches. Kids cherish the corkscrew slide into the outdoor pool. The Altamar restaurant serves mainly pastas, pizzas, and sandwiches. ✉ *Av. Las Piminelas 763,* ☎ *32/857–100 or 800/800–480,* FAX *32/857–200,* WEB *www. hippocampusresort.cl. 88 rooms. Restaurant, bar, in-room data ports, minibars, 2 pools, massage, sauna, health club, shop, baby-sitting, playground, business services, meeting rooms. AE, DC, MC, V.*

$$ 🏨 **Mantagua.** Set apart from from the vacationing masses, this cluster of cabañas has a relaxed, family-oriented atmosphere. The complex is about ½ km (¼ mi) from the wide, quiet beaches, accessible by crossing a vast tract of dunes—have fun reenacting scenes from *The English Patient.* Beige stucco cabañas have little yards with partial views of the sea. A big playground and a a stable of horses delight kids. Although it's not luxurious, Mantagua is like being away at summer camp. ✉ *Camino Quintero Km 3,* ☎ FAX *32/811–415,* WEB *www.mantagua.cl. 27 cabañas. Restaurant, bar, room service, pool, miniature golf, horseback riding, volleyball, shop, playground. AE, DC, MC, V.*

Nightlife and the Arts

Jamaica Jamaica, on the south end of town across from the Roca Oceánico, is a multi-level outdoor disco offering views of the bay.

Outdoor Activities and Sports

BEACHES

The southernmost beach in Concón, **Playa Los Lilenes** is a tiny yellow-sand cove with calm waters. After the fisherman's wharf comes **Playa Las Bahamas,** favored by surfers and windsurfers. At the north end of town is the gray-sand **Playa La Boca** (Mouth Beach), so named because the Río Anconcagua flows into the Pacific here. In the river itself, shore birds crowd a sandy inlet that curls from the north side.

HORSEBACK RIDING

There are stables right off the highway 2 km (1 mi) north of Concón where you can rent horses for about $5 per half hour.

Zapallar

★ ⑲ *48 km (30 mi) north of Concón.*

An aristocratic enclave for the past century, Zapallar doesn't promote itself as a summer retreat. In fact, it's always been a bit reticent about strangers. After traveling around Europe, Olegario O'Valle decided to re-create the Riviera on the Chilean coast. He allotted plots of land to friends and family with the provision that they build European-style villas. Today the hills above the beach are dotted with these extravagant mansions.

Walking south along the beach you reach the **Caleta de Zapallar,** where fishermen sell their catch and then settle in for dominoes. Farther on, the beach ends in a long peninsula jutting out into the ocean. This promontory looks bare but for a single, perfectly shaped tree—in fact, it is a small cluster of trees. The early steps are steep and hard, but the views make it a worthwhile climb. If you continue south, you soon reach **Plaza del Mar Bravo** (Rough Sea Square). This playground often has mules the kids can ride.

A sanctuary for Magellan and Humboldt penguins, **Isla Chachagua** is about 3 km (2 mi) south of Zapallar. No one is allowed on the island, but you can ride around in the small boats that depart from the pier in the town Zapallar. You can also get within 50 yards of the island by walking to the north end of the beach in the town of Chachagua. A pair of binoculars will help you watch the penguins wobble around the perimeter of the island.

Dining and Lodging

$$–$$$ ✕ **Cesar Restaurant.** At the southern edge of Playa Zapallar you can take a break on this terrace covered by a thatched roof. Inside is a plant-filled grotto. Try the *albacora* (swordfish) in caper sauce. ⊠ *Playa Zapallar,* ☎ *no phone. No credit cards.*

$$ ✕ **El Chiringuito.** At this remarkable seafood restaurant, the tables—thick slabs of polished wood surrounded by comfortable chairs fashioned from tree trunks—are set out on an abutment with a panoramic view of the bay. Pelicans linger among the fishing boats anchored below. For starters choose machas, camarones, or ostiones cooked *al vapor* (with wine sauce), *al pil pil* (with chili sauce and garlic), *a la parmesana* (with cheese), or *con salsa holandesa* (with a cream sauce). ⊠ *Caleta de Zapallar,* ☎ *33/741–024. No credit cards.*

$$$–$$$$ ✕▣ **Isla Seca.** A trail of black-and-white tiles leads you through a din-
★   ing room onto a tented terrace with white cast-iron furniture. From your table you can gaze out past an elegant pool to the blue of the Pacific. This restaurant's stylish refinement and simplicity rival anything in Miami Beach or Nice. While prices here are the same as almost all restaurants on the coast, the setting and the service are nearly unsurpassed. The hotel is notable for its well-appointed, spacious rooms and an atmosphere of languorous chic matched by gracious manners. Two nearly identical moss-green buildings set not far from each other are landscaped with bougainvillea and cypress trees. ⊠ *Camino Costanero s/n,* ☎ *33/741224,* ⅏ *33/741228. 34 rooms, 5 suites. Restaurant, bar, piano bar, minibars, pool, playground, business services, meeting room. AE, DC, MC, V .*

Papudo

⑳ *11 km (7 mi) north of Zapallar.*

In a letter dated October 8, 1545, Spanish conquistador Pedro Valdivia wrote: "Of all the lands of the New World, the port of Papudo has a goodness above any other land. It's like God's Paradise: it has a gentle temperate climate; large, resounding mountains; and fertile lands . . ."

For years Papudo was connected to Santiago by a train that no longer runs, thus the town's boastful sobriquet: "a resort with history." You can still find bits of that history in the quiet resort town. A block from the beach is the **Palacio Recart,** a yellow palace dating from 1910. The building, declared a national monument in 1996, hosts occasional art and history exhibitions.

Dining and Lodging

$$ ✕ **El Barco Rojo.** In 1913, a French ship called the *Ville de Dijon* sank
★ off the coast of Papudo. The beams, doors, stairways, and other sundry
parts were salvaged to build El Barco Rojo (The Red Ship). Poet Pablo
Neruda, among those who frequented the spot, admired the colorful
floor tiles. The ceiling is papered with love letters to the restaurant writ-
ten by past patrons. Each table has different color tablecloths, and the
chairs are a delightful hodgepodge. The menus—which list great em-
panadas made with cheese and *albahaca* (basil)—look like high-school
arts projects. A tiny bar is eclectically and lovingly furnished with bric-
a-brac. ⊠ *Av. Irarrazaval 300,* ☎ *33/791–488. No credit cards.*

$$ ✕ **Gran Azul.** Beside the fishermen's caleta on Playa Chica, this restaurant is the best choice for relaxed dining in Papudo. From inside the
Gran Azul's A-frame—of course it's painted blue—you're afforded
panoramic views of the Pacific. The best choices here are the seafood
chowders, king crab, and shrimp. The desserts are made on the premises.
⊠ *Av. Irarrazaval 86,* ☎ *33/791–584. AE, DC, MC, V.*

$$ ☷ **Hotel Carande.** By far the most respectable hotel in town, the
Carande has simple if not exciting rooms. Ask for one on the third floor,
as these have sea views. A fireplace warms the lobby all winter. ⊠ *Cho-
rillos 89,* ☎ *33/791–105,* ⨳ *33/791–118. 30 rooms. Restaurant, bar,
refrigerators, pool. AE, DC, MC, V.*

Los Molles

★ ㉑ *32 km (20 mi) north of Papudo on Ruta 5.*

Upon first inspection, Los Molles seems rather drab: a row of houses
on a street leading to the beach. But the nearby landscape, a desert-
like sanctuary of cacti and other hearty plants, is truly splendid. Fal-
cons, vultures, sparrows, and turtledoves fly past. Grab your binoculars
and follow Avenida Las Jaibas uphill to its end.

A 15-minute walk along the coast brings the screeches of the **Isla de
los Lobos Marinos,** a rocky island filled with boisterous sea lions. A
little farther you are waylaid by the terrifying sound of **Puquén,** a blow-
hole whose name means "mouth of the devil." There is, without a doubt,
a diabolical hiss. The spume can launch 50 meters in the air on blus-
tery weather. For a simpler natural encounter, follow Avenida Los
Pescadores past the north end of the beach to **Las Terrazas.** These ter-
races of chiseled rock are a great vantage point for the tempestuous
swells below.

Dining and Lodging

$$ ✕ **Caleta Pirata.** The Jolly Roger flies outside this fun beach restaurant run by a Chilean and a Swiss-Hungarian. The menu is original,
as in the reineta served in aluminum foil with potato and zucchini in
an herb butter sauce. There's a view of the fishing boats along the shore.
⊠ *La Caleta s/n,* ☎ *33/791–788. AE, DC, MC, V.*

$$ ✕☷ **Hosteria Kon-Tiki.** Reserved for Chilean army officers in January
★ and February, this retreat north of Los Molles is open to everyone the
rest of the year. Far from being a drab military base, it's the best lodg-
ing on the north end of the Central Coast. Identical cabañas at the mouth
of the bay have terraces, full kitchens, and rooms with bunk beds for
children. Across the street, a three-story stucco building has tasteful,
very comfortable modern rooms with balconies or terraces. The ele-
gant dining room serves corvina cooked six ways, and offers a good
selection of Chilean wines. Across the street a bar set in the stone promon-
tory has panoramic views. Most folks don't know about this hideaway—
let it be your secret. ⊠ *Av. Costanera s/n, Pichidangui,* ☎ *53/531–103,*
⨳ *02/693–5522. 32 rooms, 24 cabañas. Restaurant, bar, in-room*

data ports, minibars, 2 pools, massage, sauna, business services, meeting room. AE, DC, MC, V.

$ 🏠 **Cabañas Los Molles.** Just uphill from the beach, these cabañas—more like small houses—are the newest and most comfortable accommodations in town. They have brick and wood interiors, big living rooms, full kitchens, and sleeping quarters upstairs. They're spotless, too. ✉ *Calle Las Jaibas, corner of Calle O'Higgins,* ☎ *32/379–1787,* FAX *2/201–2184 (Santiago). 6 cabañas. Kitchenettes, playground. No credit cards.*

$ 🏠 **Cabañas Lourdes.** About 100 yards from the beach on the main road is this family-oriented stopover. The cabañas aren't much from the outside, but are spacious inside and have modern furniture. ✉ *Av. Los Pescadores s/n,* ☎ *32/791–783. 6 houses, 9 cabañas, 10 suites. Restaurant, bar, kitchenettes, refrigerators, in-room data ports. No credit cards.*

Outdoor Activities and Sports
DIVING

Hernan Labarca at **H. L. Divers** (✉ Neruda 11, ☎ 33/791–762 or 09/ 637–5113), one of only five authorized dive centers in Chile, offers classes, rents equipment and boats, and organizes trips. If you can't dive, you can take a boat trip to swim with sea lions.

THE SOUTHERN BEACHES

Once a dominion of solitude and sea, the stretch of coastline south of Valparaíso has seen much development, not all of it well planned, over the past few decades. Here you'll find a quick succession of towns catering to the hordes that head to the beaches in January and February.

The main reason to visit—and it's a great one—is to take a look at Pablo Neruda's hideaway at Isla Negra. The poet's house, perched on a bluff overlooking the ocean, displays the treasures—from masks and maps to seashells—he collected over the course of his remarkable life.

Quintay

㉒ *30 km (19 mi) south of Valparaíso.*

Not so long ago, migrating sperm whales could still be seen from the beaches at Quintay. The creatures were all but exterminated by the whaling industry that sprung up in Quintay in 1942. Whaling was banned in 1967, and the town went quiet again. Just past the handful of brightly colored fishing boats on the little beach is the abandoned **whaling factory.** Walking around its nearly abandoned skeletal remains— parts now used as an open-air shellfish hatchery—is likely to be the memory you take home of Quintay.

Escuela San Pedro de Quintay, the town's elementary school, serves as a makeshift museum dedicated to Quintay's whaling past. Jose Daniel Barrios, a former whaler, maintains the humble display; his whaling contract is among the exhibits. Others include photos of the plant, a whale gun, whale teeth, and a harpoon. Also here are some pottery and skeletons from the indigenous Aconcagua people, who inhabited the region around 1300. ✉ *Calle Escuela San Pedro,* ☎ *no phone.* 🎫 *Donation.* ⊙ *Jan.–Feb., daily 10–noon, 2–6; Mar.–Dec., hrs vary.*

Dining and Lodging
$$ ✕ **Los Pescadores.** Echoing the colors of the fishing boats below, this seafood restaurant has yellow walls, a bright blue terrace, and wooden floors painted green. As you watch the rugged fishermen with their catch, it's easy to imagine whales being hauled in a few decades ago. There's a good wine selection and attentive service, and the seafood is dynamite. ✉ *Av. Costanera s/n,* ☎ *32/362–068. AE, DC, MC, V.*

$ ⊞ **Residencial Mónica.** Quintay has a couple of residenciales, but it really isn't set up for overnighters. This private home is the best option in town. Open only in summer, it has basic but well-maintained rooms. ⊠ *Merino s/n,* ☎ *32/362–090. 10 rooms. No credit cards.*

Outdoor Activities and Sports

BEACHES

Until a few years ago, a thick pine forest made **Playa Grande** one of the most beautiful, as well as secluded, beaches on the coast. New apartment buildings are where the woods used to be. There are two ways to reach the beach: through the town, following Avenida Teniente Merino, or through the gated community of Santa Augusta. Teepee-like huts selling crafts and food are set up along the beach in summer.

DIVING

Chile's coastline is home to an array of interesting shipwrecks. Two are off the shores of Quintay, including *Indus IV,* a whaling ship that went down in 1947. There are no dive shops in Quintay, but in nearby Los Molles, **H. L. Divers** (⊠ Neruda 11, Los Molles, ☎ 33/791–762 or 09/637–5113) is an excellent coastal dive center. **Poseidon** (⊠ Av. Andrés Bello 2909, Santiago, ☎ 2/231–3597), a dive shop in Santiago, offers excursions to Quintay.

GOLF

The **Club de Golf Santa Augusta** (☎ 32/362–149, FAX 32/362147) is an excellent 18-hole course with a driving range and putting green, three tennis courts, and a restaurant.

Algarrobo

㉓ *35 km (22 mi) south of Quintay.*

The largest town south of Valparaíso, Algarrobo is the first of a long string of balnearios. Though Algarrobo isn't the prettiest place, it has a winding coastline of yellow-sand beaches that attract a great number of summer visitors.

The statue of Saint Peter in the sand next to fishermen's wharf marks **Playa San Pedro,** the town's largest beach. On Playa San Pedro you'll find a private yacht club, **Club de Yates Algarrobo.** In February, boats from all over the country participate in one of Chile's most important nautical events, the Regata Mil Millas Náuticas.

The **Cofradía Náutica,** another private marina, harbors some of the country's top yachts. Through this marina you can reach **Isla de los Pájaros Niños,** a penguin sanctuary connected to the dock that is home to more than 300 Humboldt and Magellan penguins. The upper crags of the island are dotted with hundreds of little caves dug by the penguins using their legs and beaks. If you can't access the island through the marina, grab your binoculars and take the moderately difficult path up the nearby hill.

Dining and Lodging

$$ ✕ **Los Patitos.** Two large, simple dining rooms look across the dunes of Playa Algarrobo Norte. Locals recommend the filling *caldos* (soups) served in clay bowls. *Ostiones a la parmesana* (scallops served in their shell in a butter sauce, topped by grated Parmesan) is a tasty appetizer. Those with big appetites should try the good-size servings of albacora. ⊠ *Av. Carlos Alessandri 278,* ☎ *35/481–778. No credit cards.*

$$ ✕ **Restaurante Algarrobo.** The only beachfront restaurant in Algarrobo has a terrace overlooking tiny, misnamed Playa Grande. Hot butter crackles as it's poured over corvina, reineta, and other excellent fish

served *a la mantequilla* (grilled with butter). The service is very good. ✉ *Av. Carlos Alessandri 1505,* ☎ FAX *35/481–078. No credit cards.*

$$ ✕⊞ **Der Münchner Hof.** This guest house, south of town in El Quisco, sits right on the shore. The spotless accommodations, with separate bedrooms with two single beds, have stunning views. Ask for Room 3, which comes with a terrace overlooking the beach. Though German-owned, the restaurant's menu doesn't include many Bavarian dishes. However, your hankering for old Munich might be staved with a *pernil ahumado* (smoked ham) and a Löwenbräu. There's a lunch buffet on weekends. ✉ *Av. Costanera 111, El Quisco,* ☎ *35/471–660,* FAX *35/ 471–704. 4 rooms. Restaurant, bar, room service. AE, DC, MC, V.*

$$–$$$ ⊞ **Pao Pao.** Kids will be mesmerized by the four llamas eating all the flowers at this lodging in the northern reaches of town. Spread across well-kept lawns, the comfortable cabañas have ocean views from beneath a canopy of pine trees. Choose between basic cabañas and suites with *camas de matrimonio* (double beds), hot tubs, fireplaces, and kitchens with microwaves. The restaurant, open in summer only, is one of the best in town—a nice feature since you have a long walk to reach the rest of Algarrobo. ✉ *Camino Mirasol s/n,* ☎ FAX *35/482–145 or 35/481–264. 21 cabañas. Restaurant, bar, room service, 2 pools, playground, baby-sitting, laundry service, meeting rooms. AE.*

$$ ⊞ **Hotel Pacífico.** This is the most modern hotel south of Valparaíso on the Central Coast. A block from Playa Las Cadenas on the town's main road, it has a wide lawn with swings and a large pool. Make sure to get a room in the newer part of the hotel—the older wing has seen better days. The lobby is used for art expositions on weekends. ✉ *Av. Carlos Alessandri 1930,* ☎ *35/481–040,* FAX *35/481–040. 79 rooms. Restaurant, bar, pool, playground, convention center, meeting rooms. AE, DC, MC, V.*

Outdoor Activities and Sports

BEACHES

Playa El Canelo and **Playa Canelillo,** separated by a small rocky jag, have fine yellow sand, clear green water, and a backdrop of pines. Except for a few snack stands there are no businesses in sight. Outside of January and February you're likely to find the beaches deserted. La Peñablanca, the large, white rocky outcropping at the end of the beach that is a favorite of seagulls, marks the southern end of town. **Playa San Pedro,** next to the fisherman's wharf, is the town's busiest beach. To the north, the popular **Playa Las Cadenas** is flanked by a few inexpensive restaurants. Las Cadenas, or "the chains," refers to the thick, rusted metal links that mark the seafront promenade at the beach's north end. They were recovered from a shipwreck off Algarrobo Bay.

DIVING

Diving Center Cinco Oceanos Chile at Hotel Pacífico (✉ Av. Carlos Alessandri 1930, ☎ 09/448–3784) rents equipment, offers classes, and leads dives.

GOLF

A few miles outside of town, you can play 18 holes of golf at the residential country club **Santa María de Algarrobo** (✉ Carretera Casablanca-Algarrobo Km 5, ☎ 35/481–673).

Isla Negra

24 *4 km (2 mi) south of Algarrobo.*

"I needed a place to work," Chilean poet and Nobel Laureate Pablo Neruda wrote in his memoirs. "I found a stone house facing the ocean, a place nobody knew about, Isla Negra." Neruda, who bought the house in 1939, found much inspiration here. "Isla Negra's wild coastal strip, with its turbulent ocean, was the place to give myself passionately to the writing of my new song," he wrote.

★ A mecca for Pablo Neruda's ardent admirers, **Casa-Museo Isla Negra** is a shrine to his life, work, and many passions. Although he spent much time living and traveling abroad, Neruda made Isla Negra his primary residence. Late in life, Neruda wrote his memoirs from the upstairs bedroom; the last pages were dictated to his wife before he departed for a Santiago hospital, where he died. Neruda and his last wife are buried in the prow-shape tomb area behind the house.

Just before Neruda's death in 1973, a military coup put Augosto Pinochet in command of Chile. Neruda's home was closed off and all access denied. Over the years, Neruda devotees chiseled their tributes into the wooden gates surrounding the property. After decades of neglect, the Neruda Foundation restored the house and it opened as a museum in 1989. Here you'll find his collections displayed as they were while he lived here. The living room contains—among numerous other oddities—a number of maidenheads from ships hanging from the ceiling and walls. Neruda called them his "girlfriends."

There are wonderful English-language tours of the property every half hour. Tours are necessary to comprehend the relevance of Neruda's many obsessions, from the positioning of guests at the dinner table to the east-west alignment of his bed. Objects had a spiritual and symbolic life for the poet, a fact that the tours make evident. On the premises, **Café Rincón del Poeta** (Poet's Corner Café) is a relaxed nook with simple fare—your best bet for a bite in town. ⊠ *Camino Vecinal s/n,* ☎ FAX *35/461–284* 🖃 *Admission.* ⊙ *Tues.–Sat. 10–7, Sun. 10–5.*

Dining and Lodging

$$ ✕🖬 **La Candela.** Abusing its proximity to Neruda's home, and taking advantage of a lack of competition (it's the only restaurant and lodging in Isla Negra), La Candela is one of the most expensive restaurants on the coast. Although there are claims to the contrary, the views of the ocean a block away are obstructed. To make up for this, perhaps, the cloth napkins are bordered in lace, and a fireplace burns all year. Despite its overblown air, little can go wrong with seafood in these parts. The attached *hostería* (small hotel) has 16 clean and simple rooms. ⊠ *Calle de la Hostería 67,* ☎ FAX *35/461–254. 16 rooms. AE, DC, MC, V.*

Outdoor Adventure and Sports

BEACHES
There are two small yellow-sand beaches at Isla Negra; swimming is prohibited at both. The most famous is directly behind Neruda's house, with its characteristic abutment of shoreline boulders. A couple of blocks south, behind La Candela, is a wider, more private stretch of shoreline.

HORSEBACK RIDING
You can rent horses for about $5 per half hour at the stables off the highway just north of Casa-Museo Neruda.

CENTRAL CHILE A TO Z

To research prices, get advice from other travelers, and book travel arrangements, visit www.fodors.com.

AIR TRAVEL
The Central Coast is served by Santiago's Aeropuerto Comodoro Arturo Merino Benítez, an hour and a half from Viña del Mar and Valparaíso. Aeropuerto Torquemada near Concón is for private flights only.
➤ AIRLINES AND CONTACTS: **Avant** (⊠ Ecuador 31, Viña del Mar, ☎ 32/251–441). **Ladeco** (⊠ Esmerelda 1048, Valparaíso, ☎ 32/216–

355; ✉ Ecuador 80, Viña del Mar, ☎ 32/979–089; ✉ 15 Norte 961, Viña del Mar, ☎ 32/690–365). **LanChile** (✉ Esmerelda 1048, Valparaíso, ☎ 32/251–441; ✉ Ecuador 80, Viña del Mar, ☎ 32/690–365).

BUS TRAVEL

There's excellent bus service between Santiago and Valparaíso and Viña del Mar for about $2. Tur-Bus and other companies leave from Santiago's Terminal Alameda. Smaller companies serving the other beach resorts depart from Santiago's Terminal Santiago.

Most bus companies with routes along the Central Coast pick up passengers at Valparaíso's Terminal Rodoviario, across from the Congreso Nacional and Viña's Terminal Rodoviario two blocks from Plaza Vergara. Pullman Bus serves most coastal towns south of Valparaíso. Tur-Bus heads north to Cachagua, Zapallar, Papudo, and other towns. Sol del Pacífico also runs buses to the northern beaches.

➤ BUS TERMINALS: **Terminal Rodoviario** (✉ Av. Pedro Montt 2800, Valparaíso, ☎ 32/213–246). **Terminal Rodoviario** (✉ Av. Valparaíso and Quilpué, Viña del Mar, ☎ 32/882–661).

➤ BUS COMPANIES: **Pullman Bus** (☎ 32/680–424). **Tur-Bus** (☎ 32/ 212–028). **Sol del Pacífico** (☎ 32/288–577).

CAR TRAVEL

Since it's so easy to get around in Valparaíso and Viña del Mar, there's no need to rent a car to explore these cities. But if you want to travel to other towns on the coast, renting a car is advisable. To rent from one the larger chains, you'll probably have to do so in Santiago. Hertz also has an office in Viña del Mar. Chilean companies Euroval, Mach, Mazdaval, and Unión have offices in Valparaíso, while Bert has offices in both Valparaíso and Viña del Mar.

➤ CAR RENTAL: **Bert** (✉ Victoria 2675, Valparaíso, ☎ 32/254–842; ✉ Av. Libertad 892, Viña del Mar, ☎ 32/681–151). **Euroval** (✉ Av. Brasil 1910, Valparaíso, ☎ 32/211–964). **Hertz** (✉ Quillota 766, Viña del Mar, ☎ 32/97–1625). **Mach** (✉ Viña Las Heras 428, Valparaíso, ☎ 2/601–9421). **Mazdaval** (✉ 5 Norte 650, Viña del Mar, ☎ 32/686–820). **Unión** (✉ Independencia 2771, Valparaíso, ☎ 32/213–977).

FESTIVALS AND SEASONAL EVENTS

The annual *Festival Internacional de la Canción* (International Song Festival) takes place over a week in mid-February in Viña del Mar. The concerts are broadcast live on television. Most towns have colorful processions on the *Día de San Pedro* on June 29. A statue of Peter, patron saint of fishermen, is typically hoisted onto a fishing boat and led along a coastal procession. Thousands turn out for the event in Valparaíso.

INTERNET

The only Internet cafés on the Central Coast are in Valparaíso and Viña del Mar. There are a few good choices in Valparaíso. Café Riquet charges less than $2 an hour and is open daily (except Sunday) 10–10. Cheery Café Color charges slightly more and is open daily 9–9. In Viña del Mar, 286 Rue Valparaíso is open daily past midnight and offers headphones so you can make free international calls.

➤ INTERNET CAFÉS: **286 Rue Valparaíso** (✉ Av. Valparaíso 286, ☎ 32/ 710–140). **Café Color** (✉ Calle Papudo 526, ☎ 746–136). **Café Riquet** (✉ Plaza Anibal Pinto 1199, ☎ 32/213–171).

MAIL AND SHIPPING

Perhaps because it is so close to Santiago, the postal system along the Central Coast is fairly efficient. On average, letters take five to seven days to reach the United States or Europe.

➤ POST OFFICES: **Valparaíso** (⊠ southeast corner of Plaza Sotomayor). **Viña del Mar** (⊠ north side of Plaza Vergara).

MONEY MATTERS

It's wise to bring sufficient cash when exploring the coast away from the cities. Most small towns do not have banks or ATMs, and many restaurants and hotels don't accept credit cards.
➤ ATMs: **Banco Santander** (⊠ Esmerelda 939, Valparaíso, ☎ 32/ 207–900). **Citibank** (⊠ 1 Norte 633, Viña del Mar, ☎ 32/338–500).

SAFETY

Like most port cities, Valparaíso has its share of street crime. Avoid deserted areas and be on the lookout for suspicious characters. It's best not to walk alone at night. In both Valparaíso and Viña del Mar you should always be alert to the possibility of pickpockets, especially in tourist areas. Keep on eye on cameras and other valuables.

TAXIS

In Valparaíso and Viña del Mar you can hail a taxi on the street. If you prefer to phone a cab, reputable companies include Radio Taxis Turismo and Taxis Francia in Valparaíso, and Radio Taxi in Viña del Mar. Most smaller towns have a taxi stand on the main road.
➤ TAXI COMPANIES: **Radio Taxi** (☎ 32/690 227). **Radio Taxis Turismo** (☎ 32/212–885). **Taxis Francia** (☎ 32/257–015).

TELEPHONES

There are several different telephone companies in the Central Coast, and each has their own public telephones. Calling cards for each company can be purchased in many shops and newsstands. Much easier than calling from the street is to call from one of the many Entel or Telefónica offices located in town.

TOUR OPERATORS

You'll need a tour guide to really get to know the twisting streets of Valparaíso. Claudia Acevedo of Claudia Tours lets you see the city through the eyes of a local. Her contacts get you inside private homes and other place you might have otherwise missed.

Also in Valparaíso, Agentur, Vaniatur, and Turismo Internacional are reputable travel agencies. In Concón, try Nortesur. In Viña del Mar, Sky Tour can help can you arrange airline tickets and rental cars. Chile Guias offers English tours throughout the country. Turismo Aventura specializes in adventure sport outings.
➤ TOUR COMPANIES: **Agentur** (⊠ Esmerelda 940, Valparaíso, ☎ 32/ 252–775). **Chile Guias** (⊠ Av. Valparaíso 507, Viña del Mar, ☎ 32/ 688–768). **Claudia Tours** (⊠ Valparaíso, ☎ 32/256–854 or 09/665– 6333). **Nortesur** (⊠ 7 Calle 390, Concón, ☎ 32/903–181). **Sky Tour** (⊠ Av. Valparaíso 595, Viña del Mar, ☎ 32/688–180. **Turismo Aventura** (⊠ Calle Angamos 185, Viña del Mar, ☎ 32/890–517). **Turismo Internacional** (⊠ Esmerelda 1074, Valparaíso, ☎ 32/255–774). **Vaniatur** (⊠ Esmerelda 1034, Valparaíso, ☎ 32/211–464).

TRAIN TRAVEL

Merval, a commuter train linking Viña de Mar and Valparaíso, is an excellent way to shuttle between the two cities. In Valparaíso the main station is at the Muelle Prat. In Viña del Mar, it's south of Plaza Vergara. The ride costs about a quarter.
➤ TRAIN STATIONS: **Estación Puerto** (⊠ Plaza Sotomayor, ☎ 32/217– 108). **Estación Viña del Mar** (⊠ Plaza Sucre, ☎ no phone).

VISITOR INFORMATION

Viña del Mar has the best tourist office on the coast. Near Plaza Vergara, it's open Monday through Saturday 9–7. There's also an office at the Rodoviario bus terminal that's open weekdays 10–2 and 3–6. In Valparaíso, the Departamento de Turismo is not far from Plaza Victoria. It's open weekdays 8:30–2 and 3–5. There are also two information booths, one at Rodoviario bus terminal and the other at the Prat Dock. The latter gives walking tours and a video presentation. Sernatur, the Chilean tourism agency, has offices in Valparaíso and Viña del Mar.

➤ VALPARAÍSO INFORMATION: **Prat Dock Information Booth** (✉ Muelle Prat, ☎ 32/236–222). **Rodoviario Information Booth** (✉ Av. Pedro Montt 2800, ☎ 32/213–246). **Sernatur** (✉ Esmerelda 1051 (☎ 32/234–475). **Valparaíso Departamento de Turismo** (✉ Condell 1490, ☎ 32/939–108).

➤ VIÑA DEL MAR INFORMATION: **Sernatur** (✉ Av. Valparaíso 507 ☎ 32/882–285). **Viña del Mar Central de Turismo** (✉ Av. Libertad and Av. Arlegui, ☎ 32/883–154).

4 EL NORTE CHICO

Chile's Little North is anything but small. Stretching for hundreds of miles, it's a vast land of sun-scarred hills and emerald green valleys. It was in El Norte Chico's ports that English pirates raided the riches of a budding nation. It was here that great fortunes were won and lost within a few weeks during the great silver boom. And it was here that South America's first Nobel laureate, Gabriela Mistral, composed her verses to a land of incomparable beauty and solitude.

by Gregory
Benchwick

F OR HUNDREDS OF YEARS, people have journeyed to El Norte Chico for the riches that lay buried deep within the earth. First came the Incas, who wandered the burnt hills in search of gold. The Spanish who arrived on these shores a century later also were seeking this precious metal. Prospectors flocked here in the 19th century when the silver boom reaped great rewards. Today it is yet another metal, copper, that yields the majority of the region's income. No wonder locals once called this "the land of 10,000 mines."

But El Norte Chico's appeal isn't purely metallurgical. The coastline boasts some of the best beaches in the country. Offshore there are rocky islands that shelter colonies of penguins and sea lions. Shimmering mountain lakes are home to huge flocks of flamingos. Even the parched earth flourishes twice a decade in a phenomenon called *el desierto florido,* or the flowering desert. During these years, the bleak landscape gives way to a riot of colors—flowers of every hue imaginable burst from the normally infertile soil of the plain.

In a land where water is so precious, it's not surprising that the people who migrated here never strayed far from its rivers. In the south, La Serena sits at the mouth of the Río Elqui. El Norte Chico's most important city, La Serena's colonial architecture and European flavor make it the region's cultural center as well. Nearby, in the fertile Elqui Valley, farmers in tiny villages grow the grapes to make pisco, the potent brandy that has become Chile's national drink. Those in search of the region's history will head to Valle de Encanto, a large collection of ancient petroglyphs.

On El Norte Chico's northern frontier is the Río Copiapó. This is the region that grew up and grew rich during the silver boom. The town of Copiapó, this area's most important center for trade, serves as an excellent starting place for those intent on exploring the hinterland. Inland lies Parque Nacional Nevado Tres Cruces, where you'll discover snowcapped volcanoes and dazzling white salt flats. Head to the ocean and you'll come to Parque Nacional Pan de Azúcar, home to some of El Norte Chico's most stunning coastal scenery.

Pleasures and Pastimes

Beaches

El Norte Chico's seemingly endless beaches lure tourists from around the world. The sugary sand, the turquoise water, and the warm breezes make these beaches among the best in the country. During the summer months of January and February you may have to fight for a place in the sun. If a little tranquility is what you seek, plan your trip for another part of the year. The weather is fine, the prices are cheaper, and it's not hard to find a stretch of shoreline that's completely deserted. Some of El Norte Chico's beaches are not safe for swimming due to dangerous currents or pollution. These are marked by large signs reading: NO APTA PARA BANARSE.

Dining

El Norte Chico is not known for its gastronomy, but the food here is simple, unpretentious, and often quite good. Along the coast you'll find abundant seafood. Don't pass up the *merluza con salsa margarita* (hake with butter sauce featuring almost every kind of shellfish imaginable) or *choritos al vapor* (mussels steamed in white wine). Inland you come across country-style *cabrito* (goat), *conejo* (rabbit), and *pinchones escabechadas* (baby pigeons). Don't forget to order a pisco sour, the frothy concoction made with the brandy distilled in the Elqui Valley.

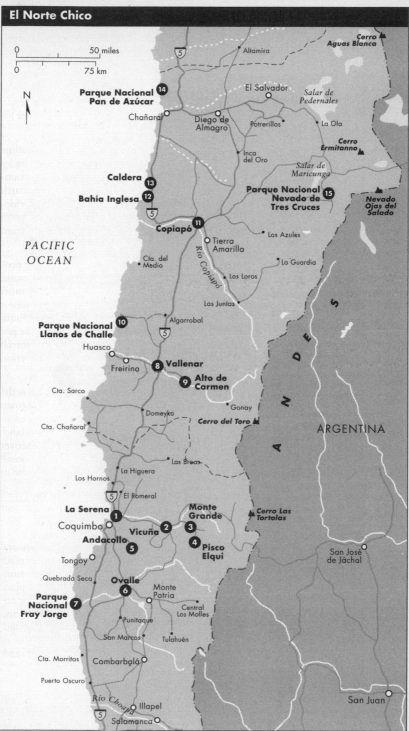

El Norte Chico

0 — 50 miles
0 — 75 km

N

PACIFIC
OCEAN

Altamira

Cerro
Aguas Blanca

**Parque Nacional
Pan de Azúcar** 14

El Salvador

Salar de
Pedernales

Chañaral

Diego de
Almagro

Potrerillos

La Ola

Inca
del Oro

Cerro
Ermitanno

Caldera 13

Salar de
Maricunga

Bahía Inglesa 12

**Parque Nacional
Nevado de
Tres Cruces** 15

Nevado
Ojos del
Salado

Copiapó 11

Tierra
Amarilla

Los Azules

Cta. del
Medio

Río Copiapó

La Guardia

Los Loros

Las Juntas

**Parque Nacional
Llanos de Challe** 10

Algarrobal

Huasco

Freirina

Vallenar 8

Cta. Sarco

**Alto de
Carmen** 9

Cta. Chañaral

Domeyko

Gonay

Cerro del Toro

ARGENTINA

Las Breas

La Higuera

Los Hornos

El Romeral

La Serena 1

Coquimbo

**Monte
Grande**

Cerro Las
Tortolas

Vicuña 2 3

Andacollo 5

4 **Pisco
Elqui**

Tongoy

San José
de Jáchal

Quebrada Seca

Ovalle 6

Monte
Patria

**Parque
Nacional
Fray Jorge** 7

Central
Los Molles

Punitaque

San Marcos

Tulahuén

Cta. Morritos

Combarbalá

Puerto Oscuro

Río Choapa

Illapel

San Juan

Salamanca

A N D E S

People in El Norte Chico generally eat a heavy lunch at around 2 PM that can last two hours, followed by a light dinner around 10 PM. Reservations are seldom needed, except in the fanciest restaurants. Leave a 10% tip if you enjoyed the service. For approximate entrée costs, *see* the dining price chart *in* Smart Travel Tips A to Z.

Lodging

The good news is that lodging in El Norte Chico is relatively inexpensive. Your best bet is often the beach resorts, which offer everything from nice cabañas to high-rise hotels. The bad news is that away from the areas that regularly cater to tourists you may have to make do with extremely basic rooms with shared baths. For approximate room costs, *see* the lodging price chart *in* Smart Travel Tips A to Z.

Shopping

El Norte Chico has some items you won't find elsewhere in Chile. In the Elqui Valley you'll find beautiful ceramics of the Diaguita people. In La Serena, jewelry and other items made from the locally mined marble called *combabalita* are particularly beautiful. The best places to shop are usually the *ferias artesenales* (artisan fairs). Here you'll find local people selling all types of handmade items.

Exploring El Norte Chico

El Norte Chico is a vast region—there are some 700 km (435 mi) between Río Aconcagua to Río Copiapó. You'll need more than one base if you want to explore the entire area. In the south, La Serena is a good place to start if you're going to the Elqui Valley. Vallenar, on the Río Huasco, is where you'll want to be if your destination is the flowering desert. Copiapó, near the region's northern border, is a convenient stop if you're headed to Parque Nacional Nevado de Tres Cruces.

Great Itineraries

IF YOU HAVE 5 DAYS

Five days isn't long enough to explore all of El Norte Chico, so make ⊡ **La Serena** ① your home base. Spend your first day exploring the whitewashed churches and lively markets of this quaint colonial town. The next morning head inland to **Vicuña** ②, birthplace of poet Gabriela Mistral. In the afternoon stop by the idyllic village of **Pisco Elqui** ④. A pisco sour here is almost obligatory. Explore the cloud forest of **Parque Nacional Fray Jorge** ⑦ on the fourth day. On your last day, head to **Ovalle** ⑥ to see the petroglyphs of the Valle del Encanto. End the day by taking a relaxing dip in the hot springs at the Termas de Socos.

IF YOU HAVE 7 DAYS

With a couple of extra days you'll be able to explore much more of El Norte Chico. Start out in ⊡ **La Serena** ①, which you'll use as your base for exploring the Elqui Valley. On day five head up to ⊡ **Copiapó** ⑪, perhaps taking a side trip to the **Parque Nacional Llanos de Challe** ⑩. Visit the remote mountain lakes of **Parque Nacional Nevado Tres Cruces** ⑮ or the coastal splendor of **Parque Nacional Pan de Azúcar** ⑭ on your sixth day. On your last day, relax on the sandy beaches near **Bahía Inglesa** ⑫.

When to Tour

During the summer months of January and February, droves of Chileans and Argentinians flee their stifling hot cities for the relative cool of El Norte Chico's beaches. Although it is an exciting time to visit, prices go up and rooms are hard to find. Make your reservations at least a month in advance. For a little tranquility, visit when the high season tapers off in March. Moving inland you'll find the weather is mild all year. The almost perpetually clear skies explain why the region has the largest concentration of observatories in the world. The temperatures drop quite a bit when you head to the mountains.

THE ELQUI VALLEY

It's hard to believe that hidden by the dusty brown hills of El Norte Chico is a sliver of land as lush and green as the Elqui Valley. The people who live along the Río Elqui harvest everything from olives to avocados. The most famous crop is the grapes distilled to make Chile's national drink: pisco. A village named after this lovely elixir, Pisco Elqui, sits high up the valley.

The Elqui Valley is renowned not only for its grapes, but also for its unusually clear skies, which have brought scientists from around the world to peer through the telescopes of the area's many observatories. The stars also attracted many New Agers who decided that the planet's spiritual center had shifted from the Himalayas to the Elqui Valley. Many who came here to check out the vibes decided to stay.

The Elqui Valley has been inhabited for thousands of years. First came the Diaguitas, whose intricate pottery is among the most beautiful of pre-Columbian ceramics. The Molles, who are believed to have carved the fascinating petroglyphs in the Valle de Encanto, followed. The Incas, who came here 500 years ago in search of gold, are relative newcomers. The clues these cultures left behind are part of what makes the Elqui Valley so fascinating.

La Serena

❶ *270 km (168 mi) north of Santiago.*

La Serena, Chile's second-oldest city, got off to a shaky start. Founded by Spanish conquistador Pedro de Valdivia in 1544, La Serena was destroyed by the Diaguitas only four years later. But the Spaniards weren't about to give in, and rebuilt the city on its original site. Situated near the mouth of the Río Elqui, La Serena slowly grew until it was visited by British pirate Bartholomew Sharp, who sacked and burned it in a three-day rampage in 1680. Once again the city was rebuilt. By the time of the silver boom in the late 19th century, it was thriving.

One of the most striking features of La Serena is the number of churches. Dating as far back as the late 16th century, most have survived fires, earthquakes, and pirate attacks. The largest church is the imposing **Iglesia Catedral,** which faces the beautiful Plaza de Armas. This behemoth was built in 1844 by French architect Jean de Herbage. On Cordovez you'll find the **Iglesia Santo Domingo,** a pretty church built in 1673 and then rebuilt after a pirate attack in 1755. One of La Serena's oldest churches, **Iglesia San Francisco,** on Balmaceda and de la Barra, has a baroque facade and thick stone walls. The exact date of the church's construction is not known, as the city archives were destroyed in 1680.

La Serena's pleasant streets, hidden plazas, and well-preserved colonial buildings are the fruition of one man's dream. Gabriel González Videla, then president of Chile, instituted his "Plan Serena" in 1940. He mandated that all new buildings be in the colonial style. The **Museo Histórico Gabriel González Videla,** his former home, was turned into a museum in 1984. It features exhibits about the ex-president, as well as showings of works by Chilean artists. ✉ *Matta 495,* ☎ *51/215-082.* ▨ *Admission.* ⊘ *Tues.–Sat. 9–noon and 4–7, Sun. 10–1.*

Housing many fascinating artifacts—including an impressive collection of Diaguita pottery—the **Museo Arqueológico** is a must-see for any-

one interested in the history of the region. The museum, inaugurated
in 1943, houses one of the world's best collections of precolonial ceramics. Also here is a moai (a carved stone head) from Easter Island.
✉ *Cordovez and Cienfuegos,* ☎ *51/224–492.* ✉ *Admission.* ☉ *Tues.–
Fri. 9–1 and 4–7, Sat. 10–1 and 4–7, Sun. 10–1.*

One of the most complete mineral collections in the world is housed
in the **Museo Mineralógico.** ✉ *Anfión Muñoz 870,* ☎ *51/204–096.* ✉
Free. ☉ *Weekdays 9:30–12:30.*

A pleasant place to pass an afternoon is **Parque Japones,** a Japanese
garden in the heart of Latin America. Here you will find koi-filled ponds,
intricate bridges, and a network of paths. The park was built by a mining company as a good-will gesture to its Japanese trading partners.
✉ *Pedro Pablo Muñoz and Cordovez,* ☎ *51/217–013.* ✉ *Admission.*
☉ *Daily 10–8.*

Dining and Lodging

$$$ ✕ **La Casona del Guatón.** This European-style steak house serves up
★   everything from shish kebab to steak with eggs. With several intimate
dining areas off the main salon, this is a great place to enjoy a romantic,
candlelit meal. The service, although friendly, is a bit doting. ✉ *Brasil
750,* ☎ *56/211–519. Reservations essential. AE, DC, MC, V.*

$$$ ✕ **Restaurant Velamar Beach.** Enjoy a seaside *parrillada* (barbecue) after
battling the waves of La Serena's beach. The restaurant literally sits
on the sand, so it's a great place to watch the sunset. ✉ *Av. del Mar
2300,* ☎ *56/215–461. No credit cards.*

$$–$$$ ✕ **El Cedro.** In a courtyard protected from the elements by a glass roof,
this pleasant restaurant offers an innovative international menu that
focuses on Middle Eastern fare. A large-screen TV gives the place a
sports-bar ambience on game day. The service tends to be a bit slow.
✉ *Brasil 451,* ☎ *56/214–300. AE, DC, MC, V.*

$$$ 🏨 **Hotel Casa Real.** Despite its neoclassical design, Hotel Casa Real has
all the modern touches you expect in an executive-class hotel—business
center, meeting rooms, and Internet access. The spotless rooms, filled with
wood and glass furniture, have a homey feel. The staff is friendly and
attentive. A breakfast buffet is included. ✉ *Av. Francisco de Aguirre 170,*
☎ *56/221–010,* ℻ *56/221–122,* 🌐 *www.regiondecoquimbo.cl/costareal.
51 rooms. Restaurant, bar, minibars, pool, laundry service, business
services, meeting rooms. AE, DC, MC, V.*

$$ 🏨 **Hotel Francisco de Aguirre.** La Serena's most venerable hotel, the
colonial-style Hotel Francisco de Aguirre is a block from the Plaza de
Armas. In a rambling three-story building, the lovely hotel is filled with
European charm. Cool off in the pool tucked away in a lush courtyard. Rates include a breakfast buffet. ✉ *Cordovez 210,* ☎ *56/222–
991,* ℻ *56/222–991. 85 rooms. Restaurant, bar, minibars, room service, pool, laundry service. AE, DC, MC, V.*

$ 🏨 **Hotel del Cid.** Run by a Scottish/Chilean couple, this colonial-style
★   bed-and-breakfast is a great value. The bright courtyard is the place
to lounge in the sun on a beach chair. The rooms are warm and cozy,
making you feel right at home. Breakfast is served in the courtyard or
in the breakfast nook. ✉ *O'Higgins 138,* ☎ *56/212–692,* ℻ *56/222–
289. 20 rooms. Laundry service, free parking. AE, DC, MC, V.*

Nightlife and the Arts

La Serena's nightlife is a little subdued, fitting perfectly with the city's
conservative nature. There are very few bars in the city proper. A huge
palm dominates the central courtyard at **Café del Patio** (✉ Prat 470, ☎
no phone), a small pub in the center of town. This is a great place to grab
a snack and listen to live jazz and blues. The majority of the city's pubs
and discos lie near the beach on glitzy Avenida del Mar. **Brooklyn's** (✉

Av. del Mar 2150, ☎ 56/212–891) is a big, impersonal pub with a dance floor. Just off Avenida del Mar is **Kamikaze** (✉ Av. Cuatro Esquinas s/n, ☎ 56/218–515). Part of a popular chain of Asian-themed discos, it livens things up late night. There's a Japanese fighter-plane lodged inside.

Outdoor Activities and Sports

La Serena's attractive sandy beach stretches all the way south to the neighboring town of Coquimbo. **Playa Peñuelas** is overrun with tourists during high season. There are several other pleasant places to catch some rays. **La Herradura,** 2 km (1 mi) south of Coquimbo, has a small but excellent beach. **Playa Totoralillo,** 17 km (11 mi) south, has beautiful green waters and a white-sand beach.

Shopping

Mercado La Recova, on the corner of Cienfuegos and Cantournet, is a modern market housed in a pleasant neoclassical building. Here you can buy dried fruits and handicrafts. The Diaguita-style ceramics and the trinkets made from the locally mined marble called combabalita are particularly stunning.

Vicuña

❷ *62 km (38 mi) east of La Serena.*

As you head into the Elqui Valley, the first town you come to is Vicuña, famous as the birthplace of one of Chile's most important literary figures, Gabriela Mistral. Her beautiful, haunting poetry often looks back on her early years in the Elqui Valley. Mistral's legacy is unmistakable as you wander through town. In the Plaza de Armas there is a chilling stone replica of the poet's death mask.

★ The **Museo Gabriela Mistral** has various artifacts pertaining to the poet, such as original copies of her books as well as handwritten letters and poems. There's also a replica of the adobe house where she was born. ✉ *Calle Gabriela Mistral 759,* ☎ *51/411–223.* 🎫 *Admission.* ☉ *Jan.– Feb., daily 10–7; Mar.–Dec., Tues.–Sun. 10–7.*

· Facing the central square, the 1909 **Iglesia de la Inmaculada Concepción** is topped by a huge steeple. Next to the church is **Torre Bauer,** a wooden tower painted fire-engine red. Named after a former mayor, it was prefabricated in Germany in 1905. On the central square is **Teatro Municipal,** noted for its art deco flourishes.

The **Casa de los Madariaga** offers a look into a historic, colonial-era home of the region, complete with antique furnishings, including ornate furniture and pictures of the Madariaga family. ✉ *Calle Gabriela Mistral 683,* ☎ *51/411–220.* 🎫 *Admission.* ☉ *Daily 10–1 and 3–5.*

As this is the Elqui Valley, you'll pass vineyards growing the grapes that make pisco. **Planta Capel,** a pisco distillery, is just across the Elqui River. Here you can tour the bottling facility and even taste the results. ✉ *Camino a Peralillo s/n,* ☎ *51/411–391.* 🎫 *Admission.* ☉ *Jan.–Feb., daily 9:30–6:30; Mar.–Dec. weekdays 9:30–12:30 and 2:30–6, weekends and holidays 9:30–12:30.*

★ **Observatorio Cerro Mamalluca** is Chile's only observatory specifically intended for public use. The facility, 9 km (6 mi) north of Vicuña, offers nightly viewings through a 12-inch telescope. ✉ *Tour office at Gabriela Mistral 260,* ☎ *51/411–352.* 🎫 *Admission.* ☉ *Mon.–Sat. 9 AM–10 PM, Sun. 10–10.*

Dining and Lodging

$$$ ✕ **Club Social Vicuña.** Specializing in local dishes such as goat and rabbit, the Club Social Vicuña offers decent country food at an afford-

able price. This is definitely a family place, as the owner's children play their games in the corner where their parents can keep an eye on them. There's also dining in the rather drab courtyard. ✉ *Gabriela Mistral 445,* ☎ *51/411–853. No credit cards.*

$$$ ✕ **Restaurant Halley.** With open-air dining under a straw roof, this restaurant gives you the feeling that you're having a picnic. The menu focuses on hearty country fare. ✉ *Gabriela Mistral 404,* ☎ *51/411–225. AE, V.*

$$ ⬚ **Hosteria Vicuña.** This large hotel's claim to fame is that Gabriela Mistral once slept here. There is an inviting parlor and bar area complete with piano, and a tree-shaded garden. The restaurant is quite good and serves up Elqui Valley specialties such as goat and rabbit as well as international fare. The ambience is a step above most eateries in El Norte Chico—theré are even cloth napkins. ✉ *Sargento Aldea 101,* ☎ *51/411–301. 25 rooms. Restaurant, bar, café, pool, tennis courts, laundry service, meeting room. AE, MC, V.*

$ ⬚ **Hotel Halley.** Housed in a pretty colonial house with wood trim and
★ white walls, this inn offers carefully decorated rooms filled with authentic circa-1950s radios and more doilies than you could possibly imagine. There is a small, rather shallow pool in the back. ✉ *Gabriela Mistral 542,* ☎ *51/412–070,* ☎ *51/412–070. 10 rooms. Restaurant, pool. AE, MC, V.*

Nightlife and the Arts

There's occasional live music at **Pub Kharma** (✉ Gabriela Mistral 417, ☎ no phone), a bar that plays Bob Marley almost exclusively. The decor consists of posters of the reggae legend himself.

Outdoor Activities and Sports

The **Cerro de la Virgen** is a place of pilgrimage for those devout to the Virgen de Lourdes, the town's patron saint. This hill overlooking the city offers a great view of Vicuña. It's a 2-km (1-mi) hike north of the city via a path on Baquedano between Independencia and Yungay.

Shopping

The **Poblado Artesenal** is a collection of artisan stands where you can buy local handicrafts, especially ceramics and jewelry. It's on the Plaza de Armas.

Monte Grande

❸ *34 km (22 mi) west of Vicuña.*

A tiny village in the rugged Elqui Valley, Monte Grande recalls a time of simpler pleasures. This picturesque village is home to two of the world's purest vices: pisco and poetry. Gabriela Mistral, born in nearby Vicuña, grew up in Monte Grande. Her family lived in the old schoolhouse where her older sister taught. The **Casa Escuela** has been turned into a museum and displays some relics from the poet's life. Her tomb is on a nearby hillside. ✉ *Central plaza,* ☎ *no phone.* ▱ *Admission.* ☉ *Tues.–Sun. 10–1 and 3–6.*

Dining

$$$ ✕ **El Meson de Fraile.** This is a good place to stop for lunch on your way to Pisco Elqui. A cozy place with stone walls and large wooden tables, El Meson de Fraile offers basic but tasty food. The ever-changing menu features local favorites such as cabrito and conejo. The service is superb. ✉ *Montegrande s/n,* ☎ *no phone. No credit cards.*

Pisco Elqui

4 *43 km (26 mi) west of Vicuña.*

The village, perched on a sun-drenched hillside, was once known as La Unión. It received its current moniker in 1939. Gabriel González Videla, at that time the president of Chile, renamed the village in a shrewd maneuver to ensure that Peru would not gain exclusive rights over the term "pisco." The Peruvian town of Pisco also produces the heady brandy.

★ This idyllic village of fewer than than 600 residents is home to two pisco plants. The **Solar de Pisco Elqui,** on the main road, is Chile's oldest distillery. It produces the famous Tres Erres brand, perhaps Chile's finest. In the older section of the plant, maintained strictly for show, you can see the antiquated copper cauldrons and wooden barrels. There's a tour followed by tastings where you can sample a pisco sour. About 4 km (2 mi) past Pisco Elqui you come upon the **Los Nichos** distillery, which also offers free daily tours and tastings.

Dining and Lodging

$$ ✕🖅 **El Tesoro de Elqui.** Beautiful gardens surround this hotel's nicely
★ decorated cabañas. El Tesoro de Elqui's German owner obviously has a green thumb, as she produces flowers of every imaginable shape and size. There is a beautiful pool where you can laze around in the world-famous Elqui Valley sunshine. From here you have a panoramic view of the Andes. The restaurant, which serves as a meeting place for travelers, features an international menu. The tasty spaghetti Bolognese makes a welcome change from Chilean country cuisine. The owner also makes a mean pisco sour. ✉ *Prat s/n,* ☎ *51/451–958,* 🖳 *www.pisco.de. 5 rooms. Restaurant, pool. AE, MC, V.*

$$ 🖅 **Complejo Turístico Gabriela Mistral.** The cabañas at this hotel are comfortable, although some are a bit dark. The pool is shallow, but can be a great place to wallow after a day of exploring the sun-drenched valley. ✉ *Prat 59,* ☎ *51/451–086. 6 cabañas. Restaurant, pool. No credit cards.*

$$ 🖅 **Misterios de Elqui.** These six grass-roof cabañas are situated around a pleasant pool. The views of the mountains are outstanding. ✉ *Prat s/n,* ☎ *51/451–126. 6 cabañas. Restaurant, pool. DC, MC, V.*

Nightlife and the Arts

There isn't much to do at night in Pisco Elqui but lie on your back and enjoy the brilliant stars. **Restaurante Los Jugos,** on the corner of the plaza, offers incredible fresh fruit drinks. Try a *jugo de frambuesa* (raspberry juice).

Shopping

Fresh fruit marmalade and preserves are sold in the town's main plaza. You can also head to the pisco distilleries to pick up a bottle of freshly brewed pisco.

Andacollo

5 *54 km (34 mi) southeast of La Serena.*

An important gold and silver mining center since the 16th century, Andacollo is a pleasant stopover between Ovalle and La Serena. The compact town is home to one of Chile's most famous religious icons. The wooden image of the Virgen de Andacollo, deemed miraculous by the Vatican in 1901, draws some 150,000 pilgrims to the town each year from December 23 to 26. During the Fiesta Grande de la Virgen, the statue is decorated and paraded through the streets.

★ The Virgen de Andacollo sits on a silver altar in the small **Templo Antiguo,** on Plaza Videla, the town's main square. This church, built in the 17th century, has a museum of the offerings given to the virgin in hopes of her miraculous assistance. The **Basilica,** which was inaugurated in 1893 after nearly 20 years of construction, is by far the largest structure in the town. With a 40-meter-high dome and two giant towers, it towers over everything else.

Ovalle

❻ *34 km (21 mi) southeast of Andacollo.*

Ovalle, a modern town southeast of La Serena, serves as a good base for trips to the Monumento Natural Pichasca or the Valle de Encanto. The shady **Plaza de Armas** is a pleasant place to pass an afternoon. On the main square, the **Iglesia San Vicente Ferrer** is worth a visit. It was constructed in 1849 but damaged by an earthquake in 1997.

Unlike geoglyphs, which are large-scale figures chiseled into the landscape, petroglyphs are small pictures carved onto the rock surface. One
★ of Chile's densest collections of petroglyphs is found in **Valle de Encanto.** The 30 images in the Valley of Enchantment were most likely etched by the El Molle culture between AD 100 and 600. The figures wear ceremonial headdresses hanging low over large, expressionist eyes. There are about 30 petroglyphs in the valley. On occasion a guide will show you the best of the carvings. To reach the site, take Ruta 45 west from Ovalle. About 19 km (12 mi) from the town head south for 5 km (3 mi) on a rough, dry road. ⊠ *24 km (15 mi) west of Ovalle.* 🎫 *Free.* ☉ *Daily 8–7:30.*

A tourist complex cut from the rough land, **Termas de Socos** is a very pleasant hot springs. The waters, which spout from the earth at 28°C (83°F), are said to have incredible healing powers. Curative or not, the waters here are extremely relaxing. ⊠ *24 km (15 mi) west of Ovalle.* 🎫 *Admission.* ☉ *Daily 8–8.*

Heading towards the Andes you come across **Monumento Natural Pichasca,** a forest of petrified tree trunks. These play host to dozens of fossils, such as imprints of leaves and outlines of small animals. Nearby is a cave beneath a stone overhand that housed indigenous peoples thousands of years ago. Inside you'll find some cave paintings by the Molle people. ⊠ *50 km (31 mi) northeast of Ovalle.* 🎫 *Admission.* ☉ *Daily 8:30–4:30.*

Dining and Lodging

$$$ ✕ **Bavaria.** Because of the country's large number of German immigrants, most Chilean cities have at least one Bavarian-theme restaurant. This one, part of a national chain, evokes the Old Country with wood beams and checkered yellow tablecloths. Entrées like *pollo a la plancha* are a bit bland, but wholesome and filling. ⊠ *Vicuña Mackenna 401,* ☎ *53/630–578. AE, MC, V.*

$$$ 🏨 **Hotel Termas de Socos.** This rustic hotel, located about 33 km (21 mi) west of Ovalle, allows you unlimited access to the hot springs at Termas de Socos. The rooms have large, comfortable beds and many have expansive picture windows looking out over the surrounding desert. Also available are relaxing massages and private hot tubs. The service, unfortunately, is a little inattentive. All meals are included. ⊠ *Termas de Socos,* ☎ *53/681–021. 26 rooms. AE, MC, V.*

$$ 🏨 **Hotel El Turismo.** A pleasant hotel in the center of town, Hotel El Turismo offers spacious and well-kept rooms. Ask for a room facing the Plaza de Armas. ⊠ *Victoria 295,* ☎ *53/623–536,* 📠 *53/623–536. 30 rooms. Restaurant. AE, MC, V.*

Parque Nacional Fray Jorge

❼ *110 km (68 mi) south of La Serena.*

★ The thought of a patch of land that is rich with vegetation and animal life in the heart of El Norte Chico's dry, desolate landscape seems to defy logic. Parque Nacional Fray Jorge, a UNESCO world biosphere reserve since 1977, is home to a small cloud forest similar to those found in Chile's damp southern regions. The forest, perched 600 meters (1,968 ft) above sea level, receives its life-giving nourishment from the *camanchaca* (fog) that constantly envelopes it. Within this forest you will come across ferns and trees found nowhere else in the region. A slightly slippery boardwalk leads you on a half-hour tour. ⊠ *At Km 383 of the Pan-American Hwy., take dirt road 18 km (11 mi) west,* ☎ *no phone.* 🖼 *Admission.* ⊙ *Jan.–Mar., Thurs.–Sun. 8:30–6; Apr.–Dec. weekends 8:30–6.*

THE HUASCO VALLEY

At least twice a decade the desert bursts to life in a phenomena called the desierto florido. If you are lucky enough to visit the area during these times, you will see the desert covered with colorful flowers, some of which only exist in this region. Parque Nacional Llanos de Challe on the coast is an excellent place to view the flowering desert.

Climbing into the Andes from Vallenar, the region's largest city, you reach the Upper Huasco Valley. The Valle de Carmen houses several quaint villages, such as Alto de Carmen and San Felix.

Vallenar

❽ *188 km (116 mi) north of La Serena.*

Vallenar, the transportation hub of the Huasco Valley, was founded in 1789 by Ambrosio O'Higgins. He named the town after his home in Ballinagh, Ireland. There aren't many sights that lure travelers off the highway—most who stop here are headed to the Parque Nacional Llanos de Challe. The large **Plaza O'Higgins** is a pleasant place for an early evening stroll. The **Iglesia Porroquial,** on the main square, is worth a visit for its huge copper dome.

The **Museo de Huasco** offers a small collection of artifacts of indigenous peoples found in the region. There are also pictures of the flowering desert for those not lucky enough to see it in person. ⊠ *Sargento Aldea 742.* 🖼 *Admission.* ⊙ *Weekdays 10–1 and 3–6, Sat. 10–12:30.*

Dining and Lodging

$$$ ✕ **Il Boccato.** Opposite the Plaza de Armas, Il Boccato is your best bet for a quick bite. A small corner restaurant with a brightly lit interior, this pizza place has a family atmosphere. Chose from myriad menu options, including a zesty pollo a la plancha. There's also a wide selection of seafood entrées. ⊠ *Plaza de Armas,* ☎ *51/614–609. No credit cards.*

$$$ ✕ **La Casona.** The menu of this comfortable restaurant features pizzas and pastas. Housed in a two-story wooden house painted blue, La Casona also has a cozy bar. ⊠ *Serrano 1475,* ☎ *51/611–600. No credit cards.*

$$$ ✕ **Moros y Christianos Restaurant.** This Mediterranean-style restaurant, named for an annual festival commemorating a battle between the Moors and the Christians, serves up flavorful Spanish fare. Try the paella for two for an authentic taste of Valencia. ⊠ *Pan-American Hwy.,* ☎ *51/614–600. Reservations essential. AE, MC, V.*

$$ 🏨 **Hostería de Vallenar.** The best lodging in Vallenar, this comfortable hosteria offers basic rooms with wood furniture. The staff is friendly

and helpful. ⊠ *Alonso de Ercilla 848,* ☎ *51/614–379. 30 rooms. Minibars. AE, MC, V.*

$ ☷ **Hotel Cecil.** A pleasant garden with a pool makes Hotel Cecil a good budget alternative. The rooms are spotless, but the baths are a bit small. ⊠ *Prat 1059,* ☎ *51/614–071. 18 rooms. Pool. No credit cards.*

Nightlife and the Arts

La Taberna (⊠ Prat 1059, ☎ no phone) is an English-style pub with live music on weekends. The friendly staff will tell you about the history of the region and proudly show off pictures of the desierto florido. **La Casona** (⊠ Serrano 1475, ☎ 51/611–600) gets things going with dancing on the weekends.

Alto del Carmen

❾ *40 km (25 mi) north of Vallenar.*

The Huasco Valley has far fewer visitors than the Elqui Valley, giving you the feeling that you've gotten here before the crowds. Not far from where the El Transito and San Felix rivers join to form the Huasco you'll find Alto del Carmen, a quaint town whose inhabitants dedicate themselves to cultivating the muscat grapes used to make pisco. **The Planta Pisquera Alto del Carmen,** just outside of town, offers free tours and tastings from 8 AM to 8 PM. In addition to pisco, the town is famous for making *pajarete,* a sweet wine.

About 26 km (16 mi) farther into the Valle de Carmen you'll find the precious town of **San Felix,** whose central plaza, whitewashed church, and pleasant markets shouldn't be missed.

Parque Nacional Llanos de Challe

❿ *99 km (62 mi) north of Huasco.*

There is no better place in El Norte Chico to view the desierto florido than this desolate coastal park. Every four or five years it is transformed into a carpet of reds, greens, and blues when there's sufficient rainfall to awaken the dormant bulbs below the dry, cracked earth. The park, spanning 450 square km (174 square mi), was formed to protect the *Garra de León,* a rare plant with an intoxicating red bloom that grows in abundance in the Huasco region. There are also a number of unusual species of cactus in the park—pacul, napina, and quisco flourish here. ⊠ *About 17 km (11 mi) north of Vallenar, turn west off the Pan-American Hwy. Take this road 82 km (51 mi) to the coast.* ☷ *Free.*

THE COPIAPÓ VALLEY

The region once known as Capayapú, meaning "cup of gold" in the Quechua language, was first inhabited by the Diaguitas around 1000. The Incas arrived several hundred years later in search of gold. Conquistador Diego de Almagro, who passed this way in 1535, was the first European to see the lush valley. Almagro didn't stop here for long; he continued on to Peru via the Inca Royal Road on his bloody conquest of the region.

During the 19th century the Copiapó Valley proved to be a true cup of gold when prospectors started large-scale mining operations in the region. Today, the residents of the valley make there living primarily from copper.

The northernmost city in the region, Copiapó, lies at the end of the world. Here's where the semi-arid region of El Norte Chico gives into the wiles of the Atacama Desert. Continuing north from Copiapó there is little but barren earth for hundreds of miles.

Copiapó

⑪ *145 km (90 mi) north of Vallenar.*

Copiapó was officially founded in 1744 by Don Francisco Cortés, who called it Villa San Francisco de La Selva. Originally a *tambo*, or resting place, Copiapó was where Diego de Almagro recuperated after his grueling journey south from Peru in 1536. The 19th-century silver strikes solidified Copiapó as an important city in the region. In the center of Copiapó lies **Plaza Prat,** a lovely park lined with 100-year-old pepper trees. Facing the central square, the neoclassical **Iglesia Catedral Nuestra Señora del Rosario** was built in the middle of the 19th century by English architect William Rogers. **Iglesia San Francisco** is a red-and-white candy cane of a church built in 1872. The adjacent Plaza Godoy has a statue of goatherd Juan Godoy, who accidently found huge silver deposits in nearby Chañarcillo.

The **Museo Mineralógico** offers a geological history of the region and what is perhaps the country's largest collection of rocks and minerals. There are more than 2,000 samples, including some found only in the Atacama Desert. It even displays a few meteorites that fell in the area. ⊠ *Colipí and Rodriguez,* ☎ *no phone.* 🎫 *Admission.* ☉ *Mon.–Sat. 10–1 and 2:30–7.*

The **Museo Histórico Regional,** dedicated to the natural history of the area, is housed in the historic home that belonged to the wealthy Matta family. Regional archives suggest that the house was originally built by mining engineer Felipe Santiago Matta between 1840 and 1850. ⊠ *Atacama 98,* ☎ *no phone.* 🎫 *Admission.* ☉ *Weekdays 9–7, Sat. 11–2 and 4–9, Sun. 11–2.*

The **Museo Ferravario** is in the old train station built in 1854. It displays pictures of South America's first railway, which ran between Copiapó and Caldera. ⊠ *Martinez s/n,* ☎ *no phone.* 🎫 *Free.* ☉ *Hrs vary.*

Dining and Lodging

$$$ ✕ **El Corsario.** A pleasant courtyard enlivened with a babbling fountain and numerous caged birds is where you'll find this local favorite. It has an interesting menu of regional dishes, including pinchones escabechadas. ⊠ *Atacama 245,* ☎ *52/215–374. No credit cards.*

$$$ ✕ **El Quincho.** This place serves seafood, but the only reason to come here is for the barbecued meats. The menu has virtually every cut of beef imaginable. The fire-red dining room gives you the feeling that you've descended into a barbecue bit. ⊠ *Atacama 109,* ☎ *52/214–647. No credit cards.*

$$ ✕ **El Cisne.** This locally recommended seafood restaurant specializes in shellfish. The *ostiones a la parmesana* (oysters with grated cheese) is particularly good. The eclectic ambience is highlighted by chairs padded with black velvet and prints of works by the old masters on the wall. ⊠ *Colipí 220,* ☎ *no phone. No credit cards.*

$$ 🏨 **Hotel Chagall.** Although it appears a little run-down on the outside, this business hotel has clean, modern rooms. Ask to see a few before you decide, as some are very dark. The bar, decorated with lots of kelly green, is reminiscent of an Irish pub. You won't find Guinness on tap here, so you'll have to settle for a well-made pisco sour. Breakfast is included. ⊠ *O'Higgins 760,* ☎ *52/213–775,* 📠 *52/211–527. 34 rooms. Bar, minibar, free parking. AE, DC, MC, V.*

$$ 🏨 **Hotel Diego de Almeida.** Stepping through the pleasant tiled entryway and into the elegantly furnished lobby, it's clear that Hotel Diego de Almeida is a step above the rest. It offers everything you would expect from a hotel catering to corporate travelers, from meeting rooms to business services. The rooms are pleasant, if a bit bland. Inquire about a room in the back, as those facing the street can be quite noisy. A breakfast buffet is included. ✉ *O'Higgins 656,* ☎ *52/212–075,* FAX *52/212–075. 20 rooms. Restaurant, bar, pool, business services, meeting rooms. AE, DC, MC, V.*

$$ ⭐ 🏨 **Hotel La Casona.** Set among beautiful gardens, this quaint country inn with a red facade is a good budget alternative. Entering through wooden doors you reach the sunny lobby. To one side is a dining area with oak furniture and red-and-white-checked tablecloths, an excellent place to enjoy your complimentary pisco sour. The rooms, decorated in blue, can get a little hot in the summer. Breakfast is included. ✉ *O'Higgins 150,* ☎ *52/217–277,* FAX *52/217–278. 10 rooms. Restaurant, bar, minibars, free parking. AE, DC, MC, V.*

$$ 🏨 **Hotel Miramonte.** Located in the center of town, Hotel Miramonte has clean, modern rooms decorated in the same shade of mauve that you'll find in the lobby and hallways. The staff here is friendly and helpful. Arched-backed wooden chairs and blue tablecloths give the restaurant a country atmosphere. The international menu is heavy on seafood, and serves up great merluza and ostiones. ✉ *Ramón Freire 731,* ☎ *52/210–440,* FAX *52/210–440,* WEB *www.chilenet.cl/miramonte. 47 rooms. Restaurant, minibars, recreation room. AE, DC, MC, V.*

Nightlife and the Arts

Because there are lots of students in town, nightlife in Copiapó can get lively. Outside of town, the **Drive-In Esso Pub** (✉ Near the exit ramp from the Pan-American Hwy., ☎ 52/211–535) is perhaps the most innovative bar in northern Chile—it's in a converted gas station. Near Plaza Prat, **La Tabla** (✉ Los Carrera 895, ☎ 52/233–029) has live music and very expensive drinks. There are also a few of discos in town that rage all night to salsa beats. **Discoteque Splash** (✉ Juan Martinéz 46, ☎ 52/215–948), is your best bet for late-night dancing.

Shopping

The **Casa de la Cultura** (✉ O'Higgins 610, on Plaza Prat, ☎ no phone) has craft workshops and a gallery displaying works by local artists. On Fridays there is a frenzied **fruit market** in the normally tranquil Plaza Godoy.

Bahía Inglesa

⑫ *68 km (42 mi) northwest of Copiapó.*

Originally known as Puerto del Inglés because of the number of English buccaneers using the port it as a hideaway, Bahía Inglesa has some of the most beautiful beaches of El Norte Chico. It is not just the beautiful white sand that sets these beaches apart, it is also the turquoise waters, the fresh air, and the fabulous weather. Combine this with the fact that the town has yet to attract large-scale development and you can see why so many people flock here in the summer. If you are fortunate enough to visit during the low season, you will experience a tranquility rarely felt in Chile's coastal towns.

Lodging

$$ 🏨 **Apart Hotel Playa Blanca.** If you are tired of indistinguishable chain hotels, a cabaña at Playa Blanca may just do the trick. These cabins are more like condos, complete with kitchens and living rooms. Relax on a chaise longue by the pool, an asymmetrical beauty. This is a great place for kids, as there is a play area with slide and jungle gym. ✉ *Camino de Martín 1300,* ☎ *52/316–044,* FAX *52/316–468. 10 rooms. Pool, free parking. No credit cards.*

$$ ⭐ 🏨 **Hotel Rocas de Bahia.** This sprawling modern hotel, straight from *The Great Gatsby,* offers rooms with huge windows facing the sea. Take a dip in the glistening waters of the bay, or head up to the roof-top pool. Rooms have huge beds and Southwestern-style furniture. A breakfast buffet is included. ⊠ *Av. El Morro s/n,* ☎ *52/316–005,* FAX *52/316–032. 36 rooms. Restaurant, pool, meeting rooms. DC, MC, V.*

Nightlife and the Arts

There are no true bars in Bahía Inglesa except in the hotels. Outside of the city, on your way north to Caldera, there are several discos that are always packed during high season. **Discoteque Loreto** (⊠ Camino Bahia Inglesa, ☎ no phone) is midway between the two towns. Nearby **Taqueo** (⊠ Camino Bahia Inglesa s/n, ☎ no phone) attracts a slightly more mature crowd.

Outdoor Activities and Sports

BEACHES

There are several easily accessible beaches around Bahía Inglesa. **Playa La Piscina** is the town's main beach. The rocky outcroppings give it a Mediterranean feel. **Playa Machas,** the town's southernmost beach, is especially relaxing because few tourists have discovered it.

WATER SPORTS

There are all types of water sports in the area. **Morro Ballena Expeditions** (⊠ El Morro s/n, ☎ no phone), offers fishing, kayaking, and scuba-diving trips.

Caldera

⑬ *74 km (45 mi) northwest of Copiapó.*

An important port during the silver era, Caldera today is a slightly run-down town with decent beaches and friendly people. The echoes of piracy still haunt the port, which is used today to export grapes and copper.

Near the beach is the recently restored **Estacion Ferrocarril,** once the terminus of Chile's first railroad. Here you can find a tourist information kiosk. The large, Gothic-towered **Iglesia de San Vincente** on the town's main square was built in 1862.

Dining and Lodging

$$$ ✕ **Nuevo Miramar.** This excellent seafood restaurant has huge windows overlooking the pier. One of the most elegant eateries in Caldera, it features tables with fine linens and cloth napkins. Bow-tied waiters, all extremely attentive, will tell you the catch of the day. ⊠ *Gana 90,* ☎ *52/315–381. Reservations essential. No credit cards.*

$$$ ✕ **Tierras Lejanas.** If you're in the mood for seafood, this restaurant
★ features just about every variety imaginable. Ask your waiter for the freshest fish, and he'll top it with a succulent margarita sauce. There is a thatched-roof bar where you can enjoy a pisco sour while waiting for your table. There is also an extensive wine list featuring Chilean wines. ⊠ *Edwards 425,* ☎ *no phone. No credit cards.*

$$ 🖭 **Motel Portal del Inca.** This string of red cabañas has tennis courts and an inviting pool surrounded by lounge chairs. There's also a playground, making this an excellent choice if you are traveling with children. ⊠ *Carvallo 945,* ☎ *52/315–252. 34 cabañas. Bar, coffee shop, pool, tennis courts, business services, meeting rooms. MC, V.*

$ 🖭 **Hostería Puerta del Sol.** With a view of the bay, this group of A-frame cabañas feature small kitchens and dining areas. The showers pour out incredibly hot water, a nice touch after a long day of exploring. There is also a pool, which could be quite pleasant if it were filled to the top. ⊠ *Wheelwright 750,* ☎ *52/315–205. 7 cabañas. Bar, pool. AE, DC, MC, V.*

Nightlife and the Arts

Many of Caldera's bars are only open during the summer, when the town is packed with vacationing South Americans. **Bartalameo** (⊠

Wheelwright 747, ☎ 52/316–413) offers a funky atmosphere. If you're hungry, chow down on the Asian and Mexican food. **La Caleta** (✉ Wheelwright 485, ☎ no phone), with a terrace overlooking the port, is a good place to enjoy the sunset. There is live music on weekends, although it's often just a man playing a keyboard.

Outdoor Activities and Sports

BEACHES

The town's main beach is **Playa Copiapina.** North of the pier, **Playa Brava** stretches as far as you can see. About 4 km (2 mi) to the south you come upon the pleasant sandy beach of **Playa Loreto.**

Parque Nacional Pan de Azúcar

⑭ *91 km (57 mi) north of Caldera.*

★ Some of Chile's most spectacular coastal scenery is in Parque Nacional Pan de Azúcar, a national park that stretches for 40 km (25 mi) along the coast north of Chañaral. Steep cliffs fall into the crashing sea, their ominous presence broken occasionally by white-sand beaches. These isolated stretches of sand make for excellent picnicking. Be careful if you take a dip, as there are often dangerous currents.

Within the park you will find an incredible variety of flora and fauna. Pelicans can be spotted off the coast, as can sea lions and sea otters, cormorants, and plovers (similar to sandpipers but with shorter beaks). There are some 20 species of cacti in the park, including the rare copiapoa. The park also contains a variety of rare predators, including the desert fox. In the pueblo of Caleta Pan de Azúcar, a tiny fishing village, you can get information from the Conaf-run kiosk.

Offshore from Caleta Pan de Azúcar is a tiny island that a large colony of Humboldt penguins calls home. You can hire local fishermen to take you there. Negotiate the price, which should be around $10. About 10 km (6 mi) north of the village, Mirador Pan de Azúcar offers spectacular views of the coastline. Another 30 km (19 mi) to the north is Las Lomitas. This 700-meter (2,296-ft) cliff is almost always covered with the *camanchaca* (fog), which rolls in from the sea. There is a huge net here used to catch the fog and condense it into water. ✉ *An unpaved road north of the cemetery in Chañaral leads to Caleta Pan de Azúcar,* ☎ *no phone.* 🎟 *Admission.* ⊙ *Conaf kiosk open daily 8–1 and 2–6.*

Dining and Lodging

$$ ✕🏨 **Hostería Chañaral.** When visiting Parque Nacional Pan de Azúcar you will probably stay in the neighboring town of Chañaral. Leaps and bounds above the other places in town, the hotel offers well-maintained rooms and clean baths with plenty of hot water. There's a restaurant on the premises that serves up tasty seafood. ✉ *Muller 268,* ☎ *52/480–050,* 🖷 *52/480–554. 34 rooms. No credit cards.*

Parque Nacional Nevado de Tres Cruces

⑮ *200 km (124 mi) east of Copiapó.*

Heading inland from Copiapó you climb high into the Andes before reaching Parque Nacional Nevado Tres Cruces. The national park lies in the inhospitable altiplano some 4,000 meters (13,000 ft) above sea level. Until just recently, few tourists dared to venture here. Created in 1994, this park is home to three of the world's four species of flamingos. Guanacos and vicuñas roam the arid region in search of food.

There are two beautiful Andean lakes within the park's borders. At Laguna San Francisco, at the main entrance, you'll find flamingos as well as some species of ducks. Along the grassy banks it is not uncommon to come across an occasional Andean fox. Farther into the park you come to Laguna Santa Rosa and the salt flat of El Salar de Maricunga.

Near the border of Argentina you come to the beautiful waters of Laguna Verde. This shallow lagoon, colored green by microorganisms, is the lifeblood of the region. Many species of birds and animals—including flamingos, guanacos, and desert foxes—make their home along its banks. On the southern shore of the lake there is a natural hot springs pool, which is free and open to the public. To the south is Ojos del Salado, the world's highest active volcano. Rising 6,893 meters (22,600 ft) above sea level, it's an awe-inspiring sight.

To visit the park you will need a four-wheel-drive vehicle. If you are driving, be sure to bring extra fuel, as gas stops are few and far between in this region. ⊠ *Take Ruta 31 from Copiapó to Paso de San Francisco, then head south on the rough road marked Quebrada Cienaga Redonda,* ☎ *no phone.* ⊡ *Admission.*

EL NORTE CHICO A TO Z

To research prices, get advice from other travelers, and book travel arrangements, visit www.fodors.com.

AIR TRAVEL

Since there are no international airports in El Norte Chico, you can't fly here directly from the North America, Europe, or Australia. You can fly into Santiago and transfer to an Avant or LanChile flight to La Serena and Copiapó. Round-trip flights from Santiago to El Norte Chico can run up to $200. Round-trip flights between cities in the north range from $40 to $150.

Copiapó's Aeropuerto Chamonate is 15 km (10 mi) east of the city. In La Serena, Aeropuerto Gabriela Mistral is 5 km (3 mi) east of the center of town.

➤ AIRLINES: **Avant** (⊠ Colipí 510, ☎ 52/217–285 in Copiapó). **LanChile** (⊠ Colipí 101, ☎ 52/213–512 in Copiapó; ⊠ Balmaceda 400, ☎ 55/221–551 in La Serena).

➤ AIRPORTS: **Aeropuerto Gabriela Mistral** (☎ 51/221–531 in La Serena). **Aeropuerto Chamonate** (☎ 51/214–360 in Copiapó).

BUS TRAVEL

There is a terminal in every major city in El Norte Chico, and there are frequent departures to other cities as well as smaller towns in the area. Keep in mind that there may be no bus service to the smallest villages or the more remote national parks.

No bus company has a monopoly, so there are often several bus stations in each city. Because many companies may be running buses along the same route, shop around for the best price. The fare for a 300-km (186-mi) trip usually runs around $20. For longer trips find a bus that has a *salon semi-cama*. The comfortable seats make all the difference.
➤ BUS STATIONS: **Copiapó** (⊠ Chañarcillo 680, ☎ 52/213–793). **Ovalle** (⊠ Maestranza 443, ☎ 53/626–707). **La Serena** (⊠ Av. El Santo and Amunátegui, ☎ 51/224– 573). **Vallenar** (⊠ Av. Matta and Prat).

CAR TRAVEL

Because of the distances between cities, a car is definitely the best way to truly see El Norte Chico. Many national parks can be visited only by car, preferably a four-wheel-drive vehicle. There are car-rental agencies in La Serena and Copiapó at the airport and in the city, and most hotels will help you arrange for a rental.

Driving can be a little hectic in Copiapó and La Serena, where drivers don't seem to observe the rules of the road. But once you get out on the open road driving is considerably easier. Ruta 5, more familiarly known as the Pan-American Highway, bisects all of northern Chile. Ruta 41 snakes along from La Serena through the Elqui Valley to Vicuña. Ruta D485 will take you to Pisco Elqui. Ruta 31 takes you inland from Copiapó.

➤ CAR RENTAL INFORMATION: **Avis** (✉ Rómulo Peña 102, Copiapó, ☎ 51/213–966; ✉ Av. Francisco de Aguirre 68, La Serena, ☎ 51/227–171). **Budget** (✉ Ramón Freire 466, Copiapó, ☎ 51/218–802; ✉ Balmaceda 3850, La Serena, ☎ 51/226–933). **Hertz** (✉ Copayapu 127, Copiapó, ☎ 51/213–522; ✉ Av. Francisco de Aguirre 225, La Serena, ☎ 51/225–471).

FESTIVALS AND SEASONAL EVENTS

Every town in El Norte Chico celebrates various annual events, such as the days honoring certain patron saints. One fiesta that you should not miss is Andacollo's Fiesta Grande de La Virgen, in which some 150,000 devout pilgrims converge on the small town to celebrate its miraculous statue of the Virgin de Andacollo (December 23–26). Also in Andacollo, the more subdued Fiesta Chica is the first Sunday of October.

HEALTH

Altitude sickness–which is marked by difficulty breathing, dizziness, headaches, and nausea—is a danger for visitors to the high elevations of the antiplano. The best way to ward off altitude sickness is to take it slow. Try to spend a day or two acclimatizing before undergoing any physical exertion. When hiking or climbing, rest more often and drink as much water as possible. If symptoms continue, return to a lower altitude.

The tap water in the major cities and even most smaller communities is drinkable. In general, the water is safer on the coast than in some towns farther inland. To be on the safe side, stick to bottled water.

MAIL AND SHIPPING

Although most cities in El Norte Chico have a post office, you'll often encounter long lines that move at a snail's pace. Your best bet is to ask your hotel to post a letter for you. But don't expect your letter to get there quickly. Mail headed out of the country can often take weeks.

➤ POST OFFICES: **Copiapó** (✉ Los Carreras 691). **Ovalle** (✉ Plaza de Armas). **La Serena** (✉ Mackenna and Granaderos). **Vallenar** (✉ Plaza O'Higgins).

SAFETY

El Norte Chico is generally a very safe area. It experiences very little violent crime. Nevertheless, visitors should use the same precautions as anywhere else. Women traveling alone should be careful, especially at night. It's best to travel in pairs or in groups.

TAXIS

Taxis are the most efficient way to get around any city in El Norte Chico. Taxis are easy to hail on the streets, but late at night you might want to ask someone at a hotel or restaurant to call one for you. Taxis often function as *colectivos*, meaning they will pick up anybody going in the same direction. The driver will adjust the price accordingly. Almost no taxis have meters, but many have the price posted on the windshield. Make sure you establish the price before getting inside. Prices range from $1 to $10, depending on the distance traveled and whether the taxi is a colectivo. Prices rise an average of 20% at night. Taxi drivers often will rent out their services for the day for a flat fee.

TELEPHONES

There are several different telephone companies in El Norte Chico, and each has its own public telephones. Calling cards for each company can be purchased in many shops and newsstands. Much easier than calling from the street is to call from one of the many Entel or CTC offices in every city. Here you can dial direct or collect to anywhere in the world.

TOURS

El Norte Chico has travel agencies in most major cities, as well as in some of the smaller ones. Shop around to make sure that you are getting the best itinerary and the best price. In La Serena check out Talinay for tours to national parks and the interior. In Copiapó you can arrange trips to the antiplano through Turismo Atacama, Peruvian Tour, and Cobre Tour. Limtur offers trips in the Ovalle area. In Caldera you can arrange trips with Turismo Tour Mar.

➤ TOUR OPERATORS: **Cobre Tour** (✉ O'Higgins 640, Copiapó, ☎ 51/211–072). **Limtur** (✉ Vicuña Mackenna 370, Ovalle, ☎ 53/630–057). **Peruvian Tour** (✉ Infante 530, Copiapó, ☎ 51/216–309). **Talinay** (✉ Prat 470, La Serena, ☎ 51/218–658). **Turismo Atacama** (✉ Carreras 716, Copiapó, ☎ 51/212–712). **Turismo Tour Mar** (✉ Diego de Almeyda 904, Caldera, ☎ 51/316–612).

VISITOR INFORMATION

Every major city of El Norte Chico has an office run by Sernatur, the Chilean tourism agency. They offer informative brochures of the region and other assistance for travelers. The staff speaks some English.
➤ INFORMATION: **Copiapó** (✉ Los Carrera 691, ☎ 52/231–510). **La Serena** (✉ Matta 461, ☎ 51/225–199). **Vallenar** (✉ Pan-American Hwy. exit, ☎ 51/619–215).

5 EL NORTE GRANDE

Terrifying in its austerity and vastness, Chile's Great North is a bleak patch of sand and rock that seems to stretch for eternity. This is the Atacama Desert, the driest place on earth. Yet people have inhabited this desolate land since time immemorial. Here you'll discover clues of the past, from ancient mummies to astounding geoglyphs. You'll also find soaring volcanoes, vast salt flats, and crumbling ghost towns.

By Gregory
Benchwick

A LAND OF ROCK AND EARTH, El Norte Grande is one of the world's most desolate regions. Spanning some 1,930 km (1,200 mi), it stretches from the Río Copiapó to the borders of Peru and Bolivia. Here you will find the Atacama Desert, so dry that in many parts no rain has ever been recorded.

The heart of El Norte Grande lies not in its geography, but in its people. The indigenous Chinchorro people eked out a meager living from the sea more than 8,000 years ago, leaving behind the magnificent Chinchorro mummies, the oldest in the world. High in the Andes, the Atacameño tribes traded livestock with the more sophisticated cultures of the Tijuanacota and the Inca. Many of these people still cling to their way of life, though much of their culture was lost during the colonial period.

Although the Spanish first invaded the region in the 16th century, El Norte Grande was mostly ignored by Europeans until the 1800s when huge deposits of nitrates were found in the Atacama region. The "white gold" brought boom times to towns like Pisagua, Iquique, and Antofagasta. Because most of the mineral-rich region lay beyond its northern border, Chile declared war on neighboring Peru and Bolivia in 1878. Chile won the five-year battle and annexed the land north of Antofagasta, a continuing source of national pride for most Chileans. With the invention of synthetic nitrates, the market for these fertilizers dried up and the nitrate barons abandoned their opulent mansions and returned to Santiago. El Norte Grande was once again left on its own.

What you'll see today is a land of both growth and decay. The glory days of the nitrate era are gone, but copper has stepped in to help fill that gap (you'll find here the world's largest open-pit copper mine). El Norte Grande still is a land of opportunity for fortune-seekers, as well as for tourists looking for a less-traveled corner of the world. It is a place of beauty and dynamic isolation, a place where the past touches the present in a troubled yet majestic embrace.

Pleasures and Pastimes

Beaches
El Norte Grande is home to some of Chile's best beaches, and during the summer months of January and February they are packed with vacationing South Americans. The stretches of shoreline near Arica and Iquique are pristine, while those around Antofagasta are, for the most part, dirty and overcrowded. Though in recent years the Chilean government has done much to clean up polluted waters, many of El Norte Grande's beaches are not safe for swimming. Those with pollution or dangerous currents are marked by large signs saying NO APTA PARA BANARSE (not suitable for swimming). Many locals, however, ignore the warnings.

Dining
The food of Norte Grande is simple but quite good. Along the coast you can enjoy fresh seafood and shellfish, including *merluza* (hake), *corvina* (sea bass), *ostiones* (oysters), and *machas* (similar to razor clams but unique to Chile), to name just a few. *Ceviche* (a traditional Peruvian dish made with marinated fish) is also available in much of El Norte Grande, but make sure the fish has been cooked. Fish may be ordered *a la plancha* (grilled in butter and lemon) or accompanied by a sauce like *salsa margarita* (a butter-based sauce comprising almost every shellfish imaginable). As you enter the interior region, the heartier meals include *cazuela de vacuno* (beef stew served with corn on the cob and

El Norte Grande

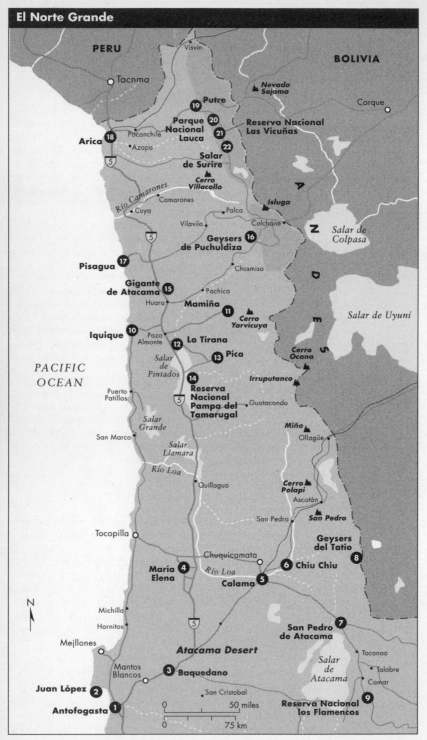

PERU

BOLIVIA

Visvin

Tacnma

Nevado
Sajama

Corque

19 Putre

20

Poconchile

21

Parque
Nacional
Lauca

Reserva Nacional
Las Vicuñas

18 Arica

Azapa

22

Salar
de Surire

*Cerro
Villacollo*

Isluga

Río Camarones

Camarones

Palca

Cuya

Vilavila

Colchane

*Salar de
Colpasa*

Geysers
de Puchuldiza **16**

Chusmisa

17 Pisagua

Gigante
de Atacama **15**

Pachica

Huara

Mamiña

*Cerro
Yarvicuya*

11

Salar de Uyuní

10 Iquique

Pozo
Almonte

12 La Tirana

13 Pica

*Cerro
Ocana*

*PACIFIC
OCEAN*

*Salar
de
Pintados*

14

Irruputanco

Reserva
Nacional
Pampa del
Tamarugal

Guatacondo

Miño

Puerto
Patillos

Ollagüe

*Salar
Grande*

*Salar
Llamara*

San Marco

*Cerro
Polapi*

Río Loa

Ascotán

Quillagua

San Pedro

San Pedro

Tocopilla

Geysers
del Tatio **8**

Chuquicamata

6 Chiu Chiu

Michilla

María
Elena **4**

Río Loa

5

Calama

Hornitos

7

San Pedro
de Atacama

Mejllones

Atacama Desert

*Salar
de
Atacama*

Toconao

Talabre

Mantos
Blancos

3 Baquedano

Camar

Juan López **2**

San Cristobal

Antofogasta **1**

0 ————— 50 miles

0 ————— 75 km

Reserva Nacional
los Flamencos **9**

N

vegetables) and *chuleta con arroz* (beef with rice). More heavily touristed areas, such as San Pedro de Atacama, also offer international fare.

People in the north generally eat a heavy lunch at around 2 PM that can last two hours, followed by a light dinner around 10 PM. Reservations are seldom needed, except in the poshest of locales. Leave a 10% tip if you enjoyed the service. For approximate entrée costs, *see* the dining price chart *in* Smart Travel Tips A to Z.

Lodging

Lodging in El Norte Grande is relatively inexpensive. Hotels in the larger cities offer all the amenities you would expect from similar establishments back home, such as business centers, laundry service, pools, cable television, and minibars. Unfortunately, many that bill themselves as "luxury" hotels haven't been remodeled or painted in years. Ask to look at a room before deciding. In small towns there is generally no such thing as a hotel, and you will have to make do with guest houses with extremely basic rooms with a shared bath. For approximate room costs, *see* the lodging price chart *in* Smart Travel Tips A to Z.

Shopping

The best places to shop in El Norte Grande are the local *mercados* (markets) and *ferias artesenales* (artisan fairs) where you'll find handmade jewelry and leather goods. Traditional Andean clothing and textiles can be purchased in most cities, but tend to be more authentic farther off the beaten path. It is illegal to export antiques from Chile, so the textiles are never more than 20 years old, and newer ones are often mass-produced in Peru. Though bargaining is acceptable, it is less common than in other parts of South America.

Exploring El Norte Grande

Only those who enjoy the solitude and desolation of the desert should venture into El Norte Grande, the region dominated by the mammoth Atacama Desert. Only on rare occasions will you see a swath of green cutting through the empty landscape. The driest desert in the world, the Atacama is barren until it explodes in a riot of color known as *el desierto florido*. The flowering desert takes place every four or five years when unusual amounts of rain awaken dormant bulbs.

For those not lucky enough to see the flowering desert, there are more mysteries to behold in the desert, along the barren coastline, and among the peaks of the world's longest mountain chain. The *altiplano,* or high plains, rests between two giant branches of the Andes and houses such natural marvels as crystalline salt flats, geysers, and volcanos. You'll also spot flocks of flamingos and such mammals as the vicuña, a cousin to the llama.

Great Itineraries

IF YOU HAVE 5 DAYS

You'll have to hustle to see much of El Norte Grande in less than a week. Start off by spending at least two days in ⌂ **San Pedro de Atacama** ⑦, visiting the incredible sights such as the bizarre moonscape of the Valle de la Luna and the desolate salt flats of the Salar de Atacama. On the third day, soak in the hot springs in the tiny town of **Pica** ⑬. Stay in the nearby city of ⌂ **Iquique** ⑩. The next day head to the nitrate ghost town of Humberstone. On your last day, take a side trip to the **Gigante de Atacama** ⑮, the world's largest geoglyph.

IF YOU HAVE 7 DAYS

Seven days will allow you to visit El Norte Grande at a more relaxed pace. Follow the five-day itinerary. On the sixth day cruise up to ⌂

Arica ⑱, the coastal town that bills itself as the "land of eternal spring." Make sure to visit the Museo Arqueológico de San Miguel de Azapa to see the Chinchorro mummies. On your last day, journey to the altiplano, taking in the flamingos at **Parque Nacional Lauca** ⑳ or the vicuñas, llamas, and alpacas of **Reserva Nacional Las Vicuñas** ㉑.

When to Tour

In the height of the Chilean summer, January and February, droves of Chileans and Argentines mob El Norte Grande's beaches. Although this is a fun time to visit, prices go up and finding a hotel can be harder. Book your room a month or more in advance. The high season tapers off in March, an excellent time to visit if you are looking for a bit more tranquility. If you plan to visit the altiplano, bring the right clothing. Winter can be very cold, and summer sees a lot of rain.

THE NITRATE PAMPA

The vast *pampa salitrera* is an atmospheric introduction to Chile's Great North. Between 1890 and 1925 this region was the site of more than 80 *oficinas de salitre,* or nitrate plants. The invention of synthetic nitrates spelled the end for all but a few. Crumbling nitrate works lay stagnant in the dry desert air, some disintegrating into dust, others remaining a fascinating testament to the white gold that for a time made this one of Chile's richest regions.

Antofagasta

❶ *565 km (350 mi) north of Copiapó.*

Antofagasta is the most important—and the richest—city in El Norte Grande. It was part of Bolivia until 1879, when it was annexed by Chile in the War of the Pacific. The port town became an economic powerhouse during the nitrate boom. With the rapid decline of nitrate production, copper mining stepped in to keep the city's coffers filled.

Most travelers end up spending a night in Antofagasta on their way to the more interesting destinations like San Pedro de Atacama, Iquique, and Arica, but a few sights here are worth a look. High above Plaza Colón is the **Torre Reloj,** the clock tower whose face is a replica of London's Big Ben. It was erected by British residents in 1910.

The historic customs house, the town's oldest building, dates from 1866. Housed inside is the **Museo Regional de Antofagasta,** which displays clothing and other bric-a-brac from the nitrate era. ⊠ *Bolívar 1888,* ☎ *55/227–016.* ▣ *Admission.* ⊙ *Tues.–Sat. 10–1 and 3:30–6:30, Sun. 11–2.*

Dining and Lodging

$$$ ✕ **Club de Yates.** Featuring nice views of the port, this seafood restaurant caters to yachting types, which may explain why the prices are a bit high. The food is quite good, especially the *ostiones a la parmesana* (oysters with Parmesan cheese). The maritime theme is taken to the extreme—the plates, curtains, tablecloths, and every decoration imaginable come in the mandatory navy blue. The service is excellent. ⊠ *Balmaceda 2705,* ☎ *56–55/263–942. Reservations essential. AE, MC, V.*

$$$ ✕ **Restaurant Arriero.** Serving up traditional dishes from Spain's Basque ★ country, this restaurant is the place to go for good barbecued meats. You'll dine in a pleasant Pyrenees-style inn decorated with the traditional cured hams hanging from the walls. The restaurant's owners play jazz on the piano almost every evening. ⊠ *Condell 2644,* ☎ *55/264–371. AE, DC, MC, V.*

$ ✕ **Don Pollo.** This rotisserie restaurant serves up some of the best chicken in Chile (good thing, because it's the only item on the menu). The thatched-roof terrace is a great place to kick back after a long day of sightseeing. ⊠ *Ossa 2594,* ☏ *no phone. No credit cards.*

$$$ ⊞ **Hotel Antofagasta.** Part of the deluxe Panamericana Hoteles chain,
★ this high-rise on the ocean offers all the first-class luxuries, from an elegant bar with a grand piano to a lovely kidney-shape pool. The rooms are comfortably furnished, and some have ocean views. A semi-private beach is just steps from the hotel's back door. ⊠ *Balmaceda 2575,* ☏ *55/228–811,* 𝐅𝐀𝐗 *55/268–415,* 𝗪𝗘𝗕 *www.panamericanahoteles.cl. 163 rooms. Restaurant, bar, pool, hair salon, health club, laundry service, business services, meeting rooms. AE, MC, V.*

$ ⊞ **Marsal Hotel.** This modern and clean hotel faces busy Calle Arturo Prat, so make sure to ask for one of the pleasant rooms in the back. The service here is quite friendly—the staff goes out of its way to recommend restaurants and arrange excursions. A Continental breakfast is included. ⊠ *Arturo Prat 867,* ☏ *55/268–063,* 𝐅𝐀𝐗 *55/221–733. 21 rooms. Minibars, business services, meeting rooms. MC, V.*

Nightlife and the Arts

Nightlife in El Norte Grande often means heading to the *schoperias,* beer stands where the almost entirely male clientele downs a type of draft beer called *schop.* The drinking generally continues until everyone is reeling drunk. If this is your idea of fun, check out the myriad schoperias in the center of town around the Plaza Colón.

For those not quite ready for the schoperia experience (not the most pleasant places to spend an evening), there are also a few bars where you can have a quiet drink. Antofagasta's elite head to **Wally's Pub** (⊠ Antonino Toro 982, ☏ 55/223–697), an American-style bar with American-style prices. **Nueva Raíces** (⊠ Condell 3033, ☏ no phone) has a funky, friendly atmosphere steeped in northern Chilean culture. Ask the bartender to show you how to play *cacho,* a dice game popular with locals. Weekends you'll enjoy live music.

Shopping

On the corner of Manuel A. Matta and Maipú you'll find the pink-walled fruit and vegetable market called **Mercado Central.** Across the street is the **Plaza del Mercado,** where artisan stalls sell handmade jewelry and healing crystals.

Juan López

❷ *38 km (23 mi) north of Antofagasta.*

Those turned off by the hustle and bustle of Antofagasta will likely be charmed by Juan López, a hodgepodge of pastel-color fishing shacks and a picturesque *caleta* (wharf). In high season, January and February, the beaches are crowded and dirty. The rest of the year you may have the white, silken sand to yourself.

On the coast about 13 km (8 mi) south of Juan López lies **La Portada,** an offshore volcanic rock that the sea has carved into an arch. It's one of the most photographed natural sights in the country.

Dining and Lodging

$$ ✕ **Restaurant Vitoco.** This restaurant, decorated with native textiles, offers a fixed meal of chicken or grilled fish. The food is good and the kitchen is spotless. ⊠ *Manzana 8,* ☏ *55/383–071. No credit cards.*

$ ⊞ **Hosteria Sandokan.** The nicest place to stay in Juan López, Hosteria Sandokan is set in an airy garden complete with chirping caged birds. It offers basic but clean rooms with shared baths. The hotel's terrace restaurant, which serves excellent seafood, has great views of the pelicans going about their business. ⊠ *Fernando Bull s/n*, ☎ *56–55/223–302. 6 rooms with shared bath. Restaurant. No credit cards.*

Outdoor Activities and Sports

People come to Juan López for the beaches, and there are plenty from which to choose. The most popular beach is **Balneario Juan López,** a small strip of white sand near the center of town. Picturesque **Playa Acapulco** is in a small cove north of Balneario Juan López. South of town there are several larger beaches easily reached by car. **Playa Rinconada,** about 5 km (3 mi) down the coast, is lauded by locals for its warm water.

Baquedano

❸ *72 km (45 mi) northeast of Antofagasta.*

Once an important railway transfer station, Baquedano today sees only a fraction of the freight that passed through during its heyday. There are few reasons to stop besides an open-air railroad museum that hints about the village's past importance. The **Museo Ferroviario** is a testament to the greatness of the nitrate era. Old locomotives sit silently, waiting for the next boom. Hop aboard one of these paralyzed monsters and relive the days when they roared across the barren pampa. ⊠ *South of the current depot.* ▱ *Free.* ☉ *Daily 8–12:30 and 2–7.*

In this region locals know as the pampa salitrera there were some 80 nitrate plants in operation between 1890 and 1925. Many of the plants, as well as the company towns that housed their workers, still survive. A mysterious dot on the desert landscape, the ghost town of
★ **Chacabuco** is a decidedly eerie place. More than 7,000 employees and their families lived here when the Oficina Chacabuco was in operation between 1922 and 1944. Today you'll find tiny houses, their tin roofs flapping in the wind and their walls collapsing. You can wander through many of the abandoned buildings and tour a museum with photographs of the town.

Chacabuco did not remain closed forever. During the first years of Augusto Pinochet's military regime, it was used as a concentration camp for political dissidents. The artwork of prisoners still adorns many of the walls. Do not walk around the town's exterior, as land mines from this era are still buried there. ⊠ *26 km (16 mi) northeast of Baquedano on the Pan-American Hwy.* ▱ *Admission.* ☉ *Daily 7 AM–8 PM.*

María Elena

❹ *148 km (92 mi) north of Baquedano.*

The 8,000 people who live in María Elena are proud of their history—nearly every house has a picture of the town hanging inside. Founded by a British company in 1926, it's home to the employees of the region's last two nitrate plants. Maria Elena is a dusty place that warrants a visit if you want to see a functioning nitrate town.

The tiny but informative **Museo Arqueológico,** on the town's run-down main plaza, houses many artifacts from the nitrate boom as well as a few from the pre-Columbian era. ⊠ *Av. Ignacio Carrera Pinto*, ☎ *55/632–935.* ▱ *Free.* ☉ *Mon.–Sat. 9–1 and 4–7, Sun. 10–1 and 5–8.*

Lodging

$ ▣ **Residencial Chacance.** If you need lodging in Maria Elena, this is the best choice by far. The inn offers basic rooms with shared baths.

There's also a pleasant, albeit neglected, garden. ✉ *Claudio Vicuña 437,* ☎ *55/639–524. 10 rooms with shared bath. No credit cards.*

Calama

❺ *213 km (132 mi) northeast of Antofagasta.*

The discovery of copper in the area turned Calama into the quintessential mining town, and therein lies its interest. People from the length of Chile flock to this dusty spot on the map in hopes of striking it rich. A modern-day version of the boomtowns of the 19th-century American West, Calama is rough around the edges, but it does possess a certain energy.

The world's largest open-pit mine, **Chiquicamata** is the lifeblood of Chile's copper industry. Heavy machinery roars in the bottom of the pit, producing 600,000 metric tons of copper yearly. Chiquicamata's immense size—4 km (2½ mi) long and 3 km (2 mi) wide—is the result of nearly a century of continuous mining. Experts say the mine will continue to yield copper for the next 45 years. ✉ *16 km (10 mi) north of Calama,* ☎ *no phone.* ✆ *Admission.* ⊙ *Guided tours begin at 9* AM.

Founded as a *tambo,* or resting place, at the crossing of two Inca trails, Calama still serves as a stopover for people headed elsewhere. Most people traveling to San Pedro de Atacama end up spending the night here. But the town does have a few attractions of its own. On Plaza 23 de Marzo, the gleaming copper roof of **Catedral San Juan Bautista** (✉ Calle Ramírez and Av. Granaderos) is testament to the importance of mining in this region.

The **Museo Arqueológico y Ernologico,** a natural history museum in the well-manicured Parque El Loa, depends heavily on dioramas to explain region's pre-Columbian past. Nearby is a replica of the quaint church in neighboring Chiu Chiu. ✉ *South of town on Av. O'Higgins,* ☎ *55/ 632–731.* ✆ *Admission.* ⊙ *Tues.–Fri. 10–1:30 and 2:30–6, weekends 11–6:30.*

Dining and Lodging

$$$ ✗ **Las Brasas de Juan Luis.** With a pleasant country atmosphere, Las Brasas de Juan Luis is known around the region for its delicious *parrilladas* (barbecued meats). Try a mixed grill, which includes a variety of cuts. ✉ *Balmaceda 1972,* ☎ *55/344–366. Reservations essential. AE, DC, MC, V. No dinner Sun.*

$$$ ✗ **Plaza Restaurant.** Excellent seafood, such as the merluza con salsa margarita, make this centrally located restaurant a good choice. The grilled meat is also tasty. The atmosphere, though tasteful, is a bit antiseptic. ✉ *Abaroa 1859,* ☎ *55/362–631. No credit cards.*

$$$$ 🛏 **Park Hotel Calama.** This top-notch hotel is frequented by international mining consultants, and it's easy to see why. The rooms have giant beds made up with luxurious linens. The steaming showers feel great after exploring the surrounding desert. There's a pool, a lovely garden, and an excellent restaurant serving international cuisine. ✉ *Camino Aeropuerto 1392,* ☎ *55/319–900,* FAX *55/219–901,* WEB *www.parkplaza.cl. 102 rooms. Restaurant, bar, minibars, pool, tennis, health club, laundry service, meeting rooms, business services, free parking. AE, DC, MC, V.*

$$ 🛏 **Hotel El Mirador.** Around the corner from Plaza 23 de Marzo, this
★ friendly bed-and-breakfast is a charmer. A tastefully decorated salon with antique furnishings leads to an enclosed courtyard where you can enjoy the sun while sipping a pisco sour. The cheerful yellow rooms are clean and comfortably furnished. A Continental breakfast is served at a nearby Bavarian restaurant. ✉ *Sotomayor 2064,* ☎ *55/340–329. 14 rooms. Laundry service. AE, DC, MC, V.*

Nightlife and the Arts

Calama is the land of the schoperia—locals say there are more schoperias than people. Come payday at the mine, these drinking halls fill up with beer-swilling workers. For a less raucous evening, try one of the schoperias near Plaza 23 de Marzo. On weekends head to **Direccion Obligada** (✉ Granaderos 2663, ☎ 55/345–834), an upscale bar that attracts foreigners and locals alike. Pop and cumbia are played here at top volume, so bring your earplugs.

Cine Teatro Municipal (✉ Ramírez 2034, ☎ 55/342–864) shows recent Hollywood movies. It also stages the occasional play or concert.

Shopping

There are covered markets where locals sell clothing and jewelry off the pedestrian mall of Calle Ramírez. There are also markets on Calle Vargas between Latorre and Vivar.

Chiu Chiu

⑥ *33 km (20 mi) east of Calama.*

Not far from sprawling industrial center of Calama, Chiu Chiu is a vision of the region's agrarian past. This pastoral town, whose inhabitants still make their living growing carrots and other vegetables, is in a lush valley near the Río Loa. Across from Chiu Chiu's main square is the **Iglesia de Chiu Chiu.** Built in 1674, it's one of the oldest churches in the altiplano. The squat building's whitewashed adobe walls are topped with a cactus-shingle roof. No nails were used in its construction—rafters and beams are lashed together with leather straps. On October 4, things get lively when the 500 inhabitants congregate in the central plaza to celebrate the town's patron saint.

San Pedro de Atacama

⑦ *100 km (62 mi) southeast of Calama.*

The most popular tourist destination in El Norte Grande, San Pedro de Atacama is in the midst of some of the most breathtaking scenery in Chile. A string of towering volcanoes, some of which are still active, stand watch to the east. To the west is La Cordillera de Sal, a mountain range composed almost entirely of salt. Here you'll find such marvels as the Valle de la Luna (Valley of the Moon) and the Valle de la Muerte (Valley of Death). The desolate Salar de Atacama, Chile's largest salt flat, lies to the south. The number of attractions in the Atacama area does not end there: alpine lakes, steaming geysers, colonial villages, and ancient fortresses all lie within easy reach.

The area's history goes back to pre-Columbian times, when the Atacameño people scraped a meager living from the fertile delta of the San Pedro River. By 1450 the region had been conquered by the Incas, but their reign was cut short by the arrival of the Europeans. Spanish conquistador Pedro De Valdivia, who eventually seized control of the entire country, camped here in 1540 while waiting for reinforcements. By the 19th century San Pedro had become an important trading center, and was a stop for llama trains on their way from the altiplano to the Pacific coast. During the nitrate era, San Pedro was the main resting place for cattle drives from Argentina.

With its narrow streets lined with whitewashed and mud-color adobe houses, San Pedro centers around a small Plaza de Armas teeming with artisans, tour operators, and others who make their living catering to tourists. The 1744 **Iglesia San Pedro,** to the west of the square, is one of the altiplano's largest churches. It was miraculously constructed without the use of a single nail—the builders used cactus sinews to tie the roof beams and door hinges. ⊠ *Padre Le Paige s/n,* ☎ *no phone.* ☒ *Free.* ☽ *Daily 8–8.*

★ The **Museo Arqueológico Gustavo Le Paige** is an awe-inspiring collection of artifacts from the region, including fine examples of textiles and ceramics. The majority was gathered by the founder, Jesuit missionary Gustavo Le Paige. The museum traces the history of the region from pre-Columbian times through the Spanish colonization. The most impressive exhibit is the well-preserved, fetal-positioned Atacameño mummy with her swatch of twisted black hair. ⊠ *Calle Padre Le Paige and Paseo Artesenal,* ☎ *55/851–002.* ☒ *Admission.* ☽ *Weekdays 9–noon and 2–6, weekends 10–noon and 2–6.*

Just 3 km (2 mi) north of San Pedro lies the ancient fortress of **Pukara de Quitor.** The group of stone structures at the entrance to the Valle de Catarpe was built in the 12th century to protect the Atacameños from invading Incas. It wasn't the Incas but the Spanish who were the real threat. Spanish conquistador Pedro de Valdivia took it by force in 1540. The crumbling buildings were carefully reconstructed in 1981 by the University of Antofagasta. ⊠ *On the road to Valle Catarpe,* ☎ *no phone.* ☒ *Free.*

The archaeological site of **Tulor,** 9 km (6 mi) southwest of San Pedro, marks the remains of the oldest known civilization in the region. Built around 800 BC, the village of Tulor was home to the Linka Arti people, who lived in small mud huts resembling igloos. Undiscovered until the middle of the 20th century, the site was excavated from a sand dune by Jesuit missionary Gustavo Le Paige. Archaeologists hypothesize that the inhabitants left because of climatic changes and a possible sand storm. Little more about the village's history is known, and only one of the huts has been completely excavated. As one of the well-informed guides will tell you, even this hut is sinking back into the obscurity of the Atacama sand. ⊠ *9 km (6 mi) southwest of San Pedro, then 3 km (2 mi) down the road leading to the Valle de la Luna,* ☎ *no phone.* ☒ *Admission.* ☽ *Daily 8–8.*

Dining and Lodging

$$–$$$ ✕ **Casa Piedra.** This rustic stone house offers views of the world-famous Atacama skies from its central courtyard. As at most San Pedro eateries, a blazing fire keeps you company. The food here is simple and good, mixing international and local dishes. Mexican entrées are served once a week. ⊠ *Caracoles 225,* ☎ *55/851–447. AE, DC, MC, V.*

$–$$$ ✕ **Paacha.** Loved by locals, Paacha doesn't attract as many tourists as other restaurants. It offers a good selection, including excellent steak dishes such as a *lomo montado* (fried tenderloin with eggs). Costumed performers play the *charango* (an altiplano version of the mandolin) and drums every night. ⊠ *Domingo Atienza 4452,* ☎ *55/851–152. AE, MC, V.*

$$$$ ▥ **Hotel Explora.** Is it a modern monstrosity or an expressionist show-
★ piece? Hotel Explora, built by the same company that constructed the much-lauded Hotel Salto Chico in Parque Nacional Torres del Paine, attracted much criticism for not fitting in with the local architecture. On the other hand, it has also won architectural prizes for its skewed lines and sleek courtyard. The hotel, which offers three-, four- and seven-day all-inclusive stays (tours, meals, and drinks included), delivers the best service and amenities of any hotel in northern Chile. Whether or not you stay here, the hotel is worth a visit to see it for yourself. ⊠ *Domingo Atienza s/n,* ☎ *56/206–6060,* FAX *56–2/228–4655,* WEB *www.explora-chile.com. 52 rooms. Restaurant, bar, pool, massage, sauna, library, baby-sitting, laundry service, meeting rooms. AE, DC, MC, V.*

$$$ ⊞ **Hotel Terrantai.** An architectural beauty with river-stone walls, Hotel
★   Terrantai is just a block away from the Plaza de Armas. The high-ceilinged
      rooms offer beautiful tile floors and big beds piled with down comforters.
      Throw open the huge windows to let in the morning breeze. The can-
      dlelit restaurant, perfect for a romantic dinner, serves international
      fare. There's also a tiny, natural-rock plunge pool in the center. ⊠ *To-*
      copilla 411, ☎ *55/851–140,* FAX *55/851–037,* WEB *www.adex.cl. 12*
      rooms. Restaurant, laundry service. AE, DC, MC, V.

$$ ⊞ **Hotel Kimal.** A good budget alternative a few blocks from the Plaza
      de Armas, the adobe-walled Hotel Kimal has pleasant rooms set around
      a sandy courtyard dotted with shrubbery. Breakfast is served at the restau-
      rant next door. ⊠ *Domingo Atienza 452,* ☎ *56/851–152,* FAX *56/851–*
      030. 10 rooms. Restaurant, shop, laundry service, meeting rooms.
      AE, DC, MC, V.

Nightlife and the Arts

The bohemian side of San Pedro gets going after dinner and generally
ends around midnight, when the town's generator switches off and the
city goes black. The majority of the bars are on Caracoles. **La Estaka**
(⊠ Caracoles 259B, ☎ no phone) is a hippie bar with funky decor, including a sculpted dragon hanging on one of the walls. Reggae music
rules. **Café Adobe** (⊠ Caracoles 211, ☎ no phone) is usually more *tran-*
quilo, although it occasionally offers live music. At night there's seating around a bonfire on the courtyard. During the day the latticed roof
around the edges protects you from the sun's rays. **Tambo Carnaval**
(⊠ Toconao s/n, ☎ no phone) offers dancing and a livelier atmosphere.

Outdoor Activities and Sports

San Pedro is an outdoor enthusiast's dreams. There are great places
for biking, hiking, and horseback riding in every direction. Extreme-
sports enthusiasts can try their hand at sand-boarding on the dunes of
the Valle de la Muerte. Climbers can take on the nearby volcanoes. The
only trouble is the crowds. At the Valley of the Moon, for example,
you'll sometimes encounter a caravan of 20 or 30 tourists scurrying
towards the top of the large sand dune to watch the sunset.

Whatever your sport, keep in mind that San Pedro lies at 2,400 meters (7,900 ft). If you're not acclimated, you'll feel tired much sooner
than you think. Also remember to slather on the sunscreen and drink
plenty of water.

BIKING

An afternoon ride to the Valle de la Luna is unforgettable, as is a quick
trip to the ruins of Tulor. You can also head to the Salar de Atacama.
Bike rentals can be arranged at most hotels and in most tour agencies.

HIKING

There are hikes in all directions from San Pedro. Good hikes include
trips through the Valle de la Muerte, as well as to the ruins of Pukara
de Quitor. **Cosmo Andino Expediciones** (⊠ Calle Caracoles s/n, San Pedro
de Atacama, ☎ 56/851–069) offers excellent tours with well-informed
guides.

HORSEBACK RIDING

San Pedro has the feeling of a Wild West town, so why not hitch up
your horse and head out on an adventure? Although the sun is quite
intense during the middle of the day, sunset is a perfect time to visit
Pukara de Quitor or Tulor. An overnight journey to the Salar de Atacama or the Valle de La Luna is a great way to see the region at a relaxed pace. **Turismo el Sol** (⊠ Tocopilla 432, San Pedro de Atacama,
☎ 56/851–230) provides horses and guides.

Shopping

Just about the entire village of San Pedro is an open-air market. The **Feria Artesenal,** just off the Plaza de Armas, is bursting at the seams with artisan goods. Here, you can buy high-quality knits from the altiplano, such as sweaters and other woolen items. **La Manada** (⊠ Caracoles 192, ☎ no phone) sells jewelry made by local artisans. **Mal-lku** (⊠ Caracoles s/n, ☎ no phone) is a pleasant store with traditional altiplano textiles, some up to 20 years old.

Geysers del Tatio

8 *95 km (59 mi) north of San Pedro.*

The world's highest geothermal field, Geysers del Tatio are a breath-taking natural phenomenon. The sight of dozens of *fumaroles,* or gey-sers, throwing columns of steam into the air is unforgettable. A trip to El Tatio usually begins at 4 AM, when San Pedro is still cold and dark. After a three-hour bus trip on a relentlessly bumpy road you reach the high plateau at about daybreak. The jets of steam are already shooting into the air as the sun slowly peaks over the adjacent cordillera. The rays of light illuminate the steam in a kaleidoscope of chartreuses, violets, reds, oranges, and blues. The vapor then silently falls onto the sulfur-stained crust of the geyser field. As the sun heats the cold, bar-ren land, the force of the geysers gradually diminishes. Now you can explore the mud pots and craters formed by the escaping steam. Be care-ful, though—the crust is thin in places and people have been badly burned falling into the boiling-hot water.

Reserva Nacional los Flamencos

9 *10 km (6 mi) south of San Pedro.*

Many of the most astounding sights in El Norte Grande lie within the boundaries of the protected Reserva Nacional los Flamencos. This sprawling national reserve, which lies to the south and east of San Pedro, encompasses a wide variety of geographical features, including alpine lakes, salt flats, and volcanoes. You can get information about the park at the station run by Conaf, the Chilean forestry service. ⊠ *Conaf sta-tion near Laguna Chaxa,* ☎ *no phone.* 🎟 *Admission.* ☉ *Daily 8:30–1 and 2:30–6:30.*

About 10 km (6 mi) south of San Pedro you arrive at the edge of the **Salar de Atacama,** Chile's largest salt flat. The rugged crust measur-ing 3,000-square-km (1,158-square-mi) formed when salty water flow-ing down from the Andes evaporated in the stifling heat of the desert. Unlike other salt flats, which are chalkboard-flat surfaces of crys-talline salt, the Salar de Atacama is a jumble of jagged rocks. **Laguna Chaxa,** in the middle of Salar de Atacama, is a very salty lagoon that is home to three of the world's four species of flamingos. The elegant pink and white birds are mirrored by the lake's glassy surface. Near Laguna Chaxa, beautiful plates of salt float on the calm surface of **La-guna Salada.**

One of the most impressive sights in Reserva Nacional los Flamencos is the 4,350-meter-high **Laguna Miscanti.** The awe-inspiring blue lake is enough to merit a few hours of rest and repose. Laguna Miñeques, a smaller lake adjacent to Laguna Miscanti, is also spectacular. Here you will find vicuña and huge flocks of flamingos.

Very few places in the world can compare to the **Valle de la Luna** (⊠ 14 km [9 mi] west of San Pedro). This surreal landscape of barren ridges, soaring cliffs, and pale valleys could be from a canvas by Salvador Dalí.

Originally a small corner of a vast inland sea, the valley rose up with
the Andes. The water slowly drained away, leaving deposits of salt and
gypsum that were folded by shifting of the earth's crust and then worn
away by wind and rain. Visit Valle de la Luna in the late afternoon to
take advantage of the incredible sunsets visible from atop the immense
sand dune. Not far from the Valle de la Luna are the reddish rocks of
the **Valle de la Muerte.** Jesuit missionary Gustavo Le Paige, the first
archaeologist to explore this desolate area, found many human bones.
He hypothesized that people may have gone here to die.

IQUIQUE AREA

Iquique is the capital of Chile's northernmost region, but it wasn't always so important. For hundreds of years it was a tiny fishing community. After the arrival of the Spanish the village grew slowly,
eventually becoming a shipping port. The population, however, never
totaled more than 100. It was not until the great nitrate boom of the
19th century that Iquique became the major port. Many of those who
grew rich on nitrate moved to the city and built opulent mansions, almost all of which still stand today. The boom went bust, and those who
remained turned again to the sea to make a living. Today Iquique is
the world's largest exporter of fish meal.

Iquique itself is rather dreary, but the area holds many sights that merit
a visit. A stone's throw from Iquique, nitrate ghost towns like Humberstone sit in eternal silence. Farther inland you encounter the charming hot spring oases of Pica and Mamiña and the desolate, beautiful
Parque Nacional Volcán Isluga.

Iquique

10 *390 km (242 mi) northwest of Calama.*

At the base of a coastal mountain range, Iquique is blessed with year-
round good weather. Perhaps that's why in recent years the city has
become a mecca for vacationing Chilean families. The long stretches
of white beaches are one draw. Another is the *zona franca,* or duty-
free zone. Life in the city revolves around the **Plaza Prat,** where children ride bicycles along the sidewalks and adults chat on nearly every
park bench. The 1877 **Torre Reloj,** with its gleaming white tower and
Moorish arches, stands in the center of the plaza.

Unlike most cities, Iquique's cathedral is not on the main plaza. Here
instead you'll find the sumptuous **Teatro Municipal,** built in 1890 as
an opera house. On the Corinthian-columned facade you'll find lovely
statues representing the four seasons. If you're lucky you can catch a
play or musical performance here. ⊠ *Plaza Prat,* ☎ *57/411–292.* ☞
Admission. ⊙ *Daily 8–7.*

Many of the old mansions are badly in need of repair, leaving the city
with a rather worn-down feeling. For a tantalizing view into the opu-
★ lence of the nitrate era, visit the Georgian-style **Palacio Astoreca.** This
palace, built in 1903, features the likeness of Dionysus, the Greek god
of revelry. There's also a giant billiards table, a beautiful skylight over
the central hall, and an art and natural history museum on the upper
level that houses modern works by Chilean artists and artifacts including
pottery and textiles. ⊠ *O'Higgins 350,* ☎ *57/425–600.* ☞ *Free.* ⊙
Tues.–Fri. 10–1 and 4–7:30, Sat. 10–1:30, Sun. 11–2.

Along the historic Calle Baquedano is the **Museo Regional,** a natural
history museum of the region. It houses pre-Columbian artifacts such
as deformed skulls and arrowheads, as well as an eclectic collection

from the region's nitrate heyday. ⊠ *Baquedano 951,* ☎ *57/411–034.* ▣ *Admission.* ⊙ *Mon.–Sat. 9:30–1 and 3–6:30.*

The **Museo Naval** can be found in the old customs house. Inside are displays about the Battle of Iquique in 1879, when the Chileans claimed Iquique from their neighbors to the north. Here you can get a glimpse at what the soldiers wore during the war and at the antiquated English arms used by Chilean soldiers. ⊠ *Sotomayor and Anibal Pinto.* ▣ *Free.* ⊙ *Weekdays 9:30–12:30 and 3–6.*

Dining and Lodging

$$$–$$$$ ✕ **Casino Español.** This venerable gentleman's club on Plaza Prat has
★ been transformed into a palatial restaurant. The beautiful Moorish architecture calls to mind the Alhambra Palace in Granada. The service is good, though rather fussy, and the food is extravagant in the traditional Andalucian style. The paella Valenciana is quite good. ⊠ *Plaza Prat 584,* ☎ *57/423–284. Reservations essential. AE, MC, V.*

$$$–$$$$ ✕ **Restaurant Nautico Cavancha.** Located away from the center of the city, Restaurant Nautico Cavancha treats you to views of Playa Cavancha. It's very stylish, right down to the cloth napkins (a rarity in El Norte Grande). Try the paella for two, served by friendly bow-tied waiters. ⊠ *Los Rieles 110,* ☎ *57/432–896. Reservations essential. DC, MC, V.*

$$$–$$$$ ✕ **Restaurant Protectora.** Next to the Teatro Municipal, this elegant restaurant has a soaring molded ceiling and huge chandelier. There's an international menu featuring such succulent items as lamb cooked in mint sauce—an excellent choice. The service, though a bit doting, is top-notch. ⊠ *Thompson 207,* ☎ *57/390–571. AE, DC, MC, V.*

$$–$$$ ✕ **Boulevard.** This intimate, candlelit French restaurant features excellent seafood served a variety of ways. The cuisine is an interesting mélange of French and Chilean recipes—try hake served with a creamy sauce. There is also live music on weekends. ⊠ *Baquedano 790,* ☎ *57/413–695. Reservations essential. MC, V.*

$$ ✕ **Timber House.** This bar, housed in a rough-hewn building from the nitrate era, gives you the feeling of being in a saloon from the Wild West. Timber House offers tasty Mexican dishes such as enchiladas and quesadillas. The service is quite friendly to boot. ⊠ *Bolívar 553,* ☎ *57/422–583. AE, DC, MC, V.*

$$$ ▥ **Sunfish.** On Playa Cavancha, Sunfish has very large, very modern rooms, many with views of the beach. Though the hotel lacks character, the royal blue exterior will certainly catch your eye. There's a small roof-top pool, but it's surrounded by a tacky artificial-grass terrace. A breakfast buffet is included. ⊠ *Amunategui 1990,* ☎ *57/419–000,* ℻ *57/419–001,* ⎁ *www.sunfish.cl. 45 rooms. Restaurant, minibars, pool, business services. AE, DC, MC, V.*

$$ ▥ **Hotel Arturo Prat.** In the heart of Iquique's historic district, Hotel Arturo Prat faces the central square. The only thing this luxury hotel lacks is access to the ocean. To make up for this, it has a very pleasant roof-top pool area decorated with white umbrellas and navy-blue sails. The rooms are all comfortable and modern, though some look out onto the parking lot—ask for one with a view of the square. The restaurant sits right on the Plaza Prat and serves good, but somewhat uninspired, fare. A breakfast buffet is included. ⊠ *Anibal Pinto 695,* ☎ *57/427–000,* ℻ *57/429–088,* ⎁ *www.hotelarturoprat.cl. 92 rooms. Restaurant, bar, minibars, laundry service, business services. AE, DC, MC, V.*

$$ ▥ **Hotel Carlos Condell.** A beautiful nitrate-era mansion complete with wrought-iron balconies and a rickety elevator, this restored landmark is a great budget alternative. This friendly bed-and-breakfast has lots of character, from the model sailboats in the reception area to the flower-

print comforters in the rooms. It's clean, although the baths are a bit small and run-down. A Continental breakfast is included. ⊠ *Baquedano 964,* ☏ *57/313–027. 27 rooms. Minibars. AE, MC, V.*

$ ⊡ **Hotel Atenas.** Housed in a venerable nitrate-era mansion on the beach,
★ Hotel Atenas is truly a taste of the city's history. Rooms are decorated with antiques and decked out with wood furnishings. The honeymoon suite has a giant tub where you can imagine the nitrate barons bathing in champagne. There are more modern rooms in the back, but these are not nearly as charming. There's also a pleasant pool in the garden. ⊠ *Los Rieles 738,* ☏ *57/431–100,* ℻ *57/431–100,* ₩₣₿ *www.iquiqueonline.cl/atenas. 40 rooms. Minibars, pool, hot tub, laundry service, free parking. AE, DC, MC, V.*

Nightlife and the Arts

Iquique really gets going after dark. Young people stay out all night and then spend the next day lazing around on the beach. Bars, most of which feature folk and jazz performances, get crowded around midnight. One of the most popular is **Circus Pub** (⊠ Thompson 123, ☏ 57/427–804) where the walls are decorated with cheesy art deco murals. It has live music and a very friendly staff.

At about 2 AM the beachfront discos start filling with a young, energetic crowd. Check out the discos along Playa Brava. **Kamikaze** (⊠ Playa Brava s/n, ☏ 57/381–001), part of a popular chain of discos, is jam-packed on weekends with young people dancing to salsa music. **Pub 35 mm** (⊠ Patricio Lynch 302, ☏ no phone) is the only disco in the center of town. Catering to a younger crowd, it has a two-tiered dance floor and plays pop and techno beats mixed with the occasional salsa or cumbia twist.

Outdoor Activities and Sports

BEACHES

Just south of the city center on Avenida Balmaceda is **Playa Cavancha,** a long swath of white, sandy beach. A great place for families, you can stroll along the boardwalk and pet the llamas and alpacas at the small zoo. Since it's so close to town, it can often get crowded. If you're craving solitude, follow the coast south for about 3 km (2 mi) on Avenida Balmaceda to reach **Playa Brava,** a pretty beach that's often deserted. The currents here are quite strong, so swimming is not a good idea. **Playa Blanca** 13 km (8 mi) south of the city center on Avenida Balmaceda is another sandy spot that you may have to yourself.

Shopping

Many Chileans come to Iquique with one thing on their minds—shopping. About 3 km (2 mi) north of the city center the **Zona Franca,** the only duty-free zone in the country's northern tip. Known to locals as the Zofri, this big, unattractive mall is stocked with with cheap cigarettes, alcohol, and electronic goods. Remember that large purchases, such as personal computers, are taxable upon leaving the country. ⊠ *Av. Salitrera Victoria,* ☏ *57/214–129.* ☺ *Mon. 4–9, Tues.–Fri. 10–9, Sat. 10–2 and 5–9.*

En Route   One of the last nitrate plants in the region, **Humberstone** closed in 1960 after being in operation for nearly 200 years. Now it's a ghost town where ancient machines creak and groan in the wind. You can wander through the central square and along the streets of the company town, where almost all of the original buildings survive. The theater, with its rows of empty seats, is particularly eerie. ⊠ *45 km (28 mi) east of Iquique on the Pan-American Hwy.,* ☏ *no phone.* ✉ *Free.*

Mamiña

⑪ *125 km (77 mi) east of Iquique.*

An oasis cut from the brown desert, the tiny village of Mamiña is home to hundreds of hot springs. Renowned throughout Chile for their curative powers, these springs draw people from around the region. A fountain called the **Vertiente del Radium,** near the Baños Ipla, is said to cure every type of eye malady. Every hotel in the town has the thermal water pumped into its rooms, so you are can enjoy a soak in the privacy of your own *tina,* or bathtub.

For those who like to wallow in the mud, **Barros El Chino** (✉ near the Mamiña bottler, ☎ no phone) offers soothing mud baths in a secluded setting. After your bath you can bake in the sun on one of the drying racks. Leap into one of the plunge pools to wash the stinky brown stuff off your skin. The valley also has also a number of public pools fed by thermal springs. **Baños Ipla** (✉ near the Mamiña bottler, ☎ no phone) lets you soak in large tinas.

The town itself is perched on a rocky cliff above the terraced green valley where locals grow alfalfa. In the central plaza, the charming **Iglesia Nuestra Señora del Rosario** is a simple church dating from 1632. Its twin bell towers are unique in Andean Chile. Unfortunately, a garish electric sign mars the front of the building.

A two-hour hike from the Mamiña, **Pukara del Cerro Inca** is a great place to watch the sunset. Here you'll find interesting petroglyphs left by the Incas and an excellent view of the valley. To find it, head west on a trail found a block west of the bottlery.

Dining and Lodging

$$$ ✕⊡ **Hotel los Cardenales.** This hotel features a lovely garden and
★ pool covered to protect you from the fierce rays of the sun. All rooms have private tubs filled with spring water—most are a little smallish, but the one in the honeymoon suite is big enough for two. The restaurant has a pleasant terrace where you can enjoy views of the valley. A fixed menu features a soup or cazuela and grilled meat. ✉ *Camino Barros El Chino s/n,* ☎ *09/545–1091. 10 rooms. Pool. No credit cards.*

$$$ ✕⊡ **Hotel Refugio del Salitre.** On the hill in the northern part of the valley, you reach the Hotel Refugio del Salitre by a series of flower-lined walkways. Although the rooms here have seen better days, the tubs are big and the king-size towels are luxurious. The views of the alfalfa-laden valley from your bath are also quite nice. Your stay includes all meals, which are served in the wood-floored restaurant. The menu features grilled fish or meat. ✉ *Av. El Tambo 1,* ☎ *57/751–203,* FAX *57/751–203,* WEB *www.aeroplan.cl/fichas/refugiosalitre.htm. 40 rooms. Restaurant, bar, pool. No credit cards.*

La Tirana

⑫ *72 km (44 mi) southeast of Iquique.*

An oasis of tamarugo trees in the forbidding Atacama Desert holds this hodgepodge of adobe and concrete houses. La Tirana, a village of 250 people, is usually a quiet place. The sleepy town awakens each year from July 12 to 18, when 80,000 people in colorful masks and costumes converge on the town, filling the square with riotous dancing. The object of all his merriment is one of Chile's most important religious icons, the Virgen del Carmen. The statue is found inside the rather run-down **Santuario de la Tirana.**

On Tirana's main plaza, the **Museo del Salitre** is a family-run museum that houses artifacts from the nitrate era, including ice-cream makers and a film projector. There are also other odd items, such as a stuffed condor. ✉ *Opposite the Sanctuario de la Tirana on the main plaza,* ☎ *no phone.* 🎟 *Free.* ⊙ *Mon.–Sat. 8:30–1 and 3–8.*

Pica

⑬ *114 km (70 mi) southeast of Iquique.*

From a distance, Pica appears to be a mirage. This oasis cut from the gray and brown sand of the Atacama Desert is known for its fruit—the limes used to make pisco sours are grown here. The town's chief pleasure is sitting in the Plaza de Armas and sipping a *jugo natural,* fresh-squeezed juice of almost any fruit imaginable, including mangos, oranges, pears, and grapes.

Most people come to Pica not for the town itself but for the incredible hot springs at **Cocha Resbaladero.** This lagoonlike pool is cut out of the rock and surrounded by tropical green flora. Nearby caves beckon to be explored. It is quite a walk, but well worth the effort. ✉ *Calle Gen. Ibañez,* ☎ *no phone.* 🎟 *Admission.* ⊙ *Daily 8–8.*

Dining and Lodging

$$$$ ✕ **El Eden de Pica.** Pica's only upscale restaurant, El Eden del Pica offers an innovative menu. It should, as the chef has published his own book on the cuisine of the region. Ask him to recommend an entrée and he'll claim they're all his favorites. The lamb is a good choice, though. The straw-mat roof gives the restaurant a rather musty odor, but the tranquil atmosphere more than makes up for this. ✉ *Riquelme 12,* ☎ *04/171–788. No credit cards.*

$$ ✕ **San Andres.** Recommended by locals, the family-style restaurant at the Hotel San Andres serves up a fixed lunch. The northern Chilean fare, featuring a cazuela and chicken or beef entrée, is delicious. ✉ *Balmaceda 197,* ☎ *57/741–319. No credit cards.*

$ 🏨 **Hotel los Emelios.** A family-owned bed-and-breakfast, Hotel Los Eme-
★ lios is your best bet in Pica. The chirping birds in the garden and the refreshing plunge pool make it a comfortable and homey place to stay. The small rooms have nice linens on the somewhat lumpy beds. Breakfast is served on the terrace in the back, where you'll enjoy bread with marmalade and tea or coffee. ✉ *L. Cochrane 213,* ☎ *57/741–126,* FAX *57/741–126. 7 rooms. Pool. No credit cards.*

Reserva Nacional Pampa del Tamarugal

⑭ *96 km (60 mi) southeast of Iquique.*

The tamarugo tree is an anomaly in the almost lifeless desert. These bushlike plants survive where most would wither because they are especially adapted to the saline soil of the Atacama. Over time they developed extensive root systems that search for water deep beneath the almost impregnable surface. Reserva Nacional Pampa del Tamarugal has dense groves of tamarugos, which were almost wiped out during the nitrate era when they were felled for firewood. At the entrance is a Conaf station. ✉ *24 km (15 mi) south of Pozo Almonte on the Pan-American Hwy.,* ☎ *57/751–055.* 🎟 *Free.*

★ The amazing **Cerros Pintados** (Painted Hills), within the Reserva Nacional Pampa del Tamarugal, are well worth a detour. Here you'll find the largest group of geoglyphs in the world. These figures, which scientists believe ancient peoples used to help them navigate the desert, date from AD 500 to 1400. They are also enormous—some of the figures are decipherable only from the air. Drawings of men wearing pan-chos were probably intended to point out the route to the coast to the llama caravans coming from the Andes. More than 400 figures of birds, animals, and geometric patterns adorn this 4-km (2½-mi) stretch of desert. There is a Conaf kiosk on a dirt road 2 km (1 mi) west of the Pan-American Highway. ⊠ *45 km (28 mi) south of Pozo Almonte,* ☎ *57/ 751–055.* ▣ *Admission.* ☉ *Daily 9:30–6.*

Gigante de Atacama

⑮ *84 km (52 mi) northeast of Iquique.*

The world's largest geoglyph, the Gigante de Atacama, measures an incredible 86 meters (282 ft). The Atacama Giant, thought to repre-sent a chief of an indigenous people, looks more like a space alien. It is adorned with a walking staff, a cat mask, and a feathered headdress that resembles rays of light bursting from his head. The exact age of the figure is not known, but it certainly hails from before the arrival of the Spanish. The geoglyph is best viewed just before dusk, when the long shadows make the outline clearer. ⊠ *Cerro Unita, 13 km (8 mi) west of the turnoff to Chusmiza,* ☎ *no phone.* ▣ *Free.*

Geysers de Puchuldiza

⑯ *211 km (130 mi) from Iquique.*

Truly a sight to behold, the Geysers de Puchuldiza constantly throw steam into the air, the vapor falling in misty cascades to the sulfur-crusted earth. In the winter months between May and September this area is particularly beautiful because of the huge ice monoliths that form. These towers of ice, reaching heights of up to 15 meters (50 ft), are an in-tense blue. You won't have to stand in line to get that perfect shot of the geysers because very few people visit this natural wonder. Walk with care, as the crust is very thin in places. ⊠ *Turn north 60 km (37 mi) past the turnoff to Chusmiza, then proceed for 19 km (12 mi),* ☎ *no phone.* ▣ *Free.*

Pisagua

⑰ *132 km (82 mi) north of Iquique.*

Pisagua, one of the region's most prominent ports during the nitrate era, at one time sustained a population of more than 8,000 people. Many of the mansions built at that time are still standing, although others have fallen into disrepair. During Pinochet's regime Pisagua was the site of a concentration camp now used as a hotel. The town's most famous sight, the **Torre Reloj,** stands on a hill overlooking the city. Built in 1887 from Oregon pine, its blue and white paint is peeling in the hot coastal sun. This clock tower, which some insist was constructed by Gustave Eiffel, is an excellent place to catch views of the town and its port.

Right on the edge of the sea, the **Teatro Municipal** is a testament to the wealth the town once possessed. Built in 1892 at the height of the ni-trate boom, the once-lavish theater has grand touches, such as the painted cherubs dancing across the ceiling. Waves crash against the walls of the theater, throwing eerie echoes through the empty, forgotten audi-torium. Get the key to the theater and a very informative free tour from a woman in the tourist kiosk opposite the theater.

Dining and Lodging

$$–$$$ ✕ **Restaurant La Picada de Don Gato.** This terrace restaurant, recom-
★ mended by locals, serves up simple but exquisite seafood. The shell-fish dishes, especially the ostiones a la parmesana, are particularly

delicious. One odd thing is the plastic chairs, which look like they belong in a bus station. ⊠ *Prat 127,* ☎ *57/731–511. No credit cards.*

$$ ⊡ **Hotel Pisagua.** In the two-story warden's residence at the former prison, the wood-frame Hotel Pisagua has a bit of a sinister feeling. Despite this, the hotel is also the nicest place to stay in town. The restaurant serves excellent seafood. ⊠ *At the entrance to town,* ☎ *57/731–509. Restaurant. No credit cards.*

ARICA AREA

At the very tip of Chile, Arica is the country's northernmost city. This pleasant community cut from the rocky coast once belonged to Peru. In 1880 Chilean soldiers stormed El Morro, a fortress set high atop a cliff in Arica. Three years later, much of the land north of Antofagasta that was once part of Peru and Bolivia belonged to Chile. Though the Arica of today is fervently Chilean, you can still see the Peruvian influence in the streets and market stalls of the city. Indigenous women still sell their goods and produce in the town's colorful markets.

Inland from Arica, the Valle Azapa cuts its way up into the mountains, a strip of green in a land of brown. The excellent Museo Arqueológico de San Miguel de Azapa is home to the world's oldest mummies. They were left behind by the Chinchorro people who inhabited Chile's northern coast during pre-Hispanic times. Ascending farther up the mountains towards the Bolivian border you pass through the pleasant indigenous communities of Socoroma and Putre. These towns, though far from picturesque, are good resting points for those planning to make the journey to the 4,000-meter-high Parque Nacional Lauca and the neighboring Reserva Nacional Las Vicuñas. The beautiful Lago Chungará, part of Parque Nacional Lauca, lies near Bolivia, creating what is probably the country's most impressive border crossing.

Arica

⑱ *301 km (186 mi) north of Iquique.*

Arica boasts that it is "the land of the eternal spring," but its temperate climate is not the only reason to visit this small city. On Plaza Colón is the **Iglesia de San Marcos,** constructed entirely from iron. Gustave Eiffel (who designed the Eiffel Tower) had the individual pieces cast in France erected them in Arica in 1876. Across from Parque General Baquedano, the **Aduana de Arica,** the city's former customs house, is another of Eiffel's creations. It currently houses the town's cultural center where you can find exhibits about northern Chile, old photographs of Arica, and works by local painters and sculptors. North of Parque General Baquedano is the defunct **Estacion Ferrocarril,** the train station for the Arica-La Paz railroad. Though trains no longer run across the mountains to the Bolivian capital, this 1913 building houses a small museum with a locomotive and other remnants of the railroad.

Hanging over the town, the fortress of **El Morro de Arica** is impossible to ignore. This former Peruvian stronghold was the site of one of the key battles in the War of the Pacific. The **Museo de las Armas,** which commemorates that battle, is housed in the old fortress. As you listen to the proud drumroll of military marches you can wander among the uniforms and weapons of past wars. ⊠ *Reached by footpath from Calle Colón,* ☎ *58/254–091.* ⊡ *Admission.* ☉ *Daily 8:30–8.*

★ The **Museo Arqueológico de San Miguel de Azapa,** a short drive from Arica, is a must for any visitor to El Norte Grande. In an 18th-century olive-oil refinery, this museum houses an impressive collection of artifacts from the cultures of the Chinchorros (a coastal people) and Tijuanacotas (a group that lived in the antiplano). Of particular interest are the Chinchorro mummies, the oldest in the world, dating back to 6,000 BC. The incredibly well-preserved mummies are arranged in the fetal position, which was traditional in this area. To look into their wrinkled, expressive faces is to get a glimpse at a history that spans more than 8,000 years. ⊠ *12 km (7 mi) south of town,* ☏ *58/232–067.* 🖃 *Admission.* ⊙ *Daily 10–6.*

Dining and Lodging

$$$–$$$$ ✕ **Maracuyá.** With wicker furniture that enhances its cool South Pacific atmosphere, this pleasant beachfront restaurant offers an international menu that focuses on seafood. The food, lauded by locals, is always fresh; ask the waiter what fish was caught that day. ⊠ *Av. Comandante San Martin,* ☏ *56/227–600. AE, DC, MC, V.*

$$–$$$ ✕ **Casino La Bomba.** In the old fire station, Casino La Bomba is more of a cultural curiosity than a culinary one. That said, the traditional food isn't bad, and the service is friendly. You'll have to maneuver around the parked fire trucks to get inside, where you are greeted by wagon-wheel furnishings and a menu heavy on the grilled fish. ⊠ *Colon 357,* ☏ *58/232–983. No credit cards.*

$$–$$$ ✕ **Club de Deportes Náuticos.** This old yacht club with views of the port serves up succulent seafood dishes in a relaxed terrace setting. One of the friendliest restaurants in town, this former men's club is a great place to meet the old salts of the area. Bring your fish stories. ⊠ *Thompson 1,* ☏ *58/254–738. DC, MC, V.*

$$ ✕ **El Rey de Mariscos.** Locals call this the best seafood restaurant in town, and they are right. The merluza con salsa margarita is a winner. On the second story of a cement-block building, the dreary fluorescent lights and tacky furnishings give the restaurant an undeserved down-at-the-heel air. ⊠ *Colon 565,* ☏ *58/229–232. AE, MC, V.*

$$$ ✕🖃 **Hotel Arica.** The finest hotel in Arica, this first-class establishment
★   is on the ocean between Playa El Laucho and Playa Las Liseras. There's a lovely swimming pool, tennis courts, and plenty of activities for the kids. The rooms have everything you would expect—clean showers with lots of hot water, minibars, and cable television. The courteous and attentive staff can help set up sightseeing tours or book a table at a local eatery. The hotel's tony restaurant, which looks onto the ocean, features fresh seafood cooked to order. ⊠ *Av. Comandante San Martin 599,* ☏ *56–58/254–540,* 🖷 *56–58/231–133,* 🖳 *www.panamericanahoteles.cl. 114 rooms. Restaurant, minibars, pool, tennis, laundry service, convention center, meeting rooms. AE, DC, MC, V.*

$$ 🖃 **Hotel El Paso.** This modern lodging in the center of Arica surrounds a landscaped courtyard and a pool with a swim-up bar. Though not on the ocean, it's a short walk from any of the city's beaches. There are plenty of diversions here, including a petting zoo that kids will love. The superior rooms, with new furnishings and larger televisions, are a far better value than the standard ones. A breakfast buffet is included. ⊠ *Av. General Velasquez,* ☏ *58/230–808,* 🖷 *58/231–965,* 🖳 *www.hotelelpaso.cl. 81 rooms. Restaurant, tennis, laundry service. AE, DC, MC, V.*

$ 🖃 **Hotel Plaza Colon.** A dimly lit lobby welcomes you into this centrally located hotel. It's a good budget option if you don't mind being so far from the beach. The pink-walled rooms are small but clean, and each has a small television with cable. A Continental breakfast is included. ⊠ *San Marcos 261,* ☏ *56–58/254–424,* 🖷 *56–58/231–244. Minibars. AE, DC, MC, V.*

$ 🖃 **Hotel Saint Georgette.** Although it's quite a hike from Arica's city center, this pleasant ocean-front hotel is great for weary travelers who simply want to relax on the beach. Although some of the common areas feel a bit run-down, the rooms are fine. Many have their own hot tubs. Breakfast is served on a terrace overlooking the sea. ⊠ *Av. Comandante San Martin 1020,* ☎ *58/257–697,* FAX *58/229–187,* WEB *hotelstgeorgette.tripod.com. Restaurant, pool. AE, DC, MC, V.*

Nightlife and the Arts

Join the locals for a beer at one of the cafés lining the pedestrian mall of 21 de Mayo. These low-key establishments, many with outdoor seating, are a great place to spend an afternoon watching the passing crowds. In the evening you won't have trouble finding the city's many watering holes. For a more refined setting, try the lively **Barrabas** (⊠ 18 de Septiembre 520, ☎ 56/252–127), which has a funky atmosphere that attracts Arica's younger set. The beachfront **Puesto del Sol** (⊠ Raul Pey 2492, ☎ 56/216–150) plays '80s tunes and appeals to a slightly older crowd. It has a pleasant terrace where you can enjoy live music on weekends. Near Playa Chinchorro, **Discoteca SoHo** (⊠ Buenos Aires 209, ☎ 56/215–892) livens things up on weekends with the sounds of pop and cumbia.

Outdoor Activities and Sports

Part of the reason people flock to Arica is the beaches. South of El Morro, **Playa El Laucho** is the closest to the city, and thus the most crowded. South of Playa El Laucho you'll find **Playa Brava.** It has a pontoon that keeps the kids occupied. A little more secluded is **Playa Chinchorro,** 2 km (1 mi) north of the city. At this white sandy beach you can rent Jet Skis in high season.

Shopping

Calle 21 de Mayo is a good place for window-shopping. Just off Calle 21 de Mayo, **Calle Bolognesi** is crowded with artisan stalls offering handmade goods. The **Feria Internacional** on Calle Máximo Lira sells everything from bowler hats (worn by Aymara women) to blankets to batteries. Next to the market, the **Terminal Pesquero** offers an interesting view of El Norte Grande's predominant industry. The **Poblado Artesenal,** located outside of the city in the Azapa Valley, is an artisan cooperative designed to resemble an altiplano community. This is a good place to pick up traditionally styled ceramics and leather.

Putre

⑲ *145 km (90 mi) east of Arica.*

In a valley protected by two snowcapped mountains, Putre can be described only as *tranquilo* (tranquil). As tourism has yet to take root in this Andean village, it's still possible to witness traditional Aymara culture. On an ancient Inca trail later used by the Spanish to transport gold from Bolivia, Putre is still a stop along the road for people heading elsewhere, such as to Parque Nacional Lauca and Reserva Nacional de Las Vicuñas. Worth a visit is the lovely **Iglesia de Putre,** on the northeast corner of the main plaza. The church was built in 1670 but had to be reconstructed in 1871 after an earthquake destroyed the interior.

Dining and Lodging

$ ✕ **Pub Kuchu Marka.** The funky, eclectic atmosphere makes Pub Kuchu Marka a nice place to pass an evening playing a game of cacho or sipping a *mate de coca* (medicinal tea made with leaves from the coca plant). Grab a cold beer and plan your excursion for the next day. The pub serves local specialty dishes such as cazuela and, on certain days, llama steaks. ⊠ *Calle Baquedano,* ☎ *no phone. No credit cards.*

$$ ✕▦ **Hotel Las Vicuñas.** This row of older buildings, originally used as a miners' camp, is the best lodging in town. You'll find clean, basic

rooms with space heaters (essential, as it gets chilly in the Andes). With Andean textiles serving as tablecloths, the restaurant serves typical fare for the region: expect a fixed menu with cazuela and then a meat dish. Breakfast and your choice of lunch or dinner are included. ⊠ *Calle Baquedano,* ☎ *56/251–354 or 56/228–564. 112 rooms. Restaurant, bar, Ping-Pong. No credit cards.*

$$ 🏠 **Casa Barbarita.** This friendly bed-and-breakfast has only two rooms, so you're sure to get personalized service. Accommodations have comfy flannel sheets and heaters to keep you warm on chilly nights, and the baths have steaming hot showers. You can get the scoop on the area from the owner, naturalist Barbara Knapton. There is a kitchen for those wishing to prepare their own food. Breakfast is included. ⊠ *Calle Baquedano,* ☎ *58/300–013,* FAX *56–58/300–013,* WEB *www.birdingaltoandino.com. 2 rooms. No credit cards.*

Parque Nacional Lauca

⑳ *47 km (29 mi) southeast of Putre.*

★ On a plateau more than 4,000 meters (13,000 ft) above sea level, the magnificent Parque Nacional Lauca offers flora and fauna found few other places in the world. The landscape is dotted with cacti, grasses, and a brilliant emerald-green moss called *llareta.* Playful vizcacha, rabbitlike rodents with long tails, laze in the sun. You'll see not just llamas, but graceful vicuñas and alpacas as well. About 10 km (6 mi) into the park you come upon a Conaf station with informative brochures. ⊠ *Off Ruta 11,* ☎ *no phone.* 🎫 *Free.*

Within the park is the altiplano village of **Parinacota** (⊠ off Ruta 11), one of the most beautiful in all of Chile. In the center of the village sits the whitewashed Iglesia Parinacota, dating from 1789. Inside you come across murals depicting sinners and saints and a mysterious "walking table," which parishioners have chained to the wall for fear that it will steal away in the night. Opposite the church you'll find crafts stalls run by Aymara women in the colorful shawls and flat-topped hats worn by many altiplano people. Only 18 people live in the village, but many more make a pilgrimage here for annual festivals such as the Fiesta de las Cruces, held on May 3, and the Fiesta de la Virgen de la Canderlaria, a three-day romp that begins on February 2.

About 8 km (5 mi) east of Piranacota are the beautiful **Lagunas Cotacotani,** which means "land of many lakes" in the Quechua language. Sitting in a desolate moonscape formed by volcanic eruptions, this string of ponds attracts many species of bird, including Andean geese.

On the the Bolivian border, **Lago Chungará** sits at an amazing altitude of 4,600 meters (15,180 ft) above sea level. It is home to hundreds of flamingos. Volcán Parinacota, at 6,330 meters (20,889 ft), casts its shadow onto the lake's glassy surface. There is a Conaf-run office at Lago Chungará. ⊠ *From Ruta 11, turn north on Ruta A-123,* ☎ *no phone.* 🎫 *Free.* ☉ *Daily 8–8.*

Reserva Nacional Las Vicuñas

㉑ *121 km (75 mi) southeast of Putre.*

★ Although it attracts far fewer visitors than neighboring Parque Nacional Lauca, Reserva Nacional Las Vicuñas offers some incredible sights—salt flats, high plains, and alpine lakes. You can enjoy the vistas without running into buses full of tourists. The reserve, which stretches some 100 km (62 mi), has a huge herd of graceful vicuñas. Although quite similar to their larger cousins, llamas and alpacas, vicuñas have not been domesticated. Their incredibly soft wool, among the most prized in the world, led to so much hunting that these creatures were threatened with extinction. Today it is illegal to kill vicuña. Getting to this reserve, unfortunately, is quite a challenge. There is no public transportation, and the roads are only passable in four-wheel-drive vehicles. Many people choose to hook up with a tour in Arica. ⊠ *From Ruta 11, take Ruta A-21 south to park headquarter,* ☎ *no phone.* 🖪 *Free.*

Salar de Surire

㉒ *126 km (78 mi) southeast of Putre.*

After passing through the high plains, where you'll spot vicuña, alpaca, and the occasional desert fox, you'll catch your first glimpse of the sparkling **Salar de Surire.** Seen from a distance, the salt flat appears to be a giant white lake. Unlike its southern neighbor, the Salar de Atacama, it's completely flat. Three of the world's four species of flamingos live in the nearby lakes. ⊠ *South from Reserva Nacional Las Vicuñas on Ruta A-235,* ☎ *no phone.* 🖪 *Free.*

EL NORTE GRANDE A TO Z

To research prices, get advice from other travelers, and book travel arrangements, visit www.fodors.com.

AIR TRAVEL

Since there are no international airports in El Norte Grande, you can't fly here directly from the United States, Canada, Europe, or Australia. You must fly into Santiago and transfer to a flight headed to Antofagasta, Calama, Iquique, and Arica. Avant and LanChile fly from Santiago to El Norte Grande. Round-trip flights can run up to $300. Since the cities in El Norte Grande are far apart, taking planes between them can save you both time and a lot of hassle. Both airlines offer service between the major cities. Prices range from $40 to $150.

You can also get here from other South American countries. LanChile offers a number of direct flights to El Norte Grande to and from the neighboring countries of Bolivia and Peru.

Antofagasta's Aeropuerto Cerro Moreno is 25 km (16 mi) north of the city. Calama's Aeropuerto El Loa is found 5 km (3 mi) south of the city center. Iquique's Aeropuerto Diego Aracena is a little far from the center of the city, about 40 km (25 mi) to the south. Arica's Aeropuerto Internacional Chacalluta lies 18 km (11 mi) north of the center. ➤ AIRLINES: **Avant** (☎ 55/452–050 in Antofagasta). **LanChile** (☎ 55/265–151 in Antofagasta; ☎ 55/313–927 in Calama; ☎ 57/427–600 in Iquique; ☎ 58/251–641 in Arica). ➤ AIRPORTS: **Aeropuerto Cerro Moreno** (☎ 55/269–077 in Antofagasta). **Aeropuerto El Loa** (☎ 55/312–348 in Calama). **Aeropuerto Diego Aracena** (☎ 57/424–547 in Iquique). **Aeropuerto Internacional Chacalluta** (☎ 58/ 211–116 in Arica).

BUS TRAVEL

Getting around by bus in El Norte Grande is easy. There is a terminal in every major city with frequent departures to the other cities as well as smaller towns in the area. Keep in mind that there may be no bus service to the smaller villages or the more remote national parks.

No bus company has a monopoly, so there are often several bus stations in each city. Because many companies may be running buses along the same route, shop around for the best price. The fare for a 300-km (186-mi) trip usually runs around $20. For longer trips find a bus that has a *salon semi-cama.* The comfortable seats make all the difference.

CAR TRAVEL

A car is definitely the best way to see El Norte Grande. If you want to get far off the beaten path, there is no other way to travel. You can rent cars in Antofagasta, Calama, Iquique, and Arica at both the airport and downtown. Most hotels will also help you arrange a rental.

Driving in the cities can be a little hectic, but once you get on the highway it is usually smooth sailing. The roads of the north are generally well maintained. The farther from major population centers you travel— such as the remote national parks like Parque Nacional Lauca and Reserva Nacional Las Vicuñas—the worse the roads become. Destinations like these require a four-wheel-drive vehicle. Ruta 5, more familiarly known as the Pan-American Highway, bisects all of Northern Chile. Ruta 1, Chile's answer to California's Highway 101, is a beautiful coastal highway between Antofagasta and Iquique. Calama is reached by Ruta 25.

Avis, Budget, and Hertz have offices in most major cities in northern Chile. The best deals are probably in Iquique. However, cars rented here cannot be taken out of the Iquique area.

➤ RENTAL AGENCIES: **Avis** (✉ Balmaceda 2556, Antofagasta, ☎ 55/ 319–797; ✉ Latorre 1498, Calama, ☎ 56/319–797; ✉ Manuel Rodriguez 734, Iquique, ☎ 56/472–392). **Budget** (✉ Baquedano 300, Antofagasta, ☎ 56/283–667; ✉ Granaderos 2875, Calama, ☎ 56/346– 868; ✉ Bolívar 615, Iquique, ☎ 56/407–034). **Hertz** (✉ Balmaceda 2566, Antofagasta, ☎ 55/269–043; ✉ Latorre 1510, Calama, ☎ 55/ 341–380; ✉ Souper 650, Iquique, ☎ 57456–519; ✉ Hotel El Paso, Baquedano 999, Arica, ☎ 58/231–487).

FESTIVALS AND SEASONAL EVENTS

El Norte Grande's festivals are most often tied to Catholicism. Every town celebrates the day honoring its patron saint. Most are small gatherings attended mostly by locals, but a few are huge celebrations that attract people from all over the country. One fiesta not to be missed takes place in La Tirana from July 12 to 18. During this time some 80,000 pilgrims converge on the town to honor the Virgen del Carmen with riotous dancing in the streets.

HEALTH

Because of El Norte Grande's extremely varied topography, visitors should be prepared for many different weather conditions. Those heading up into the Andes should remember to bring along warm clothes, even during the warmer months. A weather phenomenon called Bolivian winter, which actually takes place in the summer, brings rains and even snow to the region. The Atacama Desert, where some areas have never recorded any rainfall, can take its toll on unsuspecting tourists. Bring sunblock, a wide-brimmed hat, and plenty of water.

Altitude sickness—which is marked by difficulty breathing, dizziness, headaches, and nausea—is a danger for visitors to the high elevations of the antiplano. The best way to ward off altitude sickness is to take it slow. Spend a day or two acclimatizing before any physical exertion. When hiking or climbing, rest more often and drink as much water as possible. If symptoms continue, return to a lower altitude.

The tap water in the major cities and even most smaller communities is drinkable. In general, the water is safer on the coast than in some towns farther inland. To be on the safe side, stick to bottled water.

MAIL AND SHIPPING

Mailing letters and packages from El Norte Grande is a formidable task. Although most cities have a post office, you often are faced with long lines that move at a snail's pace. Your best bet is to ask your hotel to post a letter for you. But don't expect your letter to get there quickly. Mail headed out of the country can often take weeks.

➤ POST OFFICES: **Antofagasta** (✉ Washington 2613). **Arica** (✉ Arturo Prat 305). **Calama** (✉ Mackenna and Granaderos). **Iquique** (✉ Bolívar 485).

SAFETY

El Norte Grande experiences very little crime. Nevertheless, visitors should use the same precautions as anywhere else. Women traveling alone should be careful, especially at night. It's best to travel in pairs or groups.

TAXIS

Taxis are the most efficient way to get around any city in El Norte Grande. Taxis are easy to hail on the streets, but late at night you might want to ask someone at a hotel or restaurant to call one for you. They often function as *colectivos,* meaning they will pick up anybody going in the same direction. The driver will adjust the price accordingly. Almost no taxis have meters, but many post the price on the windshield. Make sure you establish the price before getting inside. Prices range from $1 to $10, depending on the distance traveled and whether the taxi is a colectivo. Prices rise an average of 20% at night. Taxi drivers often will rent out their services for the day for a flat fee.

TELEPHONES

There are several different telephone companies in El Norte Grande, and each has its own public telephones. Calling cards for each company can be purchased in many shops and newsstands. Much easier than calling from the street is to call from one of the many Entel or CTC offices in every city. Here you can dial direct or collect to anywhere in the world.

TOURS

Tours can be arranged in the major cities and a number of the smaller towns. It's a good idea to shop around to make sure that you are getting the best itinerary and the best price.

In Antofagasta, Desertica Expediciones offers trips into the interior, including trips to Parque Nacional Pan de Azucar. In Calama, Turismo Buenaventura offers trips to Chiu Chiu and the San Pedro area. There are myriad tour agencies in San Pedro de Atacama. Cosmo Andino Expediciones offers excellent tours with well-informed guides. Turismo el Sol also offers tours. In Iquique and Arica, a well-respected agency called Geotour offers trips to Parque Nacional Lauca, the Salar de Surire, and the Reserva Nacional las Vicuñas. In Putre, Birding Alto Andino features an Alaskan naturalist who leads birding expeditions.

➤ TOUR OPERATORS: **Birding Alto Andino** (✉ Calle Baquedano, Putre, ☎ 58/300–013). **Cosmo Andino Expediciones** (✉ Calle Caracoles s/n, San Pedro de Atacama, ☎ 56/851–069). **Desertica Expediciones** (✉ La Torre 2732, Antofagasta, ☎ 55/386–877). **Geotour** (✉ Baquedano 982, Iquique, ☎ 57/428–984; ✉ Bolognesi 421, Arica, ☎ 56/253–927). **Turismo Buenaventura** (✉ Sotomayor 1959, Calama, ☎ 09/799–5122). **Turismo el Sol** (✉ Tocopilla 432, San Pedro de Atacama, ☎ 56/851–230).

VISITOR INFORMATION

Most major cities in El Norte Grande have an office of Sernatur, Chile's tourism agency. Here you'll find helpful information about the region, including maps and brochures. Some members of the staff speak English.

➤ SERNATUR OFFICES: **Antofagasta** (✉ Maipú 240, ☎ 55/264–044). **Arica** (✉ Arturo Prat 305, ☎ 58/254–606). **Calama** (✉ Latorre and Vicuña, ☎ 56/364–176). **Iquique** (✉ Serrano 145, ☎ 57/427–686).

6 THE CENTRAL VALLEY

This slender valley just south of Santiago
is one of the most fertile places on earth,
especially when it comes to growing grapes.
The vineyards that spread like a quilt across
these gently rolling hills produce some of the
best cabernet sauvignons and merlots in
the world. Often the wineries are centered
around centuries-old haciendas that provide
a glimpse into a way of life that has, for the
most part, completely vanished.

By Michael
de Zayas

A QUIET NOBILITY is maintained by the people of the Central Valley. Perhaps it is because wine-making traditions have been passed from generation to generation for hundreds of years. This land certainly has ties to other great wine regions, but it has a personality all its own. If Bordeaux has its châteaux, the Central Valley has its haciendas. In the central part of the country, the traditional hacienda—the main structure on a farm—became more than an economic and agricultural center; it was the glue that maintained a family's structure and a manifestation of a family's honor. Many of these grand manor houses have been preserved as museums.

The Central Valley is also home to the *huaso,* a cousin of the Argentine gaucho and a distant relation of the American cowboy. Chilean rodeo began here, and on weekends it's still easy to catch an afternoon of riding and roping. While traveling through the region, you're likely to see horses and others beasts of burden being used as they have for centuries, sometimes even penetrating into the area's major cities: Rancagua, Curicó, Talca, Chilán, and Concepción.

Pleasures and Pastimes

Dining
Even the most informal meal in the Central Valley is likely to be centered around an excellent local wine. Lunch in Santa Cruz may be accompanied by a cabernet from Viña Santa Laura, while dinner in Curicó might mean a merlot from Viña San Pedro. Knowing a handful of wine-related words will doubtless come in handy. *Vino* is the Spanish word for wine; red is *tinto* (never *rojo*) and white is *blanco*. *Desgustación* and *cata* both refer to a formal wine tasting.

Cuisine in the Central Valley is not unlike what you'll find to the north in more cosmopolitan Santiago. Just about any type of seafood you could desire is abundant, fresh, and inexpensive. For a chart that explains the cost of meals at the restaurants listed throughout this chapter, *see* Dining *in* Smart Travel Tips.

Lodging
Each sizeable town in this region has one or two respectable hotels, usually near the central square. But with the notable exception of Hacienda Los Lingues near Rancagua, the lodgings in the Central Valley can't match those you'll find in Santiago. It may be an unfair comparison, however, as hotels here often have a charm all their own. For a chart that explains the cost of accommodations listed throughout this chapter, *see* Lodging *in* Smart Travel Tips.

Outdoor Activities
From September to April, San Clemente, a town 16 km (10 mi) southeast of Talca, hosts the best rodeo in the region. The national championship selections take place here towards the end of the season. The events take place weekends 11–6. Besides riding and roping, you'll find food, dances, and beauty queen competitions. Beyond San Clemente, you'll find important *medialunas* (corrals) in Talca, Pelarco, Curicó, Molina, Pencahue, Los Niches, and Linares.

Wineries
Chile recognizes five distinct wine regions. By far the most important of these, in terms of quality and quantity, is the Región del Valle Central, which begins near Santiago and extends for 300 km (186 mi) to the south. The wineries of this sprawling region grow mostly cabernet sauvignon, merlot, sauvignon blanc, and chardonnay. However, two

The Central Valley

PACIFIC OCEAN

San Antonio
Talagante
Melipilla
Paine
Graneros
Sewell
Rancagua **1**
Peumo
Termas de
Cauquenes
Pichilemu
San Fernando
Bucamlemu
Santa Cruz **2**
Cerro
Sosneado
Llico
Chimbarongo
Vichuquén **4**
Iloca
Hualañé
Curicó **3**
Gualleco
Molina
Las Leñas
Constitución
Peteroa
Rio Maule
Talca **5**
San Clemente
Descabezado
Grande
San Javier **6**
Villa Allegre
Colbún **7**
Rio Chico
Chanco
Linares
Cauquenes
Longaví
Cobquecura
Parral
Nevado
Longaví
Quirihue
San Carlos
Coelemu
Chillán **8**
Tomé
Pinto
Chillán
Talcahuano
Bulnes
San Pedro
Concepción **10**
Recinto
Termas de
Chillán **9**
Isla
Santa
María
Pemuco
Lota
Cabrero
Las Ovejas
ARGENTINA
Arauco
Yungay
Curanilahué
Parque
Nacional
Laguna
de Laja
Lebú
Nacimiento
Quilleco
Parque
Nacional
Nahuelbuta
La Laja
Los Angeles
Antuco
Cañete
Munchen
Copahue
Copahue
Contulmo
Angol
Collipulli
Termas de
Pemehue
Puren
Victoria
Isla
Mocha
Traiguén
Parque
Nacional
Tolhuaca
Lonquimay
Lautaro
Curacautín
Las Lajas
Carahue
Vilcún
Parque
Nacional
Conguillio
Nehuentehué
Llama
Las Lajas
Nueva
Imperial
Temuco

0 — 50 miles
0 — 75 km

N

PAN. AMERICAN HWY.

ANDES

Rio Bío Bío

increasingly popular red varietals are malbec and carmenère—a grape only grown in Chile. When visiting *viñas* (vineyards) you're likely to come across these Spanish words: *barrica* (barrel), *fundo* (estate), *botella* (bottle), and *bodega* (cellar). The phrase *ruta del vino* refers to a region where you can tour various vineyards.

Exploring the Central Valley

Bordered on the east by the volcanic cones of the Andes and on the west by smaller mountain ranges running along the Pacific coast, the Central Valley is a straight shot down the Pan-American Highway. The landscape in between is unpredictably hilly. It's about a six-hour drive from Santiago to Concepción, although most people choose to stop somewhere along the way.

Great Itineraries

IF YOU HAVE 3 DAYS

If you can afford it, spend at least a day at Hacienda Los Lingues. The restored ranch near Rancagua will leave you with a sense of what life was like for the aristocrats who lived here centuries ago. Otherwise head to Santa Cruz, where you can explore another perfectly preserved hacienda outside of town at the Museo San José del Carmen de El Huique. You won't want to leave without taking a tour of the area's vineyards. Spend the night in Santa Cruz, then get an early start as you drive south to Chillán. You'll find handicrafts from all over the country at the city's Feria de Chillán. By evening head east to the Termas de Chillán. Spend your third day exploring the mountains or soaking in the hot springs.

IF YOU HAVE 5 DAYS

If you enjoy visiting vineyards, budget more time in Santa Cruz, where you can thoroughly explore the Valle de Colchagua. You'll also want to stop in Curicó, where you can easily spend a day at the Miguel Torres and San Pedro vineyards south of town, or in Talca, where the Domaine Oriental and Balduzzi wineries make excellent excursions.

When to Tour

There is no real high season in the Central Valley except in the Termas de Chillán, when snow attracts skiers from June to September. If you don't ski, you're probably headed to the Central Valley for the wineries. February and March are when the grapes are picked, making these months the best time to visit a vineyard. Tours during this time show you everything from crushing to bottling. The Fiesta de la Vendimia, the annual harvest festival, is celebrated with particular zest in Santa Cruz and Curicó. The four-day fiesta in Curicó takes place the first weekend in March and includes grape-stomping contests and the selection of a queen, whose weight is measured out in grapes on a massive scale. In the religious festival called the Fiesta de San Francisco, held October 4 in the small town of Huerta de Maule, 38 km (24 mi) southwest of Talca, more than 200 huasos gather from all over Chile for a day of horseback events, including races around the central square.

THE WINE COUNTRY

Within the vast Región del Valle Central are the four subregions that you'll most commonly find on a bottle of Chilean wine: Valle del Maipo (south of Santiago), Valle del Rapel (west of Rancagua), Valle de Curicó (around Curicó), and Valle del Maule (south of Talca). These four subregions are further subdivided, but save for moments of inspired snobbery these aren't found on labels. An exception is the Valle del Rapel, which is divided into the Valle del Cachapoal and the Valle de Colchagua.

The Pan-American Highway bisects the Central Valley, passing through most of the wine-growing areas. Just south of Santiago is the Valle del Rapel, where you'll find some of the area's most prestigious wineries. After exploring the valley's vineyards, relax in the hot springs at the Termas de Cauquenes.

Don't overlook the wineries along the banks of the Río Maule. There are two official wine regions here, the Valle de Curicó and the Valle del Maule. You'll also find some wonderful national parks, such as Reserva Nacional Radal Siete Tazas.

Rancagua

❶ The Rancagua region was first settled by the indigenous Picunche people, then by the Incas. A hanging bridge built over the Río Cachapoal by the Incas was later used by Spanish colonists led by José Antonio Manso de Velasco. He founded Villa Santa Cruz de Triana, later renamed Rancagua, here in 1745.

In 1814, the hills around the city were the site of a battle known as the *Desastre de Rancagua* (Disaster of Rancagua). Chilean independence fighters, including Bernardo O'Higgins, held off the powerful Spanish army for two days before being captured. In a resulting blaze, much of the town was destroyed.

Today's Racagüinos spend their evenings in the city's central square, the **Plaza de los Héroes**. A block north of the plaza along Calle Estado is **Iglesia de la Merced,** a church that has been declared a national monument. It was in this bell tower that O'Higgins waited in vain for reinforcements during the battle for independence.

A few blocks south of Plaza de los Héroes is the **Museo Regional de Rancagua** (⊠ Estado and Ibieta, ☎ 72/221–254), which has three rooms that re-create a typical 18th-century home, complete with period furniture and religious artifacts. Across the street from the Museo Regional de Rancagua is **Casa de Pilar de Esquina** (⊠ Estado and Ibieta, ☎ no phone), a house that belonged to independence fighter Fernando Errázuriz Aldunate.

A 15,000-acre national reserve 54 km (34 mi) east of Rancagua, **Reserva Nacional Río de los Cipreses** has numerous trails leading through thick forests of cypress trees. Occasionally you'll reach a clearing where you'll be treated to great views of the mountains above. Conaf, the national parks service, has an office here with informative displays and maps. Just south of the park is the spot where a plane carrying Uruguayan high school students crashed in 1972. The story of the group, part of which survived three months in a harsh winter by resorting to cannibalism, was told in the 1993 film *Alive.* ⊠ *Carretera del Cobre,* ☎ 72/297–505. 🎟 *Admission.* ◷ *Dec.–Mar., daily 8:30–8; Apr.–Nov., daily 8:30–6.*

On the southern banks of the Río Cachapoal about 31 km (19 mi) east of Rancagua, the **Termas de Cauquenes** spout mineral-rich water that has been revered for its medicinal properties since colonial days. The Spanish discovered the 48°C (118°F) springs in 1646. José de San Martín, who masterminded the defeat of Spanish forces in Chile, is said to have relaxed here before beginning his campaign. Naturalist Charles Darwin, who visited in 1834, wrote that the springs were situated in "a quiet, solitary spot, with a good deal of wild beauty." To reach the springs, take Ruta 32 to Coya and then head south. ⊠ *Carretera del Cobre,* ☎ 72/899–010. ◷ *Daily 8–6:30.*

Dining and Lodging

$$$$ ✕🔲 **Hacienda Los Lingues.** One of the country's best preserved colo-
★   nial haciendas is northeast of Rancagua on lands deeded to Santiago's
first mayor by Spanish King Felipe III in 1545. The estate, which has
remained in the same family for four centuries, is now run as a five-star
hotel. But you won't feel as if you're staying in a hotel, because rooms
are filled with portraits and other items belonging to the family. A stay
here includes mountain biking and hiking on an 8,000-acre property
of rolling hills. Fishing aficionados can catch rainbow trout in a private lake just beyond the main building. The restaurant, which pairs
Chilean cuisine with regional wines, is well worth a trip. ✉ *Panamericana Sur Km. 124, San Fernando,* ☎ *2/235–5446,* FAX *2/235–7604,* WEB
*www.relaischateaux.com/loslingues. 22 rooms. Restaurant, bar, minibars,
room service, pool, recreation room, laundry service. AE, DC, MC, V.*

$$$ ✕🔲 **Hotel Termas de Cauquenes.** This hotel on the Río Cachapoal draws
tourists who come to enjoy the therapeutic waters of the Termas de
Cauquenes. The marble bathtubs dating from 1885 have been preserved
in many rooms, but the rest of the facilities are completely modern.
The grounds include a colonial chapel and manicured gardens. The ac-
complished father-daughter team of René and Sabine Acklin serve up
typical Chilean cuisine in the restaurant overlooking the river. ✉ *Car-
retera del Cobre,* ☎ *72/899–010,* FAX *72/899–009. 50 rooms. Restau-
rant, bar, room service, pool, mineral baths, recreation room, laundry
service. AE, DC, MC, V.*

Santa Cruz

➋ *104 km (65 mi) southwest of Rancagua.*

Reminiscent of many small towns in the grape-growing regions of
Spain, Santa Cruz has a central square, a few streets lined with shops,
and vineyards radiating out in all directions. In the center of the palm-
lined **Plaza de Armas** is a colonial-style bell tower with a carillon that
chimes every 15 minutes; inside the tower you'll find the town's tourist
office. Facing the central square is the fortresslike **Iglesia Parroquial,**
an imposing white stucco structure.

★ **Museo de Colchagua.** The entire history of the region is the focus of
this impressive new museum. It's the largest private natural history col-
lection in the country, and second only in size to Santiago's Museo Na-
cional de Historia Natural. The display of amber is the only one of its
kind in the country; through special lenses you can glimpse fossilized
insects that have since become extinct. The collection of silver fashioned
by the indigenous Mapuche people is the largest anywhere. The mu-
seum also displays the only known original copy of the country's in-
dependence proclamation, the equivalent of the U.S. Declaration of
Independence. Outside, under a series of handsome colonial-style pavil-
ions, is a collection of early automobiles, tractors and trucks, and wine-
making implements. The collection, which belongs to Santa Cruz native
Carlos Cardoén, began to come together after he found arrowheads and
other artifacts here as a child. A dramatic video introduces the museum's
collection to English speakers, as the placards are only in Spanish. ✉
Av. Errázuriz 145, ☎ *72/821–050,* WEB *www.museocolchagua.cl.* 🔲 *Ad-
mission.* ☾ *Tues.–Sun. 10–6.*

★ **Museo San José del Carmen de El Huique.** This 2,600-acre country es-
tate is one of Chile's most important national monuments. The ranch,
about 16 km (10 mi) from Santa Cruz, was owned by the same fam-
ily since 1756. Federico Errázuriz Echaurren, president of Chile from
1896 to 1901, once made this hacienda his home. The rooms are pre-
served exactly as they were when Errázuriz lived here—the one stipu-

lation when the family handed the property to the government in 1975. Sumptuous suites contain collections of opal glass, lead crystal, bone china, and antique furniture collected from years in Europe, as well as photographs and family portraits. In one of the many kitchens, smoke residue from years of cooking is caught in the roof's beams, and the provocative scents evoke the aristocratic life in Chile 150 years ago. Today's tour guides know a lot about the estate, as they are descendents of the hundreds of people who worked for the Errázuriz family. Call ahead to arrange for an English-speaking guide. A highlight of a tour of the grounds is the 1852 chapel, which has Venetian blown-glass balustrades ringing the altar and the choir loft. Visit on Sunday morning, when mass is said at 11:30. ⊠ *El Huique,* ☎ *72/933–083.* ⊠ *Admission.* ☼ *Oct.–Feb., Wed.–Sun. 11–6; Mar.–Sept., Wed.–Sun. 11–5.*

Unlike most other small towns in the Central Valley, Santa Cruz has capitalized on the burgeoning interest in the region's viticulture. The **Ruta del Vino** (⊠ Plaza de Armas 140, ☎ FAX 72/823–199, WEB www.chilevinos.cl/rutadelvino) offers detailed information about the valley's vineyards. Others wine routes have sprouted up in the past few years, probably because of the success Santa Cruz has had in attracting tourists. You can join a guided tour that includes lunch, or grab a map and strike out on your own. One of the best times to visit is in early March, when the Fiesta de la Vendimia celebrates the harvest. Around that time of year you can see much of the process of turning the grapes into wine.

One of the most attractive wineries in the Valle de Colchagua is **Viña Bisquertt,** where a 200-year-old farmhouse with a Spanish-tile roof makes you feel as if you've stepped back in time. The property once belonged to Federico Errázuriz Zañartu, Chile's president from 1871 to 1876, and his carriage is part of a beautiful collection of 19th-century coaches at the vineyard. This family-run business oversees 1,200 acres of plantings. A tour will take you through the cellars, which feature 16 15-ft-tall wooden casks dating from the 1940s, as well as the new stainless-steel tanks that replaced them. Tours should be arranged through the Ruta del Vino office. ⊠ *Camino a Lihueimo s/n,* ☎ *2/233–6681,* WEB *www.bisquertt.cl.* ⊠ *Free.* ☼ *Open for tours.*

Viña Santa Laura is a small winery on lands where grapes have been grown for over a century and a half. The likeness of Laura Hartwig, the elegant owner of the estate, is beautifully drawn on the winery's labels by the famous Chilean artist Claudio Bravo. Hartwig's brother owns Viña Bisquertt, a family tie not uncommon among Chilean wineries. After a tour of the facilities, don't forget to sample the carmenère, a type of wine grown only in Chile. It has more character than merlot but is not as full bodied as cabernet sauvignon. Also try the malbec, which has a lasting finish, a sensation compared by a winery guide to "kissing Sean Connery." Tours should be arranged through the Ruta del Vino office. ⊠ *Camino Barreales s/n,* ☎ *72/823–179,* WEB *www.bisquertt.cl.* ⊠ *Free.* ☼ *Open for tours.*

Dining and Lodging

$–$$ ✕ **Club Social de Santa Cruz.** Many towns in Chile have their own Club Social, which always offers a good meal at good price. Most, like this one, are found on the town's main square. In summer, the courtyard fills with locals lunching under the shady pergola. Try the *plateada guisada* (beef stew) or *riñones al jerez* (kidneys in a sherry sauce). Only the bravest gourmands will sample the house specialty, *criadillas a la orden* (lamb testicles). ⊠ *Plaza de Armas 178,* ☎ *72/824–548. No credit cards.*

$–$$ ✕ **Los Varietales.** It's no surprise that the town's best restaurant is in the beautiful Hotel Santa Cruz Plaza. The name refers to varieties of grapes, a motif reflected in the magnums set atop the fireplace mantel, the bar shaped like an antique barrel, and the wine list, where you will find all of the Valle de Colchagua's labels. Select from the array of seafood and meats on the menu, as well as a large selection of sandwiches. Try the cream of smoked salmon soup or the conger eel with sautéed shrimp, tomatoes, and onions. In warmer months, the trellised terrace is a popular spot. ⊠ *Plaza de Armas 286,* ☎ *72/821–010,* WEB *www.hotelsantacruzplaza.cl. AE, DC, MC, V.*

$$–$$$ 🏨 **Hotel Santa Cruz Plaza.** When it opened in 2000, this beautiful colo-
★   nial-style hotel changed the face of Santa Cruz. Serving for years as a gateway to the nearby vineyards, Santa Cruz suddenly became a destination in its own right. The bright yellow facade has porches supported by rustic wooden columns and wrought-iron balconies overlooking the Plaza de Armas. Behind the main building, two small footbridges cross the creek that runs through town. Here you'll find a curvaceous pool wrapping around lush gardens and a large gazebo. There is a fine wineshop on the premises with every Valle de Colchagua wine arranged in handsome vitrines. If you have a suite, you can also sample the wines at your private bar. All the guest rooms are lovely, with walls painted in pales oranges and French doors you can throw open to catch the breeze. Before departing, don't miss the remarkable mosaic-tile map of the region. ⊠ *Plaza de Armas 286,* ☎ *72/821–010; 2/242–1030 in Santiago,* FAX *72/823–445; 2/242–1044 in Santiago,* WEB *www.hotelsantacruz-plaza.cl. 41 rooms, 3 suites. Restaurant, bar, snack bar, wineshop, in-room data ports, in-room safes, 4 pools, sauna, gym, baby-sitting, laundry service, convention center. AE, DC, MC, V.*

Shopping

Near the Viña La Posada on Avenida Rafael Casanova, the **Asociación de Artesanos** sells high-quality leather goods, embroidered tapestries, and clay figurines. If you want a souvenir you can't find elsewhere, head to **La Lajuela,** a hamlet 8 km (5 mi) southeast of Santa Cruz. Residents here weave *chupallas,* straw hats made from a fiber called *teatina* that is cut, died, dried, and braided by hand.

Curicó

❸   *113 km (71 mi) south of Rancagua.*

Founded in 1743, Curicó is the gateway to the Valle de Curicó. The bustling industrial town has a few attractions of its own, however. The lovely **Plaza de Armas** has a pretty fountain ringed by statues of nymphs. Nearby is an elaborate bandstand that was constructed in New Orleans in 1904. Five blocks east of the central plaza is the **Iglesia San Francisco,** where you'll find a statue of the Virgen de la Velilla that was brought from Spain in 1734. It's been named a national monument.

The Molina Vineyard that surrounds **Viña San Pedro** is the largest in Latin America. Viña San Pedro is one of Chile's oldest wineries, as the first vines were planted here in 1701. It's also among the most modern, with 28 half-million-liter stainless-steel tanks producing more wine than any other competitor except Concha y Toro. San Pedro makes the premium lines of Cabo de Horbos and Castillo de Molino as well as the ubiquitous Gato Negro and Gato Blanco brands. The bottling plant has a sleek glass dome and a second-floor viewing platform. Excellent tours can be arranged with a one-week notice. ⊠ *Ruta 5 S, Km 205,* ☎ *75/492–770; 2/235–9144 in Santiago,* WEB *www.vinosdechile.cl.* 🎫 *Admission.* ⊙ *Weekdays 9:30–5:30.*

Immediately off the Pan-American Highway is **Viña Miguel Torres,** one of Chile's most visitor-savvy vineyards. An orientation video providing a glossy overview of the winery all but nominates owner Don

Miguel Torres for sainthood. The Spanish vintner may actually deserve the honor, as he single-handedly began the wine revolution in Chile. When he set up shop here in 1972, all the equipment needed to make wine had to be imported from Spain. Now the methods he introduced to the region are taken for granted. Also from his native country came the idea for an annual fiesta: Torres established the wine harvest festival that takes place in Curicó's main square each year. ⊠ *Ruta 5 S, Km 195, Curicó,* ☎ *75/310–455,* ℻ *75/312–355,* WEB *www.migueltorres.cl.* ☜ *Free.* ⊙ *Weekdays 9–7, weekends 10–2.*

A 20-acre national reserve 70 km (44 mi) southeast of Curicó, **Reserva Nacional Radal Siete Tazas** is famous for the unusual "Seven Teacups," a series of pools created by waterfalls along the Río Claro. From the park entrance, where you'll find a Conaf station, the falls are a short hike away. Farther along the trail are two other impressive sprays of water, the Salto Velo de la Novia (Bride's Veil Falls) and Salto de la Leona (Lioness Falls). Visible throughout the park is the *loro tricahue,* an endangered species that is Chile's largest and most colorful parrot. Camping is permitted in the park, which is snowed over in winter. October to March is the best time to visit. ⊠ *Camino Molina–Parque Inglés,* ☎ *71/228–029.* ☜ *Admission.* ⊙ *Daily.*

Vichuquén

❹ 112 km (70 mi) west of Curicó.

An hour's drive from Curicó, this isolated community is now a popular country retreat for Santiago business executives rich enough to helicopter in for the weekend. With just a few streets and very little traffic, it retains a remote feeling. Until recently the entire journey was over dirt roads, and today the last 13 km (8 mi) is still unpaved. Black-necked swans are a common sight on meandering Lago Vichuquén. Swimming isn't permitted, but windsurfing and fishing are popular pastimes.

The **Museo Colonial de Vichuquén** (⊠ Av. Manuel Rodríguez s/n, ☎ 75/400–045, ⊙ daily 10–1 and 4–5) displays ceramics, stone tools, and other artifacts collected from pre-Hispanic peoples.

Dining and Lodging

$$ ✕🏨 **Hotel Playa Aquelarre.** This two-story structure of native woods offers unmatched views of Lago Vichuquén, with many rooms overlooking the lake from private decks. The hotel has excellent water-sports facilities, with jet ski classes available. The discotheque is extremely popular—many guests arrive by motorboat. The restaurant here is among the best in the area. ⊠ *Sector Aquelarre, Lago Vichuquén,* ☎ ℻ *75/400–018. 12 rooms. Restaurant, lake, boating, jet skiing, nightclub. AE, DC, MC, V.*

$$ ✕🏨 **Marina Vichuquén.** Boasting its own marina, the comfortable Marina Vichuquén has an enviable location right on the shore. Many rooms have nice views of the lake and the surrounding pine forests. There are plenty of opportunities for water sports, including a sailing school for children. If you want to explore the nearby countryside, you can also rent horses. ⊠ *Sector Aquelarre, Lago Vichuquén,* ☎ *75/400–265,* ℻ *75/400–274,* WEB *www.marinavichuquen.cl. 18 rooms. Restaurant, pub, pool, lake, tennis, gym, horseback riding, boating, jet skiing, marina, bicycles, baby-sitting. AE, DC, MC, V.*

Talca

❺ *56 km (35 mi) south of Curicó.*

Straddling the banks of the Río Claro, Talca is one of the most attractive towns in the Central Valley. Founded in 1692, it is laid out on a regimented grid pattern extending out from the Plaza de Armas. It's di-

vided into quadrants—*poniente* means west and *oriente* east; *sur* means
south and *norte* north. You can make out the city's orderly colonial
design from **Cerro de la Virgen,** a hill that affords a panoramic view
of the city and the vineyards in the distance.One of the most pleasant
stretches of green is **Avenida O'Higgins,** a cedar-lined boulevard popular with joggers, skaters, and strolling couples. At its western tip is
the Balneario Río Claro, where you can hire a boat to paddle down
the river. Near the Plaza de Armas, the **Museo O'Higgiano** (⊠ 1 Norte
and 2 Oriente, ☎ no phone) is a pink colonial mansion that belonged
to Albano Pereira, a tutor of national hero Bernardo O'Higgins. As
Chile's first president, O'Higgins signed the country's declaration of
independence in this house in February 1818. Declared a national
monument in 1971, it is now home to the city's fine arts museum, which
has a collection of more than 500 paintings by local artists. The museum is open Tuesday to Friday 9:15 to 6 and weekends 10 to 2.

There may be no better way to get to know the Central Valley than by
taking a ride on Chile's only remaining *ramal* (branch-line railroad), which
runs from Talca to the coastal city of Constitución. The 100-km (63-mi)
Ramal Talca–Constitución makes a slow trip to the coast (it's 2½ hours
each way), stopping for about 15 minutes at each of the small towns en
route. In Constitución you'll be able to explore the rocky cliffs, gaze at
the picturesque yellow tugboats, and dine at one of the string of inexpensive seafood restaurants along the coast. The train departs from the
station in Talca daily at 7:30 AM, returning at 6 PM. In high season the
train also leaves at 11 and returns at 9. Tickets are $2 one-way.

Dining and Lodging

$$ ✕ **Rubén Tapío.** One of the best restaurants in all the Central Valley,
★   Rubén Tapío is renowned for the staff's attention to the little details.
The fine service makes a ceremony even of pouring a glass of wine (choose
from a large list of local vintages). With comfortable dining rooms up-
stairs and down, you feel like you're a guest in someone's home. The
signature dish here is a fish soup called *caldillo de congrio dorado* (Pablo
Neruda's own recipe, the menu says). Other standouts include *filete
de corvina* (sea bass fillet served with a seafood sauce) and *chupe de
locos* (creamy abalone chowder topped with shredded cheese). Bread
is delivered to your table with three spreads, including a delicious
olive pâté. ⊠ 2 Oriente 1339, ☎ 71/237–875. No credit cards.

$–$$ ✕ **El Alero de Gastón.** A simple dining room with Spanish tiles over-
hanging the bar—calling to mind the name "Gaston's Eaves"—is the
setting of this traditional restaurant. The cuisine is literally all over the
map—try the Argentine *parillada* (barbecue) or the Ecuadorian *ca-
marónes ecuatoriano al ajillo* (shrimp in garlic sauce). The steak tartare
with a mustard sauce is tasty, too. The terrace is a good spot for a romantic meal in the summer. ⊠ 2 Norte 858, ☎ 71/237–875. MC, V.

$ ✕ **Club Social.** Extremely inexpensive, consistently delicious food is what
you can expect at this unpretentious eatery near the Plaza de Armas.
A popular choice is the *paila marina* (seafood chowder), served here
with beef and chicken. The selection of bottled wines from the surrounding vineyards is very good, but you can also order a *(copa)* of
the excellent house selection for about 30¢. Service is attentive and unpretentious. The dining room is admittedly humble, with a television
always blaring, but you'll emerge with a real dose of Talca. After a meal,
club members retire to the billiard room across the enormous main hall.
⊠ 3 Oriente, between Sur 1 and Sur 2, ☎ 71/221–583. No credit cards.

$$ ▥ **Hotel Terrabella.** Just off the Plaza de Armas, the Hotel Terrabella has
a sprightly air about it. While not especially bright and by no means spa-
cious, the rooms are clean and comfortable. The attractive lounge and
the cafeteria with a view of the swimming pool make for a pleasant, if

not luxurious, stay. ⊠ *1 Sur 641,* ☎ FAX *71/226–555. 22 rooms, 1 suite. Cafeteria, in-room safes, meeting room, free parking. AE, DC, MC, V.*

Outdoor Activities and Sports

Horseback-riding enthusiasts should contact **Achibueno Expediciones** (⊠ Ruta L-4 Km 8, Llancanao, ☎ 73/214–861, WEB www.achibueno-expediciones.cl), which leads guided excursions to the Andes, taking in waterfalls, thermal baths, and archaeological sites along the way. A minimum two-day trip costs $140 per person.

Shopping

The city's market, damaged by a fire in 2001, is currently being reconstructed. In the meantime you can stroll among the stands of fresh produce at the **Vega Municipal** at the eastern end of Avenida O'Higgins.

San Javier

❻ *21 km (13 mi) south of Talca.*

After crossing the Río Maule you come to the small but bustling town of San Javier. It serves as the gateway to the vineyards of the Valle del Maule. On one of its one-way streets you'll find the headquarters of the **Valle del Maule Ruta del Vino** (⊠ Calle Sargento Aldea 2491, ☎ 73/323–657, WEB www.chilewineroute.com). The small office, open 9:15–1:30 and 2:30 to 6:15, arranges tours of a dozen small wineries in the Maule Valley, which stretches from Talca to Chillán. These wineries are often family-run establishments where the owners hand-label each bottle.

The **Domaine Oriental** winery is named for its location east of the city. After a long drive over a dirt road, you arrive at a massive iron gate bearing the winery's initials. The vineyards themselves climb, unimpeded, up into the Andes. Kept moist by mountain streams, the land requires little artificial irrigation. The Donoso family owned this estate for many generations before it was purchased in 1989 by four Frenchmen who live in Tahiti cultivating black pearls. The oenological work is done by a skilled Chilean staff, and the results are auspicious. The Casa Donoso label's blend of cabernet sauvignon, which lends the structure, and carmenère, which brings out the soft edges, is one of Chile's most promising reserves. As in many vineyards here, the colonial adobe walls lock in the cold and humidity, so underground storage isn't necessary. ⊠ *Camino a Palmira Km 3.5,* ☎ *71/242–506,* WEB *www.domaineoriental.cl.* ⊞ *Admission.* ☉ *Weekdays 9–6.*

In San Javier itself is **Viña Balduzzi.** Albano Balduzzi, who came from generations of wine makers in Italy, built the 40-acre estate here in 1906. His grandson, Jorge Balduzzi, still lives here, making a million liters of wine each year. The premium label features varietals such as cabernet sauvignon, sauvignon blanc, carmenère, merlot, and a sweet late-harvest chardonnay. There's no need to call ahead for tours, which include a look at the cellars that stretch underneath the property, the collection of antique machinery, and a tasting. ⊠ *Av. Balmacaeda 1189,* ☎ *73/332–138,* WEB *www.balduzzi.cl.* ⊞ *Free.* ☉ *Weekdays 9–6.*

Colbún

❼ *50 km (31 mi) east of Talca.*

Heading east on Ruta 115 you reach the tiny town of Colbún. It sits near a 93-square-km (36-square-mi) lake formed after a hydroelectric dam was built on the Río Maule in 1985. The largest such plant in Chile, it produces half the country's electrical power. The lake, stocked with trout, is an especially popular destination for fly-fishing aficionados. You can also rent motorboats and jet skis.

Hikers will love the **Reserva Nacional Alto de Lircay,** which has lengthy trails that cut through native oak forest on their way to the volcanic cones of the Andes. To reach the park, which is administered by Conaf, the national park service, head east on Ruta 115, which is called the Camino Internacional Paso Pehuenche. Turn left at the signs past the hamlet of Corralones. About 25 km (15 mi) farther is the reserve. The park is snowed over July–September.

Lodging

$$ ⊡ **Cabañas Lago Colbún.** Nestled in a pine forest besides Lago Colbún, this small complex consists of wooden cabañas that can accommodate six people, making them a good choice for families seeking a quiet retreat. Each cabin has its own kitchen and a large deck that looks out at the lake. You can rent boats, canoes, and kayaks. The location is 7 km (4 mi) down a dirt road from the main highway. ⊠ *Camino a la Represa, Km. 7,* ☎ ℻ *71/221–750. 8 cabanas. Kitchenettes, boating. AE, DC, MC, V.*

$$ ⊡ **Casas el Colorado.** The lovingly restored 19th-century hacienda is set among fields of grazing horses. On the grounds is the simple wood-and-brick chapel of Santa Teresita de los Andes, where mass is still said on Sundays. It was constructed over the foundations of a Jesuit church dating from 1790; you can visit the ruins in the basement. The restaurant here is the best in the area; grilled salmon and filet mignon are house specialties. All meals are included in the rate. ⊠ *Km 46, Colorado,* ☎ ℻ *71/221–750. 16 rooms. Restaurant, grocery, golf, tennis, heliport. AE, DC, MC, V.*

RÍO BÍO BÍO

The mighty Río Bío Bío empties into the Pacific Ocean at the regional capital of Concepción, a coastal city with a population of about 500,000. The area's other major community, Chillán, is an easygoing town known for its attractive handicrafts market.

Chillán

❽ *157 km (98 mi) south of Talca.*

Friendly, tranquil Chillán is worth a stop for its historic resonance and colorful markets. At the Feria de Chillán you'll find crafts from all over Chile. Across the street is the main market, with extremely inexpensive eateries clustered inside and out. Each of the vendors has dozens of locally produced sausages called *longaniza* hanging from their stalls. The sight of thousands of these dangling rings of pork make clear that this delicacy is a staple of the local diet.

The heart of Chillán is the verdant **Plaza de Armas,** the city's pretty main square. A plaque honors Bernardo O'Higgins, who was born here in 1778. The modern **Catedral de Chillán,** on the east side of the central square, is constructed of nine parabolic arches. All ornamentation is eschewed inside and out, except for a crucifix above the altar, the stations of the cross in the spaces between the arches, and the mosaic above the entrance. A huge cement cross, even taller than the church itself, stands outside.

After an earthquake devastated Chillán in 1939, Pablo Neruda, then Chile's ambassador to Mexico, arranged a visa allowing Mexican painter David Alfaro Siqueiros to travel to Chile. He painted an incendiary mural in the **Escuela México** (⊠ Av. O'Higgins and Vega de Saldias), about five blocks from the Plaza de Armas. The mural depicts indigenous peoples being murdered by the Spanish conquistadors. Neruda lost his job because of the resulting scandal, but the mural still remains.

Dining and Lodging

$$ ✕ **Centro Español.** This building on the Plaza de Armas was intended to house the Spanish Friends Society, which still meets here. The exterior curves gracefully, as if it is reacting to the sinuous form of the neighboring cathedral. Spanish touches on the exterior, such as iron lanterns and window grilles, give way to an interior graced by two large fireplaces and elegant chandeliers. Count on traditional favorites like paella and *arroz a la valenciana*, a Spanish rice dish. ✉ *Calle Arauco 555*, ☎ *2/777–8740. AE, DC, MC, V.*

$$ ▥ **Hotel Las Terrazas.** Steps from the Plaza de Armas, the newest hotel in town occupies the fifth and sixth floors of an attractive shopping center. Some rooms have memorable views of the Andes. Enjoy a drink in the the sixth-floor lobby, which has pillowy furniture that invites you to linger. After Chile's president stayed here, Las Terrazas replaced the Gran Hotel Chillán as the premier hotel in Chillán. ✉ *Constitución 664, 5th floor*, ☎ *42/227–000*, FAX *42/227–001*, WEB *www.lasterrazas.cl. 35 rooms, 2 suites. Cafeteria, bar, in-room safes, minibars, room service, meeting room, free parking. AE, DC, MC, V.*

Shopping

At the sprawling **Feria de Chillán** (✉ Av. 5 de Abril between Calles Maipón and Arturo Prat) you'll find dozens of vendors selling woven clothing, pottery, jewelry, and handicrafts. It's open daily until sunset.

Termas de Chillán

❾ *78 km (49 mi) east of Chillán.*

Billed as the continent's "most complete ski resort," Termas de Chillán has a mountainside location that rivals Valle Nevado and Portillo. A total of nine lifts carry you to 28 groomed runs, including one that is the longest in South America. There's snowmobiling and snowboarding, as well as more unusual activities such as Alaskan malamute sledding.

Separating Termas de Chillán from the pack, rooms at the two hotels here can only be arranged in seven-night or four-night packages. Rates include lift tickets and half-board (breakfast and dinner).

Lodging

$$$$ ▥ **Gran Hotel Termas de Chillán.** This new five-star facility has comfortable rooms in a stepped, eight-story building. There are three pools fed by hot springs, one indoor and two outdoor. What really sets the hotel apart, however, is its excellent spa with modern treatments such as aromatherapy and hydrotherapy as well as traditional therapies like massages and mud baths. ✉ *Termas de Chillán*, ☎ *42/223–887; 2/233–1313 in Santiago*, WEB *www.termaschillan.cl. 120 rooms. Restaurant, bar, room service, 1 indoor pool, 2 outdoor pools, hair salon, hot springs, massage, mineral baths, sauna, spa, health club, racquetball, cross-country skiing, ski shop, baby-sitting, laundry service, convention center, meeting rooms. AE, DC, MC, V.*

$$$$ ▥ **Hotel Pirigallo.** This two-story sibling of the larger Gran Hotel Termas de Chillán offers comfortable but not luxurious rooms. The Pirigallo also has its own outdoor pool. ✉ *Termas de Chillán*, ☎ *42/223–887; 2/233–1313 in Santiago*, WEB *www.skichillan.com. 48 rooms. Restaurant, bar, room service, pool, cross-country skiing, ski shop, baby-sitting, laundry service. AE, DC, MC, V.*

Concepción

❿ *112 km (70 mi) southwest of Chillán.*

Earthquakes have devastated this coastal city since it was founded in 1551. The latest few, in 1939 and 1960, destroyed pretty much any historic building still standing. The regional capital is a mishmash of modern buildings, many in disrepair and most aesthetically awry. The city straddles the Río Bío Bío, with two mile-long bridges (Puente Viejo and Puente Nuevo) crossing to the other side. **Plaza de la Independencia,** also called Plaza de Concepción, is the heart of the city, with pedestrian shopping streets radiating from its borders. Governmental buildings are located here, as is an abstract modern church.

Cerro Caracol, or Conch Hill, overlooks the city from the southeast. Largely covered by pine trees, the hill is popular with joggers, hikers, and mountain bikers. You can reach the hill by heading south on Calle Tucapel. Park along the mossy cobblestone streets and wander among the many footpaths that lead into the woods. Running parallel to the hill is Parque Ecuador. Here you'll find the **Museo de la Historia de Concepción** (✉ Lamas and Lincyán, ☎ 41/231–830), which depicts regional history through a dozen dioramas, including the 1939 earthquake that devastated the city; battles between the Spanish invaders and the indigenous Mapuche people; and Alonso de Ercilla writing the epic poem "La Auraucana" in 1557. Rooms upstairs are dedicated to changing art exhibitions. The museum is free and is open Tuesday to Sunday 10–1 and 3–6:30.

★ The **Casa del Arte,** at the Universidad de Concepción, is home to the country's largest, and arguably best, collection of classical Chilean paintings. The museum is most famous for the striking mural by Mexican artist Jorge González Camarena. Unaware of the presence of a protruding staircase until he saw the room, González incorporated it into the work. It now bears the snaky form of Quetzalcoatl, a symbol of Aztec culture. Climb Quetzalcoatl to the galleries displaying selections from the collection of more than 1,600 works, including major canvases by Alfredo Valenzuela Puelma. Past shows in the three halls downstairs have included included exhibits of works by Picasso and the promising young painter, sculptor, and designer José Fernández Covich. ✉ *Av. Chacabuco at Av. Paicavi,* ☎ *41/204–126.* ⊙ *Free.* ⏱ *Tues.–Fri. 10–6, Sat. 10–4, Sun. 10–1.*

Dining and Lodging

$ ✕ **El Faro Belén.** While it may not appear like much from the outside, this nautically themed restaurant serves some of the best seafood in Concepción. A towering wooden mermaid surveys the dining room, which overflows with locals on weekday afternoons. Ask for the *plato americano,* a selection of seven seafood dishes including sea bass, shrimp, salmon, and clams, all served cold. A more intimate dining room is tucked away upstairs. ✉ *Av. Bulnes 382,* ☎ *41/243–430. AE, DC, MC, V. No dinner Sun.*

$ ✕ **Julio's.** Carnivores should head directly to this Argentine parrillada for juicy *costaleta argentina* steaks. The restaurant, three blocks from Plaza Independencia, also has great homemade pastas and pizzas. The setting is informal (paper place mats, for instance) but the big booths are a great place to relax after a day of sightseeing. ✉ *Barros Arana 337,* ☎ *41/228–207. AE, DC, MC, V.*

$$–$$$$ 🛏 **Hotel El Araucano.** Still considered the best hotel in the city, Hotel El Araucano wins out primarily because of its excellent location, well-regarded restaurant, and good views of Plaza de la Independencia and the Río Bío Bío. Yet the city's downturned fortunes have clearly left this hotel without the funds to keep current. The minibars, though functional, are relics from an earlier era. Baths are on the small side. ✉ *Caupolicán 521,* ☎ FAX *41/230–606,* WEB *www.carrera.cl. 138 rooms, 6 suites. Restaurant, room service, indoor pool, sauna, laundry service, convention center, meeting rooms, free parking. AE, DC, MC, V.*

$$–$$$ 🛏 **Hotel Terrano.** From Avenida Bernardo O'Higgins, this hotel looks small and uninviting, but don't be fooled. It's actually quite specious, with a taller wing hidden in the back that provides room for a restaurant and

even a cavernous convention hall. Inside are bright and cheerful rooms with comfortable beds. The baths are fairly large, with extras like hair dryers and phones. Upper-floor rooms have views of the surrounding hills. ⊠ *Av. O'Higgins 340,* ☎ FAX *41/240–078,* WEB *www.hotelterrano.cv.cl. 68 rooms, 2 suites. Restaurant, gym, laundry service, convention center, meeting rooms, free parking. AE, DC, MC, V.*

Outdoor Activities and Sports

The **Club de Tenis de Concepción** (⊠ Parque Ecuador, at Av. Lamas and Caupolicán, ☎ 41/230–671) has 10 clay tennis courts.

Shopping

Almacenes París (⊠ Castellón and Barros), part of the major department store chain, is found in the city's newest and most modern building, a five-floor glass structure that's impossible to miss.

THE CENTRAL VALLEY A TO Z

To research prices, get advice from other travelers, and book travel arrangements, visit www.fodors.com.

AIR TRAVEL TO AND FROM THE CENTRAL VALLEY

Concepción's Aeropuerto Carriel Sur—5 km (3 mi) northwest of town—is the only major airport in the region. LanChile and its domestic subsidiary Ladeco fly here, as does Aerocontinente. The airport is a good choice if you plan to explore the area around the Río Bío Bío. Otherwise it may be more convenient to fly into Santiago.

CARRIERS
➤ AIRLINES & CONTACTS: **Aerocontinente** (⊠ Aeropuerto Carriel Sur, ☎ 41/732–030). **LanChile** (⊠ Barros Arana 600, ☎ 41/521–092 or 41/229–138; ⊠ Aeropuerto Carriel Sur, ☎ 41/732–005).
➤ AIRPORTS: **Aeropuerto Carriel Sur** (☎ 41/732–000).

BUS TRAVEL WITHIN THE CENTRAL VALLEY

The two big bus companies in the region, Tur-Bus and Pullman Bus, offer frequent service between major cities such as Rancagua, Talca, Chillán, and Concepción. Smaller companies run buses to towns not along the Pan-American Highway.
➤ BUS COMPANIES: **Pullman Bus** (☎ 2/779–2026). **Tur-Bus** (☎ 2/270–7500).
➤ BUS TERMINALS: **Chillán Terminal Marí Teresa** (⊠ Av. O'Higgins 10, ☎ 42/272–149). **Concepción Terminal Puchucay** (⊠ Terminal Principal Collao Calle Tegualda 860, ☎ 41/311–511). **Rancagua Terminal Sur** (⊠ Dr. Salinas 1165, ☎ 72/230–340). **Talca Terminal de Buses** (⊠ 12 Oriente and 2 Sur, ☎ 71/243–270).

CAR RENTALS

Most visitors to the Central Valley who rent a vehicle do so in Santiago. If you find you need a car while traveling in the region, Avis and Hertz both have agencies at Aeropuerto Carriel Sur and downtown Concepción.
➤ LOCAL AGENCIES: **Avis** (⊠ Aeropuerto Carriel Sur, ☎ 41/480–089; ⊠ Av. Chacabuco 726, Concepción, ☎ 41/235–837). **Hertz** (⊠ Aeropuerto Carriel Sur, ☎ 41/480–088; ⊠ Av. Arturo Prat 248, Concepción, ☎ 41/230–341).

CAR TRAVEL

The Central Valley is sliced in half by Chile's major highway, the Pan-American Highway. With the exception of Concepción, it passes through all of the major towns in the region. Since so many of the sights are off the beaten path, traveling by car is often the most convenient way to see the region. The speed limit here is 100 kph (62 mph), which may be a bit slower than you're used to driving. Be aware that road conditions vary greatly. Many of the secondary roads in the region remain unpaved.

INTERNET
In the major cities in the Central Valley, there are always one or two Internet cafés. In smaller towns, however, they are much harder to find. In Talca, Planet Café is a well-run Internet café across from the tourist information office. It's open daily 8:30 AM to 11 PM. In Concepción, Moonblass Café is one of many inexpensive places to get online. It's open Monday to Saturday 9:30 AM–10:30 PM, and Sunday 4–9.
➤ INTERNET: **Moonblass Café** (⊠ Aureliano Manzano 538, Concepción, ☎ 41/910–233). **Planet Café** (⊠ 1 Poniente 1282, Talca, ☎ 71/210–775).

MAIL AND SHIPPING
You'll find at least one post office in every town in the Central Valley. Because of the proximity to Santiago, mail service is quicker here than in other regions.
➤ POST OFFICES: **Chillán** (⊠ Calle Libertad 505, ☎ 42/223–272). **Concepción** (⊠ Calle Colo Colo 417, ☎ 41/235–666). **Curicó** (⊠ Carmen s/n, ☎ 75/310–000). **Rancagua** (⊠ Calle Campos at Calle Cuevas, ☎ 72/230–413). **Talca** (⊠ 1 Oriente 1150, ☎ 71/227–271).

MONEY MATTERS
Because it's the largest city in the region, Concepción has the most banking options. Besides Chilean banks, you can also find the international banks such as Citibank. Here you can exchange currency, get cash advances on credit cards, and withdraw money from a 24-hour ATM.
➤ BANKS: **Banco Concepción** (⊠ Constitución 550, Chillán, ☎ 42/221–306). **Banco del Estado** (⊠ 1 Sur 971, Talca, ☎ 71/223–285). **Banco Sudamericano** (⊠ Independencia at Bueras, Rancagua, ☎ 72/230–413). **Citibank** (⊠ Av. O'Higgins 499, Concepción, ☎ 41/233–870).

TELEPHONES
Public phones in the region accept coins and phone cards that can be purchased at shops and newsstands.

TOUR OPERATORS
In Concepción, Publitur and Turismo Cocha arrange trips around the region. In Chillán, Centrotur is a reputable company.
➤ TOUR COMPANIES: **Centrotur** (⊠ 18 de Septiembre 342, Chillán, ☎ 42/221–306). **Publitur** (⊠ Anibal Pinto 486, Concepción, ☎ 41/240–800). **Turismo Cocha** (⊠ Av. O'Higgins, Concepción, ☎ 41/237–303).

TRAIN TRAVEL
Although service in much of the rest of the country has been gutted, the train remains an excellent way to travel among towns in the Central Valley. Trains from Santiago travel through the cities of Rancagua, Curicó, Talca, Chillán, Concepción, and Temuco, with stops in the smaller towns of San Bernardo, San Javier, Linares, Parral, San Carlos, Bulnes, Cabrero, Monte Aguila, Yumbel, San Rosendo, Talcamavida, Hualqui, Laja, Santa Fe, Renaico, Mininco, Collipulli, Victoria, and Lautaro.
➤ TRAIN INFORMATION: **Chillán** (⊠ Av. Brasil at Libertad, ☎ 42/222–424). **Concepción** (⊠ Av. Arturo Prat at Calle Barros Arana, ☎ 41/226–925). **Curicó** (⊠ Maipú 567, ☎ 75/310–028). **Rancagua** (⊠ Av. Viña del Mar at Carrera Pinto, ☎ 72/225–239). **Talca** (⊠ 11 Oriente and 2 Sur, ☎ 71/226–254).

VISITOR INFORMATION
Sernatur has outstanding offices with English-speaking staff in Rancagua, Talca, and Concepción. The offices are open weekdays 8:30–6.
➤ INFORMATION: **Concepción** (⊠ Anibal Pinto 460, Plaza de Armas, ☎ 41/227–976 or 41/244–999). **Rancagua** (⊠ German Riesco 277, ofc. 2 and 3, ☎ 72/230–413). **Talca** (⊠ 1 Poniente 1281, ☎ 71/226–254).

7 THE LAKE DISTRICT

Densely forested national parks crisscrossed with hiking paths, a dozen large lakes (and scores of smaller ones) ideal for water sports, and perfectly conical volcanoes providing a dazzling backdrop—the Lake District is the Chile you came to see. While the rest of the country reflects a blending of Spanish and indigenous cultures, this region adds German, Austrian, and Swiss immigrants to the mix. With so many Bavarian-style buildings you might just think you're in the Alps.

A S YOU TRAVEL THE WINDING ROADS of the Lake District, the snowcapped shoulders of volcanoes emerge, mysteriously disappear, then materialize again, peeping through trees or towering above broad valleys. The sometimes difficult journey through breathtaking mountain passes is almost inevitably rewarded by views of a glistening lake, vibrant and blue. Often, there are hot springs in which tired travelers can soak stiff muscles.

By Jeffrey
Van Fleet

The Lake District is the historic homeland of Chile's indigenous Mapuche people. The Mapuche revolted against the early Spanish colonists in 1598, driving them out of the region. They kept outsiders out of the region for nearly three centuries. Though small pockets of the Lake District were controlled by Chile after it won its independence in 1818, most people viewed the forbidding region south of the Río Bío Bío as a separate country. But after the last Mapuche war in 1881, Santiago began to recruit waves of German, Austrian, and Swiss immigrants to settle the so-called empty territory and offset indigenous domination. The Lake District took on the Bavarian sheen still evident today.

Pleasures and Pastimes

Beaches
Despite its long coastline, this part of southern Chile historically looks inward rather than to the sea. Development is sparse along the coast, except for a couple of beach communities near Valdivia and Puerto Montt. Most tourists seeking fun in the sun concentrate on the inland lakes. Chileans from the north flock to the gray-sand beaches on Lago Llanquihue, Lago Villarrica, and others.

Dining
Meat and potatoes characterize the cuisine of this part of southern Chile. The omnipresent *cazuela* (a plate of rice and potatoes with beef or chicken) and *pastel de choclo* (a corn, meat, and vegetable casserole) are solid, hearty meals. Though more associated with Chiloé, the southern Lake District dishes up its own *curanto,* a fish stew served with lots of bread. Mercifully, you'll probably never have occasion to sample *ñache,* a thick mass of lamb or goat blood, lemon juice, and coriander. It's a delicacy in remote rural areas.

Arguably the greatest gift from the waves of German immigrants were their tasty *küchen,* rich fruit-filled pastries. (Raspberry is a special favorite here.) Sample them during the late afternoon *onces,* the coffee breaks locals take in the afternoons to tide them over until dinner. The Germans also brought their beer-making prowess to the New World; Valdivia, in particular, is recognized as Chile's brewing center, home to the popular Kunstmann brand. For approximate entrée costs, *see* the dining price chart *in* Smart Travel Tips A to Z.

Lodging
If you've traveled in Europe, you'll immediately feel at home in the Lake District, where most of the lodgings resemble old-world hotels. Many hostelries, even the newly built ones, are constructed in Bavarian-chalet style echoing the region's Germanic heritage. A handful of lodgings—Temuco's Hotel Continental, Pucón's Hotel Antumalal, and Puerto Octay's Hotel Centinela—are also historic landmarks that shouldn't be missed. The owners of many smaller places are couples in which one spouse is Chilean and the other is German, combining what one such pair calls "the best of both worlds: Chilean warmth and Germanic efficiency."

The Lake District

Central heating is a much-appreciated feature in most lodgings here during the winter and on brisk summer evenings. Rates usually include a Continental breakfast of coffee, cheese, bread, and jam. While the majority of the places listed here stay open all year, call ahead to make sure the owners haven't decided to take a well-deserved vacation during the April–November off-season. For approximate room costs, *see* the lodging price chart *in* Smart Travel Tips A to Z.

Nightlife

An early-to-bed, early-to-rise ethic brought by the Germans, combined with years of curfews under the former government, didn't infuse the region with a wild nightlife. That said, the streets are quite lively on summer evenings, with everyone out dining, strolling, shopping—businesses keep much later hours during the December–March high season—and enjoying the glorious sunsets that don't fade until 10 PM.

Shopping

The Lake District offers the best shopping options for traditional wares of two of Chile's strongest regional cultures, one native to this part of the country, the other not. The best selection of woolen blankets and ponchos of the indigenous Mapuche people is found in the markets of Temuco, most notably in the Mercado Municipal. Chilote woolens come from nearby Chiloé, but the best place to buy these handicrafts is not the island itself, but at the market stalls of Caleta Angelmó near Puerto Montt.

Exploring the Lake District

The Lake District's altitude descends sharply from the towering peaks of the Andes on the Argentine border, to forests and plains, finally to sea level, all in the space of about 200 km (120 mi). The Pan-American Highway runs straight down the middle, making travel to most places in the region relatively easy. It connects the major cities of Temuco, Osorno, and Puerto Montt, but bypasses Valdivia by 50 km (30 mi). A drive from Temuco to Puerto Montt should take under four hours. Flying between the hubs is a reasonable option. A Temuco–Osorno ticket, for example, costs $24.

Great Itineraries

IF YOU HAVE 3 DAYS
Fly directly to ▨ **Temuco** ① and spend the afternoon shopping for Mapuche handicrafts at the city's Mercado Municipal. Rise early the next morning and drive to ▨ **Pucón** ④ or ▨ **Villarrica** ③, where you can spend the day exploring one of the Lake District's most beautiful areas, maybe taking a dip in any of the nearby thermal springs. The next day take a hike up Volcán Villarrica.

IF YOU HAVE 5 DAYS
Spend your first day in ▨ **Temuco** ①. On your second day head south to ▨ **Valdivia** ⑧, where you can spend the afternoon visiting the modern art and history museums on Isla Teja. Catch an evening cruise along the Río Valdivia. Rise early the next day and drive to the Bavarian-style village of ▨ **Frutillar** ⑬ on Lago Llanquihue. Visit the Museum of German Colonization and wind up the afternoon partaking of the Chilean *onces* ritual with coffee and küchen. Head for ▨ **Puerto Varas** ⑭ the next day for a thrilling rafting excursion on the nearby Río Petrohué. Head to **Puerto Montt** ⑯ the final day, and spend the afternoon shopping for handicrafts in the Angelmó market stalls. Finish out the day with a seafood dinner at one of the market's lively restaurants.

When to Tour

You'll find all the standard high-season, low-season trade-offs in the Lake District. Seemingly everyone heads here during southern Chile's glorious summer between December and March. Visiting during the off-season is no hardship, though. An increasing number of smog-weary Santiaguinos flee the capital in the winter to enjoy the Lake District's brisk, clear air. Just be prepared for rain and some snow at higher elevations.

LA ARAUCANÍA

The tourism industry uses the term "Lake District" to denote the 400-km (240-mi) stretch of land beginning in Temuco and running south to Puerto Montt, but Chileans only call the southern part of this region Los Lagos ("The Lakes"). To the north is the fiercely proud La Araucanía, whose regional government seems to emblazon its name on everything possible.

La Araucanía is the historic home of the Araucano, or Mapuche, culture. The Spanish both feared and respected the Mapuche, especially legendary Chief Lautaro. He cunningly adopted a know-thy-enemy strategy that proved tremendously successful in fending off the colonists. This nomadic society, always in search of new terrain, was a moving target that the Spaniards found impossible to defeat. Beginning with the 1598 battle against European settlers, the Mapuches kept firm control of the region for 300 years. After numerous peace agreements failed, a treaty signed near Temuco ended hostilities in 1881 and paved the way for the German, Swiss, and Austrian immigration that would transform the face of the Lake District.

It may not be called Los Lagos, but La Araucanía contains some of Chile's most spectacular lake scenery. Several volcanoes, among them Villarrica and Llaima, two of South America's most active, loom over the region. Burgeoning Pucón, on the shore of Lago Villarrica, has become the tourism hub of southern Chile. Other quieter alternatives exist, however. Lago Calafquén, farther south, begins the seven-lake Siete Lagos chain that stretches across the border to Argentina.

Temuco

❶ *675 km (405 mi) south of Santiago.*

The south's largest city, and Chile's fastest-growing metropolis, Temuco has a more Latin flavor than the communities farther south. (It could be the warm weather and the palm trees swaying in the pleasant central park.) This northern gateway to the Lake District is an odd juxtaposition of modern architecture and indigenous markets, of traditionally clad Mapuche women darting across the street and business executives talking on cell phones, but oddly enough, it all works. This is big-city life Chilean style, and it warrants a visit of a day or two.

Bustling **Plaza Aníbal Pinto,** Temuco's central square, is ringed with imported palm trees, a rarity in this part of the country. A monument to the 300-year struggle between the Mapuche and the Spaniards sits in the center. The city's modern **Catedral de Temuco** sits on the northwest corner of the square, flanked by an office tower emblazoned with a cross. Lined with lime and oak trees, a shady secondary square called **Plaza Teodoro Schmidt** sits six blocks north of the Plaza Aníbal Pinto. It's ruled over by the 1906 Iglesia Santa Trinidad, an Anglican church that is one of the city's oldest surviving structures.

Housed in a 1924 mansion, the **Museo Regional de la Araucanía** covers the history of the area. It has an eclectic array of artifacts and relics, including musical instruments, utensils, and the country's best collection of indigenous jewelry. Upstairs exhibits document the Mapuche people's three-century struggle to keep control of their land. The presentation could be more evenhanded: the rhetoric dismisses the Central European colonization of this area as the *pacificación de la Araucanía* ("the taming of the Araucanian territories"). But the museum gives you a reasonably good Spanish-language introduction to Mapuche history, art, and culture. ⊠ *Av. Alemania 84,* ☎ *45/211–108.* 🖺 *Admission.* ⊙ *Weekdays 9–5, Sat. 11–4:45, Sun. 11–2.*

Part of Chile's national park system, the imposing **Monumento Natural Cerro Ñielol** sits near downtown. The hill was the site of the signing of the 1881 treaty between the Mapuche and the Chilean army, allowing for the city of Temuco to be established. The trails bloom with bright red *copihues,* Chile's national flower, during the March–May autumn season. ⊠ *Av. Prat, 5 blocks north of Plaza Teodoro Schmidt.* 🖺 *Admission.* ⊙ *Jan.–Mar., daily 8 AM–11 PM; Apr.–Nov., daily 8:30–12:30, 2:30–6.*

Dining and Lodging

$$–$$$ ✕ **El Fogón.** This place decorated with primary colors—yellow walls, red tablecloths, and blue dishes—certainly stands out in pastel-hued Temuco. The Chilean-style *parrillada,* or grilled beef, is the specialty of the house. You'll notice the barbecue here uses subtler spices than its better-known Argentine counterpart. The friendly owners gladly take the time to proudly explain the menu to the uninitiated. Though close to downtown, splurge on a a cab if you're coming to this dark street at night. ⊠ *Aldunate 288,* ☎ *45/952–163. MC, V.*

$$–$$$ ✕ **La Estancia.** North of the city, this rustic restaurant features reindeer heads on the walls and cured hams hanging from the ceiling. It offers good southern beef in the form of steaks, roasts, and barbecues in a traditional country atmosphere. ⊠ *Rudecindo Ortega 02340-A Interior,* ☎ *45/220–287. AE, DC, MC, V. No dinner Sun.*

$$–$$$ ✕ **La Pampa.** Frequented by the wealthy professionals of this bustling city, this upscale modern steak house serves huge, delicious cuts of beef and the best *papas fritas* (french fries) in Temuco. While most Chilean restaurants douse any kind of meat with a creamy sauce, this is one of the few exceptions: the entrées are served without anything but the simplest of seasonings. ⊠ *Caupolicán 0155,* ☎ *45/329–999. Reservations essential. DC, MC, V.*

$$ ✕ **Bavaria.** Part of a national chain, this café offers three types of parrilladas and the most unusual vegetarian pizza you'll ever experience—two kinds of cheese, green beans, pickles, tomatoes, olives, red pepper, and oregano, all on a cakey crust. Bavaria also has coffee drinks, sweets, and all the other traditional Chilean staples. ⊠ *Manuel Rodríguez 1075,* ☎ *45/215–569. No credit cards.*

$$ ✕ **Café Artesanía Raíces Indoamericanas.** Though the city is full of reminders that it was once the center of Mapuche territory, this is one of the few restaurants in Temuco where you can sample traditional Mapuche dishes. Corn reigns, as in any Mapuche community. Try the pastel de choclo (a meat and vegetable casserole) or the *humita* (steamed ground corn prepared in its own husk). ⊠ *Manuel Montt 645,* ☎ *45/232–434. DC, MC, V. Closed Sun.*

$$ ✕ **Centro Español.** This is the headquarters of an association that promotes Spanish culture in Temuco, but it opens its basement dining room to all for lunch and dinner. You have your choice of four of five rotating prix-fixe menus. There will always be something Spanish, something seafood, and something meaty to choose from. *Jamón de Serrano,*

Close-Up

THE PEOPLE OF THE LAND

THE MAPUCHE PROFOUNDLY affected the history of southern Chile. For almost 300 years this indigenous group fought to keep colonial powers out of their land. The Spanish referred to these people as the Araucanos, from a word in the Quechua language meaning "brave and valiant warriors." In their own Mapudungun language, today spoken by some 400,000 people, the word Mapuche means "people of the land." In colonial times only the Spanish missionaries, who were in close contact with the Mapuche, seemed to grasp what this meant. "There are no people in the world," one of them wrote, "who so love and value the land where they were born."

Chilean schoolchildren learning about the Mapuche are likely to read about Lautaro, a feared and respected young chief whose military tactics were instrumental in driving out the Spanish. They are less likely to hear about the tightly knit family structure or nomadic lifestyle of the Mapuche. Even the region's two museums dedicated to Mapuche culture, located in Temuco and Valdivia, have traditionally focused on the three-century war with the Spaniards. They toss around terms like *pacificación* (meaning "to pacify" or "to tame") to describe the waves of European immigrants who settled in the Lake District at the end of the 1800s, the beginning of the end of Mapuche dominance in the region.

Life has been difficult for the Mapuche since the signing of a peace treaty in 1881. Their land was slowly taken by the Chilean government. Some 200,000 Mapuche today are living on 3,000 *reducciones* (literally meaning "reductions"), operated much like reservations in the United States. Other Mapuche have migrated to the cities, in particular fast-growing Temuco, in search of employment. Many have lost their identity in the urban landscape, scraping together a living as handicraft vendors.

A new resurgence in Mapuche pride these days takes several forms, some peaceful, some militant. Mapuche demonstrations in the cities are now commonplace, many calling attention to deplorable conditions on the reducciones. Some are seeking the return of their land, while others are fighting against the encroachment of power companies damming the rivers and logging interests cutting down the forests. News reports occasionally recount attacks and counterattacks between indigenous groups and farmers in remote rural areas.

But awareness of Mapuche history is rising. Both major museums are devoting more of their space to the art, language, and culture of this people who, according to the latest census figures, make up about 1 million of Chile's population of 16 million. Both institutions spend ample time these days discussing the group's distinctive textiles, with their bold rhomboid, triangular, and zigzagging lines. Both museums also devote considerable space to traditional animal-shape pottery.

There is also a new interest in the Mapuche language and its seven dialects. Mapudungun poetry movingly describes the sadness and dilemma of integration into modern life, of becoming lost in the anonymity of the urban landscape. Never understood by others who shared their land, the Mapuche may finally make their cause known.

–Jeffrey Van Fleet

a salty type of ham, is a specialty. ⊠ *Brunes 483,* ☎ *45/217–700. AE, DC, MC, V. Closed Sun.*

$$ ✕ **Mercado Municipal.** In the central market around the produce stalls are small stands offering such typical Chilean meals as cazuela and pastel de choclo. Many have actually taken on the trappings of sit-down restaurants, and a few even have air-conditioning. The complex closes at 8 in the summer and 6 the rest of the year, so late-night dining is not an option. ⊠ *Manuel Rodríguez 960,* ☎ *no phone.*

$–$$ ✕ **Confitería Central.** Coffee and homemade pastries are the specialties of this café and salón de té, but sandwiches and other simple dishes are also available. Piping-hot empanadas are served on Sundays and holidays. ⊠ *Bulnes 442,* ☎ *45/210–083. DC, MC, V.*

$–$$ ✕ **Grill de la Piscina Municipal.** The Municipal Pool Grill has a pretty utilitarian name, but this open-air steak restaurant is an excellent place to stop for lunch, especially if you're traveling with children. You can savor a good meal and the pleasant view while the kids splash around in the water. ⊠ *Av. Pablo Neruda 1080,* ☎ *45/248–189. No credit cards. Closed Mon. in winter.*

$$ ✕▥ **Hotel Frontera.** This lovely old hotel is really two in one, with "nuevo" and "clásico" wings facing each other across Avenida Bulnes. Tastefully decorated rooms have double-paned windows to keep out the street noise. If you're on a budget, opt for the less expensive rooms in the newer wing. La Taberna ($$–$$$), the downstairs restaurant on the clásico side, has excellent international dining, as well as an orchestra and dancing on weekends. ⊠ *Bulnes 733–726,* ☎ *45/200–400,* FAX *45/200–401,* WEB *www.hotelfrontera.cl. 60 rooms, 2 suites. Restaurant, bar, minibars, indoor pool, convention center, meeting room. AE, DC, MC, V.*

$ ✕▥ **Hotel Continental.** Chile's oldest lodging, the Hotel Continental
★   first flung open its doors in 1890. Temuco's grande dame is definitely showing her age, but that's part of the charm. The hotel has hosted a slew of historical figures, including Nobel laureates Pablo Neruda and Gabriela Mistral and former presidents Salvador Allende and Pedro Aguirre Cerda. Checkered in black and white tiles, the lobby is adorned with leather furniture, antique bronze lamps, and handsome trim in woods like *alerce* and *raulí*. Rooms, tastefully painted in ash-blue and cream tones, have hardwood floors and lofty ceilings. In honor of the Alzuget family, which has run the establishment for 70 years, the restaurant ($$–$$$) serves very good French cuisine. Good choices include the steak au poivre and the salade Niçoise. ⊠ *Antonio Varas 708,* ☎ *45/238–973,* FAX *45/233–830,* WEB *www.continental.nt.cl. 40 rooms, 18 with bath. Restaurant, bar, meeting room. AE, DC, MC, V.*

$$$ ▥ **Hotel Terraverde.** Part of Chile's Panamericana chain, Temuco's most luxurious lodging combines all the comforts of a modern hotel with a hunting-lodge decor. The dramatic, glass-enclosed spiral staircase has a view of Cerro Ñielol. Cheerful rooms have lovely wood furnishings. Rates include a huge breakfast buffet, a nice change from the roll and coffee served at most other lodgings in the region. ⊠ *Av. Prat 220,* ☎ *45/239–999; 2/234–9610 in Santiago,* FAX *45/239–455; 2/234–9608 in Santiago,* WEB *www.panamericanahoteles.cl. 74 rooms, 10 suites. Restaurant, piano bar, in-room safe, minibars, no-smoking rooms, pool, convention center, meeting rooms. AE, DC, MC, V.*

$$ ▥ **Don Eduardo Hotel.** Orange outside and inside, this pleasant nine-story hotel is made up entirely of cozy furnished apartments. All have two or three bedrooms and kitchenettes. An eager-to-please staff tends to your needs. ⊠ *Bello 755,* ☎ *45/214–133,* FAX *45/215–554. 33 apartments. Business services. AE, DC, MC, V.*

$$ ▥ **Holiday Inn Express.** Adjoining a shopping mall on the northern outskirts of town, this hotel is one of four of the chain's outlets in Chile.

It comes complete with U.S.-style comforts, including the do-it-your-self breakfast for which the chain is known. ⊠ *Av. Rudecindo Ortega 1800,* ☎ *45/223–300,* FAX *45/224–100,* WEB *www.hiexpress.com. 62 rooms. Pool, gym, business services. AE, MC, V.*

$$ ⊞ **Hotel Aitué.** The outside is unimposing, but this small, pleasant business-class hotel has bright, airy rooms with a tan and lavender color scheme. They come complete with minibars and music systems. ⊠ *Antonio Varas 1048,* ☎ *45/211–917,* FAX *45/212–608. 34 rooms. Bar, minibars, meeting rooms, business services. AE, DC, MC, V.*

$$ ⊞ **Nuevo Hotel Turismo.** Originally established as a budget accommodation, this three-story hotel retains its bland facade. The interior has been upgraded, with a comfortable lobby and rooms with their own music systems. A lime-green color scheme reigns throughout. ⊠ *A. Lynch 563,* ☎ *45/213–151,* FAX *45/232–902,* WEB *www.nuevohotelturismo.cl. 30 rooms. Bar, restaurant, laundry service. AE, DC, MC, V.*

$ ⊞ **Hotel Espelette.** This simple hotel a few blocks from the main square has rooms surrounding a large lobby overflowing with knickknacks. The decor throughout—flowers all over the wallpaper and drapes—echoes the Basque origins of the owners. The rooms are large and airy. Soft beds compensate for hard pillows the size of watermelons. ⊠ *Claro Solar 492,* ☎ FAX *45/234–805. 9 rooms, 4 with bath. Breakfast room. AE, DC, MC, V.*

Shopping

The **Mercado Municipal** is one of the best places in the country to find Mapuche woolen ponchos, pullovers, and blankets. The interior of the 1930 structure has been extensively remodeled, giving the place a more spacious feel. The low-key artisan vendors share the complex with butchers, fishmongers and fruit sellers. There is no bargaining, but the prices are fair. ⊠ *Manuel Rodríguez 960.* ☉ *Dec.–Mar., Mon.–Sat. 8–6, Sun. 8:30–3.*

A little more rough-and-tumble than the Mercado Municipal is the **Feria Libre.** You can bargain hard with the Mapuche vendors who sell their crafts and produce in the blocks surrounding the railroad station and bus terminal. Leave the camera behind, as the vendors aren't happy about being photographed. ⊠ *Barros Arana and Miraflores.* ☉ *Mon.–Sat. 9–2.*

Outdoor Activities and Sports

Conaf (⊠ Av. Bilbao 931, ☎ 45/236–312 or 45/238–900) provides maps and other information about nearby national parks. In the summer it also organizes hikes in Parque Nacional Conguillío. The agency is strict with permits to ascend the nearby volcanos, so expect to show evidence of your ability and experience.

Parque Nacional Conguillío

❷ *91 km (54 mi) east of Temuco.*

Volcán Llaima, which erupted as recently as 1994, is the brooding centerpiece of Parque Nacional Conguillío. The 3,125-meter (10,200-ft) monster, one of the continent's most active volcanos, has altered the landscape—much of the park's southern portion is a moonscape of hardened lava flow. But in the 610-square-km (235-square-mi) park's northern sector you'll find thousands of umbrella-like araucaria pines, often known as monkey puzzle trees.

The Sierra Nevada trail is the most popular for short hiking. The three-hour trek begins at park headquarters on Laguna Conguillío, continuing northeast to Laguna Captrén. The inaugural section of the Sendero de Chile, a hiking and biking trail, opened in 2001. Skirting the shores of Laguna Captrén, it will eventually span the entire length of the country.

Heavy snow can cut off the area in winter, so November to March is the best time to visit the park's eastern sector. Conguillío's western sector, Los Paraguas, comes into its own in winter because of a small ski center. ⊠ *Entrances at Melipeuco and Curacautín,* ☏ *45/298–221 in Temuco.* 🖃 *Admission.* ⊙ *Dec.–Mar., daily 8 AM–10 PM; Apr.–Nov., daily 8–5.*

Lodging

$$–$$$ 🏠 **Cabañas Conguillío.** The only accommodation available close to the park, Cabañas Conguillío rents basic four- or six-person cabins built around the trunks of araucaria trees. There's also a restaurant. ⊠ *Laguna Conguillío,* ☏ *45/213–291 or 45/214–363. 10 cabins. Restaurant. No credit cards. Closed Apr.–Nov.*

Villarrica

❸ *87 km (52 mi) southeast of Temuco.*

Villarrica was founded in 1552, but the Mapuche wars prevented extensive settlement of the area until the early 20th century. Today, the pleasant town on the lake of the same name is the first community you'll encounter in one of the loveliest, least spoiled areas of the southern Andes. Villarrica lives in the shadow of Pucón, its flashier neighbor a few miles down the road. Many travelers drive through without giving Villarrica a glance, but they're missing out. Villarrica has some wonderful hotels that won't give you high-season sticker shock. Well-maintained roads and convenient public transportation make Villarrica a good base for exploring the area.

The municipal museum, the **Museo Histórico y Arqueológico de Villarrica,** displays an impressive collection of Mapuche ceramics, masks, leather, and jewelry. A replica of a traditional indigenous hut, called a *ruca,* graces the front yard. It's made of thatch so tightly entwined that it's impermeable to rain. ⊠ *Pedro de Valdivia 1050,* ☏ *45/413–445.* 🖃 *Admission.* ⊙ *Jan.–Mar., Mon.–Sat. 9–1 and 6–10, Sun. 6–10; Apr.– Dec., weekdays 9–1 and 3–7.*

Dining and Lodging

$$–$$$ ✕ **Café 2001.** For a filling sandwich, a homemade küchen, and an espresso or cappuccino brewed from freshly ground beans, this is the place to stop in Villarrica. Pull up around a table in front or slip into one of the quieter booths by the fireplace in the back. The *lomito completo* sandwich—with a slice of pork, avocado, sauerkraut, tomato, and mayonnaise—is one of the best in the south. ⊠ *Camillo Henríquez 379,* ☏ *45/411–470. AE, DC, MC, V.*

$$–$$$ ✕ **The Travellers.** This restaurant's owners met by happenstance and decided to open a place serving food from their far-flung homelands. The result is a place that serves one or two dishes from Thailand, Italy, Mexico, and many countries in between. While you chow down on an enchilada, your companions might be having spaghetti with meatballs and sweet-and-sour pork. Dining on the front lawn under umbrella-covered tables is the best option for a summer evening. ⊠ *Valentín Letelier,* ☏ *45/412–830. AE, DC, MC, V.*

$$ 🏠 **El Parque.** Set amid 20 acres of forest, this 70-year-old rustic retreat offers commanding views of Lago Villarrica from just about everywhere—the plush lobby, the sitting area, and the restaurant. With a bed-and-breakfast atmosphere, rooms in the main house are decorated with warm earth tones. Eleven modern cabins amble down the hill to private beach and dock. Each cabin, which accommodates 2 to 10 peo-

When you pack your MCI Calling Card, it's like packing your loved ones along too.

Your MCI Calling Card is the easy way to stay in touch when you travel. Use it to call to and from over 125 countries. Plus, every time you call, you can earn frequent flier miles. So wherever your travels take you, call home with your MCI Calling Card. It's even easy to get one. Just visit **www.mci.com/worldphone**.

EASY TO CALL WORLDWIDE

1. Just enter the WorldPhone® access number of the country you're calling from.
2. Enter or give the operator your MCI Calling Card number.
3. Enter or give the number you're calling.

Argentina	0800-222-6249
Belize	815
Brazil	000-8012

Chile	800-207-300
Colombia ◆	980-9-16-0001
Costa Rica ◆	0800-012-2222
Ecuador ⁑	999-170
El Salvador	800-1567
Guatemala ◆	99-99-189
Honduras ⁑	8000-122
Mexico	01-800-021-8000
Nicaragua	166
Panama	00800-001-0108
Venezuela ◆ ⁑	800-11140

◆ Public phones may require deposit of coin or phone card for dial tone. ⁑ Limited availability.

EARN FREQUENT FLIER MILES

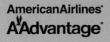

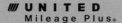

SEE THE WORLD
IN FULL COLOR

Fodor's Exploring Guides bring all the great sights
vividly to life with hundreds of photographs,
fascinating historical background, and colorful
anecdotes. Detailed maps and practical information
keep you headed in the right direction.

Pair a **Fodor's** Exploring Guide with your trusted
Gold Guide for a complete planning package.

ple, comes with kitchen, fireplace, and terrace. ⊠ *Camino Villarrica–Pucón Km 2.5,* ☎ *45/411–120,* FAX *45/411–090,* WEB *www.hotelelparque.cl. 8 rooms, 11 cabins. Restaurant, pool, tennis court, meeting room. AE, MC, V.*

$$ ⊞ **Hostería de la Colina.** The friendly American owners are among the
★ many reasons for staying at this half-century-old lodging on a hill south of town. Besides attentive service, Glen and Beverly Aldrich provide little touches like homemade ice cream. Rooms in the main house are a mix of large and small, carpets and hardwood floors, all tastefully decorated with wood furnishings. Some rooms have direct access to the terrace and its stupendous views of Lago Villarrica. Two bright, airy hillside cottages are carpeted and wood-paneled and have private patios. There's a hot tub heated by a wood-burning stove and a serene garden with a *vivero* (greenhouse) that attracts a variety of birds. Rates include a huge American breakfast. ⊠ *Las Colinas 115,* ☎ FAX *45/411–503,* WEB *www.hosteriadelacolina.com. 9 rooms, 2 cabins. Restaurant, bar. AE, DC, MC, V.*

$$ ⊞ **Hotel El Ciervo.** Villarrica's oldest hotel is an unimposing house on a quiet street, but inside you'll find elegant details such as wrought-iron fixtures and wood-burning fireplaces. Spacious rooms, some with their own fireplaces, have huge beds and sparkling bathrooms. Just outside is a lovely pool and a secluded patio. Rates include an enormous German breakfast with loads of fruit, muesli, and fresh milk. El Ciervo also offers all-inclusive seven-day tour packages. ⊠ *General Körner 241,* ☎ *45/411–215,* FAX *45/410–925,* WEB *www.villarricanet.com/elciervo. 12 rooms. Restaurant, pool, laundry service, meeting rooms. AE, DC, MC, V.*

$ ⊞ **Monteblanco Hotel.** The owner, a retired furniture maker from Italy who decided to get into the hotel business, continues to fashion many of the wood furnishings for this lodging in the center of town. The pleasant rooms upstairs all have small balconies. The tiled bathrooms are clean and bright, but the showers are tiny, with barely enough room to turn around. ⊠ *Pedro de Valdivia 1011,* ☎ *45/411–798,* FAX *45/415–136,* WEB *www.villarrica.co.cl/mtc. 12 rooms. Restaurant, bar, meeting rooms. AE, DC, MC, V.*

Pucón

❹ *25 km (15 mi) east of Villarrica.*

The trendy resort town of Pucón, on the southern shore of Lago Villarrica, attracts wealthy, fashionable Chileans. Like their counterparts in the Colorado ski resort of Vail, they come to enjoy their luxurious vacation homes, stroll along the main strip, and flock to the major night spots. But for every fan, Pucón has a detractor who laments the town's growth. A stream of ugly billboards appears at the turnoff from the Pan-American Highway and continues until you reach town. But many don't seem to mind, and Pucón remains one of Chile's top tourist draws.

Dining and Lodging

$$$–$$$$ ✕ **¡Viva Perú!** As befits the name, Peruvian cuisine reigns supreme at this restaurant in a thatch-roof house with rustic wooden tables. Try the *ají de gallina* (hen stew with cheese, milk, and peppers), or the ceviche, thoroughly cooked but served cold. You can dine on the porch or order to carry out. ⊠ *O'Higgins 761,* ☎ *45/444–285. No credit cards.*

$$$ ✕ **En Alta Mar.** The best seafood in Pucón is served here, so don't be frightened off by the nondescript decor. You'll find basic wooden tables and the ubiquitous nautical theme. ⊠ *Fresia and Urrutia,* ☎ *45/442–294. AE. Closed Sun.*

$$-$$$ ✕ **Arabian Restaurant.** It may not have a very original name, but this sidewalk café dishes up tasty falafel and shawarma, reflecting the friendly owner's Palestinian roots. There is a tiny dining area inside, but most everyone opts for the outdoor tables. ✉ *Fresia 354,* ☎ *45/ 443–469. No credit cards.*

$$-$$$ ✕ **Living Sushi.** The Lake District is awash in seafood restaurants, but not this kind. Pucón now has an honest-to-goodness sushi bar. It's very modern, with a black-and-white color scheme accented with chrome. After midnight it's transformed into Living Pucón, a late-night club playing soft rock. ✉ *O'Higgins 691,* ☎ *09/778–0022. No credit cards.*

$ ✕🏨 **¡école!** Part youth hostel and part beach house, this friendly hostería takes its name from a Chilean expression meaning "Great!" It has a cozy ambience and attentive service. The environmentally conscious folks here can organize hiking and horseback riding trips and expeditions to volcanos and hot springs, as well as arrange for Spanish lessons and massages. The vegetarian restaurant, a rarity in the Lake District, is worth a special trip. The cuisine is truly international; choose among lasagna, burritos, or moussaka. It's served in the sunny courtyard or cozy dining room, depending on the weather. ✉ *General Urrutia 592,* ☎ FAX *45/441–675,* WEB *www.ecole.cl. 25 rooms, 16 with bath. Restaurant, travel services. DC, MC, V.*

$$$$ 🏨 **Hotel Antumalal.** Perched atop a cliff overlooking Lago Villarrica,
★ this Frank Lloyd Wright–inspired masterpiece is easily one of the best hotels in Chile. Queen Elizabeth, Neil Armstrong, and Jimmy Stewart are just a few who thought so. This family-run hotel, just outside of Pucón, has the atmosphere of a country inn. The cozy rooms have fireplaces and huge windows overlooking the spectacularly landscaped grounds. If you tire of relaxing with a refreshing pisco sour on the wisteria-shaded deck, just ask owner Rony Pollak to arrange an adventure for you. Favorites include fly-fishing, white-water rafting, and volcano cave tours. ✉ *Casilla 84,* ☎ *45/441–011,* FAX *45/441013,* WEB *www.antumalal.com. 18 rooms, 2 suites. Restaurant, bar, pool, travel services. AE, DC, MC, V.*

$$$$ 🏨 **Hotel del Lago.** This glitzy hotel is a little short on charm, but has everything else you could hope for—an indoor pool, a health spa, even a movie theater. Enter through the five-story atrium lobby, then let one of the glass elevators whisk you upstairs. The rooms are simple and elegant, with blond wood and crisp white linens. The hotel is known as "the Casino" for its Las Vegas–style ground floor, complete with rows of one-arm bandits and tables for roulette and poker. ✉ *Miguel Ansorena 23,* ☎ *45/291–000; 2/232–3111 in Santiago,* FAX *45/291–200; 2/245–6008 in Santiago,* WEB *www.hoteldellago.cl. 81 rooms, 2 suites. Restaurant, bar, snack bar, minibars, 2 pools, massage, sauna, exercise room, casino, business services, meeting room. AE, DC, MC, V.*

$$$ 🏨 **Hotel Huincahue.** Close to the center of town, the elegant Huincahue has the attentive service that only a small hotel can offer. The lobby of the German-style building, warmed by a roaring fire, is brightened by lots of windows. Rates for the airy rooms include a hearty American breakfast. ✉ *Pedro de Valdivia 375,* ☎ FAX *45/443–540,* WEB *www.hotel-huincahue.cl. 20 rooms. Bar, pool, laundry service. AE, DC, MC, V.*

$$-$$$ 🏨 **Del Volcán.** In the center of Pucón, this chalet-style hotel has apartments that sleep up to six people. Many of the generously proportioned rooms also have balconies. In keeping with the region's *Mitteleuropa* atmosphere, the furnishings look like they come straight from Germany, with checked fabrics covering the carefully fluffed duvets. ✉ *Fresia 420,* ☎ *45/442–055,* FAX *45/442–053,* WEB *www.pucon.com/delvolcan. 18 apartments. In-room safes, kitchenettes, gym, free parking. DC, MC, V.*

$$-$$$ 🏨 **Gran Hotel Pucón.** This imposing hotel, Pucón's largest, has wonderful views of Lago Villarrica. Its location right on the shore provides

direct access to the beach. The rooms, however, are somewhat plain. ⊠ *Clemente Holzapfel 190,* ☎ *45/441–001; 2/353–0000 in Santiago,* FAX *2/207–4586 in Santiago,* WEB *www.granhotelpucon.cl. 145 rooms. 2 restaurants, bar, 3 pools, massage, sauna, squash. AE, DC, MC, V.*

$$ ⛱ **Hotel Gudenschwager.** Once a rural fishing lodge, this attractive three-story building has a comfortable country atmosphere. Covered with the wooden shakes typical of southern Chile, it has a view of a corner of the lake. ⊠ *Pedro de Valdivia 12,* ☎ FAX *45/441–156, 20 rooms, 1 suite. Restaurant. DC, MC, V.*

$$ ⛱ **Hotel Munich.** A Bavarian-style hotel near the center of town, Hotel Munich stands out because the owner is a stickler for good service. Each of the rooms, furnished in native woods and decorated in soft pastels, is unique. Rates include an enormous buffet breakfast. ⊠ *Gerónimo de Alderete 275,* ☎ FAX *45/442–293,* WEB *www.pucon.com/munich. 14 rooms. Bar, café, laundry service. No credit cards.*

$$ ⛱ **La Posada Plaza Pucón.** This dark-wood chalet-style house stands in an orchard on a quiet street a couple of blocks from the city center. The rooms, each with a small sitting alcove, are more modern than the knickknack-filled reading room and lobby. ⊠ *Pedro de Valdivia 191,* ☎ *45/441–088,* FAX *45/441–762,* WEB *www.hotelplazapucon.cl. 20 rooms, 4 cabins. Restaurant, bar, pool. AE, DC, MC, V.*

$$ ⛱ **Termas de San Luis.** The famous San Luis hot springs are the main attraction of this hideaway east of Pucón. Here you can rent a rustic cabin that will sleep up to six people. Rates include all meals and free use of the baths. If you're not staying here, $12 gets you a day of soaking in the thermal springs. ⊠ *Camillo Henríquez 301, Catripulli,* ☎ *63/412–880 or 63/411–388. 8 cabins. No credit cards.*

$ ⛱ **Hostería La Poza.** This friendly hotel with a family-style ambience is a good option for those on a budget. Ask for a room out of earshot of the television in the lobby, or opt for one of the secluded cabins. ⊠ *Holzapfel 11,* ☎ FAX *45/441–320. 9 rooms, 2 cabins. No credit cards.*

$ ⛱ **Kila Leufu.** Part of a growing agro-tourism trend in Chile, a Mapuche family has opened its red farmhouse, 15 minutes from Pucón, to temporary urban refugees anxious to partake of rural life. You can bake bread and milk the cows if you like, or just relax and read. Horseback riding excursions are an extra $20. ⊠ *Camino a Curarrehe, Puente Cabedane,* ☎ *09/711–8064,* WEB *www.kilaleufu.homestad.com. 5 rooms, 2 with bath. No credit cards.*

Outdoor Activities and Sports

BICYCLING

Pedal Aventura (⊠ General Urrutia 592, ☎ 45/441–675) specializes in mountain-bike rental during the summer. **Anden Sport** (⊠ O'Higgins 535, ☎ 45/441–048) is a good bet for bikes and other outdoor equipment.

WHITE-WATER RAFTING

Pucón is the center for rafting expeditions in the Lake District. In the capital, **Cascada Expediciones** (⊠ Orrego Luco 054, Santiago, ☎ 2/ 234–2274, FAX 2/233–9768) organizes white-water rafting trips in the region. William Hatcher of **Sol Y Nieve** (⊠ O'Higgins and Lincoyan, ☎ FAX 45/441–070) offers rafting trips and hiking and skiing excursions. Friendly **Aguaventura** (⊠ Palguín 336, ☎ 45/444–246) is a good bet for rafting, as well as canoeing and kayaking.

Parque Nacional Huerquehue

5 *35 km (21 mi) northeast of Pucón.*

Unless you're driving a four-wheel-drive vehicle, this 124-square-km (48-square-mi) park is accessible only during the summer. (And even then, a jeep isn't a bad idea.) It's worth a visit for the two-hour hike on the Lago Verde trail beginning at the ranger station near the park entrance. You head up into the Andes through groves of araucaria pines, eventually reaching three startlingly blue lagoons with panoramic views of the whole area, including distant Volcán Villarrica. ☎ 45/298–221 in Temuco. ☒ Admission. ☉ Dec.–Mar., daily 8 AM–10 PM; Apr.–Nov., daily 8–6.

Lodging

$$$$ ☷ **Termas de Huife.** Just outside Parque Nacional Huerquehue, this resort lets you relax in two steaming pools set beside an icy mountain stream. At the spa you can enjoy an individual bath, a massage, or both. The complex includes a handful of luxurious cabins, all of which have enormous tubs you can fill with water from the hot springs. For those just visiting for the day, there's a country house past the spa where you can soak in privacy. ☒ 33 km (20 mi) from Pucón on the road to Caburga, ☎ FAX 45/441–222, WEB www.pucon.com/huife. 10 cabins. Restaurant, bar, minibars. AE, DC, MC, V.

Parque Nacional Villarrica

★ ❻   15 km (9 mi) south of Pucón.

One of Chile's most popular national parks, Parque Nacional Villarrica offers skiing, hiking, and many other outdoor activities. The main draw, however, is the volcano that gives the 610-square-km (235-square-mi) national park its name. You don't need to have any climbing experience to reach the 3,116-meter (9,350-ft) summit of Volcán Villarrica, but a guide is a good idea. The volcano sits in the park's Sector Rucapillán, a Mapuche word meaning "house of the devil." That name is apt, as the perpetually smoldering volcano is one of South America's most active. Conaf closes off access to the trails at the slightest hint of volcanic activity. It's a steep uphill walk to the snow line, and then crampons and ice axes are needed. That equipment will be supplied by any of the Pucón outfitters that organize daylong excursions for about $60 per person. Your reward for the six-hour climb is the rare sight of an active crater, which continues to release clouds of sulfur gases and explosions of lava. You'll also be treated to superb views of the nearby volcanoes, the less-visited Quetrupillán and Lanín. ☒ 15 km (9 mi) south of Pucón, ☎ 45/298–221 in Temuco. ☒ Admission. ☉ Daily 8–6.

Camping
Volcán Villarrica–Sector Rucapillán. This camping area is in the midst of a forest of coigüe, Chile's massive red oaks. The site charges about $15 per person and provides very basic toilets. For more information, contact Conaf (☎ 45/562–313 or 45/274–141) in Temuco.

Outdoor Activities and Sports
The popular **Ski Pucón,** in the lap of Volcán Villarrica, is one of the best-equipped ski areas in southern Chile, with 20 runs for varying levels of experience, nine rope tows, three double-chair tows, and equipment rental. There's also a restaurant and coffee shop. Information about the facility can be obtained from the Gran Hotel Pucón. ☒ Parque Nacional Villarrica, ☎ 45/441–001; 2/353–0000 in Santiago, FAX 2/207–4586 in Santiago.

Lican Ray

❼   30 km (18 mi) south of Villarrica.

In the Mapuche language, Lican Ray means "flower among the stones." This pleasant, unhurried resort town is on Lago Calafquén, the first of a chain of seven lakes that spills over into Argentina. You can rent rowboats and sailboats along the shore. Lican Ray lacks Pucón's perfect manicure. With but one paved street, a lot of dust gets kicked up on a dry summer day.

Dining and Lodging

$$–$$$$ ✕ **Cábala Restaurant.** Impeccable service is the hallmark of this Italian restaurant on Lican Ray's main street. The brick-and-log building has plenty of windows where you can watch the summer crowds stroll by as you enjoy pizza and pasta. ⊠ *General Urrutia 201,* ☎ *45/431–176. AE, DC, MC, V. Closed Apr.–Nov.*

$$–$$$ ✕ **The Ñaños.** Hearty meats and stews are the offerings at Lican Ray's most popular eatery. Most people partake of their cazuelas on the plain terrace on the main street, but the wood-trimmed dining room is a lot cozier. ⊠ *General Urrutia 105,* ☎ *45/431–021. DC, MC, V.*

$$ 🏠 **Hotel Inaltulafquen.** This rambling old house sits in a garden on a quiet street fronting Playa Grande. The rooms are simple, but bright and airy and filled with plants. The cozy restaurant serves Chilean dishes. There's soft music playing in the background, but someone is bound to sit down at the piano and encourage the crowd to sing along. ⊠ *Punulef 510,* ☎ *45/431–115. 8 rooms, 6 with bath. Restaurant, bar. DC, MC, V.*

$ 🏠 **Hostal Hoffman.** An attentive German woman watches over this little house just outside town. You'll get lost in the plush chairs as you read a book in the sitting room. Rates include a huge breakfast with lots of homemade breads and pastries. ⊠ *Camino a Coñaripe 100,* ☎ FAX *45/431–109. 4 rooms. Breakfast room. No credit cards.*

Outdoor Activities and Sports

The peninsula on which Lican Ray sits has two gray-sand beaches. **Playa Chica,** the smaller of the beaches near Lican Ray, is south of town. It's popular for swimming. **Playa Grande,** to the west of Lican Ray, has rougher water.

LOS LAGOS

Los Lagos, the southern half of the Lake District, is a land of snow-capped volcanoes, rolling farmland and, of course, the shimmering lakes that give the region its name. This landscape is literally a work in progress, as it's part of the so-called Ring of Fire. Most of Chile's 55 active volcanoes are here.

For a region so conscious of its heritage, history is not much in evidence. Some of Chile's oldest colonial cities are in Los Lagos, yet you'll be disappointed if you come looking for colonial grandeur. Wars with indigenous peoples kept the Spaniards from building here for hundreds of years. An earthquake in 1960, the largest ever recorded in Chile, destroyed many older buildings around Valdivia.

Anxious to fill its *tierras baldías* (uncultivated lands), Chile worked tirelessly to promote the country's virtues to German, Austrian, and Swiss immigrants looking to start a new life. The newcomers quickly set up shop, constructing breweries, foundries, shipyards, and lumberyards. By the early part of the last century, Valdivia had become the country's foremost industrial center, aided in large part by the construction of a railroad from Santiago. To this day the region retains a distinctly Germanic feeling, and you'll swear you've taken a wrong turn to Bavaria when you pull into towns such as Frutillar or Puerto Octay.

Valdivia

❽ *120 km (72 mi) southwest of Villarrica.*

One of the Lake District's oldest and most beautiful cities, Valdivia gracefully combines Chilean wood-shingle construction with the architectural style of the well-to-do German settlers who colonized the area in the late 1800s. But the historic appearance is a bit of an illusion, as the 1960 earthquake destroyed all but a few historic riverfront buildings. The city painstakingly rebuilt its downtown area, seamlessly mixing old and new buildings. Today you can enjoy evening strolls through its quaint streets and along its two rivers, the Valdivia and the Calle Calle.

Valdivia's imposing modern **Catedral de Nuestra Señora del Rosario** faces the west side of the central plaza. A small museum inside documents the evangelization of the region's indigenous peoples from the 16th through 19th centuries. ✉ *Independencia 514,* ☎ *63/232–040.* 🎫 *Free.* ☉ *Dec.–Mar., Tues.–Sun. 10–1 and 3–7; Apr.–Nov., Tues.–Fri. 10–1 and 3–7.*

The awning-covered **Mercado Fluvial,** in the southern shadow of the bridge leading to Isla Teja, is a perfect place to soak up the sights, sounds, and smells of a real fish market. ✉ *Arturo Prat and Libertad,* ☎ *no phone.* ☉ *Mon.–Sat. 8–3.*

For a historic overview of the region, visit to the **Museo Histórico y Antropológico Maurice van de Maele,** on neighboring Isla Teja. The collection focuses on the city's colonial period, during which it was settled by the Spanish, burned by the Mapuche, and invaded by Dutch corsairs. Downstairs rooms re-create the interior of the late-19th-century Anwandter mansion that belonged to one of Valdivia's first immigrant families; the upper floor delves into Mapuche art and culture. ✉ *Los Laureles, Isla Teja,* ☎ *63/212–872.* 🎫 *Admission.*

Fondly known around town as the "MAC," the **Museo de Arte Contemporáneo** is one of Chile's foremost modern art museums. This Isla Teja complex was built on the site of the old Anwandter brewery destroyed in the 1960 earthquake. Recent exhibits include "Pintura/Fotografía," in which artists blurred the line between painting and photography. ✉ *Los Laureles, Isla Teja,* ☎ *63/221–968,* WEB *www.macvaldivia.uach.cl.* 🎫 *Admission.*

The **Jardín Botánico,** north and west of the Universidad Austral campus, is awash with flowers and plants native to the area. It's a lovely place to walk whatever the season, but it's particularly enjoyable in spring and summer. ✉ *Isla Teja,* ☎ *63/216–964.* 🎫 *Admission.*

Valdivia means beer to many Chileans, and **Cervecería Kunstmann** brews up the country's beloved lager. The Anwandter family immigrated from Germany a century-and-a-half ago, bringing along their beer-making know-how. The cervecería, on the road to Niebla, offers interesting guided tours. There's also a small museum and a souvenir shop where you can buy the requisite caps, mugs, and T-shirts. ✉ *Ruta T350 No. 950,* ☎ *63/292–969.* 🎫 *Free.* ☉ *Daily noon–6.*

OFF THE
BEATEN PATH

ISLA HUAPI – Some 20% of Chile's 1 million Mapuche live on reducciones, or reservations. One of the most welcoming communities is on Isla Huapi, a leafy island in the middle of deep-blue Lago Ranco. It's out of the way—about 80 km (48 mi) southeast of Valdivia—but worth the trip for those interested in Mapuche culture. A boat departs from Futorno, on the northern shore of the lake, at 7 AM Monday, Wednesday, and Friday, returning at 5 PM. The pastoral quiet of Isla Huapi is broken once a year in January or February with the convening of the island council, in conjunction with the Lepún harvest festival. You are welcome during the festival, but be unobtrusive with your camera.

Dining, Lodging, and Camping

$$$–$$$$ ✕ **Cervecería Kunstmann.** On the road to Niebla, this restaurant is attached to the brewery that makes Chile's celebrated Kunstmann lager. Along with the typical Chilean fare, the friendly folks serve wurst and sauerkraut and, of course, giant chilled mugs of their refreshing beers with lots of German *Gemütlichkeit* (conviviality). ✉ *Ruta T350 No. 950,* ☎ *63/292–969. DC, MC, V.*

$$$–$$$$ ✕ **Salón de Té Entrelagos.** This swanky café caters to Valdivian business executives. The specialties are sandwiches such as the Isla Teja— a grilled chicken sandwich with tomato, artichoke hearts, asparagus, olives, and red peppers—decadent crepes, and sweet-tooth goodies. ✉ *Vicente Pérez Rosales 640,* ☎ *63/218–333. No credit cards.*

$$–$$$$ ✕ **Camino de Luna.** This romantically named restaurant floats on the Río Valdivia just north of the Pedro de Valdivia bridge. As the city is only a few miles from the ocean, it's no surprise that seafood is a speciality here. The *congrío calle calle* (conger eel in a cheese-and-tomato sauce) is particularly good. Tables by the windows offer views of Isla Teja. ✉ *Av. Prat Costanera s/n,* ☎ *63/213–788. AE, DC, MC, V.*

$$–$$$ ✕ **Café Haussmann.** Valdivia was the center of German immigration at the turn of the last century, and this is one place that takes advantage of that fact. Sample the excellent *crudos* (steak tartare) and German-style sandwiches. Don't forget the delicious küchen for dessert. ✉ *O'Higgins 394,* ☎ *63/213–878. AE, DC, MC, V. Closed Mar. 15– Apr. 15.*

$$–$$$ ✕ **Café Paula.** This café is part of a chain famous for ice cream and pastries, but the Valdivia branch also offers sandwiches and other light fare. ✉ *Vicente Pérez Rosales 633,* ☎ *63/212–328. DC, MC, V.*

$$–$$$ ✕ **La Calesa.** If you're curious to try other South American cuisines, head to this well-known Peruvian restaurant near the center of town. A good introduction is the *ají* (chicken stew with cheese, milk, and peppers). Be careful not to burn your mouth, as Peruvian dishes, particularly the stews, are spicier than their Chilean counterparts. ✉ *Yungay 735,* ☎ *63/225–467. AE, DC, MC, V. Closed Sun. No lunch Sat.*

$$$ 🏨 **Hotel Pedro de Valdivia.** This pink palace near Valdivia's central
★ square is, in a word, magnificent. With pleasant views of the Río Calle Calle, the historic hotel is most notable for its elegant appointments and excellent service. All the tasteful rooms have lovely wood furniture, and some have small terraces. ✉ *Carampague 190,* ☎ *63/212– 931,* FAX *63/203–888,* WEB *www.hotelpedrodevaldivia.telsur.cl. 77 rooms, 5 suites, 7 apartments. Restaurant, bar, pool, meeting room, airport shuttle, free parking. AE, DC, MC, V.*

$$$ 🏨 **Hotel Puerta del Sur.** Lavish pampering is what you can expect at this highly regarded lodging. Spacious rooms, all with views of the river, are decorated in soft lavender tones. Play a few games of tennis, then hit the pool or relax in the hot tub. ✉ *Los Lingues 950, Isla Teja,* ☎ *63/224–500; 2/633–5101 in Santiago,* FAX *63/211–046; 2/633–6541 in Santiago. 40 rooms, 2 suites. Restaurant, 2 bars, in-room safes, pool, outdoor hot tub, sauna, tennis court, volleyball, dock, meeting room, travel services. AE, DC, MC, V.*

$$ 🏨 **Hotel Isla Teja.** Situated on the island of the same name, this affordable hotel doubles as student housing for the nearby Universidad Austral. The guest rooms are quiet and comfortable, with modern amenities. ✉ *Las Encinas 220, Isla Teja,* ☎ *63/215–014,* FAX *63/214–911. 95 rooms. Restaurant, bar, meeting room, travel services. AE, DC, MC, V.*

$$ ⊞ **Hotel Naguilán.** Seven blocks south of the city center, this charming hotel has a garden with a pool where you can relax while you watch the boats pass by on the Río Valdivia. Ask for a room in the newer building; they are bigger and have balconies. This is part of the Best Western chain, so you can expect the usual amenities. ⊠ *General Lagos 1927,* ☎ *63/212–851,* ℻ *63/219–130,* ⓦ *www.bestwestern.com. 32 rooms, 3 suites. Restaurant, bar, pool, dock, baby-sitting, laundry service, meeting room, free parking. AE, DC, MC, V.*

$ ⊞ **Hostal Centro Torreón.** Originally constructed in 1916 for a family of German settlers, this hotel offers basic lodgings inside one of Valdivia's more architecturally appealing homes. A stairway of *pellín* oak twists up to the bright second-story rooms. José Retamales Prelle, the hotel's amiable proprietor, gives discounts to Hosteling International members. ⊠ *Vicente Pérez Rosales 783,* ☎ *63/212–622,* ℻ *63/203– 217. 13 rooms. Breakfast room, café, travel services. DC, MC, V.*

$ ⊞ **Hostal Prat.** The friendly, eager-to-please owner and the reasonable rates make this one of those terrific finds that you want to keep to yourself. Rooms in this lodging near the bus station are mostly tan, but a few splashes of color liven things up. ⊠ *Valdivia 595,* ☎ *63/222–020. 10 rooms. No credit cards.*

$ ⚠ **Complejo Turístico Isla Teja.** With an attractive view of the Río Valdivia, the campsites at this facility sit in the middle of an apple orchard. There is electricity and hot showers. ⊠ *Los Cipreses 1125, Isla Teja,* ☎ *63/213–584,* ℻ *63/225–855.*

Outdoor Activities and Sports

Valdivia-based tour operator **Jumping Chile** (⊠ Pasaje 11 No. 50, ☎ 63/253–377) organizes marvelous fly-fishing trips for two to six people in the nearby rivers.

Niebla

❾ *18 km (11 mi) southwest of Valdivia.*

To protect the all-important city of Valdivia, the Spanish constructed a series of strategic fortresses at Niebla, where the Valdivia and Tornagaleones rivers meet. At the 1671 **Fuerte de Niebla,** portions of the fort and its 18 cannons have been restored. The old commander's house serves as a small museum documenting the era's military history. ⊠ *West of Niebla.* ▧ *Admission.* ⏱ *Nov.–Mar., daily 9–8; Apr.–Oct., daily Tues.–Sun. 10–5.*

Across the estuary from the Fuerte de Niebla, the 1645 **Castillo San Sebastián de la Cruz** is large and well preserved. In the January–February summer season, historic reenactments of Spanish military maneuvers take place daily at 4 and 6. ⊠ *North of Corral.* ▧ *Admission.* ⏱ *Dec.–Mar., daily 8:30 AM–10 PM; Apr.–Nov., daily 9–5.*

Outdoor Activities and Sports

Just north of Niebla you'll find the green-blue water of the popular **Playa Los Molinos.** A few more miles north, past the villages of Loncollén and Calfuco, is **Playa Curiñanco.** The waves can be a bit strong, so be cautious.

Osorno

❿ *107 km (65 mi) southeast of Valdivia.*

Workaday Osorno is the least visited of the Lake District's four major cities. It is one of the oldest cities in Chile, but the Mapuche prevented foreigners from settling here until the late 19th century. Like other communities in the region, it bears the imprint of the German settlers who came here in the 1880s. Osorno, situated in a bend of the Río Rahue, makes a convenient base for exploring the nearby national parks.

Osorno's friendly **tourist office** (⊠ Plaza de Armas, ☎ 64/264–250) offers free daily tours in summer. Each day has a different focus: walks around the city, fruit orchards, or nearby farms are a few of the offerings. Tours leave at 10:30 AM from the kiosk on the north side of the square.

The 1960 earthquake left Osorno with little historic architecture, but a **row of 19th-century houses** miraculously survived on Calle Juan Mackenna between Lord Cochrane and Freire. Their distinctively sloped roofs, to provide for adequate drainage of rain and snow, are replicated in many of Osorno's newer houses. The modern **Catedral de San Mateo Apostol** fronts the Plaza de Armas and is topped with a tower resembling a bishop's mitre. "Turn off your cell phone," the sign at the door admonishes those who enter. "You don't need it to communicate with God."

The **Museo Municipal Osorno** contains a decent collection of Mapuche artifacts, Chilean and Spanish firearms, and exhibits devoted to the German settlement of Osorno. Housed in a pink neoclassical building dating from 1929, this is one of the few older structures in the city center. ⊠ *Manuel Antonio Matta 809*, ☎ *64/238–615.* ▣ *Admission.* ☉ *Jan.–Mar., daily 11–7; Apr.–Nov., weekdays 9–noon and 2–5.*

Dining and Lodging

$$–$$$ ✕ **Club Alemán.** This was the first in a network of German associations in southern Chile. Established in 1862, it predated the first big waves of European immigration. Despite the exclusive-sounding name, anyone can dine here. Options are limited, however. There's usually a choice of four or five rotating prix-fixe menus for lunch and dinner, often including a seafood stew or a hearty cazuela, and lots of tasty küchen and other pastries for dessert. ⊠ *O'Higgins 563*, ☎ *64/232–784. AE, DC, MC, V.*

$$ ✕ **Café Central.** This diner, swathed in orange, sits on the Plaza de Armas next to the Gran Hotel Osorno. It's a great place to get a hearty American-style breakfast; burgers and sandwiches reign the rest of the day. The friendly, bustling staff speaks no English, but if it's clear you're North American an English menu will be presented with great fanfare. ⊠ *O'Higgins 610*, ☎ *64/257–711. DC, MC, V.*

$$ ▥ **Hotel García Hurtado de Mendoza.** One of Osorno's nicest lodgings, this stately hotel is two blocks from the Plaza de Armas. Its bright and airy rooms all have a stereo and VCR system. ⊠ *Juan Mackenna 1040*, ☎ *64/237–111,* FAX *64/237–115. 31 rooms. Restaurant, bar, meeting room, sauna. AE, DC, MC, V.*

$$ ▥ **Hotel Lagos del Sur.** This quiet lodging near the Plaza de Armas has sparkling white rooms splashed with a lot of warm greens and golds. The color scheme echoes the building's dark green exterior. Doubles include a small sitting room off to one side. ⊠ *O'Higgins 564*, ☎ *64/243–244,* FAX *64/243–696. 20 rooms. Bar, laundry service. AE, DC, MC, V.*

$$ ▥ **Hotel Rayantu.** With lots of large windows to let in the sun, this modern hotel feels open and airy. Many of the cheerful rooms look out onto the lovely pool in the rear. ⊠ *Patricio Lynch 1462*, ☎ *64/238–114,* FAX *64/238–116,* WEB *www.hotelrayantu.cl. 31 rooms, 6 suites. Restaurant, bar, pool, meeting rooms. AE, DC, MC, V.*

$ ▥ **Gran Hotel Osorno.** Osorno's grande dame, built in the era when art deco was all the rage, has stood the test of time. The five-story hotel has an unbeatable location on the Plaza de Armas. The rooms, although a tad dark, are clean and comfortable. Mercifully, the hotel's Power

Disco has closed, though the neon sign still blinks out front. ⊠ *O'Higgins 563,* ☏ *64/232–784,* FAX *64/234–137. 20 rooms. Restaurant, bar, laundry service, meeting room. AE, DC, MC, V.*

$ ☷ **Hotel Innsbruck.** Osorno's most Germanic hotel, the Innsbruck has half-timbered walls and cheery flower boxes in the windows. The vaulted ceilings give the simply furnished rooms a spacious feeling. ⊠ *Manuel Rodríguez 941,* ☏ *64/242–000,* FAX *64/243–490,* WEB *www.region10.cl/hotelinnsbruck.htm. 20 rooms. MC, V.*

En Route   An Osorno business executive's love for tail fins and V-8 engines led him to establish the **Auto Museum Moncopulli** about 25 km (16 mi) east of Osorno. His particular passion is the little-respected Studebaker, which account for 40 of the 50 vehicles on display. Elvis and Buddy Holly bop in the background to put you in the mood. ⊠ *Ruta 215, Puyehue,* ☏ *64/204–200.* ◪ *Admission.* ⊙ *Dec.–Mar., Tues.–Sun. 10–8; Apr.–Nov., Tues.–Sun. 10–6:30.*

Parque Nacional Puyehue

⑪ *81 km (49 mi) east of Osorno.*

Chile's most popular national park, Parque Nacional Puyehue draws crowds who come to bask in its famed hot springs. Most never venture beyond them, and that's a shame. A dozen miles east of the Aguas Calientes sector lies a network of short trails leading to evergreen forests with dramatic waterfalls. Truly adventurous types attempt the five-hour hike to the summit of 2,240-meter (7,350-ft) Volcán Puyehue. Access to the 1,070-square-km (413-square-mi) park is easy: head due east from Osorno on the highway leading to Argentina. ⊠ *Ruta 215,* ☏ *64/374–572.* ◪ *Admission.* ⊙ *Nov.–Mar., daily 8 AM–9 PM; Apr.–Oct., daily 8–7.*

Lodging

$$–$$$ ☷ **Gran Hotel Termas de Puyehue.** Probably Chile's most famous hot springs resort, this massive compound on the edge of Parque Nacional Puyehue reopened in 2001 after a much-needed remodeling and expansion. The grandiose lodge features all sorts of outdoor activities, from skiing to horseback riding to sportfishing. Most people come for a soak in the thermal pools. All-day use of the springs is $15 for nonguests. ⊠ *Ruta 215, Km 76, Puyehue,* ☏ *64/232–881; 2/231–3417 in Santiago,* FAX *64/236–988; 2/231–3582 in Santiago,* WEB *www.puyehue.cl. 132 rooms. 3 restaurants, 2 pools, mineral bath, meeting room, travel services. AE, DC, MC, V.*

Puerto Octay

⑫ *50 km (30 mi) southeast of Osorno.*

The story goes that a German merchant named Ochs set up shop in this tidy community of the northern tip of Lago Llanquihue. A phrase uttered by customers looking for a particular item, "*¿Ochs, hay . . . ?*" ("Ochs, do you have . . . ?"), gradually became "Octay." With spectacular views of the Osorno and Calbuco volcanoes, the town was the birthplace of Lake District tourism: a wealthy Santiago businessman constructed a mansion outside of town in 1912, using it as a vacation home to host his friends. (That structure is now the area's famed Hotel Centinela.) Puerto Octay doesn't have the frenetic energy of neighboring Frutillar and Puerto Varas, but its many fans enjoy its less frenzied, more authentic atmosphere.

The small **Museo El Colono** displays great old photographs and maps documenting the town's turn-of-the-last-century German settlers. An annex in a barn outside of town at the turnoff to Centinela exhibits farm machinery. ✉ *Independencia 591,* ☎ *64/391523.* ⊠ *Admission.* ☉ *Dec.–Mar., daily 9:30–1 and 3–7; Apr.–Nov., Tues.–Sun. 9:30–1 and 3–7.*

Dining and Lodging

$$ ✕ **Restaurant Baviera.** On the Plaza de Armas, this is a popular lunch stop for tour groups. It dishes up tasty German food—schnitzel, sauerkraut, sausage, and küchen are among the favorites. Beer steins and other Bavarian paraphernalia on the walls evoke the Old Country. ✉ *German Wulf 582,* ☎ *64/391–460. No credit cards.*

$$–$$$ ⊡ **Hotel Centinela.** Simple and elegant, the venerable Hotel Centinela
★ remains one of Chile's best-known accommodations. Constructed in 1912, this imposing wood-shingled lodge with a dramatic turret sits amid 20 forested acres at the tip of Península Centinela, which juts into Lago Llanquihue. Britain's Edward VII, then the Prince of Wales, was the most famous guest (but there's some mystery as to whether he was accompanied by his future wife, American divorcée Wallis Simpson). The huge rooms in the main building are furnished with imposing beds and armoires. The cabins, whose rates include meals delivered to the door, have more personality than the rooms in the lodge, but never cross the line into clutter. Don't miss the spectacular views of the lake from the lovely terrace. ✉ *Península de Centinela,* ☎ ℻ *64/391–326,* ᵂᴱᴮ *www.hotelcentinela.cl. 11 rooms, 1 suite, 18 cabins. Restaurant, bar, sauna. AE, DC, MC, V.*

$ ⊡ **Zapato Amarillo.** Backpackers make up the majority of the clien-
★ tele here, but this is no scruffy youth hostel. Located outside of town, this modern alerce-shingled house boasts a drop-dead gorgeous view of Volcán Osorno. The eager-to-please Chilean-Swiss couple that owns it will arrange guided horseback riding and cycling tours, as well as hikes up the volcano. Rates include a Continental breakfast that's a cut above the rest, tossing in fruit and locally made dairy products. Guests also have access to the kitchen. ✉ *2 km (1 mi) north of Puerto Octay on road to Osorno,* ☎ *64/391–575. 4 rooms. Breakfast room, travel services. No credit cards.*

Frutillar

🔞 *30 km (18 mi) southwest of Puerto Octay.*

Halfway down the western edge of Lago Llanquihue lies the small town of Frutillar, one of the main destinations of European immigrants in the late 19th century. The town—actually two adjacent hamlets, Frutillar Alto and Frutillar Bajo—is known for its perfectly preserved German architecture. Don't be disappointed if your first look at the town is the nondescript neighborhood on the top of the hill; head down to the charming streets that face the lake. Each January and February, the town hosts *Semanas Musicales de Frutillar,* an excellent series of mostly classical concerts (and a little jazz) in an idyllic outdoor setting.

★ You step into the past when you step into one of southern Chile's best museums, the **Museo Colonial Alemán.** Besides displays of the 19th-century agricultural and household implements, this open-air museum features full-scale reconstructions of buildings—a smithy and barn, among others—used by the original German settlers. Exhibits at this complex administered by Chile's Universidad Austral are labeled in Spanish and, *natürlich,* German, but there are also a few signs in English. A short walk up from the lake up Avenida Arturo Prat, the museum also has beautifully landscaped grounds and great views of Volcán Osorno. ✉ *Vicente Pérez Rosales at Arturo Prat,* ☎ *65/421–142.* ⊠ *Admission.* ☉ *Dec.–Mar., Mon.–Sun. 10–2 and 3–8; Apr.–Nov., Mon.–Sun. 10–2 and 3–6.*

Dining and Lodging

$$ ✕ **Club Alemán.** One of the German clubs that dot the Lake District, this restaurant in the center of town offers a selection of four or five rotating prix-fixe menus. There will always be a seafood and meat option—often steak and salmon—with soup, salad, and dessert. Don't forget the küchen. ✉ *Philippi 747,* ☎ *65/421–249. AE, DC, MC, V.*

$$ ✕ **Club de Bomberos.** Frutillar's atmospheric old fire station is a popular place for a hearty lunch. Cazuelas and pasteles de choclo are the particular favorites here. Caricatures of the firefighters decorate the walls. ✉ *Philippi 1065,* ☎ *65/421–588. No credit cards. No dinner.*

$$ ✕🏨 **Hotel Salzburg.** This Tyrolean-style lodge offers rooms commanding excellent views of the lake. Cozy cabins and slightly larger bungalows, all made of native woods, are fully equipped with kitchens and private terraces. The staff will gladly organize fishing trips. The restaurant features some of the best smoked salmon in the area. ✉ *Costanera Norte, Frutillar Bajo,* ☎ *65/421–569,* 𝖥𝖠𝖷 *65/421–599,* 𝖶𝖤𝖡 *www.salzburg.cl. 31 rooms, 9 cabins, 5 bungalows. Restaurant, bar, pool, sauna, meeting rooms, travel services. AE, DC, MC, V.*

$$ 🏨 **Hotel Elun.** This hilltop lodge just south of town gives you a spectacular view of Lago Llanquihue from just about every vantage point—the lobby, the library, and, of course, the guest rooms. Each has huge bay windows framing Volcán Osorno. The blue of the facade is repeated in rooms, which feature polished wood furniture. Rates include a large buffet breakfast. ✉ *Costanera Sur, Frutillar Bajo,* ☎ *65/420–055,* 𝖥𝖠𝖷 *65/420–170,* 𝖶𝖤𝖡 *www.hotelelun.cl. 14 rooms. Restaurant, bar, no-smoking rooms, meeting rooms. AE, DC, MC, V.*

$$ 🏨 **Hotel Klein Salzburg.** This gingerbread-style house, built in 1911, offers a cozy B&B ambience. The location, right on the lake, couldn't better. Wood-paneled rooms are tastefully decorated with flowered bedspreads and curtains. Rates include a full German breakfast. ✉ *Av. Philippi 663, Frutillar Bajo,* ☎ *65/421–201,* 𝖥𝖠𝖷 *65/421–750,* 𝖶𝖤𝖡 *www.salzburg.cl. 8 rooms. Restaurant. AE, DC, MC, V.*

$$ 🏨 **Hotel Volcán Puntiagudo.** This redwood lodge sits on a hillside a mile north of town. Decorated in soft earth tones, the rooms have views of Lago Llanquihue and Volcán Osorno. Rates, which drop for stays over three days, include a large breakfast. ✉ *Camino Fundo las Piedras, Frutillar Bajo,* ☎ *65/421–646,* 𝖥𝖠𝖷 *65/421–640,* 𝖶𝖤𝖡 *www.hotelvolcanpuntiagudo.com. 10 rooms. Restaurant, bar, pool, tennis court, meeting room. DC, MC, V. Closed May–Nov.*

Outdoor Activities and Sports

Packed with summer crowds, the gray-sand **Playa Frutillar** stretches for 15 blocks along Avenida Philippi. From this point along Lago Llanquihue you have a spectacular view due east of the conical Volcán Osorno, as well as the lopsided Volcán Puntiagudo.

Puerto Varas

⑭ *27 km (16 mi) south of Frutillar.*

A small resort town on the edge of Lago Llanquihue, Puerto Varas is known for the stunning rose arbors that bloom from December to March. Often described as the "Lucerne of Chile," the town has ice cream shops, cozy cafés, and trendy restaurants. The view of the Osorno and Calbuco volcanoes graces dozens of postcards and travel brochures for the Lake District. The town could someday soon mount a serious challenge to Pucón as the region's top vacation spot.

Dining and Lodging

$$$–$$$$ ✕ **Merlin.** Often called the best restaurant in southern Chile, this charming little establishment features a variety of fish and vegetables

Andor

Boss: Richard

combined in unusual ways. Specialities include razor clams with vegetable strips in a curry vinaigrette and beef tenderloin in a morel-mushroom sauce. For dessert look for peaches packed with almond cream. ⊠ *Walker Martínez 584,* ☎ *65/233–105. AE, DC, MC, V. No lunch.*

$$ ✕ **Restaurant Aníbal.** Although the decor in this Italian restaurant is plain, the food is anything but. The friendly staff dishes up pasta with a tangy Argentine flavor. ⊠ *Del Salvador at Santa Rosa,* ☎ *65/235–222. MC, V.*

$$$ ⌂ **Hotel Cabañas del Lago.** The rooms in this recently remodeled hotel on the lake are cozy, and most have lovely views of Volcán Osorno. But it's the cabins that make this spot special. Hidden in carefully tended gardens, each A-frame unit is decorated with lace curtains and floral patterned bedding. Accommodating five guests, the pine-paneled cabins have wood stoves and full kitchens. ⊠ *Klenner 195,* ☎ *65/23–2291,* FAX *65/232–707,* WEB *www.bestwestern.com. 63 rooms, 21 cabins, 2 suites. Restaurant, bar, indoor pool, massage, sauna, billiards, babysitting, meeting rooms. AE, DC, MC, V.*

$$$ ⌂ **Hotel Colonos del Sur.** This five-story hotel, with peaked gables that give it a Germanic look, dominates the waterfront in Puerto Varas. The views from the upper floors are magnificent. Warm alerce and pine dominate the interior, including the paneled guest rooms. ⊠ *Del Salvador 24,* ☎ *65/233–369,* FAX *65/233–394,* WEB *www.colonosdelsur.cl. 54 rooms, 2 suites. Restaurant, bar, indoor pool, sauna, meeting room. DC, MC, V.*

$$–$$$ ⌂ **Hotel Licarayén.** This rambling Bavarian-style chalet, across from the Plaza de Armas, boasts balconies overlooking Lago Llanquihue. Most of the comfortably furnished rooms have views of the lake or the garden. ⊠ *San José 114,* ☎ *65/232–305,* FAX *65/232–955. 23 rooms. Sauna, gym. No credit cards.*

$$ ⌂ **Hotel Bellavista.** An eclectic mix of traditional Bavarian and modern architectural styles, the Hotel Bellavista sits right on the lake. Most of the bright rooms have views of the nearby volcanoes, and some have their own balconies. ⊠ *Vicente Pérez Rosales 60,* ☎ *65/232–011,* FAX *65/232–013,* WEB *www.hotelbellavistachile.com. 38 rooms. Restaurant, bar, sauna. AE, DC, MC, V.*

$$ ⌂ **Hotel Westfalia.** This steep-roofed hotel in a quiet residential neighborhood is a bit removed from the action, but the trade-off is a homey feel you don't get in the center of town. Rooms and public areas contain hardwood floors decorated with colorful throw rugs. ⊠ *Estación 505,* ☎ *65/233–039,* FAX *65/233–394,* WEB *www.colonoasdelsur.com. 19 rooms. Pool. AE, DC, MC, V.*

Nightlife

The flashy **Casino de Puerto Varas** (⊠ Klenner 351, ☎ 65/232–281) dominates the center of town these days. There are all the Vegas-style trappings, from slot machines to roulette.

Outdoor Adventure and Sports

Al Sur Expediciones (⊠ Del Salvador 100, ☎ 65/287–628) is known for rafting and kayaking trips on the Class III Río Petrohué. It also offers horseback riding and fly-fishing trips. **Aqua Motion** (⊠ San Pedro 422, ☎ 65/232–747) leads rafting and kayaking excursions on the nearby Río Puetrohué.

Parque Nacional Vicente Pérez Rosales

⑮ *50 km (30 mi) east of Puerto Varas.*

Chile's oldest national park, Parque Nacional Vicente Pérez Rosales was established in 1926. South of Parque Nacional Puyehue, the 2,538-

square-km (980-square-mi) preserve includes the Osorno and lesser-known Puntiagudo volcanoes, as well as the deep blue Lago Todos los Santos. The visitor center opposite the Hotel Petrohué provides access to some fairly easy hikes. The Rincón del Osorno trail hugs the lake; the Saltos de Petrohué trail runs parallel to the river of the same name. ☎ 65/290–711. ⊠ *Admission.* ☉ *Dec.–Feb., daily 9–8; Mar.–Nov., daily 9–6.*

Lodging

$$–$$$ 🏨 **Hotel Petrohué.** This upscale rustic chalet, with vaulted ceilings and huge fireplaces, is the most comfortable lodging within the park. The hotel's tour office can set you up with cruises on nearby lakes or take you to scale Volcán Osorno if you're an experienced climber. ⊠ *Petrohué s/n,* ☎ FAX *65/258–042,* WEB *www.petrohue.com. 28 rooms. Restaurant, travel services. AE, DC, MC, V.*

Puerto Montt

⑯   *20 km (12 mi) south of Puerto Varas.*

For most of its history, windy Puerto Montt was the end of the line for just about everyone traveling in the Lake District. Now the Carretera Austral carries on southward, but for all intents and purposes Puerto Montt remains the region's last significant outpost, a small provincial city that is the hub of local fishing, textile, and tourist activity. Today the town consists of low clapboard houses perched above its bay, the Seno de Reloncaví. If it's a sunny day, head east to Playa Pelluco or one of the city's other beaches. If you're more interested in exploring the countryside, drive along the shore for a good view of the surrounding hills.

The **Museo Juan Pablo II,** east of the city's bus terminal, has a collection of crafts and relics from the nearby archipelago of Chiloé. Historical photos of Puerto Montt itself give a sense of the area's slow and often difficult growth and the impact of the 1960 earthquake, which virtually destroyed the port. Pope John Paul II, for whom the museum was renamed, celebrated mass on the grounds during his 1987 visit. One exhibit documents the event. ⊠ *Av. Diego Portales 991,* ☎ *65/344–457.* ⊠ *Admission.* ☉ *Daily 9–7.*

About 3 km (2 mi) west of downtown along the coastal road lies the **Caleta Angelmó,** Puerto Montt's fishing cove. This busy port serves small fishing boats, large ferries, and cruisers carrying travelers and cargo southward through the straits and fjords that form much of Chile's shoreline. On weekdays you'll notice small launches from Isla Tenglo and other outlying islands that arrive early in the morning and leave late in the afternoon. The fish market here offers one of the most varied selections of seafood in all of Chile.

Barely a stone's throw from Puerto Montt, the mountainous 398-square-km (154-square-mi) **Parque Nacional Alerce Andino,** with over 40 small lakes, was established to protect some 20,000 endangered alerce trees. Comparable to California's hardy sequoias, alerces grow to average heights of 40 meters (130 ft), and can reach 4 meters (13 ft) in diameter. Immensely popular for construction of houses in southern Chile, they are quickly disappearing from the landscape. Many of these are 3,000–4,000 years old. ⊠ *35 km (21 mi) east of Puerto Montt,* ☎ *65/212–036.* ⊠ *Admission.* ☉ *Daily 9–6.*

Dining and Lodging

$$$–$$$$ ✕ **Balzac.** One of Puerto Montt's finest restaurants, Balzac specializes
    ★   in seafood prepared with a French flair. Try the *jaiba de chardonnay* (a stew of king crab, Parmesan cheese, and white wine). The owner's

father—an endearing gentleman and a rich source of Chilote history—
passes his time downstairs chewing the fat with friends. Don't worry
about waking the child sleeping on the stairs inside the door—it's a
doll. ⊠ *Urmeneta 305,* ☎ *65/313–251. No credit cards. Closed Sun.*

$$$ ✕ **Club Alemán.** Part of a network of old German associations, Club
Alemán serves delicious küchen and other pastries, but the rest of the
menu doesn't recall Deutschland. Seafood—delicious clams, oysters,
and lobster—as well as freshwater trout are the specialties here. ⊠ *Antonio Varas 264,* ☎ *65/252–551. AE, DC, MC, V. No dinner Sun.*

$$–$$$ ✕ **Club de Yates.** There are no yachts here, despite the tony-sounding
name. You can't miss this place, as it sits on a high pier jutting out into
the bay. The weathered blue exterior contrasts sharply with the elegance of the interior, complete with crips linens and candlelight. Prices
are reasonable, though—you can feast on lobster for just a few dollars. ⊠ *Av. Juan Soler Manfredini 1,* ☎ *65/276–888. AE, DC, MC, V.
No dinner Sun.*

$$–$$$ ✕ **Feria Artesanal Angelmó.** A variety of small kitchens offer *mariscal*
(shellfish soup) and *caldillo* (seafood chowder), as well as *almejas*
(clams), *machas* (razor clams), and *ostiones* (scallops) with Parmesan
cheese. Separate tables and counters are located at each kitchen in this
enclosed market, which is 3 km (2 mi) west of Puerto Montt along the
coast road. ⊠ *Caleta Angelmó,* ☎ *no phone. No credit cards.*

$$–$$$ ✕ **New Harbor Café.** When you step into this café decorated with pale
woods and chrome, you might think it's a bit too trendy for its own
good. In reality it's a fun, friendly place serving sandwiches and other
light meals. It's a great destination for late-night noshing. ⊠ *San
Martín 85,* ☎ *65/293–980. No credit cards.*

$$ ✕ **Café Restaurant Amsel.** Serving breakfast, lunch, and dinner, this
two-story café has a variety of inexpensive meat and seafood dishes,
in addition to sandwiches and an extensive vegetarian selection. This
is a good spot to socialize over a well-brewed cappuccino or *cortado*
(coffee with a bit of milk) when the weather proves unfriendly. ⊠ *Diego
Portales and Pedro Montt,* ☎ *65/253–941. AE, DC, MC, V.*

$$ ✕ **Restaurant Kiel.** Hospitable German-born proprietor Helga Birkir
stands guard at this Chilean-Teutonic seafood restaurant on the coast
west of Puerto Montt. Her well-kept garden makes lunch here a delight. ⊠ *Camino Chinquihue Km 8, Chinquihue,* ☎ *65/255–010. AE.*

$–$$ ✕ **Al Passo.** Steak rules—you'll have trouble finding anything green—
at this high-ceilinged restaurant on the Plaza de Armas. This modern
establishment has all the hustle and bustle of a big-city diner. ⊠ *Antonio Varas 502,* ☎ *65/252–947. AE, DC, MC, V.*

$–$$ ✕ **Café Central.** This old-style café in the heart of Puerto Montt retains the spirit of the 1920s and 1930s. It's a good place for a filling
afternoon tea, with its menu of sandwiches, ice cream, and pastries.
⊠ *Rancagua 117,* ☎ *65/254–721. No credit cards.*

$$$ ▥ **Hotel Don Luis.** This modern lodging, next to the cathedral, has
panoramic views of the Seno de Reloncaví. It's part of the Best Western chain, so you can expect the rooms to be comfortable and clean.
There's a small salon for the big American-style breakfast included in
the rate. ⊠ *Urmeneta and Quillota,* ☎ *65/259–001,* FAX *65/259–005,*
WEB *www.bestwestern.com. 60 rooms, 1 suite. Restaurant, bar, meeting rooms. AE, DC, MC, V.*

$$$ ▥ **O'Grimm.** This four-story lodging is in the heart of Puerto Montt,
but its warmth and charm would make it equally at home in a small
town in Germany. The helpful staff makes you feel right at home. The
simple rooms are decorated in muted shades of gray, rose, and green.
⊠ *Guillermo Gallardo 211,* ☎ *65/252–845,* FAX *65/258–600,* WEB
www.ogrimm.com. 27 rooms, 1 suite. Restaurant, bar, minibars, laundry service, meeting rooms. AE, DC, MC, V.

$$$ 🏨 **Vicente Pérez Rosales.** This hotel's Bavarian-style facade resembles that of countless other Lake District lodgings, but the lobby's huge picture window overlooking the Seno de Reloncaví lets you know this place is something special. The grandest of Puerto Montt hotels, this alpine lodge has undergone a much needed face-lift, which restored its Gstaad-by-the-sea glory. ⊠ *Antonio Varas 447,* ☎ *65/252–571,* 🖷 *65/255–473,* 🕸 *www.hotelperezrosales.com. 81 rooms, 2 suites. Restaurant, bar, in-room safes, minibars, meeting room. AE, DC, MC, V.*

$$$ 🏨 **Viento Sur.** This remodeled Victorian house sits proudly on a hill, offering a majestic view of both the city and the sea. Rooms are comfortably furnished with generous use of native Chilean woods. The restaurant serves excellent Chilean seafood. ⊠ *Ejército 200,* ☎ *65/258–700,* 🖷 *65/258–701. 27 rooms, 2 suites. Restaurant, bar, sauna, laundry service. AE, DC, MC, V.*

$$ 🏨 **Hotel Burg.** Rooms in this waterfront hotel are bright and cheery, with tongue-and-groove paneling and comfortable beds. The fifth floor offers rooms with high ceilings and great views of the bay. ⊠ *Diego Portales and Pedro Montt,* ☎ *65/253–941,* 🖷 *65/253–813. 30 rooms, 1 suite. Restaurant, bar, room service, laundry service. AE, DC, MC, V.*

$ 🏨 **Hostal Pacífico.** This solid budget option, up the hill from the bus station, is a favorite of European travelers. The rooms are small, but they have comfy beds with lots of pillows. Look at a few before you pick one, as some of the interior rooms have skylights rather than windows. The staff is exceptionally friendly and helpful. ⊠ *Juan J. Mira 1088,* ☎ 🖷 *65/256–229. 22 rooms. Restaurant. No credit cards.*

$ 🏨 **Hotel Gamboa.** The floors creak, the rooms are very plain, and the bright yellow exterior looks strangely out of place in staid downtown Puerto Montt. But the sweetly fussy owner makes this second-story lodging a good budget choice. ⊠ *Pedro Montt 157,* ☎ *65/252–741. 8 rooms, 4 with bath. No credit cards.*

$ 🏨 **Hotel Raysan.** Lots of glass means lots of light streams into the rooms at this business hotel in the center of the city. The decor is eclectic, a mix of pale pastels. ⊠ *Benavente 480,* ☎ 🖷 *65/256–151. 32 rooms. Restaurant, bar, meeting room. AE, MC, V.*

CAMPING

Campgrounds, most of them located to the west of Puerto Montt, all charge around $15 per vehicle per night. **Chinquihue** (⊠ Costandera, ☎ 65/262–950), 7 km (4½ mi) west of Caleta Angelmó, has showers and views of the beach. **El Ciervo** (⊠ Costandera, ☎ 65/255–271), 1 km (½ mi) west of Angelmó, offers 20 sites with electricity, hot showers, and boat rental. **Los Alamos** (⊠ Costandera, ☎ 65/264–666), 11 km (7 mi) west of Caleta Angelmó, has fine views of the Seno de Reloncaví and Isla Tenglo and offers electricity, water, and hot showers, as well as a dock and boat rentals. **Paredes** (⊠ Costandera, ☎ 65/258–394), 6 km (4 mi) west of Caleta Angelmó, is short on shade but has a pretty beach, hot showers, and a playground.

Nightlife and the Arts
The **Casa de Arte Diego Rivera,** a gift of the government of Mexico, commemorates the famed muralist of the same name. It hosts art exhibitions, theater productions, and occasional music and film festivals. ⊠ *Antonio Varas at Quillota,* ☎ *65/261–817.* ☉ *Mon.–Sat. 8–6.*

Shopping
An excellent selection of handicrafts sold at the best prices in the country can be found in the **Feria Artesanal Angelmó.** Chileans know there's a better selection of crafts from Chiloé to be found here than in Chiloé itself. Baskets, ponchos, figures woven from different kinds of grasses and straws, and warm sweaters of raw, hand-spun, and hand-dyed wool are all offered. Much of the merchandise is geared toward

tourists, but if you look carefully you'll find more authentic offerings. Haggling is expected. ⊠ *On the coastal road near Caleta Angelmó.*

Pargua

63 km (39 mi) southwest of Puerto Montt.

Pargua is the Lake District's end of the line, the jumping-off point for ferries to nearby Chiloé. This is where you catch the boats leaving every 30 minutes to Chacao on the northern tip of Chiloé.

THE LAKE DISTRICT A TO Z

To research prices, get advice from other travelers, and book travel arrangements, visit www.fodors.com.

AIR TRAVEL

LanChile and its domestic partner Ladeco have flights from Santiago to the four major cities within the Lake District—Temuco, Valdivia, Osorno, and Puerto Montt. Some flights to Puerto Montt continue south to Balmaceda and Punta Arenas. Avant duplicates many of the Lan-Chile and Ladeco routes. ALTA operates smaller twin-propeller planes between Temuco, Puerto Montt, Valdivia, and other cities.

Osorno's Aeropuerto Carlos Hott Siebert is 7 km (4 mi) east of the city. Puerto Montt's Aeropuerto El Tepual is found 16 km (10 mi) west of the city center. Temuco's Aeropuerto Manquehue is about 6 km (4 mi) south of the city. Valdivia's Aeropuerto Pichoy lies 29 km (18 mi) north of the city.

➤ AIRLINES: **ALTA** (⊠ Aeropuerto El Tepual, Puerto Montt, ☎ 65/268–646; ⊠ Aeropuerto Manquehue, Temuco, ☎ 45/213–090; ⊠ Aeropuerto Pichoy, Valdivia, ☎ 63/228–150). **Avant** (⊠ Prat 565, Temuco, ☎ 45/270–670; ⊠ O'Higgins at Varas, Puerto Montt, ☎ 65/258–277; ⊠ Chacabuco 408, Valdivia, ☎ 63/251–431). **LanChile** and **Ladeco** (⊠ Manuel Antonio Matta 862, Osorno, ☎ 64/314–949; ⊠ San Martin 200, Puerto Montt, ☎ 65/253–315; ⊠ Bulnes 687, Temuco, ☎ 45/272–138; ⊠ O'Higgins 386, Valdivia, ☎ 63/258–840).

➤ AIRPORTS: **Aeropuerto Carlos Hott Siebert** (☎ 64/318–855) in Osorno; **Aeropuerto El Tepual** (☎ 65/294–159) in Puerto Montt; **Aeropuerto Manquehue** (☎ 45/337–703) in Temuco; and **Aeropuerto Pichoy** (☎ 63/272–224) in Valdivia.

BOAT AND FERRY TRAVEL

To drive much farther south than Puerto Montt, you've got to take a boat or ferry. Cruz del Sur operates a ferry connecting the mainland town of Pargua with Chacao on the northern tip of the island of Chiloé. Boats run every 30 minutes from early morning until late at night. The trip takes about half an hour.

Navimag operates a cargo and passenger fleet throughout the region. The M/V *Evangelistas,* a 324-passenger ferry, sails round-trip from Puerto Montt to the popular tourist destination of Laguna San Raphael, stopping in both directions at Puerto Chacabuco on the Southern Coast. The 200-passenger M/V *Alejandrina* sails from Puerto Montt to Chaitén, Quellón, and Puerto Chacabuco before making the trip in reverse.

Transmarchilay operates a cargo and passenger ferry fleet similar to that of Navimag, with ships that start in Puerto Montt and sail either to Chaitén or Puerto Chacabuco. If it's Laguna San Raphael you want to see, Transmarchilay operates the M/V *El Colono.* From early January through late February, the ship sails weekly from Puerto Montt into Laguna San Rafael and back to Puerto Montt.

The Lake District is the jumping-off point for luxury cruises, as well. Many companies that offer trips to the fjords of Chilean Patagonia are based in Puerto Montt. Skorpios, with a trio of luxurious ships, offers first-class cruises from Puerto Montt to the Laguna San Rafael. The ships carry between 70 and 130 passengers.

There are a number of companies that offer cruises on the region's lakes. Andina del Sud operates between Puerto Varas and San Carlos de Bariloche, Argentina. Boats traverse the Lago Todos los Santos.
➤ BOAT AND FERRY COMPANIES: **Andina del Sud** (⊠ Del Salvador 72, Puerto Varas, ☎ 65/232–511). **Cruz del Sur** (⊠ Puerto Montt, ☎ 64/254–731. **Navimag** (⊠ Puerto Montt, ☎ 65/432–300, WEB www.navimag.cl). **Skorpios** (⊠ Augosto Leguia Norte 118, Santiago, ☎ 2/231–1030, WEB www.skorpios.cl). **Transmarchilay** (⊠ Puerto Montt, ☎ 65/270–421, WEB www.transmarchilay.cl).

BUS TRAVEL

There's no shortage of bus companies traveling the Pan-American Highway (Ruta 5) from Santiago south to the Lake District. The buses aren't overcrowded on these long routes, and seats are assigned. Tickets may be purchased in advance, always a good idea if you're traveling during summer. Cruz del Sur and Tur-Bus connect the major cities. Buses JAC connects the resort towns of Pucón and Villarrica with Temuco and Valdivia.

In Temuco, there's no central bus terminal, but several companies are close together along Vicuña Mackenna and Lagos. Osorno, Puerto Montt, and Valdivia have their own central terminal.
➤ BUS COMPANIES: **Buses JAC** (⊠ Vicuña Mackenna 798, Temuco, ☎ 45/210–313; ⊠ Bilbao 610, Villarrica, ☎ 45/411–447; ⊠ Anfión Muñoz 360, Valdivia ☎ 63/212–925). **Cruz del Sur** (⊠ Vicuña Mackenna 671, Temuco, ☎ 45/210–701; ⊠ Anfión Muñoz 360, Valdivia, ☎ 63/213–840; ⊠ Errázuriz 1400, Osorno, ☎ 64/232–777; ⊠ Av. Diego Portales, Puerto Montt, ☎ 65/254–731). **Tur Bus** (⊠ Lagos 538, Temuco, ☎ 45/239–190).
➤ BUS TERMINALS: **Osorno** (⊠ Errázuriz 1400, ☎ 64/234–149). **Puerto Montt** (⊠ Av. Diego Portales, ☎ no phone). **Valdivia** (⊠ Anfión Muñoz 360, ☎ 63/212–212).

CAR TRAVEL

You'll see a lot more of the Lake District if you have your own vehicle. A few rental-car companies, including Hertz, will allow you to rent a car in one city and return it at another, so you can avoid the inconvenience of retracing your steps.

Much of the Pan-American Highway (Ruta 5) through the region is a well-maintained two-lane highway. Small sections of four-lane divided highway (*doble vía*) have opened, and construction is proceeding rapidly to expand the rest. With the expansion to four lanes comes an increase in the number of toll plazas, the object of scorn among most Chileans.

Once you're this far south, driving is much easier because there's less traffic, even on the major highways. Roads to most of the important tourist centers are paved, but many of the routes through the mountains are gravel or dirt, so a four-wheel-drive vehicle is ideal.
➤ CAR RENTAL INFORMATION: **Automóvil Club de Chile** (⊠ Esmeralda 70, Puerto Montt, ☎ 65/254–776; ⊠ Lautaro 703, Temuco, ☎ 45/248–903; ⊠ Bulnes 463, Valdivia, ☎ 64/232–269). **Autovald** (⊠ Portales 1330, Puerto Montt, ☎ 65/256–355). **Avis** (⊠ Urmeneta 1037, Puerto Montt, ☎ 65/253–307; ⊠ Vicuña Mackenna 448, Temuco, ☎

45/238–013). First (✉ Varas 1036, Temuco, ☎ 45/233– responsal Vicente Pérez Rosales 674, Valdivia, ☎ 52/215– (✉ Antonio Varas 126, Puerto Montt, ☎ 65/259–585; ✉ 999, Temuco, ☎ 45/235–385; ✉ Picarte 640, Valdivia, ☎ 63/218–316).

FESTIVALS AND SEASONAL EVENTS

Summer, with its better weather and ample presence of vacationers, means festival season in the Lake District. In late January and early February, Semanas Musicales de Frutillar brings together the best in classical music. Verano en Valdivia is a two-month-long celebration centered around the February 9 anniversary of the founding of Valdivia. Villarrica hosts a Muestra Cultural Mapuche in January and February that shows off Mapuche art and music.

HEALTH

The tap water is fine to drink in most places, although many people opt for bottled water. As far as food goes, the standards of hygiene are generally high. The Ministry of Health has beefed up its warnings about eating raw shellfish, citing the risk of contracting intestinal parasites.

INTERNET

You can check your e-mail at hotels in the larger towns and cities, but don't expect a fast connection. Most towns also have Internet cafés, which are generally open until at least 10 PM. Most charge between $2 and $4 per hour.

➤ INTERNET CAFÉS: **Café Phonet** (✉ Libertad 127, Valdivia, ☎ 63/341–054). **Ciber Café** (✉ Portales 888, Temuco). **Cybercafé** (✉ San Martín 232, Puerto Montt, ☎ 65/295–414). **Cyber Centro** (✉ Av. Gramado at Av. San Jose, Puerto Varas, ☎ 65/311–901). **Gea.com** (✉ Juan Mackenna 1140, Osorno, ☎ 64/207–700). **Químanche** (✉ O'Higgins 211, Pucón).

MAIL AND SHIPPING

Reasonably efficient, Correos de Chile has post offices in most towns. They are generally open weekdays 9–6 and Saturday 9–noon. Mail posted from the Lake District's four hub cities takes up to two weeks to reach North America and three to reach Europe. None of the U.S.-based international express mail services have drop-off locations in the Lake District.

➤ POST OFFICES: **Correos de Chile** (✉ Av. O'Higgins 645, Osorno; ✉ Av. Rancagua 126, Puerto Montt; ✉ Av. Diego Portales at Av. Prat, Temuco; ✉ Av. O'Higgins 575, Valdivia).

SAFETY

Volcano climbing is a popular pastime here, with Volcán Villarrica the most popular because of its easy ascent and proximity to Pucón. But Villarrica is also one of South America's most active. Conaf, the agency administering national parks, cuts off access to any volcano at the slightest hint of activity. Check with Conaf before heading out on any hike in this region.

MONEY MATTERS

All of the major cities in the Lake District have several banks that will exchange U.S. dollars. Most banks will not touch traveler's checks, which are best exchanged at a casa de cambio. Many larger hotels will also exchange currency and a few will exchange traveler's checks. ATMs at Banco Santander and Banco de Chile, part of the omnipresent Redbanc network, accept both Cirrus- and Plus-affiliated cards. The district's four main airports have ATMs and casas de cambio.

TAXIS

As elsewhere in Chile, solid black or solid yellow cabs operate as *colectivos,* or collective taxis, following fixed routes and picking up up to four people along the way. A sign on the roof shows the general destination. The cost is little more than that of a city bus. A black cab with a yellow roof will take you directly to your requested destination for a metered fare. Hail these in the street.

TELEPHONES

Entel, CTC, and Telefónica del Sur have call centers throughout the region. All allow you to place calls and send faxes. Each company also has its own network of public telephones. Phone booths use calling cards, which you can purchase at many shops and newsstands. Each works only in that company's telephones, so make sure you have the right one.

TRAIN TRAVEL

Chile's State Railway Company, the Empresa de los Ferrocarriles del Estado, has daily service southward from Santiago only as far as Temuco. It's a far cry from the journey Paul Theroux recounted in *The Old Patagonian Express.* Trains run twice daily from January to March, once daily the rest of the year. The overnight trip takes about 13 hours. Prices range from $13 for an economy-class seat to $100 for a sleeper with all the trimmings. If you prefer to rent a vehicle in Santiago, you can use the auto-train service from there to Temuco. The price is an extra $170 southbound and $130 northbound.

➤ TRAIN INFORMATION: **Empresa de los Ferrocarriles del Estado** (☎ 2/ 376–8313 or 2/376–8500 in Santiago; 45/233–522 or 45/233–416 in Temuco).

➤ TRAIN STATIONS: **Estación de Ferrocarriles** (✉ Av. Barros Arana, Temuco, ☎ 45/233–416).

VISITOR INFORMATION

The Lake District's four major cities have offices of Sernatur, Chile's national tourist office. Smaller offices, often run by local governments, can be found in most communities catering to tourists.

➤ SERNATUR OFFICES: **Osorno** (✉ O'Higgins 667, ☎ 64/237–575). **Puerto Montt** (✉ Plaza de Armas, ☎ 65/252–626). **Temuco** (✉ Claro Solar and Bulnes, ☎ 45/211–969). **Valdivia** (✉ Arturo Prat 555, ☎ 63/213– 596).

➤ TOURIST OFFICES: **Frutillar** (✉ Philippi at San Martín, ☎ 65/420– 198). **Lican Ray** (✉ General Urrutia 310, ☎ 45/431–201). **Osorno** (✉ Plaza de Armas, ☎ 64/264–250). **Panguipulli** (✉ Plaza Arturo Prat, ☎ 63/311–311). **Pucón** (✉ Brasil at Caupolicán, ☎ 45/443–388). **Puerto Montt** (✉ Antonio Varas at Plaza de Armas, ☎ 65/261–700). **Puerto Octay** (✉ La Esperanza 55, ☎ 64/391–491). **Puerto Varas** (✉ Costanera at San José, ☎ 65/233–315). **Temuco** (✉ Mercado Municipal, ☎ 45/216–360). **Valdivia** (✉ Terminal de Buses, Anfión Muñoz 360, ☎ 63/212–212). **Villarrica** (✉ Pedro de Valdivia 1070, ☎ 45/206–618).

8 CHILOÉ

Centuries of geographical, cultural, and historical isolation have left the southern archipelago of Chiloé a world unto itself. Its residents will regale you with the same myths and legends their ancestors told about these foggy green islands. Much of what is identified as Chilean folklore originated here, though the rest of the country happily embraces it as its own.

By Jeffrey
Van Fleet

S TEEPED IN MAGIC, SHROUDED IN MIST, the 41-island archipelago of Chiloé is that proverbial world apart, isolated not so much by distance from the mainland—it's barely more than 2 km (1 mi) at its nearest point—but by the quirks of history. Some 130,000 people populate 35 of these rainy islands, with most of them living on the 8,394-square-km (3,241-square-mi) Isla Grande. Almost all are descendants of a seamless blending of colonial and indigenous cultures, a tradition that entwines farming and fishing, devout Catholicism and spirits of good and evil, woolen sweaters and wooden churches.

Originally inhabited by the indigenous Chono people, Chiloé was gradually taken over by the Huilliches. Though Chiloé was claimed as part of Spain's empire in the 1550s, colonists dismissed the archipelago as a backwater. The 1598 rebellion by the Mapuche people on the mainland drove a contingent of Spanish settlers to the isolated safety of Chiloé. Left to their own devices, Spaniards and Huilliche lived side by side. Their society was built on the concept of the *minga,* a help-thy-neighbor spirit in the best tradition of the barn raisings and quilting bees of pioneer America. The outcome was a culture neither Spanish nor indigenous, but *Chilote,* a quintessential mestizo society.

Isolated from the rest of the continent, islanders had little interest in or awareness of the revolutionary fervor sweeping Latin America in the early 19th century. In fact, the mainland Spaniards recruited the Chilote to help put down rebellions in the region. When things got too hot in Santiago, the Spanish governor took refuge on the island, just as his predecessors had done two centuries earlier. Finally defeated, the Spaniards abandoned Chiloé in 1826, and the island soon joined the new nation of Chile.

These days, the isolation is more psychological than physical. Some 40 buses per day and frequent ferries make the half-hour crossing between Chiloé and Puerto Montt on the mainland.

Pleasures and Pastimes

Churches

Nothing symbolizes Chiloé like the more than 150 wooden churches that dot the eastern half of the main island. Built by Jesuit missionaries who came to the archipelago after the 1598 Mapuche rebellion on the mainland, the chapels were an integral part of the effort to convert the indigenous peoples. Pairs of missionaries traveled the region by boat, making sure to celebrate mass in each community at least once a year. Franciscan missionaries continued the tradition after the Spaniards expelled the Jesuits in 1767.

The architectural style of the churches calls to mind those in rural Germany, the home of many of the missionaries. The complete lack of ornamentation is offset only by a steep roof covered with wooden shingles called *tejuelas* and a three-tier hexagonal bell tower. An arched portico fronts most of the churches. Getting to see more than the outside of many of the churches can be a challenge. Castro's orange-and-lavender Iglesia de San Francisco, dating from 1906, opens its doors to visitors. Achao's Iglesia de Santa María de Loreto offers daily guided tours. Others are open only on Sunday for services. Many stand alone on the coast, forlorn in their solitude and locked most of the year.

A nonprofit support organization, the Fundación de Amigos de las Iglesias de Chiloé (⊠ San Martín 436, Castro; ⊠ Blanco Encalada 783, Ancud; ⊠ Victoria Subercaseaux 69, Santiago, ☎ 63/700–230), raises

Chiloé

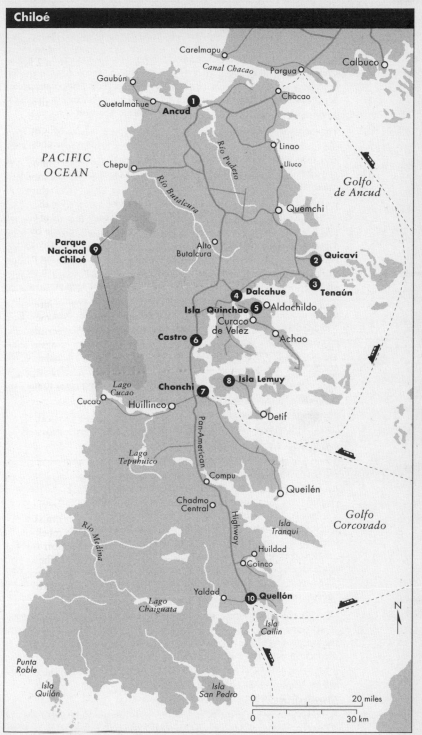

Carelmapu

Canal Chacao

Pargua

Calbuco

Gaubún

Chacao

Quetalmahue

Ancud 1

PACIFIC
OCEAN

Río Pudeto

Linao

Lliuco

Chepu

Río Butalcura

*Golfo
de Ancud*

Quemchi

Parque
Nacional
Chiloé 9

Alto
Butalcura

2 **Quicaví**

4 **Dalcahue**

3 **Tenaún**

5

Isla Quinchao

Aldachildo

Curaco
de Velez

Achao

Castro 6

8 **Isla Lemuy**

*Lago
Cucao*

Chonchi 7

Cucao

Huillinco

Detif

Pan-American

*Lago
Tepuhuico*

Compu

Queilén

Chadmo
Central

*Golfo
Corcovado*

*Isla
Tranqui*

Río Medina

Huildad

Highway

Coinco

Yaldad

10 **Quellón**

*Lago
Chaiguata*

*Isla
Cailín*

Punta
Roble

*Isla
Quilán*

*Isla
San Pedro*

N

0   20 miles

0   30 km

funds for restoration of the archipelago's churches, many of which are
in urgent need of repair.

Dining

As befits an island culture, seafood reigns in Chiloé. The signature
Chilote dish is the *curanto,* a hearty stew of fish and shellfish with chicken,
beef, pork, and lamb thrown in. It's served with plenty of potato bread.
Most restaurants here serve curanto, though not every day of the week.
Salmón ahumado (smoked salmon) is another seafood favorite.

The archipelago is also known for its tasty fruit liqueurs, usually from
the central Chiloé town of Chonchi. Islanders take mangoes, grapes,
and apples and turn them into the *licor de oro* that will often greet you
as you check into your hotel. For details on price categories, *see* Dining *in* Smart Travel Tips A to Z.

Folklore

As the southernmost outpost of Spain's empire, Chiloé was also the
"end of Christendom," as naturalist Charles Darwin wrote after his
1834 visit. But Chilote Catholicism was also tied up in magic and legend. Mythical creatures are thought to populate the coasts of Chiloé.
On the beach you might spot the beautiful blonde *Pincoya,* signaling
good fishing that day. Beware the troll-like *Trauco,* seducer of young
women. Don't go poking around caves for fear of stumbling upon a
brujo, or witch; that encounter could bode good or evil. And don't gaze
too intently out at the ocean on a foggy night, lest you catch a glimpse
of the *Caleuche,* the ill-fated ghost ship that sank on its maiden voyage and forever cruises the dark waters looking for its passengers lost
at sea.

These days, your encounter with such characters will more likely take
the form of a woven-straw figure for sale in a market in Castro or Dalcahue. But you just might run into a self-proclaimed brujo in that same
market offering an herbal cure for whatever ails you.

Lodging

There are three or four good hotels on Chiloé, but none would pass
for luxury lodgings on the mainland. That said, the islands have a selection of perfectly acceptable, reasonably priced hotels. Castro and
Ancud have the widest range of accommodations; Chonchi and Quellón less so. As in the Lake District to the north, a number of the hotels look as if they were transplanted from Germany. Many are sided
with shingles made from a type of wood called *alerce.* Much appreciated central heating and a light breakfast are standard in most better
hostelries. Few places here are equipped to handle credit cards, but with
ATM machines readily available in Castro and Ancud, paying in cash
isn't as inconvenient as you might expect.

Outside the major cities, the pickings are slim. *Hospedaje* signs seem
to sprout in front of every other house in Castro and Ancud during
the summer as home owners rent rooms to visitors. Quality varies, so
inspect the premises before agreeing to take a room from someone who
greets you at the bus station. For details on price categories, *see* Lodging *in* Smart Travel Tips A to Z.

Shopping

Baskets, ponchos, figurines woven from different kinds of grasses and
straws, and sweaters of raw, hand-spun, and hand-dyed wool all come
from Chiloé. Chilote wool processing retains the natural oils, making
the sweaters and ponchos wonderfully warm and water resistant. Castro's waterfront Feria Artesanal is the most popular place to shop for
traditional goods, but Dalcahue's Sunday-morning market also draws

the shop-till-you-drop crowd. But the best selection of Chilote hand-icrafts is not here in the archipelago at all, but in the stalls of the An-gelmó market in Puerto Montt.

Exploring Chiloé

If you're like most people, you'll explore Chiloé by car. The Pan-Amer-ican Highway that meanders through northern Chile ends at the Golfo de Ancud and continues again on Isla Grande. It connects the major cities of Ancud, Castro, and Chonchi before coming to its anticlimac-tic end in Quellón. Paved roads also connect the Pan-American to Quem-chi, Dalcahue, and Achao on Isla Quinchao.

Great Itineraries

IF YOU HAVE 3 DAYS

After crossing the Golfo de Ancud on the morning ferry, drive south to ⊞ **Ancud** ①. Soak up the port town's atmosphere that afternoon. Head to **Dalcahue** ④ the next day. If it's Sunday you can wander among the stalls of the morning market. Take the short ferry ride to **Isla Quinchao** ⑤ and visit the colorful church of Santa María de Loreto. Back on Isla Grande, head to ⊞ **Castro** ⑥. Spend the next day visiting the capital's historical and modern art museums and its lovely cathe-dral.

IF YOU HAVE 5 DAYS

With five days you have time to head to the more remote corners of Chiloé. After visiting Castro, head south to **Chonchi** ⑦, known to lo-cals as the "City of Three Stories." From there it's an easy drive to the sparsely populated Pacific coast to visit the **Parque Nacional Chiloé** ⑨, where you can enjoy one of the short hikes through the forest. On your last day head to Chiloé's southernmost town, ⊞ **Quellón** ⑩.

When to Tour

When best to visit Chiloé? In one word, summer. Weather is the pri-mary reason that most visitors descend on the archipelago from De-cember through March. The islands get only 60 days of sunshine a year, most of those during the summer. Chiloé receives some 400 centime-ters (157 inches) of rain annually, and most of that falls between April and November. You should be prepared for rain any time of year, how-ever. The high-season crowds are never overwhelming, and they give the island a festive atmosphere. Off-season Chiloé is forlorn. Admit-tedly it's not for everyone, but the mist and fog and sunless days deepen the mystery of the island.

Ancud

❶ *90 km (54 mi) southwest of Puerto Montt.*

Unless you're one of those rare visitors who approaches the archipelago from the south, Ancud is the first encounter you'll have with Chiloé. Founded in 1769 as a fortress city on the northern end of Isla Grande, Ancud was repeatedly attacked during Chile's war for independence. It remained the last stronghold of the Spaniards, and the seat of their government-in-exile after fleeing from Santiago, a distinction it retained until Chiloé was finally annexed by Chile in 1826.

Although it's the largest city in Chiloé, Ancud has a smaller-town feel than perpetual rival Castro. Both cities have their fans. Castro has a wider array of activities, but Ancud, with its hills, irregular streets, and commanding ocean views, gets raves for its quiet charm.

The fortresslike **Museo Regional de Ancud** sits uphill from the Plaza de Armas. Mythical Chilote figures, such as the Pincoya and Trauco, greet you on its terrace. The ship *La Goleta Ancud,* the museum's centerpiece, carried Chilean settlers to the Strait of Magellan in 1843. Inside is a collection of island handicrafts. ⊠ *Libertad 370,* ☎ *65/622–413.* ⚏ *Admission.* ☉ *Jan.–Feb., daily 10:30–7:30; Mar.–Dec., daily 9–1, 2:30–6.*

Northwest of downtown Ancud, the 16 cannon emplacements of the **Fuerte de San Antonio** are nearly all that remains of Spain's last outpost in the New World. The fort, constructed in 1786, was a key component in the defense of the Canal de Chacao, especially after the Spanish colonial government fled to Chiloé during Chile's war for independence. ⊠ *Lord Cohrane at San Antonio,* ☎ *no phone.* ⚏ *Free.*

Dining and Lodging

$$–$$$ ✗ **Restaurant La Pincoya.** According to Chilote legend, the presence of La Pincoya signals an abundant catch. This friendly waterfront restaurant is nothing fancy—plain wooden tables and chairs—but the views are stupendous. La Pincoya serves up an abundant fresh fish and usually whips up curanto on the weekends. ⊠ *Arturo Prat 61,* ☎ *65/622–613. No credit cards.*

$$ ✗⌂ **Hostería Ancud.** Ancud's finest hotel—some say the best in
★   Chiloé—sits atop a bluff overlooking the Fuerte de San Antonio. It's part of the Panamericana Hoteles chain, but that doesn't mean it lacks individuality. The rooms in the rustic main building, for example, have log-cabin walls. The wood-panel lobby, with a huge fireplace that invites you to linger, opens into the town's loveliest restaurant. The vaulted ceilings and picture windows give it a spacious feel. Try the *salmón del Caicavilú* (salmon stuffed with chicken, ham, cheese, and mushrooms). ⊠ *San Antonio 30,* ☎ *65/622–340,* ℻ *65/622–350,* 🕸 *hosteriancud.com. 24 rooms. Restaurant, bar, coffee shop, meeting room, travel services. AE, DC, MC, V.*

$$ ⌂ **Hotel Galeón Azul.** Formerly a Catholic seminary, the Blue Galleon is actually painted bright yellow. Perched like a ship run aground on a bluff overlooking Ancud's waterfront, this modern hotel's pleasantly furnished rooms all have big windows with great views of the sea. It's owned by the same folks who own the Hotel Unicornio Azul in Castro, and it offers the same personalized service. ⊠ *Libertad 751,* ☎ *65/622–567,* ℻ *65/622–543. 16 rooms. Restaurant. No credit cards.*

$ ⌂ **Hospedaje O'Higgins.** The nicest of the many hospedajes in Ancud, this 60-year-old home sits on a hillside overlooking the bay. You'll have your pick of eight bright rooms. The furniture in the common areas is a bit worn, but the whole place has a cozy, lived-in feel. The friendly service will make you overlook any inadequacies. ⊠ *O'Higgins 6,* ☎ *65/622–266. 8 rooms, 2 with bath. No credit cards.*

$ ⌂ **Hostal Lluhay.** Don't judge a book by its cover, the old saying goes. If you did you'd pass by this hillside hostal because of its drab exterior, missing the lobby filled with knickknacks and the dining room dominated by a 200-year-old rosewood piano. Rooms are plain, but pleasant considering the reasonable rates. The amiable owners include a buffet breakfast in the price. ⊠ *Lord Cochrane 458,* ☎ ℻ *65/622–656. 10 rooms. Bar, travel services. No credit cards.*

Quicaví

❷ *87 km (52 mi) southeast of Ancud.*

The center of all that is magical and mystical about Chiloé, Quicaví sits forlornly on the eastern coast of Isla Grande. More superstitious locals will strongly advise you against going anywhere near the coast to the south of town, where miles of caves extend to the village of Tenaún. They believe that witches, and evil ones at that, inhabit them. On the beaches are mermaids—not the beautiful and benevolent Pincoya—that lure fishermen to their deaths. And many a Quicaví denizen claims to have glimpsed Chiloé's notorious ghost ship, *El Caleuche,* roaming the waters on foggy nights, searching for its doomed passengers. Of course, a brief glimpse of the ship is all anyone dares admit, as legend holds that a longer gaze could spell death.

In an effort to win converts, the Jesuits constructed the enormous **Iglesia de San Pedro.** The original structure survives from colonial times, though it underwent extensive remodeling in the early 20th century. It's opened for services the first Sunday of every month at 11 AM, which is the only time you can get a look inside.

Tenaún

③ *12 km (7 mi) south of Quicaví.*

A small fishing village, Tenaún is notable for its 1861 neoclassical **Iglesia de Tenaún,** which replaced the original 1734 structure built by the Jesuits on the Plaza de Armas. The style differs markedly from that of other Chilote churches, as the two towers flanking the usual hexagonal central bell tower are painted a striking deep blue. You can see the interior during services on Sundays at 9:30 AM and the rest of the week at 5 PM.

Dalcahue

④ *74 km (44 mi) southeast of Ancud.*

Most days travelers who find themselves in Dalcahue stop only long enough to board the ferry that deposits them 15 minutes later on the island of Quinchao. But everyone lingers in Dalcahue if it's a Sunday morning, when they can visit the weekly artisan market. Dalcahue is a pleasant coastal town, one that deserves a longer visit.

The 1850 **Iglesia de Nuestra Señora de los Dolores,** modeled on the churches constructed during the Jesuit era, sits on the main square. A portico with nine arches, an unusually high number for a Chilote church, fronts the structure. The church contains a small museum. ⊠ *Plaza de Armas.* ⌨ *Free.* ☾ *Daily 9–6.*

Lodging

$ ⊞ **Hotel La Isla.** One of Chiloé's nicest lodgings, the wood-shingled Hotel La Isla greets you with a cozy sitting room and big fireplace off the lobby. Huge windows and vaulted ceilings make the rooms bright and airy. Rates include an ample breakfast. ⊠ *Macopulli 113,* ☏ *65/641–241,* FAX *65/641–626. 16 rooms. Bar, laundry service. No credit cards.*

Shopping

Dalcahue's Sunday-morning **Feria Artesanal,** on Avenida Pedro Montt near the waterfront municipal building, draws the crowds who come to shop for Chilote woolens, baskets, and woven mythical figures. Things get underway about 8 AM and begin to wind down about noon. Bargaining is expected, though the prices are already quite reasonable. There's fun to be had and bargains to be found, but it has a more touristy atmosphere than the ramshackle daily market in nearby Castro.

Isla Quinchao

⑤ *1 km (½ mi) southeast of Dalcahue.*

For many visitors, the elongated Isla Quinchao, the easiest to reach of the islands in the eastern archipelago, defines Chiloé. Populated by hardworking farmers and fishermen, Isla Quinchao provides a glimpse into the region's past. Most visitors head to Achao, Quinchao's largest community, to see the alerce-shingle houses, busy fishing pier, and colonial church.

★ On Achao's Plaza de Armas, the town's centerpiece is its 1706 **Iglesia Santa María de Loreto,** the oldest remaining house of worship in the archipelago. Instead of the alerce so commonly used to construct buildings in the region, the church also uses wood from cypress and *maño* trees. Its typically unadorned exterior contrasts with the deep-blue ceiling embellished with gold stars that you'll find inside. There's also an altar in a rich baroque style. Mass is celebrated Sunday at 11 AM and Tuesday at 7 PM, but docents give guided tours in Spanish while the church is open. An informative Spanish-language museum behind the altar is dedicated to the period of Chiloé's Jesuit missions. All proceeds go to much-needed church restoration—termites have taken their toll. ⊠ *Delicias at Amunategui,* ☎ *65/661–888.* ⊡ *Admission.* ⊙ *Daily 10:30–1 and 2:30–7.*

About 10 km (6 mi) south of Achao is the archipelago's largest church, the 1869 **Iglesia de Nuestra Señora de Gracia.** As with many other Chilote churches, the 60-meter (200-ft) structure sits in solitude near the coast. The church has no tours, but may be visited during Sunday mass.

Dining and Lodging

$$　✕ **Mar y Velas.** This seafood restaurant is housed in a big wood house at the foot of Achao's dock. You might not pick it out as a restaurant at first, as there's sometimes laundry hanging outside the windows. But the place serves scrumptious oysters and a panoply of other offerings from the sea. It also has the friendliest service in town. ⊠ *Serrano 2, Achao,* ☎ *65/661–375. No credit cards.*

$$　✕ **Restaurant La Nave.** On the beach, Restaurant La Nave dishes up seafood in a rambling building that arches over the street. The matter-of-fact staff dishes up curanto most days during the January–March high season, but usually only weekends the rest of the year. ⊠ *Arturo Prat at Sargento Aldea, Achao,* ☎ *65/661–219. No credit cards.*

$　🏠 **Hostal La Plaza.** This cozy private home is close to the hubbub of the Plaza de Armas, but being down an alley and behind a chocolate shop affords it a degree of privacy and quiet. Simply furnished rooms have private baths. The warm owners include breakfast in the very reasonable rates. ⊠ *Amunategui 20, Achao,* ☎ FAX *65/661–283. 10 rooms. No credit cards.*

Castro

❻ *88 km (53 mi) south of Ancud.*

Founded in 1567, Castro is Chile's third-oldest city. Castro's history has been one of destruction, with three fires and three earthquakes laying waste to the city over four centuries. The most recent disaster was in 1960, when a tidal wave caused by an earthquake on the mainland engulfed the city.

Castro's future as Isla Grande's governmental and commercial center looked promising after the 1598 Mapuche rebellion on the mainland drove the Spaniards to Chiloé, but then Dutch pirates sacked the city in 1600. Many of Castro's residents fled to the safety of more isolated parts of the island. It wasn't until 1982 that the city finally became Chiloé's administrative capital.

With a population of 120,000, Castro is Chiloé's second-largest city. Although Ancud is much larger, Castro has a more cosmopolitan atmosphere. Though hardly an urban jungle, this is big-city life, Chiloé style. Residents of more rural parts of the island who visit the capital—no more often than necessary, of course—return home with tales of traffic so heavy that it has to be regulated with stoplights.

Next to its wooden churches, *palafitos* are the best-known architectural symbol of Chiloé. These shingled houses—built on stilts and hanging over the water—are found all along the island's coast. The Pedro Montt coastal highway is the best place to see palafitos in Castro. Many of these ramshackle structures have been turned into restaurants and artisan markets.

Any tour of Castro begins with the much-photographed 1906 **Iglesia de San Francisco,** constructed in the style of the archipelago's other wooden churches, only bigger and grander. Depending on your perspective, you'll use terms like "pretty" or "pretty garish" to describe the orange-and-lavender exterior, colors chosen when the structure was spruced up before Pope John Paul II's 1987 visit. Infinitely more reserved on the inside, the dark-wood interior's centerpiece is the monumental carved crucifix hanging from the ceiling. ⊠ *Plaza de Armas,* ☎ *no phone.* ☎ *Free.* ☉ *Nov.–Feb., Tues.–Sat. 5–9, Sun. 9–12:30, 5–9; Mar.–Oct., Tues.–Sat. 5–8, Sun. 9–12:30, 5–9.*

★ The **Museo Regional de Castro,** just off the Plaza de Armas, gives the best Spanish-language introduction to the region's history and culture. Packed into a fairly small space are artifacts from the Huilliche era (primarily rudimentary farming and fishing implements) through the 19th century (looms, spinning wheels, and plows). One exhibit documents the history of the archipelago's wooden churches, and another displays black-and-white photographs of the damage caused by a 1960 earthquake that rocked southern Chile. The museum shines in its collection of observations of island culture made by outsiders. "The Chilote talks little, but thinks a lot. He is rarely spontaneous with outsiders, and even with his own countrymen he isn't too communicative," wrote one ethnographer. ⊠ *Esmeralda 205,* ☎ *65/635–967.* ☎ *Free.* ☉ *Jan.–Feb., daily 9:30–8; Mar.–Dec., daily 9–1, 3–7.*

NEED A BREAK? Grab a snack and check your e-mail at **N@vegue** (⊠ O'Higgins at Plaza de Armas, ☎ 65/635–254). This cozy Internet café is open Monday to Saturday until 11 PM. It shares space with a store called Años Luz, whose sign is much more prominent.

Northwest of downtown, the **Museo de Arte Moderno de Chiloé** is housed in five refurbished barns. Referred to locally as the "MAM," the complex in a city park exhibits works by Chilote artists. ⊠ *Pasaje Díaz 181,* ☎ *65/635–454.* ☎ *Free.* ☉ *Jan.–Mar., daily 10–7.*

Dining and Lodging

$$ ✕ **Café la Brújula del Cuerpo.** Next to the fire station on the Plaza de Armas, this little place bustles with all the commotion of a big-city diner. Sandwiches are standard fare—burgers and clubs are a favorite. Don't leave without trying one of the mouthwatering ice cream sundaes and banana splits. ⊠ *O'Higgins 308,* ☎ *65/633–229. No credit cards.*

$$ ✕ **1 Palafito Restaurant.** This is the first of five palafitos on Castro's downtown waterfront that have been converted into seafood restaurants. You really can't go wrong with the other four, but locals swear this one is the best. This is no place to escape the crowds; the cavernous restaurant can easily seat a few hundred on a bright summer night. The portions are huge; you'll never be able to finish the tasty curanto. Those with lighter appetites should order something smaller, such as clams or salmón ahumado. ⊠ *Eusebio Lillo 30,* ☎ *65/635–476. No credit cards.*

$$ ▦ **Hostería de Castro.** Looming over downtown Castro, Hostería de Castro is perched on a bluff overlooking the estuary. Its sloped chalet-style roof has a long skylight, making the interior seem bright and airy even on a cloudy day. Nice modern rooms have simply furnishings and cheery flowered bedspreads. The downstairs seafood restaurant has huge windows with great views of the Golfo de Corcovado. ✉ *Chacabuco 202,* ☎ *65/632–301,* ℻ *65/635–688. 29 rooms. Bar, restaurant, laundry service. AE, DC, MC, V.*

$$ ▦ **Hotel Esmeralda.** Just off the bustling Plaza de Armas, this hot-pink hotel is one of Castro's newest lodgings. The compact four-story building has lots of windows and all the amenities that you would expect from such a modern place. It's popular among corporate travelers because of its meeting rooms and business services. ✉ *Esmeralda 206,* ☎ *65/637–900,* ℻ *65/637–910,* ⓦⒺⒷ *www.hotelesmeralda.cl. 31 rooms, 19 with bath, 2 suites. Restaurant, bar, pool, recreation room, laundry service, meeting rooms. AE, DC, MC, V.*

$$ ▦ **Hotel Unicornio Azul.** Taking its name from a popular song by
★   Cuban singer Silvio Rodríguez, the Blue Unicorn is actually pink, though its roof is bright blue. The rambling hotel, dating from 1910, climbs the hill from the waterfront. There are lots of stairs, and many twists and turns as it makes its ascent, but there's a sitting room and reading alcove at every landing and big windows to catch the view. Furnishings in the bright rooms echo the facade's pastel hues. ✉ *Pedro Montt 228,* ☎ *65/632–359,* ℻ *65/632–808. 18 rooms. Restaurant, bar. No credit cards.*

$ ▦ **Hostal Quelcun.** An unpromising alley between two downtown storefronts opens onto a green, leafy courtyard around which you'll find this two-story wooden building, Castro's nicest budget lodging. Some of the wood-paneled rooms have improbable layouts, requiring a bit of maneuvering to get into the second bed, but all are pleasantly furnished. The staff here is friendly and eager to please. ✉ *San Martín 581,* ☎ ℻ *65/632–396. 16 rooms. Travel services. No credit cards.*

Shopping

The city's **Feria Artesanal,** a lively, often chaotic artisan market, is regarded by most as the best place on the island to pick up the woolen sweaters, woven baskets, and straw figures for which Chiloé is known. Prices are already quite reasonable, but vendors expect a bit of bargaining. The stalls share the ramshackle collection of palafitos with several seafood restaurants. ✉ *Eusebio Lillo,* ☎ *no phone.* ☉ *Daily 9–dusk.*

Chonchi

❼   *23 km (14 mi) south of Castro.*

The colorful wooden houses of Chonchi are situated on a hillside so steep that it is known as the *Ciudad de los Tres Pisos,* meaning the "City of Three Stories." The town's name means "slippery earth" in the Huilliche language, and if you tromp up the town's steep streets on a rainy day you'll understand why. Arranged around a scenic harbor, Chonchi wins raves as Chiloé's most picturesque town.

The town's centerpiece is the **Iglesia de San Carlos.** Started by the Jesuits in 1754, it was left unfinished until 1859. Rebuilt in the neoclassical style, the church is now a national monument. An unusually ornate arcade with five arches fronts the church, and inside are and intricately carved altar and wooden columns. The church contains Chonchi's most prized relic, a statue of the Virgen de la Candelaria. According to tradition, this image of the Virgin Mary protected the town from the Dutch pirates who destroyed neighboring Castro in 1600. Townspeople celebrate the event every February 2 with fireworks and gunpowder symbolizing the pirate attack. You can get a look inside during mass each Sunday at 11 AM, but it's hit and miss the rest of the week; the doors might be open, but there's no fixed schedule. ⊠ *Centenario at Plaza de Armas,* ☎ *no phone.*

The small **Museo de las Tradiciones Chonchinas** documents life in Chonchi through furnishings and photos in a 19th-century house. ⊠ *Centenario 116,* ☎ *no phone.* 🎟 *Free.* ☉ *Sept.–May, weekdays 9–7; June–Aug., weekdays 9–1.*

Dining

$ ✕ **El Trébol.** This seafood restaurant sits on the second floor of Chonchi's waterfront market. The decor is basic, and there's no view—this is the market, after all. But the food is good, and the prices are very reasonable. You have a better chance of getting curanto or salmón ahumado if you're here in high season. ⊠ *Irarrázaval s/n,* ☎ *65/671–203. No credit cards.*

Isla Lemuy

❽ *3 km (2 mi) east of Chonchi.*

Easily reached by a 15-minute ferry ride from Chonchi, Isla Lemuy seems miles away from anything. It's the third-largest of Chiloé's islands, just slightly smaller than Quinchao to the north. Jesuit churches dominate three of its villages—Ichuac, Aldachildo, and Detif—none of which are more than a handful of houses. Ichuac's church is in a sorry state of disrepair, as funds for restoration are in short supply. The Aldachildo chapel is locked most of the year, though the folks in the local telephone office can help track down someone who can open it up for you. Detif's church, open only for Sunday-morning mass, is noteworthy for its "votive boats," small wooden ship models hung in thanksgiving for a safe journey. From here there's a stunning view of Volcán Michinmahuida on the mainland.

Lodging

$ 🛏 **Lidia Pérez.** The Pérez family of Puchilco operates one of the nicer lodgings in Chiloé's Red Agroturismo Chiloé, the 19-member agrotourism network. The only accommodation on Isla Lemuy, it's just a wooden farmhouse painted a distinctive orange and green, but it offers a chance to see rural Chilote life up close—in this case, life on a sheep farm. Rooms are spartan, but pleasantly furnished with cheery green bedspreads and drapes. ⊠ *Puchilco,* ☎ *65/628–333 in Ancud. 3 rooms with shared bath. No credit cards.*

Parque Nacional Chiloé

❾ *35 km (21 mi) west of Castro.*

The 430-square-km (166-square-mi) Parque Nacional Chiloé hugs Isla Grande's sparsely populated Pacific coast. During his 1834 visit, Charles Darwin, the park's most famous visitor, marveled at the indigenous families who scratched out a living from this inhospitable land.

The park's two sections differ dramatically in terms of landscape and access. Heavily forested with evergreens, Sector Anay, to the south, is most easily entered from the coastal village of Cucao. An unpaved but passable road heads west to the park from the Pan-American Highway at Notuco, just south of Chonchi. Sector Anay is popular among backpackers who hike the short El Tepual trail, which begins at the Chanquín Visitor Center. The longer Dunas trail also begins at the same place and leads through the forest to the beach dunes near Cacao. You stand the best chance of seeing the Chiloé fox, native to Isla Grande, in your hike through the park. More reclusive is the pudú, the miniature deer found throughout southern Chile. Some 3 km (2 mi) north of the Cucao entrance is a Huilliche community on the shore of Lago Huelde. Unobtrusive visitors are welcome. ⊠ *North of Cucao,* ☎ *65/ 637–266 in Castro.* ▨ *Admission.* ☉ *Daily 7–5.*

Only accessible during the drier months of January through March, the northern Sector Chepu of Chiloé National Park is primarily wetlands created by the tidal wave that rocked the island in 1960. The sector is now home to a large bird population (most notably penguins) as well as a sea lion colony. Reaching the park is difficult—take a gravel road turnoff at Coipomó, about 20 km (12 mi) south of Ancud on the Pan-American Highway, to Chepu on the Pacific coast. From there, it's about a 90-minute hike to the park's northern border. ⊠ *South of Ancud,* ☎ *65/637–266 in Castro.* ▨ *Admission.* ☉ *Daily 7–5.*

Quellón

🔟 *99 km (60 mi) south of Castro.*

The Pan-American Highway, which begins in Alaska and stretches for most of the length of North and South America, ends without fanfare here in Quellón, Chiloé's southernmost city. Quellón was the famed "end of Christendom" described by Charles Darwin during his 19th-century visit. Just a few years earlier it had been the southernmost outpost of Spain's empire in the New World. For most visitors today, Quellón is also the end of the line. But if you're truly adventurous, it's the starting point for ferries that head to the Southern Coast.

Taking its name from a Huilliche phrase meaning "from our past," the **Museo Inchin Cuivi Ant** stands apart from other museums in Chiloé because of its "living" exhibitions: a Chilote woman spins woolens on her loom or makes empanadas in a traditional *fogón* (cooking hut). A botanical garden with herbs, plants, and trees native to Chiloé was taking root at press time. ⊠ *Ladrilleros 225,* ☎ *no phone.* ▨ *Admission.* ☉ *Daily 9–1 2:30–8.*

Dining and Lodging

$$ ✕ **Hostería Romeo Alfa.** This imposing seafood restaurant, which resembles a Bavarian chalet, sits right on Quellón's pier. Choose one of the tables along the window and watch all the comings and goings while you dine on the tasty curanto. The white tablecloths and candles make the dining room appear quite elegant, but the whole affair is really quite informal and very friendly. ⊠ *Capitán Luis Alcazar 554,* ☎ *65/680– 177. No credit cards.*

$ ⌂ **Hotel Los Suizos.** The owners pride themselves on providing Swiss-style service to their guests, which means you can expect friendliness and efficiency. The bright upstairs rooms have light-wood paneling. The cozy downstairs restaurant serves Swiss cuisine as well as seafood. ⊠ *Ladrilleros 399,* ☎ *65/681–787,* ℻ *65/680–747. 6 rooms. Restaurant, bar, laundry service. No credit cards.*

$ ⌂ **Hotel Tierra del Fuego.** This rambling alerce-shingle house sits on Quellón's waterfront. The owners added a dozen rooms, and you definitely know when you've crossed the border between old and new. Opt for one of the wood-paneled rooms in the new wing, which have sunlight streaming in through big windows. Everyone in town seems to stop by for lunch at the bustling restaurant downstairs. ⊠ *Pedro Montt 445,* ☎ *65/682– 079,* ℻ *65/681–226. 24 rooms, 12 with bath. Restaurant, bar. No credit cards.*

Shopping

Quellón's **Feria Artesanal Llauquil** doesn't have the hustle and bustle of similar artisan markets in Castro and Dalcahue, but there are some good buys to be found. The municipal government has recently restored this complex of shops stretching along Avenida Gómez García. Don't bother to bargain, as the prices are already quite reasonable.

CHILOÉ A TO Z

To research prices, get advice from other travelers, and book travel arrangements, visit www.fodors.com.

AIR TRAVEL

Chiloé has a small military airstrip, but there's no airport for either national or international flights. Most people flying to the region head to Aeropuerto El Tepual, 90 km (54 mi) northeast of Ancud in Puerto Montt. LanChile and Ladeco maintain an office in Castro.

➤ AIRLINES: **LanChile** (✉ Blanco 299, ☎ 65/632–866). **Ladeco** (✉ Blanco 299, ☎ 65/632–866).

➤ AIRPORTS: **El Tepual Airport** (✉ Puerto Montt, ☎ 65/294–159).

BOAT AND FERRY TRAVEL

Since Chiloé is an archipelago, the only way to drive here is by taking one of the frequent ferries across the Golfo de Ancud. Most visitors arrive by crossing from the mainland to the tiny town of Chacao in the north. Cruz del Sur operates the frequent ferry service connecting mainland Pargua with Chacao on the northern tip of Isla Grande. Boats leave twice an hour from early morning until late at night, and trips take about 30 minutes. Cars pay about $10.

Many fewer visitors arrive via Quellón in the south. Transmarchilay connects the southern town of Quellón with mainland Chaitén, the gateway to Chilean Patagonia, on Monday, Wednesday, and Friday, leaving Chaitén at 9 AM and Quellón at 3 PM for the five-hour crossing. Navimag connects Quellón with Chaitén eight times a month during the January–February summer season, less frequently the rest of the year. Boats usually leave Quellón at 4 PM and Chaitén at midnight, although the exact time varies greatly with each sailing. Both companies charge about $80 for a vehicle under 4 meters (13 ft) in length. Each passenger pays $14 for the crossing.

➤ BOAT AND FERRY INFORMATION: **Cruz del Sur** (☎ 65/622–265 in Ancud; 65/632–389 in Castro; 64/254–731 in Puerto Montt). **Navimag** (☎ 65/682–207 in Quellón; 65/432–300 in Puerto Montt; 65/731–570 in Chaitén). **Transmarchilay** (☎ 65/681–331 in Quellón; 65/270–421 in Puerto Montt; 65/731–272 in Chaitén).

BUS TRAVEL

Cruz del Sur and its subsidiary Transchiloé operate some 30 buses per day between Ancud and the mainland, usually terminating in Puerto Montt. Many of the routes continue north to Temuco, and a few travel all the way to Santiago. Bus service is timed to coincide with the company's frequent ferries between Pargua and Chacao.

Cruz del Sur and Transchiloé also operate hourly service along the Pan-American Highway between Ancud, Castro, Chonchi, and Quellón. Queilén Bus has service between Chiloé's major cities about 10 times daily. It also makes twice daily runs between Castro and Quemchi.

Many other companies operate small buses or comfortable minivans. Dalcahue Expreso connects Castro with Dalcahue every half hour during the week, less often on weekends. Buses Gallardo runs buses between Castro and Isla Lemuy three times a day during the week, less often on weekends. Buses Arroyo has twice-a-day service between Castro and Cucao, the gateway to Parque Nacional Chiloé.

➤ BUS INFORMATION: **Buses Arroyo** (✉ San Martín s/n, Castro, ☎ 65/

635–604). **Buses Gallardo** (✉ San Martín 667, Castro, ☎ 65/634–521).
Cruz del Sur (✉ Errázuriz at Los Carrera, Ancud, ☎ 65/622–265; ✉
San Martín 486, Castro, ☎ 65/632–389; ✉ Av. Portales at Lota,
Puerto Montt, ☎ 64/254–731). **Dalcahue Expreso** (✉ Ramírez 233,
Castro, ☎ 65/635–164). **Queilén Bus** (✉ San Martín 667, Castro, ☎
65/632–173).

CAR TRAVEL

Rather than terminating in Puerto Montt, the Pan-American Highway
(Ruta 5) skips over the Golfo de Ancud and continues through Ancud,
Castro, and Chonchi before coming to a dead end in Quellón. Paved
roads also lead to Quemchi, Dalcahue, and Achao on Isla Quinchao.
You can reach a few other communities by the so-called *ripios,* or rough
gravel roads. Plan ahead, as it's often slow going during the long rainy
season. Most of the western half of the island is inaccessible by car.

Most visitors who rent a vehicle do so on the mainland, but if you decide you need wheels after your arrival, try the local firm of ADS Rent-
a-Car in Castro.
➤ CAR RENTAL INFORMATION: **ADS Rent-a-Car** (✉ Esmeralda 260, Castro, ☎ 65/637–373).

FESTIVALS AND SEASONAL EVENTS

As elsewhere in southern Chile, Chiloé's festivals usually take place in
summer, when there's the best chance of good weather. Fiestas Cos-
tumbritsas, which celebrate Chilote customs and folklore, take place
over several weekends during January and February in Ancud and Castro. Ancud hosts a small open-air film festival the first few days in February. Every community celebrates its patron saint's day. Although they
are local affairs, outsiders are always welcome.

HEALTH

Chiloé shares Chile's generally high standard of hygiene, so eating and
drinking shouldn't cause you too much concern. The government continues to warn against eating raw shellfish. Though some visitors drink
tap water here, most stick to bottled water, especially outside Castro.

INTERNET

Internet access is not as common here as on the mainland. Castro boasts
one very friendly Internet café called N@vegue with rates of $2 per hour.
➤ INTERNET CAFÉS: **N@vegue** (✉ O'Higgins at Plaza de Armas, Castro, ☎ 65/635–254).

LODGING

Following a trend seen elsewhere in Chile, Chiloé has developed a system of so-called agro-tourism lodgings called the Red Agroturismo
Chiloé, headquartered in the northern community of Ancud. The network of 19 farms, most of them on Isla Grande, offers the adventurous Spanish-speaking traveler a chance to partake of rural life, helping
to milk the cows, churn the butter, or just relax. Rates run about $11
per person including breakfast. Accommodations are in no-frills farm-
houses, but plenty of smog- and traffic-weary Santiago residents are
lapping up the experience.
➤ TOUR AGENCIES: **Red Agroturismo Chiloé** (✉ Eleuterio Ramírez 207,
Ancud, ☎ 65/628–333, WEB www.portalsur.cl/rural/index.htm).

MAIL AND SHIPPING

Mail sent from Chiloé can take a few weeks to reach North America
or Europe. Posting from mainland Puerto Montt is a quicker option.
You can finds a Correos de Chile office in most larger cities. They are
generally open Monday to Friday from 9 to 6, Saturday from 9 to noon.

➤ POST OFFICES: **Correos de Chile** (✉ O'Higgins 388, Castro; ✉ Pudeto and Blanco Encalada, Ancud; ✉ 22 de Mayo and Ladrilleros, Quellón).

MONEY MATTERS

With few businesses equipped to handle credit cards, Chiloé is primarily a cash-and-carry economy. Banks will gladly change U.S. dollars for Chilean pesos, but most will not touch traveler's checks. But the situation is not as frustrating as it sounds; ATMs are popping up everywhere in larger cities like Castro and Ancud. You can use your Plus- or Cirrus-affiliated card to get cash at the going rate at any of the ATMs on the Redbanc network.

SAFETY

Crimes against travelers are almost unheard of in pastoral Chiloé, but the standard precautions about watching your possessions apply.

TAXIS

As is true elsewhere in the region, solid black or solid yellow cabs operate as *colectivos,* or collective taxis. They follow fixed routes with fixed stops, picking up up to four people along the way. A sign on the roof shows the general destination. The cost (less than $1 within town) is little more than that of a city bus. A black cab with a yellow roof takes you directly to your requested destination for a metered fare. You can hail them on the street.

Colectivos also operate between many of Isla Grande's communities. They may look like a regular cabs, or they may be minivans. They have fixed stops, often near a town's central bus station.

TELEPHONES

Chiloé shares Puerto Montt's area code of 65. Anywhere in the archipelago or the southern Lake District you can drop the area code and dial the six-digit number. CTC, Entel, and Telefónica del Sur are the three most prominent telephone companies. Their *centros de llamados* (call centers) are the place to make calls and send faxes. Each company also has its own network of public telephones. Make sure you have the right company's calling card to match the phone booth. Calling cards can be purchased in many shops and newsstands.

TIPPING

As elsewhere in Chile, you should add a 10% tip to your restaurant bill. Most other workers don't expect tips.

TOURS

Austral Adventures, the region's best tour operator, offers intimate guided tours of Chiloé and neighboring Patagonia. The agency's own 15-meter (50-ft) vessel, the *Cahuella,* plies the archipelago, the Chilean fjords, and Laguna San Rafael National Park, in three-, four- or eight-day tours. Austral Adventures can arrange custom-made tours of Chiloé itself, whether your tastes run to sea kayaking, church visits, or hikes in Chiloé National Park.

➤ TOUR OPERATORS: **Austral Adventures** (✉ Prat at Baquedano, Ancud, ☎ FAX 65/625–977, WEB www.austral-adventures.com).

VISITOR INFORMATION

Sernatur, Chile's national tourist office, operates a friendly, well-staffed information office on the Plaza de Armas in Ancud.

➤ INFORMATION: **Sernatur** (✉ Libertad 665, Ancud, ☎ 65/622–800).

9 THE SOUTHERN COAST

Chile's "silent south" is one of the world's last remaining frontiers. This is the thin country's thinnest region, a ragged strip of land crisscrossed by a labyrinth of channels, inlets, and fjords. Here you'll find the San Raphael glacier, one of Chile's most awe-inspiring sights. It's not the easiest place to reach, but many people endure long and difficult journeys in order to witness an icy wilderness that remains virtually untouched.

by Pete Nelson

T HE SLIVER OF LAND called the Southern Coast, stretching for 4,300-km (2,672-mi) between the tranquil valleys of the Lake District and the awesome ice fields of Patagonia, largely consists of heavily forested mountains, some rising dramatically from the shores of shimmering lakes, others directly out of the Pacific Ocean. Slender waterfalls and nearly vertical streams, often seeming to emerge from the rock itself, tumble and slide from neck-craning heights. Some dissipate into misty nothingness before touching the ground, others flow into the innumerable rivers—large and small, wild and gentle—that flow westward to the sea. Chile has designated vast tracts of this truly magnificent landscape as national parks and reserves, but most are accessible only on foot. The few roads available to vehicles are slightly widened trails or the occasional logging route navigable only by the most rugged of four-wheel-drive vehicles.

The infrequent hamlets scattered along the low-lying areas of this rugged region exist as fishing villages or small farming centers. The gradual increase of boat and ferry service to some of these towns and the expansion of the major highway called the Carretera Austral have begun to encourage migration to the region. Coihaique, the only town here of any size, offers a variety of dining, lodging, and shopping opportunities. Meanwhile, a few intrepid entrepreneurs have established world-class accommodations in remote locations that are readily accessible to spectacular mountain peaks, ancient volcanoes, and glaciers with their concomitant fjords and lakes.

Planning a visit to the region's widely separated points of interest can be challenging, as getting from place to place is often difficult. Creating a logical itinerary in southern Chile is as much about choosing how to get there as it is about where you want to go. The most rewarding trip through this region is a combination of travel by boat and by plane, with an occasional car rental if you want to get a little deeper into the hinterlands.

Pleasures and Pastimes

Dining

The Southern Coast's topography means that fish and shellfish can be found just about anywhere. Lamb and beef dishes also abound. French fries are a ubiquitous side dish, but rice is almost always available as an alternative. Locally grown vegetables and fruit are abundant. By and large, entrées are simple, hearty combinations of items, not elaborately concocted recipes. The variety of items on most menus is extensive, so many dishes are prepared from scratch when you order. Just sip your wine, or order a second beer.

Having food and drink on hand when driving along the Carretera Austral is necessary because of the distances between points of interest. The tiniest rural towns boast at least one *supermercado*. These markets are rarely "super," but the shelves typically sag under all manner of canned and packaged foods and bottled drinks. Bread of one type or another is rarely out of stock and many stores carry a small variety of deli-type meats and cheeses.

Traveling by road throughout the region, you'll see crudely printed signs with an arrow pointing to a nearby farmhouse advertising KÜCHEN, clear evidence of the many pockets of German influence. For approximate entrée costs, *see* the dining price chart *in* Smart Travel Tips A to Z.

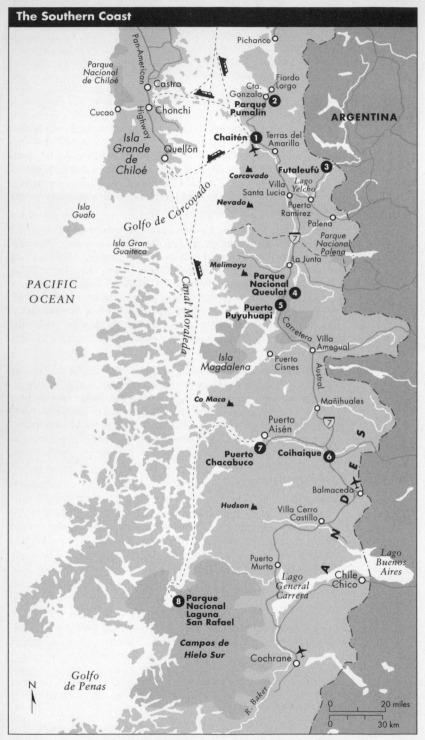

The Southern Coast

Pichanco

*Parque
Nacional
de Chiloé*

Pan-American

Castro

Cta.
Gonzalo

Fiordo
Largo

2

Cucao

Chonchi

**Parque
Pumalín**

ARGENTINA

*Isla
Grande
de
Chiloé*

Highway

Quellón

Chaitén **1** Terras del
Amarillo

Corcovado

Futaleufú **3**

Villa
Santa Lucia

*Lago
Yelcho*

*Isla
Guafo*

Nevado

Puerto
Ramirez

Palena

Golfo de Corcovado

*Isla Gran
Guaiteca*

7

*Parque
Nacional
Palena*

La Junta

Melimoyu

**Parque
Nacional
Queulat** **4**

PACIFIC
OCEAN

Canal Moraleda

**Puerto
Puyuhuapi** **5**

Carretera

Villa
Amegual

*Isla
Magdalena*

Puerto
Cisnes

Austral

Co Maca

Mañihuales

7

Puerto
Aisén

**Puerto
Chacabuco** **7**

Coihaique **6**

A
N
D
E
S

Balmaceda

Hudson

Villa Cerro
Castillo

Puerto
Murta

*Lago
Buenos
Aires*

Puerto
Murta

*Lago
General
Carrera*

Chile
Chico

8 **Parque
Nacional
Laguna
San Rafael**

*Campos de
Hielo Sur*

Cochrane

*Golfo
de Penas*

R. Baker

N

0   20 miles

0   30 km

Fishing

Fishing enthusiasts were among the first to discover the beauty of the Southern Coast. In the region's icy rivers and streams they found an abundance of fish, from brown and rainbow trout to silver and steelhead salmon. There are numerous mountain lodges where great fishing can be had right outside your door. A short boat trip can often bring you to isolated spots where you won't run into another soul the entire day.

Lodging

This region offers a surprisingly wide range of accommodations, including some of the finest resorts in the country. In many towns you'll find comfortable hotels with attractive lobbies and dining rooms that offer a complete breakfast and often even lunch and dinner. What you won't find is the blandness of chain hotels. Most of the region's establishments reflect the distinct personalities and idiosyncrasies of their owners.

Some of the most humble homes in villages along the Carretera Austral have supplemented their family income by becoming bed-and-breakfasts. A stay in one of these *hospedajes* is an ideal way to meet the people and experience the culture. These accommodations are not regulated, so the quality varies. Don't hesitate to ask to see the room—you may even have a choice. Inquire about the availability of hot water and confirm that breakfast is included. Then agree upon the rate, which might be as low as $6. Depending on how remote the village, the rate should not exceed $12. For approximate room costs, *see* the lodging price chart *in* Smart Travel Tips A to Z.

Shopping

You're likely to run across find few, if any, stalls along the roadside selling handicrafts. The major town of Coihaique, however, boasts a small artisans' market where you can find locally produced goods. Look for one interesting regional item: pottery bowls and small jugs with animal skin shrunken onto their bases to keep liquids from seeping out. Woolen items, of course, are ubiquitous.

Exploring the Southern Coast

The Southern Coast is an expansive region covered with vast national parks and reserves. By and large, this is territory for adventurous types who come for the unparalleled fishing, kayaking, and white-water rafting opportunities. The region rewards intrepid explorers with relatively untrammeled trails and rarely viewed vistas.

Part of the challenge of traveling within this region of Chile is, of course, simply the country's narrow north–south orientation. The distances between sights can be daunting. Circuits, per se, are virtually impossible. Traveling by air is a good option if your time is limited. Ferries are slow and not always scenic, particularly if skies are the least bit clouded. There are, however, a few firms offering sightseeing cruises.

The key to enjoying the Southern Coast is knowing that your trip probably won't always go as planned. Itineraries cannot be too tight as schedules are not always reliable. Meet with a professional travel operator familiar with the region and focus on your priorities.

Great Itineraries

IF YOU HAVE 7 DAYS

Unless you fly, the only way to reach the Southern Coast is by boat or ferry. On your first day head to the port town of ⚅ **Chaitén** ①. Devote a day to visiting **Parque Pumalín** ②, which features some of the most pristine landscape in the region. The third day, take the Carretera Austral to ⚅ **Puerto Puyuhuapi** ⑤. A stay at Termas de Puyuhuapi, a resort ac-

CHILE'S ROAD TO RICHES

THE PAN-AMERICAN HIGHWAY, which snakes its way through the northern half of Chile, never quite makes it to the Southern Coast. To connect this remote region with the rest of the country, former President Agusto Pinochet proposed a massive public works project to construct a highway called the Carretera Austral. But the $300 million venture had another purpose as well. Pinochet was afraid that without a strong military presence in the region, neighboring Argentina could begin chipping away at Chile's territory. The highway would allow the army easier access to an area that until then was accessible only by boat.

Ground was broken on the Carretera Austral in 1976, and in 1983 the first section, running from Chaitén to Coihaique, opened to great fanfare. The only trouble was that you still couldn't get there from the mainland. It took another five years for the extension from Chaitén north to Puerto Montt to be completed. An extension from Coihaique south to Cochrane was finished the same year.

The word "finished" is misleading, as construction continues to this day. Although the Carretera Austral is nicely paved near Puerto Montt, it soon reveals its true nature as a two-lane gravel surface that crawls inexorably southward for 1,156 km (718 mi) toward the outpost of Villa O'Higgins. And the highway isn't even contiguous. In three places the road actually ends abruptly at water's edge; ferries link these broken stretches of highway through the narrowest part of Chile.

The Carretera Austral is lauded in tourism brochures as "a beautiful road studded with rivers, waterfalls, forests, lakes, glaciers, and the occasional hamlet." This description is accurate except for the use of one critically misleading phrase: "beautiful road." In fact, the highway is still mostly unpaved. Dozens of single-lane, wide-board bridges—often sitting so high above the road surface that you have to bring your four-wheel-drive vehicle to a complete stop in order to roll onto them— cross streams and rivers. Shoulders are nonexistent or made of soft, wheel-grabbing gravel. Periodically, traffic must wend its way through construction, among heavy equipment and workers.

As you drive south along the Carretera Austral, Chile's southernmost reaches seem to simply disintegrate into a tangle of sounds and straits, channels and fjords. Here you'll find lands laden with lush vegetation or layered in fields of ice. The road struggles valiantly along this route, connecting tiny fishing hamlets and farming villages all the way from Puerto Montt to Villa O'Higgins. There, the huge Campo de Hielo Sur (Southern Ice Field) force it to a halt.

Navigating the Carretera Austral requires some planning, as communities along the way are few and far between. Some parts of the highway, especially in the southernmost reaches, are deserted. Check out your car thoroughly, especially the air in the spare tire. Make sure you have a jack and jumper cables. Bring along enough food in case you find yourself stuck far from the nearest restaurant.

What the Carretera Austral offers adventurous travelers is a chance to see a part of the world where few have ventured. The views from the highway are truly amazing, from the conical top of Volcán Corcovado near Chaitén to the sprawling valleys around Coihaique. Here you'll find national parks where the trails are virtually deserted, such as Parque Nacional Queulat and Reserva Nacional Río Simpson. The region's crowning glory, of course, is the vast glacier at Laguna San Raphael. It may be a tough journey today, but when it is eventually finished, the Carretera Austral could rival the most spectacular scenic roadways in the world.

—Pete Nelson

cessible only by boat, is a must. Head out the next morning to see the famous "hanging glacier" of **Parque Nacional Queulat** ④. On your fifth day travel down to 🛪 **Coihaique** ⑥, the only city of any size in the region. The next morning head to **Puerto Chacabuco** ⑦, where you can board a boat bound for the unforgettable **Parque Nacional Laguna San Raphael** ⑧. On your last day make your way back up the highway.

IF YOU HAVE 10 DAYS

Follow the above itinerary, but add a day or so to explore the national parks surrounding Coihaique. Then consider spending a few days on one of the boats that run along the coast.

When to Tour

Mid-summer—late November to early February—is considered high season in southern Chile; demand for accommodations is keen and advance reservations at high-end lodgings are vital. In spring (September into November) and fall (March to May) the weather is delightfully cool and hotel rooms are easier to come by. However, ferry service is reduced and sometimes even cancelled, making travel along the Carretera Austral more difficult.

Chaitén

❶ *201 km (125 mi) south of Puerto Montt.*

A century ago, Chaitén wasn't even a spot on the map. Today it's still a small port town, with a population of barely more than 3,000. Although it's not really a destination itself, Chaitén serves as a convenient base for exploring the area, including Parque Pumalín and Reserva Nacional Futaleufú.

Getting to Chaitén is fairly easy. Both Navimag and Transmarchilay operate regular ferry service between Chaitén and Puerto Montt in the Lake District and Quellón on Chiloé. Flying is also an option; a few small airlines offer flights between Chaitén and Puerto Montt.

It's also possible to drive to Chaitén from Puerto Montt via the Carretera Austral, but you have to make use of two car ferries. The first is easy, as Transmarchilay ferries make nine daily trips between La Arena and Puelche all year. The second leg is tougher because Transmarchilay's ferries between Hornopirén and Caleta Gonzalo only operate in January and February.

Isla Puduguapi, home to some 150 noisy sea lions, is an easy half-day trip from Chaitén. Toninas, a resident dolphin, may escort your boat to the island. Chaitur and other travel agencies offer tours to the island.

The emerald-green **Lago Yelcho,** one of the best places in the region to fish for brown trout, runs along the Carretera Austral south of Chaitén. Just past the village of Puerto Cárdenas you'll find Puente Ventisquero Yelcho (Glacier Bridge), the beginning of a challenging two-hour hike to Ventisquero Caví (Hanging Glacier).

The much-lauded **Termas de Amarillo,** a modest hot springs about 25 km (16 mi) southeast of Chaitén, offers a nice respite for weary muscles. The setting, along a river running through a heavily forested valley, is lovely.

Dining and Lodging

$$ ✗ **Restaurant Brisas del Mar.** This cheerful little eatery overlooks the sea from its perch on the second floor. The sheer number of items on its menu is astounding, from excellent fish dishes such as *salmón en mantequilla* (salmon braised in butter) to a variety of grilled meats. ⊠ *Corcovado 278,* ☎ *65/731–284. No credit cards.*

$ ✕ **Corcovado.** Here's one place where you won't leave hungry, as the portions of traditional fare are huge but the prices are small. This wooden building sits near the water, so you are treated to great views. ⊠ *Pedro Aguirre Cerda 5,* ☎ *65/731–221. No credit cards.*

$—$$ ☷ **Puma Verde.** Easily the finest accommodation in town, this small and comfortable B&B is half a block from the water on the town's busiest street. Puma Verde has three rooms (one much larger than the others) furnished with locally crafted furniture and woolen blankets. The baths have modern fixtures. ⊠ *O'Higgins 54,* ☎ *65/731–184. 3 rooms. Restaurant. MC, V.*

$ ☷ **Hotel Shilling.** Of the town's numerous family-run hospedajes, Hotel Shilling is the most professional and hospitable. Breakfast is included. ⊠ *Corcovado 230,* ☎ *65/731–295. 12 rooms. No credit cards.*

Parque Pumalín

★ ❷   *56 km (35 mi) north of Chaitén.*

The privately owned Parque Pumalín is an extraordinary venture that began when conservationist Doug Tompkins bought a 1,000-acre araucaria forest south of Puerto Montt. Since 1988, he has spent more than $15 million to purchase the 800,000 acres that make up Parque Pumalín. The region is home to one of the last remaining temperate rain forests in the world.

Tomkins, an American who made his fortune founding the clothing company Esprit, owns two strips of land that stretch from one side of the country to the other. He tried to buy the parcel between the two halves that would have connected them, but the sale was fiercely opposed by some government officials who questioned whether an American should own so much of Chile. Tomkins now hopes to work with the government to make Parque Pumalín part of the national park system.

Parque Pumalín encompasses some of the most pristine landscape in the region. There are a dozen or so trails that wind past lakes and waterfalls. Some two dozen campsites are available for more adventurous visitors. The entrance to the park is at Caleta Gonzalo, where the ferries from Hornopirén arrive. ⊠ *Buín 356, Puerto Montt,* ☎ *65/250–079,* FAX *65/255–145,* WEB *www.pumalinproject.org.*

Dining and Lodging

$$ ✕☷ **Cabañas Caleta Gonzalo.** Nine gray-shingled cabañas, each designed to be distinct from its neighbor, sit high on stilts against the backdrop of the misty mountains. All boast broad front porches and tall windows that let in lots of light. The interiors are rustic yet luxurious, with handcrafted furniture, handwoven woolen blankets, and fully equipped private bathrooms. The complex includes an attractive visitors center and handicraft shop stocking books, guides, and maps, as well as organic honey and jams. The adjacent café, with its welcoming copper-hooded corner fireplace, offers meals from early morning until midnight year-round. ⊠ *Caleta Gonzalo,* ☎ *65/731–364,* FAX *65/731–184. 9 rooms. Café, shop. MC, V.*

Futaleufú

❸   *159 km (99 mi) east of Chaitén.*

Near the town of Villa Lucia, Ruta 231 branches east from the Carretera Austral and winds around Lago Yelcho. About 159 km (98 mi) later, not far from the Argentine border, it reaches the tiny town of Futaleufú. Despite being barely five square blocks, Futaleufú is on many travelers' itineraries. Here, where the Río Espolón and the Río Futaleufú collide, you'll find world-class adventure-sport opportunities. It's the staging center for serious river and sea kayaking, white-water rafting, and mountain biking, as well as fly-fishing, canyon hiking, and horseback riding. Daylong trips for less-experienced travelers are available.

Lodging

$$$$ 🏨 **Hostería Río Grande.** The biggest and best lodging in Futaleufú, this sleek wooden hotel is ground zero for adventure travel in the area. It hosts the Futaleufú Adventure Center, operated by former U.S. Olympic paddler Chris Spelius. From December through March it offers four- to seven-night packages that include kayaking, rafting, and hiking trips throughout the region. All meals and activities are included. ✉ *Calle O'Higgins 397,* ☎ *65/721–320; 888/488–9082 in the U.S.,* WEB *www.expedicioneschile.com. 13 rooms. Restaurant, bar, room service, hiking, boating, fishing. AE, MC, V.*

Parque Nacional Queulat

❹ *175 km (109 mi) south of Chaitén.*

Created in 1983, the 350,000-acre Parque Nacional Queulat begins to rise and roll to either side of the Carretera Austral some 20 km (12 mi) south of the town of La Junta. The park's rugged geography is highlighted by dense virgin forests crisscrossed by rivers and streams that attract fishing aficionados from all over the world. At the higher altitudes brilliant blue glaciers can be found in the valleys between snow-covered peaks.

Less than a kilometer off the east side of the Carretera Austral you are treated to a close-up view of the **Ventisquero Colgante** (Hanging Glacier). This sheet of ice slides forward between a pair of gentle rock faces. Several waterfalls cascade down the cliffs to either side of the glacier's foot. There is an easy 15-minute walk leading to one side of the lake below the glacier, which is not visible from the overlook. Another longer hike takes you deeper into the park's interior.

A short drive farther south, where the Carretera Austral makes one of its sharp switchback turns as it climbs higher, a small sign points into the undergrowth, indicating the trailhead for the **Salto de Padre García.** There is no parking area, but you can leave your car on the shoulder. This short hike through dense forest is well worth attempting for a close-up view of a waterfall of striking proportions.

There are two Conaf stations, one at the Ventisquero Colgante overlook, the other a few kilometers north of the southern park gateway. ✉ *Carretera Austral,* ☎ FAX *67/231–065 or 67/232–599.* 🎫 *Admission.* ☉ *Daily 8:30–6:30.*

Dining and Lodging

$$–$$$ ✕🏨 **Hotel El Pangue.** Near the entrance of Parque Nacional Queulat, a driveway leads to a sprawling complex of reddish buildings on the sheltered shores of Lake Risopatrón. Several shingle-roofed cabañas, all constructed by local craftspeople from native wood, have central heating and private baths with ample hot water. The clubhouse features a fireplace and a panoramic view of the lake. The dining room offers barbecued lamb prepared on a traditional *quincho* (grill) and authentic German küchen. There is also a partially covered, heated swimming pool. Activities include trolling and fly-fishing on the lake and nearby rivers, stocked in abundance with rainbow and brown trout. Canoes, mountain bikes, and horses are available for exploring the lake and the trails through the national park. ✉ *5 km (3 mi) south of the entrance of Parque Nacional Queulat,* ☎ *67/325–128,* FAX *67/325–128.*

15 cabañas. Restaurant, bar, pool, lake, hot tub, sauna, hiking, horse-back riding, boating, fishing. AE, MC, V.

Puerto Puyuhuapi

⑤ *196 km (123 mi) south of Chaitén*

This village of a little more than 500 residents is one of the oldest along the Carretera Austral. Founded in the 1930s by German immigrants who ventured into the wilderness to clear the forests to make way for farms, it is now a convenient stopover for those headed farther south in the region. It offers a few modest hospedajes, as well as some markets and a gas station. Most people headed to Puerto Puyuhuapi stop to take the waters at **Termas de Puyuhuapi,** a hot springs south of town at the region's most prestigious hotel. In addition to its thermal waters, this resort includes a full-service spa offering thalassotherapy and other treatments.

Dining and Lodging

$$$–$$$$ ✕⌕ **Termas de Puyuhuapi.** As you drive along the Carretera Austral,
★ this world-class resort hotel is barely visible across the dark waters of the Seno Ventisquero (Glacier Sound). Accessible only by boat, Termas de Puyuhuapi gives new meaning to the word "secluded." Set between a fjord and a steep, forested mountain, its redwood structures have lots of windows to take full advantage of the views. Here you'll find carefully landscaped walkways leading to the low-roofed buildings that hold spacious bi-level rooms with decks extending over the water. Relax by the waterfalls tumbling into the outdoor pool, or choose either of the two indoor pools. The excellent restaurant offers typical Chilean fare, especially fish and shellfish. Want to catch your own? The staff is happy to organize fishing trips to nearby rivers. The hotel also leads tours throughout the region, including a trip to the Laguna San Raphael in a private catamaran. ⌂ *13 km (8 mi) south of Puerto Puyuhuapi,* ☎ *2/225–6489 in Santiago,* ⟱ *2/274–8111 in Santiago,* ⎚ *www.patagoniaconnex.cl. 28 rooms, 2 cabins. Restaurant, bar, 3 pools, spa, health club, hiking, boating. AE, MC, V.*

Shopping

Using only natural wool thread and cotton fibers, the carpets at **Alfombras de Puyuhuapi** are hand-woven by three generations of women from Chiloé. The rustic vertical looms, designed and built specifically for this shop, allow them to make carpets with a density of 20,000 knots per square meter. The shop was opened in the 1940s by several young Germans who had fled the economic ravages of World War I. Trained by his father and grandfather, current proprietor Helmut E. Hopperdietzel proudly displays the extensive stock of finished carpets of various sizes and designs. ⌂ *Calle E. Ludwig s/n,* ☎ *67/325–131,* ⎚ *www.puyuhuapi.com.*

Outdoor Activities and Sports

More than 50 rivers are within easy driving distance of Puerto Puyuhuapi, making this a cherished destination among fishing enthusiasts. Here you'll find rainbow and brown trout, silver and steelhead salmon, and local species such as the robalo. The average size is about 6 pounds, but it's not rare to catch monsters twice that size. Daily trips are organized by the staff at Termas de Puyuhuapi.

Coihaique

⑥ *224 km (140 mi) south of Puerto Puyuhuapi.*

Where Río Simpson and Río Coihaique come together you'll find Coihaique, the only community of any size on the Carretera Austral.

Its 50,000 residents make up more than half of the region's population. The prerequisite **Plaza de Armas** here is a pentagon, designed by a planner paying overzealous homage to the five-sided badges of Chile's *caribineros* (police officers). Ten streets radiate from the corners. Horn, one of the most colorful, is where you'll find the crafts stands of the Feria Artesenal. Balmaceda connects the central square with the smaller Plaza Prat. The cathedral rises between Riquelmo and Bulnes. Navigating the area around the plaza is confusing at first, but the streets, bearing those traditional names used throughout the country, soon yield to the simple grid system.

The Carretera Austral leads into the northeastern corner of this bustling town near the **Monumento al Ovejero.** On the broad median of the Avenida General Baquedano, you're welcomed by a solitary shepherd, his horse, and his dog leaning motionless into the wind behind a plodding flock of sheep.

In a small converted house, the **Museo Regional de la Patagonia** is worth the tiny fee for the black-and-white photos of early-20th-century pioneering into this region, as well as for the collections of household, farming, and early industrial artifacts from the same era. A visit is a reminder of how recently many parts of southern Chile began to develop. ⊠ *Baquedano 310, between Carrera and Prat,* ☎ *no phone.* ☞ *Admission.* ☉ *Daily 8:30–1, 2:30–6:30.*

The 5,313-acre **Reserva Nacional Coihaique,** about 4 km (2½ mi) north of Coihaique, provides hikers with some stunning views when the weather cooperates. If it's raining you can drive a 9-km (5-mi) circuit through the park.

The evergreen forests of **Reserva Nacional Río Simpson,** just north of Reserva Nacional Coihaique, are filled with with waterfalls tumbling down steep canyons walls. A lovely waterfall called the Cascada de la Virgen is a 1-km (½-mi) hike from the information center, while another called the Velo de la Novia is 8 km (5 mi) farther.

Dining and Lodging

$$ ✕ **Restaurant Histórico Ricer.** Operated by the same family for decades, this popular restaurant is a Coihaique institution. Drop by for a brief history lesson, as the walls are covered with fascinating black-and-white photos from the town's archives. Among the most popular items on the extensive menu are salmon, rabbit, and grilled leg of lamb. Lighter fare includes excellent *empanadas* (meat pies) filled with *locate* (a local mollusk). The pottery and crocheted hangings that decorate the restaurant were created by the family's matriarch. ⊠ *Horn 40 and 48,* ☎ *67/232–920 or 67/237–950. AE, MC, V.*

$–$$ ✕ **Cafetería Alemana.** Whether you're seated in one of the dining rooms (one of which conveys the aura of a small-town German restaurant, the other more like a traditional café) or outside at a table on the sidewalk, Cafetería Alemana is a great place for people-watching. The menu offers a wide array of lighter fare, including tiny *empanaditas* (small meat-filled pies). Challenge your dietary willpower by taking a look at the case full of authentic küchen. ⊠ *Condell 119,* ☎ *67/231–731. AE, MC, V.*

$–$$ ✕ **La Casona Restaurante.** A pleasant wood-burning stove in the cor-
★   ner welcomes you to this tidy little restaurant. Vases filled with fresh flowers adorn tables covered with white linen. The place is run by a small family— the mother cooks, her husband and son serve—who exude a genuine warmth to everyone who walks in the door. There's plenty of traditional fare on the menu, but the *centolla* (king crab) and *langostino* (lobster) are the standouts. ⊠ *Obispo Vielmo 77,* ☎ *67/238–894. No credit cards.*

$–$$ ✕ **La Olla.** Starched linen tablecloths lend an unmistakable aura of European gentility to this modest restaurant, operated by a courtly Spaniard and his son. Among the specialties are a fine paella and a hearty *estofado de cordero* (lamb stew). ⊠ *Av. Prat 176,* ☏ *67/234–700. AE, MC, V.*

$$$ 🏨 **Hotel Coihaique.** This nicely landscaped lodging is in a quiet corner of town, but it's within easy walking distance of the Plaza de Armas. Rooms are modestly appointed, but clean and spacious. ⊠ *Magallanes 131,* ☏ *67/231–137 or 67/231–737,* WEB *www.hotelsa.cl. 40 rooms. Restaurant, bar, minibars, room service, pool. AE, MC, V.*

$$ 🏨 **Hostal Belisario Jara.** You realize how much attention has been paid
★   to the detail here when the proprietor points out that the weather vane on the peak of the single turret is a copy of one at Chilean poet Pablo Neruda's home in Isla Negra. In the quaint lodging's various nooks and crannies, wide windows and natural woods are abundant. The artwork on the walls is created by the proprietor himself during the low season. Rooms are small, but tastefully and comfortably furnished. A country breakfast is included. ⊠ *Francisco Bilbao 662,* ☏ *67/234–150,* WEB *www.belisariojara.itgo.com. 8 rooms. Bar, dining room. No credit cards.*

Nightlife and the Arts

A father-and-son team run the popular **Piel Roja** (⊠ Moraleda 495, ☏ 67/237–832). The club, whose name translates as "Red Skin," opens at 7 PM—relatively early for Chile. This pub, famous for its pizza, is worth a visit for the funky furnishings and decor alone.

Shopping

The **Feria Artesenal** (⊠ Plaza de Armas, between Dussen and Horn) includes a number of stalls offering woolen clothing, small leather items, and pottery.

Puerto Chacabuco

❼   *68 km (43 mi) northwest of Coihaique.*

Puerto Chacabuco, an unattractive port town, is Coihaique's link to the ocean. This harbor ringed by snowcapped mountains is where you board the ferries that transport you north to Puerto Montt in the Lake District and Quellón on Chiloé, as well as boats headed south to the spectacular Laguna San Raphael.

Nearby **Puerto Aisén,** founded in 1914 to serve the region's burgeoning cattle ranches, was the original port. Devastating forest fires that swept through the interior in 1955 filled the once-deep harbor with silt, making it all but useless. The busy main street is a good place to stock up on supplies for trips to the nearby national parks.

Dining and Lodging

$$ ✕🏨 **Hotel Loberías de Aisén.** On a hill about 10 minutes from town, Hotel Loberías de Aisén offers clean, comfortable accommodations. The restaurant, popular with locals, serves the best seafood in town. ⊠ *Carrera 50, Puerto Chacabuco,* ☏ *67/351–112,* FAX *67/351–188. 26 rooms. Restaurant.*

Parque Nacional Laguna San Rafael

★ ❽ *5 hours by boat from Puerto Chacabuco.*

Nearly all of the 101,000-acre Parque Nacional Laguna San Rafael is fields of ice that are totally inaccessible. But only a handful of the people who come here ever set foot on land. Most travel by boat from Puerto Chacabuco or Puerto Montt through the maze of fjords along the coast to the expansive San Rafael Lagoon. Floating on the surface of the brilliant blue water are scores of icebergs that rock from side to side as boats pass.

The massive chunks of ice come from the Ventisquero San Rafael, the spectacular glacier extending 4 km (2½ mi) from end to end. It's a noisy beast, roaring like thunder as the sheets of ice shift. If you're lucky you'll see huge pieces of ice calve off, causing violent waves that makes you glad your boat stayed at a safe distance.

Several different companies make the trip to Laguna San Raphael. The cheapest are Navimag and Transmarchilay, which offer both two-night trips from Puerto Chacabuco and four-night trips from Puerto Montt. More luxurious are the three-night cruises from Puerto Chacabuco and the six-night cruises from Puerto Montt offered by Skorpios. For those with less time, Patagonia Express has day trips from Chacabuco on a deluxe catamaran.

THE SOUTHERN COAST A TO Z

To research prices, get advice from other travelers, and book travel arrangements, visit www.fodors.com.

AIR TRAVEL

LanChile and its domestic subsidiary Ladeco have flights to the regions from Santiago, Puerto Montt, and Punta Arenas. They arrive at the Southern Coast's only major airport, 55 km (34 mi) south of Coihaique in the town of Balmaceda. Areomet flies from Puerto Montt to a small airfield near Chaitén.

It's a good idea to make air-travel arrangements through a travel agency knowledgeable about the area. They will be invaluable if unforeseen delays force you to change your plans at the last minute.
➤ AIRLINES: **Areomet** (✉ Chaitur, O'Higgins 67, Chaitén, ☎ 65/731-429). **Lan Chile** (✉ General Parra 215, Coihaique, ☎ 67/231–188).

BOAT AND FERRY TRAVEL

There are three extensive cruise and ferry lines operating in southern Chile, all of whom can rightfully boast considerable experience sailing the interwoven fjords, rivers, and lakes of the region: Navimag, Skorpios, and Transmarchilay. Fares in high season (January and February) are dramatically higher than other times. Most cruises do not operate at all during the winter months of June, July, and August.

Navimag (short for "Navegación Magallanes") operates a rather inelegant, but highly serviceable, cargo and passenger fleet throughout the region. The M/V *Evangelistas*, a 324-passenger ferry, sails round-trip from Puerto Montt to the Laguna San Raphael, stopping in both directions in Coihaique's port of Puerto Chacabuco. The 200-passenger M/V *Alejandrina* sails from Puerto Montt to Chaitén, Quellón on Chiloé, and Puerto Chacabuco before making the trip in reverse.

Skorpios is the only firm devoted to leisure travel. Its trio of luxurious *Skorpios* ferries, which carry between 70 and 130 passengers, are designed for first-class cruises into the Laguna San Rafael. You can sail round-trip either from Puerto Chacabuco or Puerto Montt.

Transmarchilay operates a cargo and passenger ferry fleet similar to that of Navimag, with ships that start in Puerto Montt and sail either to Chaitén or Puerto Chacabuco. It also sails between Quellón and Chaitén. If it's Laguna San Raphael you want to see, Transmarchilay operates the M/V *El Colono*. From early January through late February, the ship sails weekly from Puerto Montt into Laguna San Rafael and back to Puerto Montt.

Don't overlook cruises on the deluxe catamaran *Patagonia Express*, operated by Patagonia Connection, the same company that owns the beautiful Termas de Puyuhuapi. During the peak season months of January and February, the vessel operates a full-day tour to the Laguna San Rafael from Puerto Chacabuco.

➤ BOAT AND FERRY INFORMATION: **Navimag** (✉ Presidente Ibáñez 347, Coihaique, ☎ 67/233–306, WEB www.navimag.cl). **Patagonia Connection** (✉ Puerto Puyuhuapi, ☎ 2/225–6489, WEB www.patagoniaconnex.cl). **Skorpios** (✉ Augosto Leguia Norte 118, Santiago, ☎ 2/231–1030, WEB www.skorpios.cl). **Transmarchilay** (✉ Corcovado 266, Chaitén, ☎ 65/731–272; ✉ O'Higgins s/n, Puerto Chacabuco, ☎ 67/351–144; ✉ General Parra 86, Coihaique, ☎ 67/231–971, WEB www.transmarchilay.cl).

BUS TRAVEL

Service between Puerto Montt and Cochrane is by private operators such as Turbus. Travel along the Carretera Austral is often agonizingly and inexplicably slow, so don't plan on getting anywhere on schedule.

➤ BUS INFORMATION: **Turbus** (✉ Baquedano 1171, Coihaique, ☎ 67/231–333).

CAR RENTAL

Renting a car in the Southern Coast is very expensive, and driving the Carretera Austral can be a hassle. But if you want to see the parts of the Southern Coast that are off the beaten path, there's no better way than in your own four-wheel-drive vehicle. You can stop in any of the little fishing villages and farming communities that the tour buses whiz past.

There are a few local agencies in Coihaique that rent cars for day trips. Automotriz Los Carrera and Happylandia both rent four-wheel-drive vehicles. Make certain to understand the extent of your liability for any damage to the vehicle, including routine events such as a chipped or cracked windshield. If you want to visit one of the more popular parks, check out prices of tours. They might prove far cheaper than driving yourself.

➤ CAR RENTAL INFORMATION: **Automotriz Los Carrera** (✉ Carrera 330, Coihaique, ☎ 67/231–457). **Happylandia** (✉ Condell 149, Coihaique, ☎ 67/234–730).

INTERNET

Some hotels offer Internet access, either free or for a small fee. Internet access is often available at telephone company offices such as CTC, but this is generally a more expensive option. Usually cheaper are the Internet cafés that have sprung up around Coihaique as well as in smaller towns. In Coihaique, Aysenet is friendly, helpful, and patient with visitors.

➤ INTERNET CAFÉS: **Aysenet** (✉ Prat 470, Coihaique).

MAIL AND SHIPPING

Mail service is poky here, so you might want to save that letter home until you get to a bigger city. The post office in Coihaique is on the south side of the Plaza de Armas. It's open weekdays 9–12:30 and 2:30–6, Saturday 8:30–noon.

➤ POST OFFICES: **Post office** (✉ Cochrane 202, Coihaique).

MONEY MATTERS

Converting cash can be a bureaucratic headache, particularly in smaller towns like Chaitén. A better option is using your ATM card at local banks connected to Cirrus or Plus networks. The Chilean RedBanc group is most convenient.

When you're anticipating smaller purchases, try to have coins and small bills on hand at all times, even though your pockets and purses will seem to bulge a bit. Small vendors do not always have change for large bills.

TELEPHONES

Public phones are plentiful in larger towns and are becoming more and more common in smaller villages. Some accept phone cards. Entel and CTC have offices throughout the region and both have fax and international-call capabilities.

TOUR OPERATORS

A knowledgeable tour operator or travel agent is a must for travel to the Southern Coast. In the United States, a number of companies are experienced with travel here. Among them is the Georgia-based Lost World Adventures, whose staff specializes in tailoring itineraries around your specific interests. There are many good companies in Chile as well. In Santiago, SportsTour has more than 30 years of experience. It puts together individual itineraries, as well as offering half- and full-day city tours and multi-day excursions throughout the country. Most staff members speak excellent English.

In Chaitén, American-born Nicholas La Penna runs Chaitur Excursions, the best place in town for tours, trekking, and general information about the region. Among his itineraries are full-day trips into Parque Pumalín as well as a half-day trip to the sea lion colony on Isla Puduguapi. In Coihaique, Andes Patagónicos is located adjacent to the Restaurant Histórico Ricer and owned by the same family. Gregarious Patricia Chiblé and her staff are knowledgeable and helpful. Among the regional tours they offer are flights over Laguna San Rafael and its glacier.

➤ CHILEAN COMPANIES: **Andes Patagónicos** (✉ Horn 40 and 48, ☎ FAX 67/232–920 or 67/237–950, WEB www.patagoniachile.cl/ap). **Chaitur Excursions** (✉ Diego Portales 350, ☎ 65/731–439). **SportsTour** (✉ Moneda 790, 14th floor, Santiago, ☎ 2/549–5200, FAX 2/698–2981, WEB www.chilnet.cl/sportstour).

➤ U.S. COMPANIES: **Lost World Adventures** (✉ 112 Church St., Decatur, GA 30030, ☎ 404/373–5820 or 800/999–0558, FAX 404/377–1902, WEB www.lostworldadventures.com).

VISITOR INFORMATION

➤ INFORMATION: **Sernatur** (✉ Av. Bernardo O'Higgins 254, Chaitén, ☎ 65/731–281; ✉ Bulnes 35, Coihaique, ☎ 67/231–752).

10 PATAGONIA AND TIERRA DEL FUEGO

It's no wonder that people find themselves drawn to Patagonia, where the sprawling continent finally settles into the sea. In this rugged and remote region lies one of the world's most stunning natural vistas, the soaring Torres del Paine. Its twin peaks preside over a mountain range dotted with glacial lakes of brilliant blues and greens. To the south, separated from the mainland by treacherous narrows, is the mysterious island of Tierra del Fuego. It reaches toward the rocky Islas Wollaston, the last of which is the sailor's sobering nemesis, Cape Horn.

T RADITIONAL BOUNDARIES CANNOT DEFINE Patagonia. This vast
stretch of land east of the Andes is mostly a part of Argentina,
but Chile shares its southern extremity. Geographically and cul-
by Pete Nelson turally it has little in common with either country. Patagonia, isolated
by impenetrable mountains and endless fields of ice, is really a region
unto itself.

Navigating the channel that today bears his name, conquistador Hernando de Magallanes arrived on these shores in 1520, claiming the region for Spain. Although early attempts at colonization failed, the
forbidding landscape continued to fascinate explorers. Naturalist
Charles Darwin, who sailed through the Estrecho de Magallanes (Strait
of Magellan) in 1833 and 1834, called it a "mountainous land, partly
submerged in the sea, so that deep inlets and bays occupy the place
where valleys should exist."

Because of the region's remote location, much of what Darwin described
is still relatively undisturbed. Drive north until the road peters out and
you'll reach Parque Nacional Torres del Paine, perhaps the country's
most awe-inspiring natural wonder. The snow-covered pillars of stone
seem to rise vertically from the plains below. To the east is Tierra del
Fuego, the storm-lashed island at the continent's southernmost tip. This
bleak wilderness, which still calls to adventurous types today, is literally the end of the earth.

Pleasures and Pastimes

Cruises
Patagonia's unusual topography encourages travel by water. A number of medium-size vessels take passengers on journeys ranging from
a day or two to a week or more. The vistas, such as the fantastic Avenue of the Glaciers, are breathtaking. Along this stretch of the Beagle Channel you'll pass six tremendous glaciers in rapid succession. Most
sightseeing boats traversing these waters also visit colonies of elephant
seals and penguins.

Dining
The aura of sophistication that lingers in Punta Arenas, the region's
largest city, is reflected in the variety of restaurants you can find there.
In Puerto Natales, too, you can dine well for several days without returning to the same place. In both towns, however, you will undoubtedly identify one or two restaurants that will warrant a return visit.

Menus tend to be extensive, although two items in particular might
be considered specialties: succulent *centolla* (king crab) and tender and
moist *cordero asado* (grilled lamb). King crab is always expensive, but
it is worth the splurge. Lamb is often prepared in the off-putting manner that has been used for generations: whole carcasses are roasted
spread-eagle on a vertical spit. The grill is often positioned in a restaurant's front window to tempt passersby.

Don't relegate hotel cuisine to second-class status until you've studied
the menu or chatted with the chef. Some serve up excellent local fare,
while others provide tantalizing breakfast spreads that, if you choose
to indulge, will carry you comfortably well past noon. Be careful,
though, as many restaurants close for several hours in the afternoon.
You may get hungry just as everything is closing. For a chart that explains the cost of meals at the restaurants listed throughout this chapter, *see* Dining Price Categories *in* Smart Travel Tips.

Patagonia and Tierra del Fuego

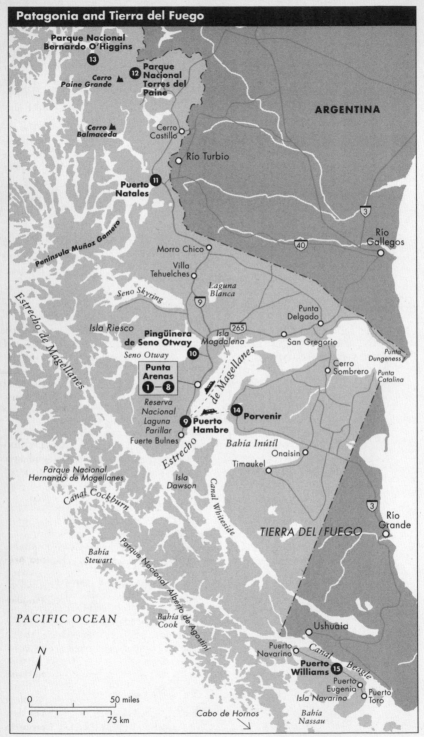

Parque Nacional Bernardo O'Higgins ⑬

Parque Nacional Torres del Paine ⑫

Cerro Paine Grande

Cerro Balmaceda

ARGENTINA

Cerro Castillo

Río Turbio

Puerto Natales ⑪

3

Península Muñoz Gamero

Morro Chico

Río Gallegos

40

Villa Tehuelches

Laguna Blanca

Seno Skyring

9

Isla Riesco

Pingüinera de Seno Otway ⑩

Isla Magdalena

265

Punta Delgado

San Gregorio

Punta Dungeness

Seno Otway

Estrecho de Magallanes

Punta Arenas ① — ⑧

Estrecho de Magallanes

Cerro Sombrero

Punta Catalina

Reserva Nacional Laguna Parillar

⑨ **Puerto Hambre**

⑭ **Porvenir**

Fuerte Bulnes

Bahía Inútil

Onaisin

Parque Nacional Hernando de Magellanes

Canal Cockburn

Isla Dawson

Timaukel

Canal Whiteside

TIERRA DEL FUEGO

3

Río Grande

Bahía Stewart

Parque Nacional Alberto de Agostini

Bahía Cook

PACIFIC OCEAN

N

Ushuaia

Puerto Navarino

Canal Beagle

Puerto Williams ⑮

Puerto Eugenia

Puerto Toro

Isla Navarino

0 — 50 miles

0 — 75 km

Cabo de Hornos

Bahía Nassau

Lodging

Patagonia offers a broad range of accommodations. Completely absent, however, are foreign chains. Because of its prosperous past, Punta Arenas has many historic hotels offering luxurious amenities and impeccable service. A night or two in one them should be part of your trip. For its size, Puerto Natales has a surprising range of options, from large hotels to intimate inns. All exude their own particular charm. There are also several excellent resorts within Parque Nacional Torres del Paine.

The terms *hospedaje* and *hostal* are used interchangeably in the region, so don't make assumptions about what type of lodging you're likely to find based on the name. Many hostals are fine hotels, just very small. By contrast, some hospedajes are little more than a spare room in someone's home. For a chart that explains the cost of accommodations listed throughout this chapter, *see* Lodging Price Categories *in* Smart Travel Tips.

Shopping

Wool is no longer king of the economy, but vast flocks of sheep still yield a high-quality product that is woven into the clothing you'll find here. Leather products are also common, but the prices are not necessarily the lowest you'll find.

Exploring Patagonia and Tierra del Fuego

The intriguing part of Patagonia is the fact that you can't travel any farther south without boarding a boat. South Africa's Cape of Good Hope lies near the 35th parallel, about the same latitude as Montevideo, Uruguay. The southernmost New Zealand territory touches the 47th parallel. Contrast those with Punta Arenas, located near the 53rd parallel. The southernmost town on the globe, Puerto Williams, is just above the 55th. It's closer to the South Pole than to the northern border of Chile.

Working out a rewarding itinerary can be relatively easy. Fly into Punta Arenas, the region's principal city, unless you elect to spend days driving south through Argentina. From there you can travel to most of the other destinations by bus or car. A few remote spots, such as Isla Magdalena or Puerto Williams, can best be reached by boat.

Great Itineraries

IF YOU HAVE 5 DAYS

With such a limited amount of time you should head to the mountains as soon as possible. After spending your first night in ⛏ **Punta Arenas** ①–⑧, drive north to ⛏ **Puerto Natales** ⑪. Take in the soaring peaks of **Parque Nacional Torres del Paine** ⑫ on the third and fourth day. On your last day head back to Punta Arenas, stopping at the **Pingüinera de Seno Otway** ⑩.

IF YOU HAVE 7 DAYS

If you have a little longer, you have time to explore the faded elegance of ⛏ **Punta Arenas** ①–⑧. You'll need two days to take in the city's major sights, and another to see nearby points of interest such as **Puerto Hambre** ⑨ and **Pingüinera de Seno Otway** ⑩. On your fourth day, head north to ⛏ **Puerto Natales** ⑪. Spend your fifth and sixth day exploring the signature **Parque Nacional Torres del Paine** ⑫. On your last day, visit the Balmacedo and Serrano glaciers in **Parque Nacional Bernardo O'Higgins** ⑬.

IF YOU HAVE 11 DAYS

If you have more time to spend, consider seeing more of the region by boat. From ⛏ **Punta Arenas** ①–⑧, the *Terra Australis* sails round-trip to **Puerto Williams** ⑮, stopping along the way at breathtaking glaciers and colonies of elephant seals and penguins. The cruise takes seven nights, leaving you plenty of time to visit 🖈 **Puerto Natales** ⑪ and **Parque Nacional Torres del Paine** ⑫.

When to Tour

Late November to early March—summer in the southern hemisphere—is considered high season in Patagonia. Demand for accommodations is highest in January and February, so advance reservations are vital. Summer weather in these latitudes is by no means warm, but rather pleasantly cool. Bring an extra layer or two, even when the sun is shining. On or near these antarctic waters, stiff breezes can be biting. In spring (September to November) and fall (March to May) the weather is usually delightfully mild, but can also feel downright cold. The region goes into virtual hibernation in the winter months of June, July, and August.

PATAGONIA

Patagonia held little appeal for the earliest explorers. Discouraged by the inhospitable climate, they continued up the coast of South America in search of gold among the Aztec and Inca civilizations. The first Spanish settlements, given only halfhearted support from the crown, were soon abandoned. The newly formed nation of Chile showed little interest in Patagonia until 1843, when other countries began to eye the region. President Manuel Bulnes sent down a ragtag group of soldiers to claim it for Chile. Five years later the town of Punta Arenas was founded.

And it was not a moment too soon, for Punta Arenas was to become a major stop on the trade route around the tip of South America. Steam navigation intensified the city's commercial importance, leading to its short-lived age of splendor from 1892 to 1914. The opening of the Panama Canal all but bumped Punta Arenas off the map. By 1920 many of the founding families decided to move on, leaving behind the lavish mansions and the impressive public buildings they had built.

Massive ranches once dominated the area around Punta Arenas. The vast flocks of sheep that dot the landscape still contribute to the local economy, but not as before. Today exploration for oil and natural gas is making the region prosperous again. Another source of income is tourism, as more and more people are drawn to this beautiful land at the bottom of the earth.

Punta Arenas

Founded a little more than 150 years old, Punta Arenas was Chile's first permanent settlement in Patagonia. This port town, no longer an important stop on trade routes, exudes an aura of faded grandeur. Plaza Muñoz Gamero, the central square, is surrounded by 19th-century structures, their dark stone exteriors recalling a time when this was one of Chile's wealthiest cities.

The newer houses here have colorful tin roofs, best appreciated when seen from a high vantage point such as the Mirador Cerro la Cruz. Although the city as a whole may not be particularly attractive, look for details: the pink-and-white house on a corner, the bay window full of potted plants, a garden overflowing with flowers.

Although Punta Arenas is 3,141 km (1,960 mi) from Santiago, daily flights from the capital make it an easy journey. As the transportation hub of southern Patagonia, Punta Arenas is within reach of Chile's Parque Nacional Torres del Paine and Argentina's Parque Nacional los

Punta Arenas

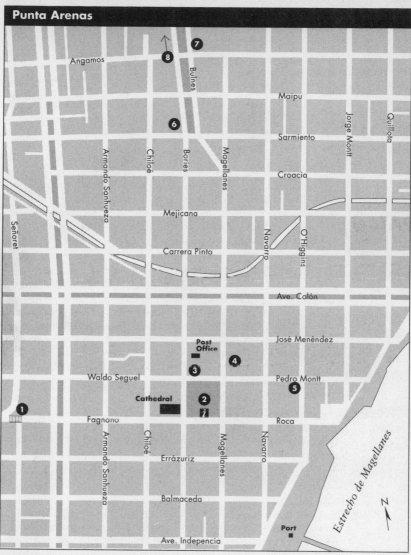

Angamos

Bulnes

Maipu

Jorge Montt

Quillota

Sarmiento

Chiloé

Bories

Magellanes

Croacia

Armando Sanhueza

Mejicana

Navarro

O'Higgins

Señoret

Carrera Pinto

Ave. Colón

José Menéndez

Post Office

Waldo Seguel

Cathedral

Pedro Montt

Fagnano

Roca

Chiloé

Armando Sanhueza

Errázuriz

Magellanes

Navarro

Balmaceda

Port

Estrecho de Magellanes

Ave. Indepencia

N

Glaciares. It is also a key point of embarkation for travel to Antarctica. But don't overlook Punta Arenas as a destination unto itself—its historic sites make it well worth allotting time for.

Numbers in white bullets in the text correspond to numbers in black bullets in the margins and on the Punta Arenas map.

A Good Walk

Get an idea of the layout of the city at **Mirador Cerro la Cruz** ①, an observation deck with a stunning view of the city. Head down the stairs and continue for three blocks to reach the cedar-lined **Plaza Muñoz Gamero** ②, the indisputable center of the city. Here you'll find a monument honoring explorer Hernando de Magallanes. In deference to the many historical and political figures they honor, streets change their names as they pass by this square. The venerable **Palacio Sara Braun** ③ overlooks Plaza Muñoz Gamero. A block east is the **Museo Regional de Magallanes** ④, commonly known as the Braun-Menéndez Museum for the family that built and occupied the mansion that houses the museum. Farther along Pedro Montt is the **Museo Naval y Maritimo** ⑤, with its overview of the all-important role of the Chilean Navy in the region's history.

A block north you'll reach Avenida Colón, one of four intersecting avenues designed to accommodate large flocks of sheep. Today the parks that run down the centers make pleasant places to stroll. Head north on Calle Bories for four blocks to reach the **Museo Salesiano de Mayorino Borgatello** ⑥. Three blocks north on Avenida Bulnes is the main entrance to the **Cementerio Municipal** ⑦. Here among the manicured gardens and tall cypress trees you'll find the grand mausoleums the town's wealthiest citizens erected in memory of themselves. Farther north on Avenida Bulnes is the **Museo de Recuerdo** ⑧.

TIMING

The walk itself will take at least 1½ hours, but budget in extra time if you wish to explore the museums. Remember that most of the museums, as well as many businesses, close for lunch about noon and reopen a few hours later. You might want to save a visit to Cerro la Cruz or the Cementerio Municipal for these times.

SIGHTS TO SEE

❼ **Cementerio Municipal.** The fascinating history of this region is chiseled into stone at the Municipal Cemetery. Bizarrely ornate mausoleums honoring the original families are crowded together along paths lined by sculpted cypress trees. In a strange effort to recognize Punta Arenas's indigenous past, there is a shrine in the northern part of the cemetery where the remains of the last member of the Selk'nam tribe are buried. Local legend says that rubbing the statue's left knee brings good luck. ⊠ *Av. Bulnes 949,* ☎ *no phone.* ☞ *Free.*

❶ **Mirador Cerro la Cruz.** From the observation deck atop the Hill of the Cross you have a truly panoramic view of the city's colorful rooftops. In the distance is the Estrecho de Magallanes. ⊠ *Fagnano and Señoret,* ☎ *no phone.* ☞ *Free.*

❺ **Museo Naval y Maritimo.** The Naval and Maritime Museum excessively extols Chile's prowess on the high seas, particularly concerning Antarctica, but its exhibits are worth a visit by anyone with even a modicum of interest in ships and sailing, merchant and military alike. Of particular appeal are the fire-bearing canoes of the indigenous peoples of the Tierra del Fuego region as well as an account of the 1908 visit to Punta Arenas by an American naval fleet. ⊠ *Pedro Montt 989,* ☎ *61/205-558.* ☞ *Admission.* ☉ *Weekdays 9:30–12:30, Sat. 10–1, Sun. 3–6.*

⑧ Museo de Recuerdo. In the gardens of the Instituto de la Patagonia, the Museum of Memory is an enviable collection of machinery and heavy equipment used during the the the late-19th- and early-20th-century pioneering era. There are exhibits of rural employment, such as a carpenter's workshop, and displays of typical home life. ✉ *Av. Bulnes*, ☎ *61/207–056.* ⊑ *Admission.* ⊙ *Weekdays 8:30–12:30, 2:30–6; Sat. 8:30–12:30.*

★ **④ Museo Regional de Magallanes.** Housed in what was once the mansion of the powerful Braun-Menéndez family, the Regional Museum of the Magallanes is an intriguing glimpse into the daily life of a wealthy provincial family at the beginning of the 20th century. Lavish Carrara marble hearths, English bath fixtures, and cordovan leather walls are among the original accoutrements. The museum also has an excellent group of displays depicting Punta Arenas's past, from the moment of European contact to its decline with the opening of the Panama Canal. ✉ *Magallanes 949*, ☎ *61/244–216.* ⊑ *Admission.* ⊙ *Tues.–Sun. 11–5.*

⑥ Museo Salesiano de Mayorino Borgatello. Commonly referred to simply as "The Salesianos," the Mayorino Borgatello Museum is operated by Italian missionaries who arrived in Punta Arenas in the 19th century. The Salesians, most of whom spoke no Spanish, proved to be daring explorers. Traveling throughout the region, they collected the artifacts made by indigenous tribes that are currently on display. They also relocated many of the people to nearby Dawson Island, where they died by the hundreds. The museum contains an extraordinary collection of everything from skulls and native crafts to stuffed animals. ✉ *Av. Bulnes 398*, ☎ *61/241–096.* ⊑ *Admission.* ⊙ *Daily 10–noon, 3–6.*

③ Palacio Sara Braun. This resplendent 1895 mansion, which once belonged to Sara Braun, was designed by French architect Nurma Meyer. All the materials were imported from Europe. The Club de la Unión, a social organization that currently occupies part of the building, opens it to the public in the afternoons on Tuesdays and Thursdays. ✉ *Av. Bories at Av. Waldo Seguel*, ☎ *no phone.* ⊑ *Admission.* ⊙ *Tues. and Thurs. 4–6.*

② Plaza Muñoz Gamero. A canopy of conifers shades this square, which is surrounded by splendid baroque-style mansions from the 19th century. A bronze sculpture commemorating the voyage of Hernando de Magallanes dominates the center of the plaza. Local wisdom has it that a kiss on the toe of one of the Fuegian people at the base of the monument will one day bring you back to Punta Arenas.

Dining

Most upscale restaurants in Punta Arenas open between noon and 3 for lunch and then close for several hours in the afternoon before they reopen for dinner. Service is courteous and careful, even in more informal eateries. Arrival of entrées, however, may seem slow because few items are prepared in advance. Hours vary with the season, the day of the week, and the whim of the owner. Many eateries are closed on Sunday, so call ahead.

$$–$$$ ✕ **Los Ganaderos.** You'll feel like a guest in a rancher's home at this
★ restaurant resembling a rural *estancia*. The manager and his waiters, dressed in authentic gaucho costumes, serve up tasty *corderos al ruedo* (spit-roasted lamb) cooked to perfection in the *salón de parilla* (grill room). Wash down your meal with something from the long list of Chilean wines. Interesting black-and-white photographs of historic and contemporary ranch life are displayed along the walls. The restaurant is several blocks north of the center of town, but it's worth the long walk or very short taxi ride to get there. ✉ *Bulnes 0977*, ☎ *61/214–597. AE, MC, V. Closed Sun.*

$$ ✕ **El Estribo.** Centered around a large fireplace used to grill the meats, this narrow restaurant is filled with intimate little tables covered with white tablecloths. The name means "The Stirrup," so the walls are adorned with tastefully arranged bridles, bits, lariats, and—of course— all manner of stirrups. This success of this longtime favorite, however, is due to its excellent regional food, including lamb, salmon, and king crab. For dessert try rhubarb pie—uncommon in these parts. ✉ *Ignacio Carrera Pinto 762,* ☎ *61/244–714. No credit cards.*

$$ ✕ **El Remezón.** Even among the many fine restaurants in Punta Arenas, this cheerful little place stands out because of its deliciously seasoned fish and meats. The unpretentious atmosphere makes you feel as if you're dining at a friend's home. The restaurant is near the port, but the terrific food and potent pisco sours make it worth the walk. ✉ *21 de Mayo 1469,* ☎ *61/241–029. AE.*

$$ ✕ **Restaurant Asturias.** Rough-hewn wood beams and white stucco walls conjure up the Asturias region of Spain. The *salmón papillote* (salmon poached in white wine with cured ham, cream cheese, and tomatoes) combines smoky aromas with flavors from the sea. The *paella castellana* varies from the traditional dish because it includes meats, and the *congrio a la vasca* (with pepper and garlic) is an imaginative rendition of Chile's ubiquitous white fish. ✉ *Lautaro Navarro 967,* ☎ *61/243– 763. AE, DC, MC, V.*

$–$$ ✕ **Sotito's.** A longtime favorite among locals, Sotito's is a virtual in- ★ stitution in Punta Arenas. The atmosphere is warm and cozy, with exposed-brick walls and wood-beam ceilings. More importantly, it serves some of the best king crab in the area. It's prepared a half dozen ways, including in an appetizer called *centolla con palta* (king crab with avocado). The restaurant is near the water a few blocks east of Plaza Muñoz Gamero. ✉ *O'Higgins 1138,* ☎ *61/243–565. AE, DC, MC, V.*

$ ✕ **Calipso.** The strong espresso and fresh pastries served at this café are certain to revive you after a day of strolling the broad avenues of Punta Arenas. More substantial fare includes moderately priced hamburgers with all the trimmings, as well as more expensive salmon and crab dinners. ✉ *Bories 817,* ☎ *61/241–782. DC, MC, V.*

$ ✕ **El Quijote.** One of the best cafés in town, El Quijote loudly announces its presence with a red neon sign. The kitchen dishes out delicious soups and sandwiches, as well as a variety of meat and seafood dishes. Stop by for the espresso drinks as well as the creative range of *liquados* (fruit and milk shakes). ✉ *Lautaro Navarro 1087,* ☎ *61/241–225. AE, DC, MC, V.*

$ ✕ **La Mamá.** Massive plates of lovingly prepared pasta served in a cozy atmosphere have made this restaurant popular with residents and visitors alike. A bulletin board in the corner is plastered with raves from every corner of the globe. ✉ *Armando Sanhueza 720,* ☎ *61/225–127. No credit cards.*

$ ✕ **Lomit's.** This bustling downtown meeting place—reminiscent of a Manhattan deli—has a fast-moving but friendly staff that serves up Chilean-style blue-plate specials. Besides traditional hamburgers you'll find the ubiquitous *completos* (hot dogs buried under mounds of toppings, from spicy mayonnaise to guacamole). Locals come here from morning to midnight, thanks to the generous portions. Lomit's is one of the few places open all day Sunday. ✉ *José Menéndez between Bories and Magallanes,* ☎ *61/243–399. No credit cards.*

Lodging

$$$$ 🏨 **Cabo de Hornos.** This imposing eight-story hotel, which dominates not only the adjacent Plaza Muñoz Gamero but the entire town, has comfortably furnished rooms and suites that afford expansive views of the Estrecho de Magallanes. The fine restaurant serves international cuisine. ⊠ *Plaza Muñoz Gamero 1025,* ☎ FAX *61/242–134,* WEB *www.hch.co.cl. 100 rooms, 1 suite. Restaurant, bar, in-room safes, minibars, room service, sauna, baby-sitting, business services, meeting rooms, travel services. AE, DC, MC, V.*

$$$$ 🔟 **Hotel José Nogueira.** Originally the home of Sara Braun, wealthy widow
★ of a wool baron, this opulent 19th-century mansion took nine years to complete. Carefully restored over many years, this Chilean monument retains the original crystal chandeliers, marble floors, and polished bronze accents that were imported from France. The rooms are rather small, but compensate with high ceilings, thick carpets, and period furniture. The ceramic-tile baths are also comfortable. ⊠ *Bories 959,* ☎ *61/248–840,* FAX *61/248–832,* WEB *www.hotelnogueira.com. 25 rooms, 3 suites. Restaurant, bar, in-room safes, minibars, laundry service. AE, DC, MC, V.*

$$$ 🔟 **Hotel Finis Terrae.** This alpine-style lodging has the all the amenities you'd expect from a modern chain hotel. Rooms are comfortable and quiet. The view from the top-floor restaurant and bar more than compensates for the uninspired decor. ⊠ *Colón 766,* ☎ *61/228–200,* FAX *61/248–124,* WEB *www.hotelfinisterrae.com. 66 rooms, 4 suites. Restaurant, bar, in-room safes, minibars, airport shuttle. AE, DC, MC, V.*

$$$ 🔟 **Hotel Isla Rey Jorge.** One block from Plaza Muñoz Gamero, this English-style hotel is a popular for its impeccable service and intimate atmosphere. The rooms, decorated in mint greens and burgundy, have lofty wood windows that let in lots of light. The hotel's richly toned linga and coigué woodwork continues down into the popular basement pub, El Galeón. ⊠ *21 de Mayo 1243,* ☎ FAX *61/248–220,* WEB *www. islareyjorge.com. 25 rooms, 4 suites. Restaurant, bar, travel services. AE, DC, MC, V.*

$$$ ✕🔟 **Hotel Los Navegantes.** This unpretentious hotel a block from the Plaza de Armas has spacious, colorfully decorated rooms. The nautical-themed restaurant, in a simple but comfortable dining room with a bright garden at one end, serves delicious grilled salmon and roast lamb. Don't pass up the shellfish appetizers. ⊠ *José Menéndez 647,* ☎ *61/244–677,* FAX *61/247–545,* WEB *www.hotel-losnavegantes.com. 50 rooms, 2 suites. Restaurant, bar, in-room safes, minibars, travel services, airport shuttle. AE, DC, MC, V.*

$$ 🔟 **Hostal de la Avenida.** The rooms of this homey guest house all overlook a garden lovingly tended by its owner, a local of Yugoslav origin. ⊠ *Av. Colón 534,* ☎ *61/247–532. 7 rooms. Breakfast room. AE, DC, MC, V.*

$$ 🔟 **Hotel Condor de Plata.** The idiosyncratic decor at the Silver Condor includes scale models of ships and photographs of old-fashioned airplanes that once traversed to the region. Rooms in the modern building are small, but clean and comfortable. ⊠ *Av. Colón 556,* ☎ *61/247–987,* FAX *61/241–149. 14 rooms. Bar, cafeteria, in-room safes, minibars, laundry service. AE, DC, MC, V.*

$$ 🔟 **Hotel Savoy.** Although lacking in architectural appeal, this squat hotel is ideally located a block from the Estrecho de Magallanes. All rooms have carpeting and wood paneling. ⊠ *José Menéndez 1073,* ☎ FAX *61/ 247–979,* WEB *www.hotelsavoy.cl. 42 rooms. Restaurant, bar, in-room safes, parking. DC, MC, V.*

$ 🔟 **Hostal del Estrecho.** A family atmosphere pervades in this guest house a block from the water. The rooms, decorated with throw rugs and frilly bedspreads, make it feel as if you're staying with friends. Breakfast featuring marmalade made by the owners is included. ⊠ *José Menéndez 1048,* ☎ FAX *61/241–011,* WEB *www.chileanpatagonia.com/estrecho. 15 rooms. Breakfast room. AE, MC, V.*

$ 🔟 **Hostal Turismo Oro Fueguino.** On a slightly sloping cobblestone street
★ near the observation deck at Cerro la Cruz, this funky little hostelry— tall, narrow, and rambling—welcomes you with lots of color. The first

thing you notice is the facade, painted bright orange and blue. Inside are wall hangings and lamp shades made of eye-catching fabrics from as far off as India that create a homey feeling. The warm atmosphere is enhanced by the personal zeal of the proprietor, Dinka Ocampo. ⊠ *Fagnano 365,* ☎ FAX *61/249–401,* WEB *www.orofueguino.com. 12 rooms. Breakfast room, laundry service, free parking. No credit cards.*

$ ⊞ **Residencial Sonia Kuscevic.** The only Punta Arenas inn affiliated with
★ Hosteling International, Residencial Sonia Kuscevic is named for its gentle, hospitable owner. She offers small, clean rooms whose gas heaters and mountains of blankets keep guests warm. Breakfast is included. ⊠ *Pasaje Darwin 175, off Angamos between Chiloé and Sanhueza,* ☎ FAX *61/248–543. 5 rooms. Breakfast room, lounge. No credit cards.*

Nightlife and the Arts

Because Punta Arenas is so far south, the sun doesn't set until well into the evening. That means that locals don't think about hitting the bars until midnight. If you can't stay up late, most hotel bars, such as **Pub 1900** (⊠ Av. Colón 716, ☎ 61/242–759), attract an early crowd. If you're in the mood for dancing, try **Abracadabra** (⊠ Bories 546, ☎ 61/224–144), where the younger set goes to party until dawn.

Shopping

About 3 km (2 mi) north of town is the **Zona Franca** (⊠ Av. Bulnes). This duty-free zone is where people from all around the region come for low-priced electronics and other consumer items. This shopper's paradise attracts a few tourists, especially those visiting the nearby Museo de Recuerdo. The Zona Franca is open Monday–Saturday 9–8.

Almacén de Antaño (⊠ Colón 1000, ☎ 61/227–283) offers a fascinatingly eclectic array of pewter and ceramics, mirrors and graphics frames. **Dagorret** (⊠ Bories 587, ☎ 61/228–692), a Chilean chain with other outlets in Puerto Montt and Puerto Natales, carries top-quality leather clothing, including *gamuza* (suede) and *gamulán* (buckskin), some with wool trim. **Quilpue** (⊠ José Nogueira 1256, ☎ 61/220–960) is a shoe repair shop that also markets *huaso* (cowboy) supplies such as bridles, bits, and spurs. Stop by for the boots you'll need for folk dancing.

Puerto Hambre

❾ *50 km (31 mi) south of Punta Arenas.*

In an attempt to gain a foothold in the region, Spain founded Ciudad Rey Don Felipe in 1584. Pedro Sarmiento de Gamboa constructed a church and homes for more than 100 settlers. But just three years later, British navigator Thomas Cavendish came ashore to find all but one person had died of hunger. He renamed the town Puerto Hambre (Port Famine). Today a tranquil fishing village, Puerto Hambre still has traces of the original settlement, a sobering reminder of the often unbridled zeal of early European explorers.

About 2 km (1 mi) west of Puerto Hambre is a small white **monolith** that marks the geographical center of Chile, the midway point between northernmost Arica and the South Pole.

In the middle of a Chilean winter in 1843, a frigate under the command of Captain Juan Williams Rebolledo sailed southward from the island of Chiloé carrying a ragtag contingent of 11 sailors and eight soldiers. In October, on a rocky promontory called Santa Ana overlooking the Estrecho de Magallanes, they built a wooden fort which they named **Fuerte Bulnes,** thereby founding the first Chilean settlement in the southern reaches of Patagonia. The fort, much of which has been restored, is 5 km (3 mi) south of Puerto Hambre.

PATAGONIA'S PENGUINS

AS THE FERRY SLOWLY approaches Isla Magdalena, you begin to make out thousands of black dots along the shore. You catch you breath, knowing that this is your first look at the 120,000 residents of Monumento Natural Los Pingüinos, one of the continent's largest penguin sanctuaries.

But the squat little birds are much closer than you think. You soon realize that on either side of the ferry are large groups of penguins catching their breakfast. They are amazingly agile swimmers, leaping almost entirely out of the water before diving down below the surface once again. A few swim alongside the boat, but most simply ignore the intrusion.

Several different types of penguins, including the Magellanic penguins found on the gently rolling hills of Isla Magdalena, make their homes along the Chilean coast. Although most favor cooler climates, small colonies can be found in the warmer waters north of Santiago. But for the thrill of seeing tens of thousands in one place, nothing beats Monumento Natural Los Pingüinos. At this reserve, a two-hour trip by boat from Punta Arenas, the birds can safely reproduce and raise their young.

Found only along the coast of Chile and Argentina, Magellanic penguins are named for Spanish explorer Hernando de Magallanes, who spotted them when he arrived on these shores in 1520. They are often called jackass penguins because of the horse braying sound they make when excited. Adults, with the characteristic black-and-white markings, are easy to distinguish from the adolescents, which are a mottled gray. Also gray are the chicks, which hide inside the burrows when their parents are searching for food. A good time to get a look at the fluffy little fellows is when their parents return to feed them regurgitated fish.

A single trail runs across Isla Magdalena, starting at the dock and ending on a hilltop at a red-and-white lighthouse. Ropes on either side keep humans from wandering too far afield. The penguins, however, have the run of the place. They waddle across the path, alone or in small groups, to get to the rocky beach. Familiar with the boatloads of people traipsing about two or three times a week, the penguins usually don't pay much attention to the camera-clutching crowds. A few of the more curious ones will walk up to visitors and inspect a shoelace or pants leg. If someone gets too close to a nest, however, they cock their heads sharply from side to side as a warning.

The Barcaza Melinka, the small ferry that makes thrice-weekly trips to the island, is run by Comapa (✉ Independencia 803, Punta Arenas, ☎ 61/224–256) The trip to the island, in the middle of the Estrecho de Magallanes, takes about two hours. The introductory video is in Spanish, but English-speaking guides can answer your questions. The island is also on the itinerary of the *Terra Australis,* a 55-cabin ship that sails round-trip between Punta Arenas and Ushuaia. It's run by Cruceros Australis (✉ Av. El Bosque Norte 0440, Santiago, ☎ 2/442–3110). However you get there, make sure to bring along warm clothing, even in summer; the island can be chilly, particularly if a breeze is blowing across the water.

An easier way to see penguins in their natural habitat is to drive to Pingüinera de Seno Otway, on the mainland about an hour northwest of Punta Arenas. Founded in 1990, the reserve occupies 2 km (1 mi) of coastline. There are far fewer penguins here—only about 7,500—but the number is still astounding. The sanctuary is run by a nonprofit group, which can provide English-language guides. Travel companies from Punta Arenas arrange frequent tours to the reserve.

–Pete Nelson

The 47,000-acre **Reserva Nacional Laguna Parillar,** west of Puerto Hambre, is centered around a shimmering lake in a valley flanked by rolling hills. It's a great place for a picnic, if the weather cooperates. There are a number of well-marked paths that offer sweeping vistas over the Estrecho de Magallanes. ✉ *Off Ruta 9.* 🎟 *Admission.* ☉ *Mid-Oct.– mid-Mar., weekdays 8:30–5:30, weekends 8:30–8:30.*

Pingüinera de Seno Otway

🔟 *50 km (31 mi) northwest of Punta Arenas.*

About 3,000 Magellanic penguins return to the Otway Sound Penguin Sanctuary between October and March to breed. From behind a rope you'll see scores of the ungainly little guys waddling to the ocean. If you're lucky you'll catch sight of one of the downy gray chicks that stick their heads out of the burrows only when their parents return to feed them. The sanctuary is a 2-km (1-mi) walk from the parking lot. It gets chilly, so bring a windbreaker. ✉ *Off Ruta 9.* 🎟 *Admission.* ☉ *Sept.–Apr., daily 8:30–8:30*

Puerto Natales

⑪ *242 km (150 mi) northwest of Punta Arenas*

The land around Puerto Natales held very little interest for Spanish explorers in search of riches. A not-so-warm welcome from the indigenous peoples encouraged them to continue up the coast, leaving only a name for the channel running through it: Seno Última Esperanza (Last Hope Sound).

It took hundreds of years for Europeans to finally establish a foothold in the region. In the late 1800s Hermann Eberhard, a German entrepreneur, founded a sheep farm at nearby Puerto Prat. The town of Puerto Natales wasn't founded until 1911.

Today this town of fading fishing and meat-packing enterprises is rapidly emerging as the staging center for visits to Parque Nacional Torres del Paine, Parque Nacional Bernardo O'Higgins, and other remote sites. The town, with 15,000 friendly and hospitable residents, is still unspoiled by the spoils of tourism.

On a clear day, an early morning walk along Avenida Pedro Montt, which follows the shoreline of the Seno Última Esperanza (or Canal Señoret, as it is called on some maps), is a soul-cleansing experience. The rising sun gradually casts a glow on the mountain peaks to the west. A few blocks east of the shore is the not-quite-central **Plaza de Armas** (Arturo Prat and Eberhard). An incongruous railway engine sits prominently in the middle of the square. Across from the Plaza de Armas is the squat little **Iglesia Parroquial** (Arturo Prat and Bulnes). Here you'll find an ornate altarpiece depicting the town's founders, indigenous peoples, and the Virgin Mary all in front of the Torres del Paine. A highlight in the small but interesting **Museo Historico Municipal** (Bulnes and Magallanes) is a room of photos featuring indigenous peoples. Another room is devoted to the exploits of German-born Hermann Eberhard, considered the region's first settler.

In 1896, German immigrant Hermann Eberhard stumbled upon a gaping cave that extended 200 meters (650 ft) into the earth. Venturing inside, he discovered the bones and dried pieces of hide of an animal he could not identify. It was later determined that what Eberhard had discovered were the extraordinarily well-preserved remains of a prehistoric herbivorous mammal, about twice the height of man, which they called a *milodón*. The cave, and a somewhat kitschy life-size fiberglass rendering of the creature, can be found about 28 km (17 mi) northwest of Puerto Natales in the **Monumento Natural Cueva de Milodón.** ⊠ *Northwest of Puerto Natales,* ☎ *no phone.* 🎟 *Admission.* ⊘ *Daily 8:30–6.*

Dining and Lodging

$$ ✕ **Centro Español.** Tables swathed in bright red and hardwood floors that would be perfect for flamenco dancing create this restaurant's subtly Spanish atmosphere. It's a bit formal, but never stuffy. There's a wide selection of simply prepared meat and fish entrées, including succulent squid, served in ample portions. ⊠ *Magallanes 247,* ☎ *61/ 411–181. AE, MC, V.*

$$ ✕ **Restaurant Edén.** This expansive venue, with tables generously ★ spaced on the white terrazzo floor, boasts floor-to-ceiling windows on two sides that give you the feeling of dining alfresco. The regional specialty, grilled lamb, sizzles prominently near the entrance. Chilean folk music plays softly in the background. ⊠ *Blanco Encalada 345,* ☎ *61/ 414–120. AE, MC, V.*

$$ ✕ **Restaurant Última Esperanza.** Named for the strait on which Puerto Natales is located, Last Hope Restaurant sounds as if it might be a bleak place. It's known, however, for its attentive service and top-quality entrées that include a wide range of meats and fish. ⊠ *Av. Eberhard 354,* ☎ *61/411–391. No credit cards.*

$–$$ ✕ **Café Melissa.** The best espresso in town is found at Café Melissa, which also serves up pastries and cakes baked on the premises. This café, in the heart of downtown, is a popular meeting place for residents and visitors alike. ⊠ *Blanco Encalada 258,* ☎ *61/411–944. No credit cards.*

$–$$ ✕ **Don Pepe.** This restaurant isn't much to look at, but it draws crowds during the summer because of its creative ways of serving seafood. Try the salmon with a crab and cream sauce, a house specialty. ⊠ *Ladrilleros 172,* ☎ *61/412–189. DC, MC, V.*

$–$$ ✕ **El Rincón del Tata.** This funky little spot's warm, welcoming atmo ★ sphere is a delight any time. The walls are covered with slabs of bark, suggesting a ski lodge. In the evenings a strolling guitarist entertains with Chilean folk songs, encouraging diners to join in. The eclectic menu includes a tasty *salmón à la mantequilla* (salmon baked in butter and black pepper) that more expensive restaurants can't match. Upstairs is a one-room museum filled with artifacts, mainly household items, from the town's early days. ⊠ *Arturo Prat 236,* ☎ *61/413–845. No credit cards.*

$$$–$$$$ 🏨 **Hotel CostAustralis.** Dominating the waterfront, this venerable hotel is considered among the finest in Puerto Natales. Designed by a local architect, it's noted for its peaked green roof topped by a turret. Rooms have wood-paneled entryways and Venetian and Czech furnishings. Some have a majestic view of the Seno Última Esperanza and the snow-capped mountain peaks beyond, while other look out over the city. ⊠ *Pedro Montt and Bulnes,* ☎ *61/412–000,* 𝔽𝔸𝕏 *61/411–881,* 🕸 *www. australis.com. 50 rooms, 2 suites. Restaurant, bar, café, in-room safes, minibars, room service, laundry service, travel services. AE, DC, MC, V.*

$$$ 🏨 **Hotel Alberto de Agostini.** The Agostini is one of the modern hotels that has cropped up in Puerto Natales in the past few years. The small rooms—some with hot tubs—are unremarkable in decor but nicely appointed. A comfortably furnished lounge on the second floor looks out over the Seno Última Esperanza. Breakfast is included. ⊠ *Calle O'Higgins 632,* ☎ *61/410–060,* 𝔽𝔸𝕏 *61/110–070. 21 rooms. Restaurant, bar, minibars, room service, sauna, free parking. AE, MC, V.*

$$$ 🏨 **Hotel Martin Gusinde.** Part of Chile's Austro Hoteles chain, this intimate inn possesses an aura of sophistication that contrasts with the laid-back atmosphere of Puerto Natales. It's across from the casino, a

block south of the Plaza de Armas. Rooms are nicely decorated with wood furniture and colorfully patterned wallpaper. ⊠ *Lautaro Navarro 1065,* ☎ *61/229–512,* FAX *61/241–042,* WEB *www.chileaustral.com/grey. 20 rooms. Breakfast room, in-room safes, room service, free parking. AE, MC, V.*

$$ ⌸ **Hostal Francis Drake.** You'll know when you see the wishing well out front that Hostal Drake is different. This clean and carefully maintained lodging, in a half-timbered house near the center of town, feels like home. The proprietor is a delightful European lady who dotes on her guests. Breakfast is included. ⊠ *Philippi 383,* ☎ FAX *61/411–553,* WEB *www.chileaustral.com/francisdrake. 8 rooms. Breakfast room, lounge, free parking. DC, MC, V.*

$$ ⌸ **Hostal Lady Florence Dixie.** Named after an aristocratic English immigrant and tireless traveler, this modern hostal with its alpine-style facade is located on the town's main street. Its bright, spacious lounge is a great people-watching perch. Guest rooms are a bit spartan. ⊠ *Bulnes 659,* ☎ *61/411–158,* FAX *61/411–943,* WEB *www.chileanpatagonia.com/ florence. 18 rooms. Breakfast room, in-room safes, free parking. AE, MC, V.*

$$ ⌸ **Hotel Capitán Eberhard.** On the Seno Última Esperanza, this local landmark was one of the first hotels in the area. A number of the clean, comfortable rooms look out over the water. The charming, gracious staff makes you feel right at home. ⊠ *Pedro Montt 58,* ☎ *61/411– 208,* FAX *61/411–209,* WEB *www.busesfernandez.com. 45 rooms. Restaurant, bar, cafeteria, laundry service. AE, DC, MC, V.*

$$ ⌸ **Hotel Glaciares.** An enduring choice in Puerto Natales, the cheery Hotel Glaciares is half a block from the Seno Última Esperanza. Rooms have lots of windows letting in the sun. The hotel also offers tours of Parque Nacional Torres del Paine in its own fleet of minivans. ⊠ *Eberhard 104,* ☎ FAX *61/411–452,* WEB *www.hotelglaciares.co.cl. 15 rooms. Restaurant, laundry service, travel services. DC, MC, V.*

Parque Nacional Torres del Paine

⑫ *125 km (75 mi) northwest of Puerto Natales.*

Some 12 million years ago, lava flows pushed up through the thick sedimentary crust that covered the southwestern coast of South America, cooling to form a granite mass. Glaciers then swept through the region, grinding away all but the ash-gray spires that make up the landscape of Parque Nacional Torres del Paine, established as a national park in 1959. Mother Nature continues to favor this part of the world, blessing it with some of her most provocative sunsets.

Among the 2,420-square-km park's most beautiful attractions are its lakes of such unlikely hues as turquoise, aquamarine, and emerald green. Another draw is its unusual wildlife. Odd creatures like the *guanaco* (a woollier version of the llama) and the *ñandú* (resembling a small ostrich) abound. They are used to visitors, and don't seem to be bothered by the incessant chatter and the snapping of cameras. Predators like the gray fox make less frequent appearances. You may also spot the dramatic aerobatics of a falcon or the graceful soaring of the endangered condor.

Although considerable walking is called for to take full advantage of Parque Nacional Torres del Paine, one need not be a hard-core backpacker. Many people take five or six days to hike El Circuito, a route that leads around the entire park, spending the nights in tents or the dozen or so *refugios* found along the trails. Others prefer to stay in one of the comfortable lodges and hit the trails for the morning or afternoon. But you need not take a step to see the sights. Driving is a great way to enjoy the park, particularly if you are a photographer with lots of equipment. Most of the more than 100 km (62 mi) of roads leading to the most popular sites are unpaved, but safe and well maintained.

The vast majority of visitors come during the summer months, which means the trails can get congested. Early spring, when wildflowers add flashes of color to the meadows, is an ideal time to visit because the crowds have not yet arrived. The park is open all year, and trails are almost always accessible. Storms can hit without warning, however, so be prepared for sudden rain or snow.

There are three entrances: Laguna Amarga, Lago Sarmiento, and Laguna Azul. You are required to sign in when you arrive at the park. *Guardaparques* (park rangers) staff six stations around the reserve. They request that you inform them when setting out on a hike. Conaf, the national forestry service, has an office at the northern end of Lago del Toro. Maps are readily available here. ⊠ *Conaf station in southern section of the park near Hotel Explora,* ☎ *61/691–931.* ☑ *Admission.* ⊙ *Daily 8–8.*

Lodging

$$$$ ⊞ **Hostería Lago Grey.** This unpretentious lodge on the edge of Lago Grey is a delight. The panoramic view past the lake to the glacier beyond is worth the journey here. Rooms are comfortable and spacious, if a bit spartan. The hostería operates its own sightseeing vessel, the *Grey II,* for close-up tours to Glaciar Grey. ⊠ *Parque Nacional Torres del Paine,* ☎ FAX *61/229–512 or 61/225–986,* WEB *www.chileaustral.com/grey. 20 rooms. Restaurant, lounge. AF, MC, V.*

$$$$ ⊞ **Hotel Explora.** Discreetly tucked away on the southeast corner of
★ Lago Pehoé, this low-slung lodge is one of the most luxurious in Chile. The interior is Scandinavian in style, with local woods used for ceilings, floors, and furniture. No expense has been spared, with bed linens imported from Spain and china brought over from England. As the focus of this hotel is exploring Parque Nacional Torres del Paine, bookings must be for a minimum of three nights. The hotel offers five different types of trips to the national park, depending on weather conditions and guests' interests. ⊠ *Lago Pehoé,* ☎ *2/206–6060 in Santiago,* FAX *2/228–4655 in Santiago,* WEB *www.explora.com. 26 rooms, 4 suites. Restaurant, bar, pool, outdoor hot tub, massage, sauna, gym, hiking, horseback riding, boating, library, baby-sitting, laundry service, business services, meeting rooms. AE, DC, MC, V.*

Parque Nacional Bernardo O'Higgins

⑬ *Southwest of Parque Nacional Torres del Paine.*

Bordering the Parque Nacional Torres del Paine on the southwest, Parque Nacional Bernardo O'Higgins is composed primarily of the southern tip of the vast Campo de Hielo Sur (Southern Ice Field). As it is inaccessible by land, the only way way to visit the park is to take a boat up the Seno Última Esperanza. The Puerto Natales tour company 21 de Mayo operates two boats here, the *21 de Mayo* and the *Alberto de Agostini.* On your way to the park you approach a cormorant colony with nests clinging sheer cliff walls; venture to a glacier at the the foot of Monte Balmaceda; and finally dock at Puerto Toro for a 1-km (½-mi) hike to the foot of the Serrano Glacier. On the trip back to Puerto Natales the crew treats you to a pisco sour served over a chunk of glacier ice. As with many full-day tours, you must bring your own lunch. Warm clothing, including gloves, is recommended year-round, particularly if there's even the slightest breeze.

TIERRA DEL FUEGO

Tierra del Fuego, a vaguely triangular island separated from the southernmost tip of South America by the twists and bends of the Estrecho de Magallanes, is indeed a world unto itself. The vast plains on its northern reaches are dotted with trees bent low by the savage winds that frequently lash the coast. The mountains that rise in the south are equally forbidding, traversed by huge glaciers slowly making their way to the sea.

The first European to set foot on this island was Spanish explorer Hernando de Magallanes, who sailed here in 1520. The smoke that he saw coming from the fires lit by the native peoples prompted him to call it Tierra del Humo, meaning "Land of Smoke." King Charles V of Spain, disliking that name, rechristened it Tierra del Fuego, or "Land of Fire."

Tierra del Fuego is literally split in half. The island's northernmost tip, well within Chilean territory, is its closest point to the continent. The only town of any size here is Porvenir. Its southern extremity, part of Argentina, points out into the Atlantic toward the Falkland Islands. Here you'll find Ushuaia, on the shores of the Canal Beagle. Farther south is Cape Horn, the southernmost bit of land before you reach Antarctica.

Porvenir

⑭ *30 km (18 mi) by boat from Punta Arenas.*

A short trip eastward across the Estrecho de Magallanes, Porvenir is the principal town on Chile's half of Tierra del Fuego. It's not much to speak of, as its population hovers just over 6,000. Located at the eastern end of narrow Bahia Porvenir, it was born during the gold rush of the 1880s. After the boom went bust, it continued to be an important port for the burgeoning cattle and sheep industries.

Porvenir's small **Museo Provincial Fernando Cordero Rusque** (⊠ Plaza de Armas, ☎ no phone) includes collections of memorabilia as eclectic as early Chilean filmmaking and the culture of the indigenous peoples. There are interesting photos of the gold rush and the first sheep ranches. The museum is the only site of particular interest in this otherwise quiet port of entry to Tierra del Fuego.

Puerto Williams

⑮ *75-minute flight from Punta Arenas.*

Located on an island southeast of the Argentine city of Ushuaia, the town of Puerto Williams is the southernmost permanent settlement in the world. Originally called Puerto Luisa, it was renamed in 1956 in honor of the military officer who took possession of the Estrecho de Magallanes for the newly founded nation of Chile in 1843. Most of the 2,500 residents of Puerto Williams are troops at the naval base, but there are several hundred civilians in the adjacent village. A tiny community of indigenous peoples makes its home in the nearby village of Ukika.

For a quick history lesson on how Puerto Williams evolved and some insight into the indigenous peoples, visit the **Museo Martin Gusinde,** named for the renowned anthropologist who traveled and studied in the region between 1918 and 1924. ⊠ *Aragay 1,* ☎ *no phone.* ▨ *Admission.* ☉ *Weekdays 10–1, 3–6; weekends 3–6.*

Weather permitting, Aerovís DAP offers charter flights over **Cabo de Hornos,** the southernmost tip of South America. Although the water looks placid from the air, strong westerly winds make navigating around Cape Horn treacherous. Hundreds of ships met their doom here trying to sail to the Pacific.

Dining and Lodging

When you arrive in Puerto Williams, your airline or ferry company will recommend a few of the hospedajes available, then take you around to see them. All are rustic inns that also serve meals.

$ ✕⌂ **Hostal Pusaki.** Run with Chilean hospitality, this humble hospedaje hosts its guests in comfortable rooms with up to four beds (including bunks). The dining room serves fine local fare. You'll enjoy a particularly pleasant dinner if the fresh *ensalada de centolla* (king crab salad) is on the menu. ✉ *Piloto Pardo 242,* ☎ *61/621–020,* ⅎ *61/621–116. 3 rooms with shared bath. No credit cards.*

Nightlife

Permanently moored at the dock is a small Swiss freighter listing slightly to port called the *Micalvi*. It's home to the rustic **Club de Yates.** Sailors stop off here for good company, strong spirits, and hearty food as they travel between the Atlantic and Pacific around Cape Horn. You don't need to be a sailor to stop by and mingle with whomever is there at the time. You'll meet Aussies, Brits, Finns, Russians, Swedes, or even the occasional American.

A world away from the cosmopolitan clubs of Santiago, **Pub El Pingüino** (✉ Centro Commercial, ☎ no phone) is a watering hole patronized by the town's civilians. Hours are irregular, but closer to the weekend it opens earlier and closes later.

Outdoor Activities and Sports

A hike to the top of nearby **Cerro Bandera** is well worth the effort if you have the stamina. The trail is well marked, but very steep. The view from the top toward the south to the Cordón Dientes del Perro (Dog's Teeth Range) is impressive, but looking northward over the Beagle Channel to Argentina—with Puerto Williams nestled below and Ushuaia just visible to the west—is truly breathtaking.

PATAGONIA AND TIERRA DEL FUEGO A TO Z

To research prices, get advice from other travelers, and book travel arrangements, visit www.fodors.com.

AIR TRAVEL

LanChile and its subsidiary Ladeco operate a number of flights daily between Punta Arenas and Santiago, Coihaique, and Puerto Montt. Another domestic airline, Aerovís DAP, has regularly scheduled flights between Punta Arenas, Porvenir, Puerto Williams, and the Argentine city of Ushuaia. Aerovís DAP also operates chapter flights over Cape Horn for about $180 per person.

Punta Arenas' Aeropuerto President Ibañez is 20 km (13 mi) north of town. Porvenir's airport is 5 km (3 mi) north of town. The airstrip in Puerto Williams is on the western edge of town. There is a small airport near Puerto Natales, but it is not open to commercial air traffic.

It's a good idea to make air travel arrangements through a reliable travel agency, if possible. That way you can rely on the company if you need to make last-minute changes in your itinerary.

➤ AIRLINES: **Aerovís DAP** (✉ Bernardo O'Higgins 891, Punta Arenas, ☎ 61/223–340). **LanChile/Ladeco** (✉ Lautaro Navarro 999, Punta Arenas, ☎ 61/241–232).

BOAT AND FERRY TRAVEL

Comapa runs a ferry three times a week between Punta Arenas and Porvenir. It also operates the ferry that takes penguin-seekers to Isla Magdalena's Monumento Natural Los Pingüinos.

Turismo 21 de Mayo operates two ships, the *21 de Mayo* and the *Alberto de Agostini,* to the Balmacedo and Serrano glaciers in Parque Nacional Bernardo O'Higgins. Passengers on these luxurious boats are treated to lectures about the region as the boat moves up the Seno Última Esperanza.

Cruceros Australis operates the elegant *Terra Australis,* a 55-cabin ship that sails round-trip between Punta Arenas and Ushuaia. On the way, the ship stops at number of sights, including the Garibaldi Glacier, a breathtaking mass of blue ice. You also ride smaller motorboats ashore to visit Isla Magdalena's colony of 120,000 penguins, and Ainsworth Bay's family of elephant seals. The cruises include lectures in English, German, and Spanish on the region's geography and history, flora and fauna.

Navimag operates an inelegant, but highly seviceable, cargo and passenger ferry fleet between Puerto Montt and Puerto Natales. These are boats designed for transportation, not touring, but they are comfortable enough for all but the most finicky travelers.

➤ BOAT AND FERRY INFORMATION: **Comapa** (⊠ Independencia 803, Punta Arenas, ☎ 61/224–256). **Cruceros Australis** (⊠ Av. El Bosque Norte 0440, Santiago, ☎ 2/442–3110, FAX 2/203–5173, WEB www.australis.com). **Navimag** (⊠ Av. El Bosque Norte 0440, Santiago, ☎ 2/442–3120, FAX 2/203–5025, WEB www.navimag.cl). **Turismo 21 de Mayo** (⊠ Ladrilleros 171, Puerto Natales, ☎ 61/411–176).

BUSINESS HOURS

Most shops in the region close for a few hours in the afternoon, usually between noon and 3. Grocery stores are the exception. Most restaurants close between lunch and dinner, which means most don't serve meals from 3 until 8 or even later.

BUS TRAVEL

The four-hour trip between Punta Arenas and Puerto Natales is service by small, private companies. One of the best is Buses Fernández, which has a fleet of first-class coaches and its own terminals in both towns.

➤ BUS INFORMATION: **Buses Fernández** (⊠ Armando Sanhueza 745, Punta Arenas, ☎ 61/221–429; ⊠ Eberhard 555, Puerto Natales, ☎ 61/411–111, WEB www.busesfernandez.com).

CAR RENTAL

Renting a car in Patagonia is not inexpensive—most companies charge about $100 per day. Compare rental rates to the cost of tours; you may find a tour is far cheaper than driving yourself. Make sure you don't rent a more expensive car than you need. Four-wheel-drive vehicles are popular and readily available, but they often aren't necessary if you're not leaving the major roads. Make certain to understand the extent of your liability for any damage to the vehicle, including routine accidents such as a chipped or cracked windshields.

Of the international chains, Budget and Hertz have an office in Punta Arenas. Reputable local companies in Punta Arenas include RUS and Payne.

➤ RENTAL AGENCIES: **Budget** (⊠ O'Higgins 964, Punta Arenas, ☎ 61/241–696). **Hertz** (⊠ O'Higgins 987, Punta Arenas, ☎ 61/248–742). **Payne** (⊠ José Menéndez 631, Punta Arenas, ☎ 61/240–852). **RUS** (⊠ Colón 614, Punta Arenas, ☎ 61/221–529).

CAR TRAVEL

Driving in Patagonia isn't as difficult as you might think. Highways are paved. Secondary roads, including those in the more popular parks, are well maintained. Be careful of gravel roads—broken windshields are common.

HEALTH

As with other parts of the country, the tap water is safe to drink. If you want to be on the extra safe side, stick to bottled water. Because of the thin ozone layer, the sun is particularly strong here. Make sure to slather yourself with sunscreen before going outdoors.

INTERNET

Some hotels and hostals offer Internet access for a small fee. Some telephone company offices also offer Internet services, but it's generally more expensive. Your best bet is usually the Internet cafés that are springing up around Punta Arenas and Puerto Natales.

In Punta Arenas, one of the most welcoming is Calafate, on Avenida Magallanes. It's open 24 hours. Rates are about $3 per hour. In Puerto Natales, El Rincón del Tata has one computer terminal in a corner of the restaurant itself as well as several more on the second floor.
➤ INTERNET CAFÉS: **Calafate** (✉ Magallanes 626, ☎ 61/241–281). **Rincón del Tata** (✉ Arturo Prat 236, ☎ 61/413–845).

MONEY MATTERS

There are any number of banks in Punta Arenas and Puerto Natales where you can exchange cash. Banco Santiago is one of the most convenient and reliable. Many banks have ATMs that accept credit cards on the Cirrus or Plus systems. Do not count on banking services in Puerto Williams.

When you're anticipating smaller purchases, try to have coins and small bills on hand at all times. Many vendors do not always have appropriate change for large bills.

TAXIS

Taxis are readily available in Punta Arenas and Puerto Natales. Ordinary taxis have yellow roofs, while *colectivos* running on fixed routes have black roofs.

TELEPHONES

Public telephones, plentiful in larger towns, are becoming more common in smaller villages. Some accept phone cards that can be purchased at nearby shops. Entel and CTC have offices throughout the region where you can send faxes and make international calls.

TOUR OPERATORS

A knowledgeable tour operator or travel agent is a must for travel to Patagonia and Tierra del Fuego. In the United States, a number of companies are experienced with travel to this region. Among them is the Georgia-based Lost World Adventures, whose staff specializes in tailoring itineraries around your specific interests. There are many good companies in Chile as well. In Santiago, SportsTour puts together individual itineraries. It also offers half- and full-day city tours and multiday excursions throughout the country. Most staff members speak excellent English.

In Punta Arenas, one of the best is Ventistur. Operated by Gonazalo Tejeda, who studied in the United States, Ventistur offers expert advice on travel throughout the region. In Puerto Natales, TourExpress operates a fleet of small vans for comfortable tours into the Parque Nacional Torres del Paine. The bilingual guides are well versed not only on the area's culture and history but on its geology, fauna, and flora. With offices in both cities, Comapa offers numerous tours all over Patagonia and Tierra del Fuego.

➤ CHILEAN COMPANIES: **Comapa** (⊠ Independencia 803, Punta Arenas, ☎ 61/200–202; ⊠ Pedro Montt 262, ☎ 61/414–300, WEB www.comapa.com). **SportsTour** (⊠ Moneda 790, 14th floor, Santiago, ☎ 2/549–5200, FAX 2/698–2981, WEB www.chilnet.cl/sportstour). **Tour-Express** (⊠ Bulnes 769, Puerto Natales, ☎ 61/410–734). **Ventistur** (⊠ José Menéndez 647, Punta Arenas, ☎ 61/241–463, FAX 61/229–081, WEB www.chileaustral.com/ventistur).

➤ U.S. COMPANIES: **Lost World Adventures** (⊠ 112 Church St., Decatur, GA 30030, ☎ 404/373–5820 or 800/999–0558, FAX 404/377–1902, WEB www.lostworldadventures.com).

VISITOR INFORMATION

Sernatur, the national tourism agency, has offices in Punta Arenas and in Puerto Natales.

➤ INFORMATION: **Sernatur** (⊠ Waldo Seguel 689, Punta Arenas, ☎ 61/241–330; ⊠ Puerto Montt s/n, Puerto Natales, ☎ 61/412–125).

11 EASTER ISLAND

The mysteries of the moais—the sad-eyed statues standing watch over the windswept landscape—will probably never be solved. Why were they carved? What did they represent? How were they raised onto their platforms? Archaeologists and anthropologists have many conflicting theories, and you'll doubtless come up with a few of your own when you first encounter these stone sentinels of Easter Island.

by Mark
Sullivan

BELCHING OUT GREAT COLUMNS OF SMOKE, the volcano pushed its way out of the Pacific Ocean about 2.5 million years ago. Poike's anger had barely subsided when it was joined by two fiery siblings, Rano Kau and Terevaka. The triangular landmass that formed between the trio is what is known today as Easter Island.

The isolated island—hundreds of miles from its nearest neighbor—was uninhabited until around 1,500 years ago. That's when, according to local legend, King Hotu Matu'a and his extended family landed on a beach on the northern shore. Exactly where they came from is still a mystery. Norwegian archaeologist Thor Heyerdahl, asserting that the fine masonry found on the island resembles that of the Incas, believed they came from South America. To prove the journey was possible, Heyerdahl set sail in 1947 from Peru in a balsa wood boat called the *Kon-Tiki*. Most archaeologists, however, believe the original inhabitants were of Polynesian descent, citing similarities in language and culture.

Its earliest inhabitants called the island Te Pito O Te Henua. They cleared the vast forests to make room for neatly cultivated fields, and fished the surrounding waters, which teemed with tuna and swordfish. As the population grew, they moved from the caves along the shore into tight-knit communities of *hare paengas*, or boat-shape houses. To communicate they created *rongo-rongo*, a beautiful script and the only written language in all of Polynesia. But their greatest achievement was the hundreds of stone heads called *moais* they erected to honor their ancestors.

Dutch explorer Jacob Roggeveen, the first European to encounter the island, gave it the name most people recognize when he landed here on Easter Sunday in 1722. Here he found a thriving community numbering in the thousands. But when British Captain James Cook anchored here in 1774, he found only several hundred people so impoverished they could barely afford to part with a few sweet potatoes. What's more, many of the moai had been toppled from their foundations. What happened during those 50 years? Archaeologists believe overpopulation and overdevelopment devastated the island. Warfare broke out between clans, who knocked down the moais belonging to their opponents.

This period pales in comparison to the devastation the island suffered in 1862, when slave traders from Peru captured more than 1,000 islanders. Forced to work in guano mines on the mainland, most of them died of hunger or disease. Religious leaders interceded, and the few that remained alive were returned to their island. They spread smallpox to the rest of the population, killing all but 110 people. Everyone who could read the rongo-rongo script died, and to this day no one has been able to decipher the language.

With the collapse of Spanish influence in South America, several countries began to covet Easter Island. In 1888 a Chilean ship raced westward and claimed the island before France or Britain could do so. Chile leased the entire island to a British sheep company, which restricted the islanders from venturing outside the little town of Hanga Roa. The sheep company left in 1953, but life didn't really begin to improve for islanders until an airport was constructed in 1967. The promise of large-scale tourism encouraged the Chilean government to make much-needed improvements on the island.

Tourism is now the biggest industry on Rapa Nui—the name locals give the island. Most of the 3,500 residents are involved in this endeavor in some way. The residents, mostly descendents of the original inhabitants, are extremely proud of the island's past. Ask anyone here about

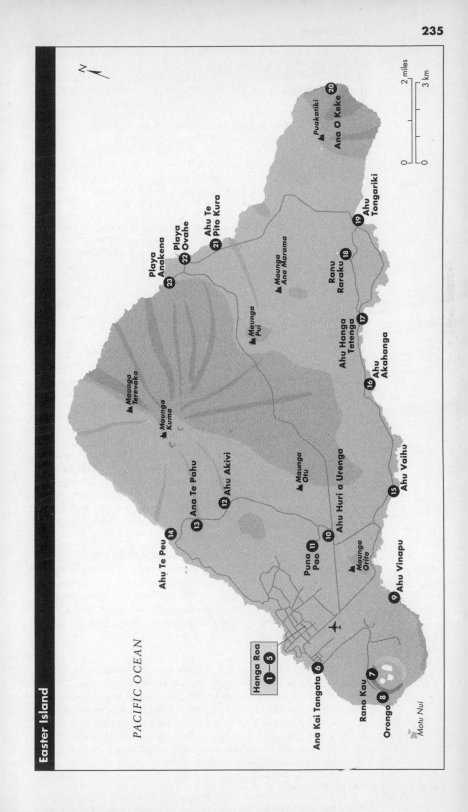

Easter Island

PACIFIC OCEAN

2 miles
3 km

Puakatiki
Ana O Keke 20

Ahu Te
Pito Kura
21

Playa
Ovahe
22

Playa
Anakena
23

Ahu Tongariki
19

Maunga
Ana Marama

Rano
Raraku
18

Maunga
Pui

Ahu Hanga
Tetenga
17

Maunga
Terevaka

Maunga
Kuma

Ahu
Akahanga
16

Ahu Te Peu
14

Ana Te Pahu
13

Ahu Akivi
12

Maunga
Ohu

Ahu Vaihu
15

Ahu Huri a Urenga
10

Puna
Pao
11

Maunga
Orito

Ahu Vinapu
9

Hanga Roa
1 — 5

Ana Kai Tangata
6

Rano Kau

Orongo
8

7

Motu Nui

Poike, the volcano that poked its head out of the Pacific so long ago, and they'll probably tell you the whole tale.

Pleasures and Pastimes

Archaeology

Even if Easter Island held not a single moai, there would still be plenty to see. Hundreds of well-preserved petroglyphs stand on the cliffs near the ancient village of Orongo, and a few are found near the ceremonial sights of Ahu Tongariki and Ahu Te Pito Kura. Cave paintings can be viewed at Ana Kai Tangata. More than 300 of the stone platforms called *ahus* line the coast, and many are worth exploring.

Dining

To eat well on Easter Island, follow the locals. If you spot an unassuming place filled with Rapa Nui residents, chances are you'll find delicious and inexpensive food. At a few places you'll see women cooking skewers of meat on outdoor grills. Barbecue of all types, especially lamb, is extremely popular. As this is an island, seafood is found on nearly every menu. Don't hesitate to ask which type is the freshest—the tuna may have been caught that morning. Meals are often accompanied by fresh fruit grown on the island, especially bananas, papayas, and intensely sweet pineapples.

All of the island's accommodations include breakfast in the price of a room. Most also offer lunch and dinner. However, if you plan to spend your days exploring the island, ask your hotel to prepare a picnic for you or stop by one of the many *supermercados* for provisions. For approximate entrée costs, *see* the dining price chart *in* Smart Travel Tips A to Z.

Lodging

Easter Island has two types of accommodations: *hoteles* and *residenciales*. A hotel is usually a large structure built specifically to house tourists, while a residencial is most often a small private home with a few rooms added to accommodate guests. If you can't get by without amenities such as a swimming pool or tennis court, opt for a hotel. You'll miss out, however, on the chance to stay with a local family at a residencial— the best option for really learning about life on Rapa Nui.

Although it's possible to show up on the island without a reservation— owners of residenciales with spare rooms crowd the waiting room of the airport—it's best to reserve in advance, especially if you are coming in January and February. Many flights arrive late in the evening, and the last thing you'll want to do is search for a place to stay. For approximate room costs, *see* the lodging price chart *in* Smart Travel Tips A to Z.

Shopping

Your first opportunity to shop comes the minute you step into the airport, where dozens of vendors hawk miniature moais in the form of paper weights or earrings. Don't worry, they'll also be here when you depart. In the meantime, you'll find plenty of shops along Avenida Atamu Tekena and Avenida Te Pito O Te Henua. Handicrafts made by locals include wood and stone carvings in the shape of moais and earrings and necklaces made from shells and seeds. Bargaining is expected, but don't expect to knock much off the price.

Exploring Easter Island

An adventurous spirit is a prerequisite for visiting Easter Island. It's possible to sign up for a package tour, but you'd visit only a handful of the sights. To fully experience the island, hire a private guide. Even better is renting a four-wheel-drive vehicle and heading out on your own. Tour buses often bypass fascinating destinations that are off the beaten path. Even in the height of the high season you can find secluded spots.

It's nearly impossible to get lost on Easter Island. The island is fairly small—just 22 km (14 mi) from end to end. Two major thoroughfares—a gravel road that winds its way around the coastline past most of the major archaeological sites, and a paved road that leads directly across the island to the beaches—traverse the island; both meet near Playa Anakena.

Great Itineraries

IF YOU HAVE 3 DAYS

In three days, you won't see everything on Easter Island, but you can visit the major sights. Spend your first full day in Hanga Roa, stopping by the Iglesia Hanga Roa, the Cementerio, and the Museo Antropológico Sebastián Englert. Finish the day with sunset at Tahai. On your second day visit the volcano of Rano Kau, where you'll find the ceremonial village of Orongo. In the afternoon head inland to the small quarry of Puna Pau and the seven moais of Ahu Akivi. Tour the coastal road on your last day, visiting the hundreds of moais in the quarry at Ranu Raraku and the 15 moais in a line at Ahu Tongariki.

IF YOU HAVE 5 DAYS

Follow the first two days of the three-day itinerary. On the third day, travel the inland route to Puna Pau, Ahu Akivi, and Ahu Te Peu. The coastal road makes a good trip for your fourth day, stopping at Ahu Vaihu, Ahu Akahanga, and Ahu Hanga Tetenga before you head to Ranu Raraku and Ahu Tongariki. On your final day visit the beaches of Playa Anakena and Playa Ovahe, checking out some of the island's most striking moais.

IF YOU HAVE 7 DAYS

If you're lucky enough to have a week here you can travel far off the beaten path. Follow the above itinerary, but reserve a day for snorkeling around the spectacular islets of Motu Nui and Motu Iti, found just off the southwestern coast. If you'd rather stay on dry land, consider a hike around the island's northern coast. Another day should be set aside for a little spelunking—see the cave paintings at Ana Kai Tangata, the hidden garden of Ana Te Pahu, and the eerie Ana O Keke, where young women were sequestered until their weddings.

When to Tour

Most people visit in summer, between December and March. Many time their visit to coincide with Tapati Rapa Nui, a two-week celebration featuring music and dancing. Temperatures can soar above 27°C (80°F) in summer. In winter, temperatures reach an average of 22°C (72°F), although brisk winds can often make it feel much cooler. Make sure to bring a light jacket. The wettest months are June and July.

Hanga Roa

Hugging the coast on the southwest side of the island is the village of Hanga Roa. About 3,500 people, most of them of Polynesian descent, make this tangle of streets their home. Very few live outside the village because the bulk of the island has been declared a national park. The population is beginning to spread out as the Chilean government cedes more land to the locals.

The two main roads in Hanga Roa intersect a block from the ocean at a puny public park. Avenida Atamu Tekena, which runs the length

238

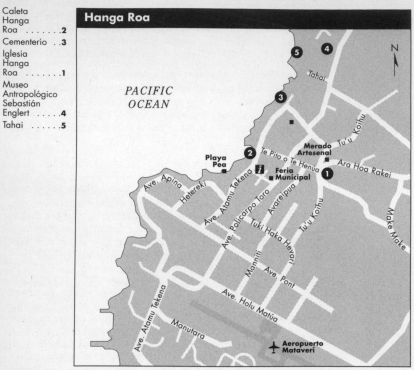

Hanga Roa

of the village, is where you'll find most of the tourist-oriented businesses. Avenida Te Pito O Te Henua begins near the fishing pier and extends two blocks uphill to the church. These two roads are paved, but most others in town are gravel.

Buildings are not numbered and street signs are nonexistent, so finding a particular building can be frustrating at first. Locals will give directions from landmarks, so it's not a bad idea to take a walk around town as soon as you arrive so you can get your bearings.

A Good Tour

Start at the **Iglesia Hanga Roa** ①, the squat colonial church near the center of Hanga Roa. Peek inside to see the carved wooden statues that put a Polynesian spin on traditional Christian iconography. Two blocks downhill on Avenida Te Pito O Te Henua you'll reach the **Caleta Hanga Roa** ②, the town's little fishing pier. To the north along the coast is the colorful **Cementerio** ③. Head east on Petero Atamu for a block, then turn north on Avenida Atamu Tekena. On your left is the **Museo Antropológico Sebastián Englert** ④, a museum with a fascinating look at the island's history. From here it's a short walk to **Tahai** ⑤, a ceremonial site where impressive moais stand with their backs to the sea.

TIMING

If you decide to walk, this tour will take most of the day. If you drive, you can take in all these sights in two or three hours. Either way, try to plan your tour to arrive at Ahu Tahai in time to watch the sunset.

Sights to See

❷ **Caleta Hanga Roa.** Colorful fishing boats bob up and down in the water at Hanga Roa's tiny pier. Here you may find fishermen hauling in the day's catch of tuna or a boatload of divers returning from a trip to the neighboring islets. Nearby is Ahu Tautira, a ceremonial platform with two restored moais. ⊠ *Av. Policarpo Toro at Av. Te Pito O Te Henua.*

❸ **Cementerio.** Hanga Roa's colorful cemetery is unlike any other in the world. Its overgrown flower beds and brightly painted tombstones lend it a cheerful feeling. The central cross is erected on a *pukao*, the reddish headdress that once adorned a moai. ⊠ *Av. Policarpo Toro at Petero Atamu.*

❶ **Iglesia Hanga Roa.** Missionaries brought Christianity to Rapa Nui, but the Rapa Nui people brought their own beliefs to Christianity. In this colonial church you'll find the two religions intertwined. The figure on the cross above the altar is obviously Christ, but it looks surprisingly similar to many ancient carvings found on the island. A bird in the hand of the statue of St. Francis of Assisi strongly resembles the god Make-Make. Try to visit during services on Sunday morning, as the hymns have a distinctly Polynesian flavor. ⊠ *Av. Te Pito O Te Henua.*

❹ **Museo Antropológico Sebastián Englert.** Named for a German priest who dedicated his life to improving conditions on Rapa Nui, the Sebastian Englert Anthropological Museum focuses on daily life. Explanations on how the islanders caught fish and cultivated the land accompany displays of ancient tools. Displays describe the various theories about how the moais were transported and set upright. The most fascinating item is an eye made of coral that was found during the reconstruction of an ahu at Playa Anakena, forever changing scientists' ideas of how the moais looked. Most of the text is in Spanish, but a guide will be happy to explain the displays. Another building in this modern complex houses a changing collection of modern art. ⊠ *Tahai s/n,* ☎ *32/100–296,* WEB *www.dibam.renib.cl.* ⊠ *Admission.* ☉ *Tues.– Fri 9:30–12:30 and 2–5:30, weekends 9:30–12:30.*

❺ **Tahai.** The ancient ceremonial center of Tahai, where much of the annual Tapati Rapa Nui festival takes place, was restored in 1968 by noted anthropologist William Mulloy, who is buried nearby. Tahai consists of three separate ahus facing a wide plaza that once served as a community meeting place. Religious and social leaders lived here in boat-shape dwellings, and you can still find the foundations. In the center is Ahu Tahai, which holds a single weathered moai. To the left is Ahu Vai Uri, where five moai, one little more than a stump, cast their stony gaze over the island. Also here is Ahu Kote Riku, holding a splendid moai with its red topknot intact. This is the one moai on the island that has had its gleaming white eyes restored. These are the only moais standing on the western coast, so this is an especially good place to come to see the blazing yellow sunsets. ⊠ *On the coast near Museo Antropológico Sebastián Englert.*

The Western Circuit

On the western tip of the island you'll find the cave paintings of Ana Kai Tangata and the petroglyphs near the ceremonial village of Orongo. You'll also be treated to a spectacular view of the crater lake inside the long-dormant volcano of Rano Kau.

A Good Tour

Heading south from Hanga Roa you soon reach **Ana Kai Tangata** ⑥, a shallow cave in a protected cove on the coast. On the cave ceiling you'll spot the remains of reddish paintings of birds. Continue south and the road suddenly winds uphill to the crater of **Rano Kau** ⑦. On its rim is the partially restored ceremonial village of **Orongo** ⑧, where islanders worshiped the god Make-Make and where you'll find amazing petroglyphs of birdlike creatures carved into the rock. Take the

Avenida Hotu Matu'a southeast to **Ahu Vinapu** ⑨, where you'll discover some of the best stonework on the island. Head back toward town, then turn northeast on the paved road leading across the island. You'll soon pass **Ahu Huri a Urenga** ⑩, a solitary moai noted for its four hands. A sign on the left marks the turnoff to **Puna Pau** ⑪, the small quarry where the rust-color topknots for the moais were carved. Several miles farther is **Ahu Akivi** ⑫, where seven moai stare toward the sea. Continuing down the same road you'll have to look hard for the entrance to the cave dwellings of **Ana Te Pahu** ⑬. Finally, as you reach the coast, you come to the ruins of the boat-shape houses at **Ahu Te Peu** ⑭.

TIMING

Because much of this tour is over rough gravel roads, it will take most of the day. Consider stopping for lunch in Hanga Roa after visiting Ahu Vinapu, or pack a lunch and picnic on the rim of Ranu Rao and take in its unmatched views of the crater.

Sights to See

⑫ **Ahu Akivi.** Restored by archaeologists William Mulloy and Gonzalo Figueroa in 1960, the seven stoic moais of Ahu Akivi are among the few that gaze out to sea. Researchers say this is only coincidental— they are actually facing a ceremonial site. ⊠ *Past Puna Pau on a gravel road branching north from the paved road to Playa Anakena.*

⑩ **Ahu Huri a Urenga.** One of the few ahus to be erected inland, Ahu Huri a Urenga appears to be oriented toward the winter solstice. Its lonely moai is exceptional because it has two sets of hands, the second carved above the first. Researchers believe this is because the lower set was damaged during transport to the ahu. ⊠ *3 km (2 mi) from Av. Hotu Matu'a on the paved road to Playa Anakena.*

⑭ **Ahu Te Peu.** As at Ahu Vinapu, the tightly fitting stones at the unrestored Ahu Te Peu recalls the best work of the Incas. The foundations for several boat-shape houses, including one that measures 60 meters (36 ft) from end to end, are clearly visible. From here you can begin the six-hour hike around the island's northern coast to Playa Anakena. ⊠ *Past Ana Te Pahu on a gravel road branching north from the paved road to Playa Anakena.*

⑨ **Ahu Vinapu.** The appeal of this crumbled ahu isn't apparent until you notice the fine masonry on the rear wall. Anyone who has seen the ancient Inca city of Macchu Picchu in the mountains of Peru will note the similarity in the stonework. This led Norwegian archaeologist Thor Heyerdahl to theorize that Rapa Nui's original inhabitants may have sailed here from South America. Most others disagree, believing that the first settlers were Polynesian. The moais here still lay where they were toppled, one staring sadly up at the sky. ⊠ *Southeast of Hanga Roa on Av. Hotu Matu'a.*

⑥ **Ana Kai Tangata.** A small sign just past the entrance of Hotel Iorana points toward Ana Kai Tangata, a seldom-visited cavern on the coast that holds the island's only cave paintings. Directly over your head are images of red and white birds in flight. Dramatic cliffs shelter the cave from the crashing surf, making this one of the most spectacular sights on the island. ⊠ *South of Hanga Roa.*

⑬ **Ana Te Pahu.** A grove of banana trees marks the entrance to these underground caverns that once served as dwellings. Partly shielded from the blazing sun, a secret garden of tropical plants thrives in the fissure where the caves begin. Below ground is a passage leading to a second cave where the sunlight streams through a huge hole. ⊠ *Past Ahu Akivi*

MYSTERIES OF THE MOAIS

WHEN EUROPEAN explorers first spotted Easter Island in 1722, they were bewildered by the dozens of massive stone heads that lined the coast. Just how the small band of islanders he encountered could have constructed these monoliths mystified Dutch explorer Jacob Roggeveen. "The stone images at first caused us to be struck with astonishment," Roggeveen wrote in his log, "because we could not comprehend how it was possible that these people, who are devoid of heavy thick timber for making any machines, as well as strong ropes, nevertheless had been able to erect such images."

When British Captain James Cook anchored here in 1774, he was also impressed by the "stupendous figures" that had been "erected in so masterly a manner." But he noted in his journal of the expedition that many had been knocked from their pedestals. By the time French Admiral Abel Dupetit-Thouars visited in 1838, almost all had been toppled. Now the question was not only how and why the massive carvings had been erected, but also how and why they had been destroyed.

After hundreds of years of study, we still know very little about these stone statues, called moais. Archaeological evidence suggests that the majority of these statues, apparently memorials to ancestors, were constructed during a period of fevered activity between 1400 and 1600. Most were erected on ahus, or stone platforms, along the coast. All but a few come from Ranu Raraku, the quarry where 397 moais can still be seen today. By studying those left behind we know that most were carved in a horizontal position, and that once finished they were moved to a nearby trench where they stood until moved to their ahus.

But how were they transported? The more than 90 moais that were abandoned en route provide few clues. Many are bro-ken, but most are intact. Most are face-down, but a few gaze up at the sky. Although theories abound, most archaeologists believe they were either dragged on wooden platforms or rolled along on top of tree trunks. It's not clear, though, how they could have been moved several miles without damaging the delicate features that were carved at the quarry.

Once they arrived at their ahus, how were the moais lifted into place? In 1955, Norwegian archaeologist Thor Heyerdahl and a team of a dozen men were able to raise the single moai on Ahu Ature Huki in 18 days. In 1960 archaeologists William Mulloy and Gonzalo Figueroa and their men raised the seven moais at Ahu Akivi. They struggled for a month to lift the first, but the last took only a week. Both teams used the same method—lifting them with a stone ramp and wooden poles. This technique would be unwieldy for lifting the larger moais, however. It also fails to explain how the pukaos, or topknots, were placed on many of the heads.

And why were the moais destroyed? The reason, ironically enough, may have been that creating the moais required a tremendous amount of natural resources. Most of the palm trees that had once covered the island were felled to move the moais. This had a devastating effect on the island—there soon was little wood for constructing dwellings or boats. Fuel for fires was increasingly hard to find. Crops were ruined as erosion washed away the soil. Archaeological evidence suggests internecine battles developed between clans that had once worked together peacefully. Bloody battles ensued, during which members of one clan toppled the moais belonging to another. In a period of about 100 years, the islanders themselves laid waste to their greatest artistic achievement. The battles eventually ended, but no more moais were ever erected.

—Mark Sullivan

on a gravel road branching north from the paved road to Playa Anakena.

★ ⑧ **Orongo.** The 48 oval huts of this ceremonial village were occupied only during the ceremony honoring the god Make-Make. The high point of the annual event was a competition in which prominent villagers designated servants to paddle small rafts to Motu Nui, the largest of three islets just off the coast. The first servant to find an egg of the sooty tern, a bird nesting on the islets, would swim back with the prize tucked in a special headdress. His master would become the *tangata manu,* or birdman, for the next year. He was honored by being confined to a cave until the following year's ceremony. Dozens of petroglyphs depicting birdlike creatures cover nearby boulders along the rim of Rano Kau. There's a ranger station at the entrance to Orongo where you pay a $10 admission good for your entire trip. ⊠ *South of Hanga Roa on Ranga Kau.* 🎟 *Admission.*

⑪ **Puna Pau.** This quarry is where scoria, the reddish stone used to make the topknots for the moai, was excavated. About two dozen finished topknots can still be found here. The views of the entire island from the top of the hill are well worth the climb. ⊠ *Off a gravel road branching north from the paved road to Playa Anakena.*

⑦ **Rano Kau.** Reached by a winding dirt road, this huge volcano on the southern tip of the island affords wonderful views of Hanga Roa. The crater, which measures a mile across, holds a lake nearly covered over by bright green reeds. The opposite side of the crater has crumbled a bit, revealing a crescent of the deep blue ocean beyond. ⊠ *South of Hanga Roa.*

The Southeastern Circuit

Most of the archaeological sites on the island are found along the southeastern coast. Driving along the southern coast you'll pass many ahus, all of them completely untouched. Busloads of tourists hurry past most of these on their way to Ahu Tongariki, where 15 moais have been restored. Also extremely popular is Ranu Raraku, the quarry where 397 moais wait in stony silence. Moais abandoned on their way to their ahus litter the fields on the northern side of the road; many appear to have been damaged en route.

A Good Tour

The coastal road starts out paved but soon disintegrates into dusty gravel, so make sure you rent a four-wheel-drive vehicle. You'll soon encounter a string of unrestored ahus—including **Ahu Vaihu** ⑮, **Ahu Akahanga** ⑯, and **Ahu Hanga Tetenga** ⑰—all worth exploring. From miles away you'll notice the dome-shape volcano of **Ranu Raraku** ⑱. As you approach, look for scores of unfinished moais covering its upper reaches. From Ranu Raraku you can see the 15 stern-faced moais of **Ahu Tongariki** ⑲. Continuing on the coastal road as it veers north, you soon pass the bare slopes of the volcano called Poike. A dirt path meandering over the hill leads to **Ana O Keke** ⑳, the Cave of the Virgins. The largest moai ever erected on an ahu lies shattered at **Ahu Te Pito Kura** ㉑, on the northern coast. At the end of the road you reach the island's two beaches, **Playa Ovahe** ㉒ and **Playa Anakena** ㉓.

TIMING
Depending on how many sights you visit, this tour will take at least a day. If you have time you might want to break it into two separate tours, visiting the sights on the southern coast on one day and those on the northern coast the next. If you want to spend more time at the beach, consider starting the tour at Playa Anakena and working your way backward.

Sights to See

⓰ **Ahu Akahanga.** This long stone platform once held four moais, which now lie facedown on the ground. Tradition holds that this is the burial site of Hotu Matu'a, the first of the island's rulers. ⊠ *2 km (1 mi) east of Ahu Viahu on the coastal road.*

⓱ **Ahu Hanga Tetenga.** The largest moai ever transported to a platform, measuring nearly 10 meters (33 ft), lies here in pieces. The finishing touches were never made to its eye sockets, so researchers believe it fell while being erected. ⊠ *3 km (2 mi) east of Ahu Akahanga on the coastal road.*

㉑ **Ahu Te Pito Kura.** The largest moai ever successfully erected—a fraction of an inch shorter than the one at Ahu Hanga Tetenga—can be found at Ahu Te Pito Kura. Also here is the perfectly round stone that Hotu Matu'a is said to have brought with him when he arrived on the island. ⊠ *9 km (6 mi) north of Ahu Tongariki on the coastal road.*

★ ⓳ **Ahu Tongariki.** One of the island's most breathtaking sights is Ahu Tongariki, where 15 moais stand side by side along the rocky southern coast. The 200-ft-long ahu, the longest ever built, was completely destroyed in 1960 when a massive tidal wave scattered the moais. The site was painstakingly restored between 1992 and 1995. The moais here, some whitened with a layer of sea salt, have holes in their extended earlobes that might have once been filled with obsidian. They face an expansive ceremonial area where you can find petroglyphs of turtles and fish. ⊠ *2 km (1 mi) east of Ranu Raraku on the coastal road.*

⓯ **Ahu Vaihu.** Eight fallen moai lay facedown in front of this ahu, the first you'll encounter on the southern coastal road. Three reddish topknots are strewn around them. Even after the ahu was destroyed this continued to be a burial chamber, as evidenced by the rocks piled on the toppled moais. ⊠ *11 km (7 mi) from Hanga Roa on the coastal road.*

⓴ **Ana O Keke.** Legend has it that young women awaiting marriage were kept here in the Cave of the Virgins so that their skin would remain as pale as possible. You need an experienced guide to find the cavern itself, which is hidden in the cliffs along the coast. Take a flashlight to see the haunting petroglyphs of flowers and fish thought to have been carved by these girls. ⊠ *Reached via a dirt road through a ranch on Poike.*

★ ㉓ **Playa Anakena.** Swaying palm trees give the beach at Playa Anakena a tropical feeling. The island's best-preserved moais can be found here on **Ahu Nau Nau.** Buried for centuries in the sand, these five moais were protected from the elements. The minute details of the carving— delicate lips, flared nostrils, gracefully curved ears—are still visible. On their backs, fine lines represent belts. The ahu itself is interesting because the head of an old moai is reused in the stonework. It was here that an eye made of white coral was found during the 1978 restoration, leading researchers to speculate that all moais once had them. That eye is now on display at the Museo Antropológico Sebastián Englert.

Staring at Ahu Nau Nau is a solitary moai on nearby **Ahu Ature Huki.** This squat little guy was the first moai to be replaced on his ahu. Thor Heyerdahl conducted this experiment to see if the techniques islanders said were used to erect the moais could actually work. It took 12 islanders nearly three weeks to lift it into position using rocks and wooden poles. ⊠ *1 km (½ mi) east of Playa Ovahe.*

㉒ **Playa Ovahe.** This beautiful stretch of pink sand is the island's best-kept secret, passed over by most tourists in favor of nearby Playa Anakena. The pile of volcanic rocks jutting out into the water is actually a ruined ahu. ✉ *10 km (6 mi) north of Ahu Tongariki on the coastal road.*

★ ⑱ **Ranu Raraku.** When it comes to moais, this is the mother lode. Researchers have counted 397 moais—nearly half of those found on the island—at the quarry in this long-extinct volcano. You first encounter those that line the outer rim, but scores more cluster inside the crater. More than 150 are unfinished, some little more than faces in the rock. Among these is El Gigante, a monster measuring 22 meters (72 ft). It's twice the height of the second tallest, which crumbled while being erected at Ahu Hanga Tetenga. Also here is one of the shortest, discovered by Thor Heyerdahl in 1955. Thought to predate most others, Moai Tukuturi is the only one in a kneeling position. ✉ *5 km (3 mi) past Ahu Hanga Tetenga on the coastal road.*

Dining

$$–$$$ ✕ **Mamá Sabina.** Pretty yellow tablecloths brighten this tiny terrace restaurant. As you watch people pass on the main street, enjoy *atun a la mantequilla* (tuna grilled with butter) served with slices of banana. The portions are generous, and the service is the friendliest in town. ✉ *Atamu Tekena s/n,* ☎ *32/100–566. No credit cards.*

$$ ✕ **Avarei Pua.** You won't leave here hungry—the portions are big enough for two. Delicious dishes such as the *lomo a la plancha* (grilled pork) are served with a mixed salad flavored with lemon juice. From the terrace near the dock you can sip a pisco sour while enjoying the views of the bay. ✉ *Policarpo Toro,* ☎ *32/100–431. No credit cards.*

$$ ✕ **La Tinita.** Little more than a handful of tables on a shady front porch, this restaurant near Plaza Policarpo Toro is a pleasant place to stop for lunch. Try the *atun a la plancha* (grilled tuna) or the *pollo con agregado* (chicken with vegetables). Wash it all down with a piscola. ✉ *Te Pito Ote Henua s/n,* ☎ *32/100–813. No credit cards.*

$$ ✕ **Playa Pea.** With its dazzling view of the bay, this seafood restaurant is one of the best places on the island to catch the sunset. People pack the veranda every evening, so get here early if you want a seat along the railing. Since much of the fish is caught at the nearby *caleta* (fishing pier), it couldn't be fresher. The standout on the menu is the lemony *atun con salsa alcaparras* (tuna with caper sauce), served with *ensalada surtida* (mixed salad) or *ensalada chilena* (tomato and onion salad). ✉ *Policarpo Toro s/n,* ☎ *32/100–382. No credit cards.*

$$ ✕ **Tunu Haoa.** To find this outdoor restaurant on the main street, look for the locals lined up for the delicious grilled beef. The restaurant won't win you over with its decor—plastic tables under a sagging green tarp—but don't let that fool you. Your most memorable meal might come straight off the grill a few feet from your table. ✉ *Atamu Tekena s/n,* ☎ *no phone. No credit cards.*

Lodging

All accommodations on the island will arrange for someone to welcome you at the airport with a garland of flowers to drape around your neck. It's a good thing, as most places would be hard to find because Hanga Roa doesn't post the street names. Breakfast is included everywhere, and you can usually arrange for other meals as well. Most places accept credit cards, but they add a surcharge because it can often take months for them to get their money from the mainland. It's best to settle on a rate beforehand and bring travelers checks.

$$$–$$$$ ▥ **Hotel Hanga Roa.** Part of the Panamericana Hoteles chain, this hotel attracts lots of tour groups. The common areas, from the spacious lobby to the more intimate bar, provide a comfortable setting. A wall of windows brightens the dining room. The newer bungalows, with private terraces overlooking the ocean, are clean and bright. The cramped older rooms, however, have seen better days. ⊠ *Pont s/n,,* ☎ *32/100–299,* WEB *www.panamericanahoteles.cl. 70 rooms, 1 suite. Restaurant, bar, in-rooms safes, minibars, pool, tennis, laundry services, meeting rooms. AE, DC, MC, V.*

$$$–$$$$ 🏨 **Hotel Iorana.** Perched high on a cliff that juts into the ocean, this hotel entices its visitors with views not found elsewhere. From your private terrace you can hear the sound of the waves crashing on the rocks. Popular among tour groups, this gleaming white hotel provides immaculate facilities, from the simply furnished rooms to the generously proportioned baths. The small triangular pool, with masses of ruby-red hibiscus flowers growing at one end, is the perfect place to relax with a fruity cocktail. The hotel is about 2 km (1 mi) south of town, so it may feel a little isolated. ⊠ *Ana Magaro s/n,* ☎ *32/100–608,* FAX *32/100–312,* WEB *www.ciudadnet.com/iorana. 32 rooms, 10 suites. Restaurant, bar, in-room safes, minibars, pool, 2 tennis courts, laundry services, meeting rooms. AE, DC, MC, V.*

$$$ 🏨 **Hotel Manutara.** Palm trees tower over this low-slung resort on the
★ southern edge of Hanga Roa. It's impossible not to relax here, whether reclining in a lounge chair by the bean-shape pool or reading in one of the deliciously overstuffed sofas in the sunny lobby. Especially nice is the shaded dining room, which has rattan tables covered with tropical-print tablecloths. The rooms overlook the lush gardens overflowing with red and orange hibiscus. Little touches, such as seashells around the mirrors in the baths, add a homey charm. ⊠ *Hotu Matu'a s/n,* ☎ *32/100–297,* FAX *32/100–768. 38 rooms. Bar, coffee shop, dining room, lounge, room service, pool, laundry service, shop, travel services, car rental. DC, MC, V.*

$$$ 🏨 **Hotel Otai.** Although the hotel is right in the center of town, its beau-
★ tiful gardens make you feel like you're miles from anywhere. From the flower-scented deck surrounding the pool you can catch a glimpse of the sea. The spacious rooms, with pretty wicker furnishing, open out onto shady wooden verandas. The wood-ceilinged dining room is cool and quiet. ⊠ *Te Pito O Te Henua s/n,* ☎ *32/100–250,* FAX *32/100–560. 31 rooms. Restaurant, bar, pool. AE, DC, MC, V.*

$$$ 🏨 **Hotel Taha Tai.** Open and airy, this hotel seems to have sunlight streaming in from everywhere. The intimate bar has a nice view of the ocean, as does the expansive dining room, which has a tropical feeling lent by its soaring arched ceiling and lazily spinning fans. Guests gather here or outside in the garden to share the sunset. Rooms in the newer building are larger than the older ones in the bungalows, but all are clean and comfortable. If you're seeking privacy, retreat to your own terrace. ⊠ *Policarpo Toro s/n,* ☎ *32/100–623,* FAX *32/100–282. 13 rooms, 10 bungalows. Restaurant, bar, pool. AE, DC, MC, V.*

$$$ 🏨 **Vai Moana.** The name of this lovely lodging means "blue sea," and
★ you'll soon discover why. A long stretch of azure can be seen from just about everywhere, from the glass-enclosed dining room to the umbrella-shaded veranda. Little white cabañas strewn around the grounds offer quite a bit of privacy—all simply furnished, with wood-beamed ceilings and wide windows. The effusive staff speaks English and French. ⊠ *Atamu Tekena s/n,* ☎ *32/100–626,* WEB *www.vai-moana.cl. 14 cottages. Bar, dining room, lounge, minibars, travel services, car rental. AE, MC, V.*

$$ 🏨 **Chez Maria Gorretti.** The beautifully manicured garden is the main draw of this guest house on the northern edge of town. The simple rooms have sliding doors that open out onto clumps of banana trees rustling in the breeze and lush vines wrapping around the trunks of the papayas. The common areas are spacious, with a comfortable lounge area on a platform overlooking the dining room. ⊠ *Atamu Tekena s/n,* ☎ *32/100–459. 18 rooms. Bar, dining room. DC, MC, V.*

$$ **Hotel Gomero.** A long drive lined by palm and papaya trees leads to this charming small hotel. Guests gather in the comfortable dining room, which features rattan furniture and beautifully carved wooden columns. The comfortable guest rooms, some with handcrafted furnishings, lead out to private terraces overlooking the colorful garden. The German/Chilean couple that owns this place runs a tight ship, so everything is spotless. ⊠ *Av. Tu'u Koihu s/n,* ☎ *32/100–313. 13 rooms. Bar, dining room, minibars, laundry service. DC, MC, V.*

$$ **Hotel Poike.** A courtyard overflowing with yellow flowers leads to the open-air lounge that is the heart of this intimate lodging. Guests settle back in the rattan chairs and chat into the evening. The friendly staff provides pleasant little extras, like bowls of fresh fruit in the simple but comfortable rooms. ⊠ *Petero Atamu s/n,* ☎ *32/100–283. 13 rooms. Dining room, lounge, minibars, travel services, car rental. MC, V.*

$$ **Hotel Victoria.** Few hotels in town have a view of the ocean, which makes this family-run hotel something special. The rooms in the low-slung main building are a bit spartan, but you'll want to sit on the covered terrace or in the leafy garden and enjoy the sliver of blue on the horizon. Shops and restaurants are a short walk away. ⊠ *Pont s/n,* ☎ *32/100–272. 7 rooms. Dining room. V.*

$$ **Martín and Anita.** Set amid papaya and banana trees, this little hostal features clean, spacious rooms. The dining room is open and airy. Owner Martín Hereveri also offers several different tours of the island. ⊠ *Simon Paoa s/n,* ☎ FAX *32/100–593,* WEB *www.hostal.co.cl. 8 rooms. Dining room, travel services, car rental. AE, DC, MC, V.*

$ **Aloha Nui.** One of the most charming accommodations on Easter
★ Island, Aloha Nui begins to feel like home even before you can unpack. The genial owner, Maria Reina Pakomio Paoa, makes you feel as welcome as one of the many cousins constantly dropping by. You'll start out in the dining room, but it probably won't be long before you're in the kitchen having breakfast with the family. The generously proportioned rooms, in a separate building behind the main house, look out onto the palm-shaded gardens. ⊠ *Atamu Tekena s/n,* ☎ *32/100–274. 6 rooms. Bar, dining room. MC, V.*

Nightlife

You're in for a late night if you want to sample the scene in Hanga Roa. Locals don't hit the bars until around midnight. The most popular place to stop for a beer is **Banana Café** (⊠ Atamu Tekena s/n, ☎ no phone), a laid-back bar on the main road. On weekends, the younger set heads to **Toroko** (⊠ Policarpo Toro s/n, ☎ no phone), a dance club a stone's throw from the beach. You won't need directions—just follow the thumping disco beat.

For a taste of the excitement of the annual Tapati Rapa Nui festival, take in a performance by the folk troupe called **Kari Kari** (☎ 32/100–595) at one of the hotels. In a dance called the *sau sau,* the music gets faster and faster and the men and women spin wildly. The exuberant movements of the dancers are punctuated by shouts of joy. Another dance called the *hoko* incorporates birdlike movements.

Outdoor Activities and Sports

Haka pei, or sliding down hillsides on banana trunks, is one of the more popular activities during the Tapati Rapa Nui festival. Another is racing across the reed-choked lake that's hidden inside the crater of Ranu Raraku. Visitors who take to the water usually prefer swimming at one of the sandy beaches or snorkeling near one of the offshore islets. Another option is to hike out to isolated spots on the northern coast.

BEACHES

Easter Island's earliest settlers are believed to have landed on idyllic **Playa Anakena.** Legend has it that the caves in the cliffs overlooking the beach are where Hotu Matu'a, the island's first ruler, dwelled while constructing his home. It's easy to see why Hotu Matu'a might have selected this spot: on an island ringed by rough volcanic rock, Playa Anakena is the widest swath of sand. Today the palm-lined beach is packed all summer with sun-worshipping tourists. Ignoring the crowds are the five beautifully carved moais standing on nearby Ahu Nau Nau. Like nearly all of the island's moais, they face away from the ocean.

On the northern coast of the island, Playa Anakena is reachable by a paved road that runs directly across the island, or by the more circuitous coastal road. You'll find no restaurants nearby, but two sisters run competing stands where you can buy soft drinks and skewers of barbecued meat.

A lovely strip of pink sand, **Playa Ovahe** isn't as crowded as neighboring Playa Anakena. But the fact that most tourists pass it by is what makes this secluded beach so appealing. Families head here on weekends for afternoon cookouts. The cliffs that tower above the beach were once home to many of the island's residents. Locals proudly point out caves where relatives were born.

The only beach in Hanga Roa is **Playa Pea,** a tiny stretch of sand near the caleta. It's a popular spot among families with small children.

DIVING

The crystal-clear waters of the South Pacific afford great visibility for snorkelers and divers. Dozens of types of colorful fish flourish in the warm waters surrounding the island's craggy volcanic rocks. Some of the most spectacular underwater scenery is at Motu Nui and Motu Iti, two adjoining islets just off the coast. **Orca Diving Center** (⊠ Caleta de Hanga Roa, ☎ 32/100–375) provides a boat, a guide, and all your diving gear for $60 per person. If snorkeling is more your speed, you can rent a mask and fins for $10.

HIKING

The breezes that cool the island even in the middle of summer make this a perfect place for hikers. Be careful, though, as the sun is much stronger than it feels. Slather yourself with sunblock and bring along plenty of water.

You can take numerous hikes from Hanga Roa. A short walk takes you to Ahu Tahai. More strenuous is a hike on a gravel road to the seven moais of Ahu Akivi, about 10 km (6 mi) north of town. One of the most rewarding treks is along a rough dirt path on the northern coast that leads from Ahu Te Peu to Playa Anakena. The six-hour journey around Terevaka takes you past many undisturbed archaeological sites that few tourists ever see. If you're planning on heading out without a guide, pick up a copy of the *Easter Island Trekking Map* at any local shop.

Shopping
Souvenir shops line Hanga Roa's two main streets, Avenida Atamu Tekena and Avenida Te Pito O Te Henua. At **Hotu Matu'a's Favorite Shop** (⊠ Atamu Tekena s/n, ☎ no phone), you'll the find the widest selection of T-shirts on the island. **Feria Municipal** (⊠ Atamu Tekena s/n, ☎ no phone), an open-air market, has good buys on handmade jewelry. Next to the church is the **Mercado Artesenal** (⊠ Ara Roa Rakei s/n, ☎ no phone), a large building filled with craft stands. Here you'll often witness local artisans whittling wooden moais or stringing together seashell necklaces.

EASTER ISLAND A TO Z

To research prices, get advice from other travelers, and book travel arrangements, visit www.fodors.com.

AIR TRAVEL

Easter Island's shoe-box-size Aeropuerto Internacional Mataveri is on the southern edge of Hanga Roa. LanChile holds a monopoly here, operating all flights from Santiago to the east and Tahiti to the west. Three or four flights a week arrive from Santiago during the high season between December and March, two the rest of the year; two flights a week arrive from Tahiti. The planes are often jammed, especially in January and February, so it's best to reconfirm your flights a day or two in advance.

Tickets to Easter Island are expensive—about $500 for a round-trip flight from Santiago. However, you'll get a better deal if you combine it with a flight to Santiago.
➤ AIRLINE: **LanChile** (✉ Av. Atamu Tekena near Av. Pont, ☎ 32/100–279).
➤ AIRPORT: **Aeropuerto Internacional Mataveri** (✉ Av. Hotu Matu'a s/n ☎ 32/100–277).

BUSINESS HOURS

Almost all of Easter Island's businesses, including those catering to tourists, close for a few hours in the afternoon. Most are open 9 to 1 and 4 to 8, but a few stay open late into the evening. Many are closed Sunday.

CAR RENTAL

None of the major international car-rental chains have offices on Easter Island, but you have many reputable local agencies from which to choose. Most of the best—Aku Aku, Insular, Kia Koe, and Tipanie–are along Avenida Atamu Tekena. Most charge about $50 for eight hours, or $90 per day for a four-wheel-drive vehicle. If you plan on visiting during the busy months of January and February, call a few days ahead to reserve a car.

You might also find a car you can rent at the restaurant where you stop for lunch or the shop where you browse for souvenirs. Your best deal might come from the owner of the guest house where you're staying. If you ask around, you may find a rate that's less than half what the rental companies charge.
➤ RENTAL AGENCIES: **Ahu Ahu** (✉ Av. Hotu Matu'a s/n, ☎ 32/100–297). **Insular** (✉ Av. Atamu Tekena s/n, ☎ 32/100–480). **Kia Koe** (✉ Av. Atamu Tekena s/n, ☎ 32/100–282). **Tipanie** (✉ Av. Atamu Tekena s/n, ☎ 32/100–480).

CAR TRAVEL

To see many of Easter Island's less traveled areas, a four-wheel-drive vehicle is a necessity. Except for the well-maintained roads leading to Rano Kau and Playa Anakena, the best you can hope for are gravel roads. The most isolated spots are reached by dusty dirt roads or no roads at all.

FESTIVALS AND SEASONAL EVENTS

The annual Tapati Rapa Nui festival, a two-week celebration of the island's heritage, takes place every year in January and February. The normally laid-back village bursts to life in a colorful festival that includes much singing and dancing.

HEALTH

The tap water in Easter Island, which comes straight from the lake inside the crater of Rano Kau, is safe to drink but has a mineral taste. Bottled water is available everywhere.

LANGUAGE

Almost all residents speak Spanish, but a good number also speak Rapa Nui. Those who work with tourists also speak English, French, German, and a smattering of other languages.

MAIL AND SHIPPING

Correos de Chile, the island's tiny post office, is on Avenida Te Pito O Te Henua across from Hotel Otai. Postage is the same as in the rest of Chile. Bear in mind that mail is sent via LanChile flights, so you're likely to travel back to the mainland on the same plane as the letter you posted. If you want an Easter Island postmark, you might want to bring your own stamps. The post office here sometimes runs out.

MONEY MATTERS

The official currency is Chilean pesos, but U.S. dollars are accepted just about everywhere. The only bank on the island is the Banco del Estado de Chile, on Avenida Tuumaheke. It's open weekdays 8 to noon. You can exchange U.S. dollars and travelers checks, or get a cash advance on your Visa card.

ATMS

There are no ATMs on the island, so make sure to get enough cash before you arrive.

CREDIT CARDS

Very few restaurants or shops accept credit cards. Almost all hotels and guest houses do, but charge a fee because it takes them months to get reimbursed. It's best to negotiate a rate for your lodging in advance and bring enough cash or travelers checks to cover it.

TAXIS

Taxis have become extremely popular among residents, so it's never difficult to find one during the day. Most destinations in Hanga Roa should cost $1. After 9 PM, the price doubles.

TELEPHONES

A handful of public phones are scattered around Hanga Roa. You can also place local and international calls from the office of Entel, across from the Banco del Estado de Chile. Because Easter Island is part of the same governmental region as the Central Coast, Valparaíso and Viña del Mar are local calls.

TIPPING

Tour guides generally expect a tip of about 10%. Locals don't tip the restaurant staff, but most tourists leave about 10%. Taxi drivers do not expect a tip.

TOUR AGENCIES

Rapa Nui is filled with companies offering tours of the island. Most offer similar half-day and full-day excursions to major archaeological sites, although a few offer "adventure" tours to lesser-known areas. Make sure to settle on the itinerary before booking a tour. If you know exactly where you want to visit, consider a private tour guide. Josefina Nahoe Mulloy and Ramón Edmunds Pacomio, both English speakers, can show you sights not on any tour-bus itinerary.

Of the dozens of tour companies in Hanga Roa, Kia Koe and Mahinatur are the two most reputable. Kia Koe attracts a lot of street traffic, so its tours are often crowded. Mahinatur generally books tours in advance, so the groups are often smaller. Both have friendly, knowledgeable guides.

➤ Tour Agencies: **Kia Koe** (✉ Atamu Tekena s/n, ☎ 32/100–282). **Mahinatur** (✉ Atamu Tekena and Hotu Matu'a, ☎ 32/100–220).

➤ Tour Guides: **Josefina Nahoe Mulloy and Ramón Edmunds Pacomio** (☎ 32/100–274 or 32/100–411).

VISITOR INFORMATION

The local office of Sernatur, the Chilean tourism agency, is run by the genial Francisco Edmunds Paoa. He used to teach local history, so he knows just about everything about the island. He and his staff can provide you with maps and lists of local businesses.

➤ Information: **Oficina de Tourismo** (✉ Tuumaheke s/n, ☎ 32/100–255).

SPANISH VOCABULARY

Words and Phrases

English	Spanish	Pronunciation
Basics		
Yes/no	Sí/no	see/no
Please	Por favor	pore fah-**vore**
May I?	¿Me permite?	may pair-**mee**-tay
Thank you (very much)	(Muchas) gracias	(**moo**-chas) **grah**-see-as
You're welcome	De nada	day **nah**-dah
Excuse me	Con permiso	con pair-**mee**-so
Pardon me	¿Perdón?	pair-**dohn**
Could you tell me?	¿Podría decirme?	po-dree-ah deh-**seer**-meh
I'm sorry	Lo siento	lo see-**en**-to
Good morning!	¡Buenos días!	**bway**-nohs **dee** ahs
Good afternoon!	¡Buenas tardes!	**bway**-nahs **tar**-dess
Good evening!	¡Buenas noches!	**bway**-nahs **no**-chess
Goodbye!	¡Adiós!/¡Hasta luego!	ah-dee-**ohss/ah**-stah-**lwe**-go
Mr./Mrs.	Señor/Señora	sen-**yor**/sen-**yohr**-ah
Miss	Señorita	sen-yo-**ree**-tah
Pleased to meet you	Mucho gusto	**moo**-cho **goose**-to
How are you?	¿Cómo está usted?	**ko**-mo es-**tah** oo-**sted**
Very well, thank you.	Muy bien, gracias.	**moo**-ee bee-**en, grah**-see-as
And you?	¿Y usted?	ee oos-**ted**
Hello (on the telephone)	Diga	**dee**-gah

Numbers

1	un, uno	oon, **oo**-no
2	dos	dos
3	tres	tress
4	cuatro	**kwah**-tro
5	cinco	**sink**-oh
6	seis	saice
7	siete	see-**et**-eh
8	ocho	**o**-cho
9	nueve	new-**eh**-vey
10	diez	dee-**es**
11	once	**ohn**-seh
12	doce	**doh**-seh
13	trece	**treh**-seh
14	catorce	ka-**tohr**-seh
15	quince	**keen**-seh

16	dieciséis	dee-**es**-ee-**saice**
17	diecisiete	dee-**es**-ee-see-**et**-eh
18	dieciocho	dee-**es**-ee-**o**-cho
19	diecinueve	**dee-es**-ee-new-**ev**-ah
20	veinte	**vain**-teh
21	veinte y uno/veintiuno	**vain**-te-**oo**-noh
30	treinta	**train**-tah
32	treinta y dos	train-tay-**dohs**
40	cuarenta	kwah-**ren**-tah
43	cuarenta y tres	kwah-**ren**-tay-**tress**
50	cincuenta	seen-**kwen**-tah
54	cincuenta y cuatro	seen-**kwen**-tay **kwah**-tro
60	sesenta	sess-**en**-tah
65	sesenta y cinco	sess-**en**-tay **seen**-ko
70	setenta	set-**en**-tah
76	setenta y seis	set-**en**-tay **saice**
80	ochenta	oh-**chen**-tah
87	ochenta y siete	oh-**chen**-tay see-**yet**-eh
90	noventa	no-**ven**-tah
98	noventa y ocho	no-**ven**-tah-**o**-choh
100	cien	see-**en**
101	ciento uno	see-**en**-toh **oo**-noh
200	doscientos	doh-see-**en**-tohss
500	quinientos	keen-**yen**-tohss
700	setecientos	set-eh-see-**en**-tohss
900	novecientos	no-veh-see-**en**-tohss
1,000	mil	meel
2,000	dos mil	dohs meel
1,000,000	un millón	oon meel-**yohn**

Colors

black	negro	**neh**-groh
blue	azul	ah-**sool**
brown	café	kah-**feh**
green	verde	**ver**-deh
pink	rosa	**ro**-sah
purple	morado	mo-**rah**-doh
orange	naranja	na-**rahn**-hah
red	rojo	**roh**-hoh
white	blanco	**blahn**-koh
yellow	amarillo	ah-mah-**ree**-yoh

Days of the Week

Sunday	domingo	doe-**meen**-goh
Monday	lunes	**loo**-ness
Tuesday	martes	**mahr**-tess
Wednesday	miércoles	me-**air**-koh-less
Thursday	jueves	hoo-**ev**-ess
Friday	viernes	vee-**air**-ness
Saturday	sábado	**sah**-bah-doh

Months

January	enero	eh-**neh**-roh
February	febrero	feh-**breh**-roh
March	marzo	**mahr**-soh
April	abril	ah-**breel**
May	mayo	**my**-oh
June	junio	**hoo**-nee-oh
July	julio	**hoo**-lee-yoh
August	agosto	ah-**ghost**-toh
September	septiembre	sep-tee-**em**-breh
October	octubre	oak-**too**-breh
November	noviembre	no-vee-**em**-breh
December	diciembre	dee-see-**em**-breh

Useful Phrases

Do you speak English?	¿Habla usted inglés?	ah-blah oos-**ted** in-**glehs**
I don't speak Spanish	No hablo español	no **ah**-bloh es-pahn **yol**
I don't understand (you)	No entiendo	no en-tee-**en**-doh
I understand (you)	Entiendo	en-tee-**en**-doh
I don't know	No sé	no seh
I am American/ British	Soy americano (americana)/ inglés(a)	soy ah-meh ree-**kah**-no (ah-meh-ree-**kah**-nah)/ in-**glehs** (**ah**)
What's your name?	¿Cómo se llama usted?	koh-mo seh **yah**-mah oos-**ted**
My name is . . .	Me llamo . . .	may **yah**-moh
What time is it?	¿Qué hora es?	keh **o**-rah es
It is one, two, three . . . o'clock.	Es la una. . . . Son las dos, tres	es la **oo**-nah/sohn lahs dohs, tress
Yes, please/No, thank you	Sí, por favor/No, gracias	**see** pohr fah-**vor**/no **grah**-see-us
How?	¿Cómo?	**koh**-mo
When?	¿Cuándo?	**kwahn**-doh
This/Next week	Esta semana/ la semana que entra	**es**-teh seh-**mah**-nah/lah seh-**mah**-nah keh **en**-trah
This/Next month	Este mes/el próximo mes	**es**-teh mehs/el **proke**-see-mo mehs
This/Next year	Este año/el año que viene	**es**-teh **ahn**-yo/el **ahn**-yo keh vee-**yen**-ay
Yesterday/today/ tomorrow	Ayer/hoy/mañana	ah-**yehr**/oy/mahn-**yah**-nah
This morning/ afternoon	Esta mañana/ tarde	**es**-tah mahn-**yah**-nah/**tar**-deh
Tonight	Esta noche	**es**-tah **no**-cheh
What?	¿Qué?	keh
What is it?	¿Qué es esto?	keh es **es**-toh

Why?	¿Por qué?	pore **keh**
Who?	¿Quién?	kee-**yen**
Where is . . . ?	¿Dónde está . . . ?	**dohn**-deh es-**tah**
the train station?	la estación del tren?	la es-tah-see-**on** del **train**
the subway station?	la estación del Tren subterráneo?	la es-ta-see-**on** del trehn soob-tair-**ron**-a-o
the bus stop?	la parada del autobus?	la pah-**rah**-dah del oh-toh-**boos**
the post office?	la oficina de correos?	la oh-fee-**see**-nah deh koh-**reh**-os
the bank?	el banco?	el **bahn**-koh
the hotel?	el hotel?	el oh-**tel**
the store?	la tienda?	la tee-**en**-dah
the cashier?	la caja?	la **kah**-hah
the museum?	el museo?	el moo-**seh**-oh
the hospital?	el hospital?	el ohss-pee-**tal**
the elevator?	el ascensor?	el ah-**sen**-sohr
the bathroom?	el baño?	el **bahn**-yoh
Here/there	Aquí/allá	ah-**key**/ah-**yah**
Open/closed	Abierto/cerrado	ah-bee-**er**-toh/ ser-**ah**-doh
Left/right	Izquierda/derecha	iss-key-**er**-dah/ dare-**eh**-chah
Straight ahead	Derecho	dare-**eh**-choh
Is it near/far?	¿Está cerca/lejos?	es-**tah sehr**-kah/ **leh**-hoss
I'd like . . .	Quisiera . . .	kee-see-ehr-ah
a room	un cuarto/una habitación	oon **kwahr**-toh/ **oo**-nah ah-bee-tah-see-**on**
the key	la llave	lah **yah**-veh
a newspaper	un periódico	oon pehr-ee-**oh**-dee-koh
a stamp	un sello de correo	oon **seh**-yo deh koh-**reh**-oh
I'd like to buy . . .	Quisiera comprar . . .	kee-see-**ehr**-ah kohm-**prahr**
cigarettes	cigarrillos	ce-ga-**ree**-yohs
matches	cerillos	ser-**ee**-ohs
a dictionary	un diccionario	oon deek-see-oh-**nah**-ree-oh
soap	jabón	hah-**bohn**
sunglasses	gafas de sol	**ga**-fahs deh sohl
suntan lotion	loción bronceadora	loh-see-**ohn** brohn-seh-ah-**do**-rah
a map	un mapa	oon **mah**-pah
a magazine	una revista	**oon**-ah reh-**veess**-tah
paper	papel	pah-**pel**
envelopes	sobres	**so**-brehs
a postcard	una tarjeta postal	**oon**-ah tar-**het**-ah post-**ahl**
How much is it?	¿Cuánto cuesta?	**kwahn**-toh **kwes**-tah

It's expensive/ cheap	Está caro/barato	es-**tah kah**-roh/ bah-**rah**-toh
A little/a lot	Un poquito/ mucho	oon poh-**kee**-toh/ **moo**-choh
More/less	Más/menos	mahss/**men**-ohss
Enough/too much/too little	Suficiente/ demasiado/ muy poco	soo-fee-see-**en**-teh/ deh-mah-see-**ah**-doh/**moo**-ee poh-koh
Telephone	Teléfono	tel-**ef**-oh-no
Telegram	Telegrama	teh-leh-**grah**-mah
I am ill	Estoy enfermo(a)	es-**toy** en-**fehr**-moh(mah)
Please call a doctor	Por favor llame a un medico	pohr fah-**vor ya**-meh ah oon **med**-ee-koh
Help!	¡Auxilio! ¡Ayuda! ¡Socorro!	owk-**see**-lee-oh/ ah-**yoo**-dah/ soh-**kohr**-roh
Fire!	¡Incendio!	en-**sen** dcc-oo
Caution!/Look out!	¡Cuidado!	kwee-**dah**-doh

On the Road

Avenue	Avenida	ah-ven-ee-dah
Broad, tree-lined boulevard	Bulevar	boo-leh-**var**
Fertile plain	Vega	**veh**-gah
Highway	Carretera	car-reh-**ter**-ah
Mountain pass, Street	Puerto Calle	poo-**ehr**-toh **cah**-yeh
Waterfront promenade	Rambla	**rahm**-blah
Wharf	Embarcadero	em-bar-cah-**deh**-ro

In Town

Cathedral	Catedral	cah-teh-**dral**
Church	Templo/Iglesia	**tem**-plo/ee-**glehs**-see-ah
City hall	Casa de gobierno	kah-sah deh go-bee-**ehr**-no
Door, gate	Puerta portón	poo-**ehr**-tah por-**ton**
Entrance/exit	Entrada/salida	en-**trah**-dah/sah-**lee**-dah
Inn, rustic bar, or restaurant	Taverna	tah-**vehr**-nah
Main square	Plaza principal	plah-thah prin-see-**pahl**
Market	Mercado	mer-**kah**-doh
Neighborhood	Barrio	**bahr**-ree-o
Traffic circle	Glorieta	glor-ee-**eh**-tah
Wine cellar, wine bar, or wine shop	Bodega	boh-**deh**-gah

Dining Out

A bottle of . . .	Una botella de . . .	**oo**-nah bo-**teh**-yah deh
A cup of . . .	Una taza de . . .	**oo**-nah **tah**-thah deh
A glass of . . .	Un vaso de . . .	oon **vah**-so deh
Ashtray	Un cenicero	oon sen-ee-**seh**-roh
Bill/check	La cuenta	lah **kwen**-tah
Bread	El pan	el pahn
Breakfast	El desayuno	el deh-sah-**yoon**-oh
Butter	La mantequilla	lah man-teh-**key**-yah
Cheers!	¡Salud!	sah-**lood**
Cocktail	Un aperitivo	oon ah-pehr-ee-**tee**-voh
Dinner	La cena	lah **seh**-nah
Dish	Un plato	oon **plah**-toh
Menu of the day	Menú del día	meh-**noo** del **dee**-ah
Enjoy!	¡Buen provecho!	bwehn pro-**veh**-cho
Fixed-price menu	Menú fijo o turistico	meh-**noo fee**-hoh oh too-**ree**-stee-coh
Fork	El tenedor	el ten-eh-**dor**
Is the tip included?	¿Está incluida la propina?	es-**tah** in-cloo-**ee**-dah lah pro-**pee**-nah
Knife	El cuchillo	el koo-**chee**-yo
Large portion of savory snacks	Raciónes	rah-see-**oh**-nehs
Lunch	La comida	lah koh-**mee**-dah
Menu	La carta, el menú	lah **cart**-ah, el meh-**noo**
Napkin	La servilleta	lah sehr-vee-**yet**-ah
Pepper	La pimienta	lah pee-me-**en**-tah
Please give me	Por favor déme	pore fah-**vor deh**-meh
Salt	La sal	lah sahl
Savory snacks	Tapas	**tah**-pahs
Spoon	Una cuchara	**oo**-nah koo-**chah**-rah
Sugar	El azúcar	el ah-**thu**-kar
Waiter!/Waitress!	¡Por favor Señor/Señorita!	pohr fah-**vor** sen-**yor**/sen-yor-**ee**-tah

INDEX

NOTES

NOTES

NOTES

NOTES

NOTES

NOTES

NOTES

NOTES

NOTES